A·N·N·U·A·L E·D·I·T·I·O·N·S

Corrections 01/02
First Edition

EDITOR

Matthew C. Leone
University of Nevada, Reno

Matthew C. Leone is associate professor of criminal justice at the University of Nevada, Reno. He earned his B.A. at San Diego State University and his M.A. and Ph.D at the University of California, Irvine. His research interests include jail crowding, juvenile corrections, and policymaker perceptions and attitudes. He has published in journals such as *Crime and Delinquency, Justice Quarterly, The Social Science Journal,* and *Federal Probation,* as well as contributed to several book chapters. He has been co-investigator on studies of prison wardens and administrators, state legislators, county sheriffs, and state parole board members.

McGraw-Hill/Dushkin
530 Old Whitfield Street, Guilford, Connecticut 06437

Visit us on the Internet
http://www.dushkin.com

Credits

1. Who Are the Prisoners?
Unit photo—Associated Press/Wide World
2. Prison Life
Unit photo—Associated Press/Wide World
3. Unusual Problems and Unusual Populations
Unit photo—Associated Press/Wide World
4. Dying on the Inside: The Death Penalty
Unit photo—Associated Press/Wide World
5. Living on the Outside: Intermediate Sanctions
Unit photo—Courtesy of Wackenhut.
6. Future Issues in Corrections
Unit photo—Courtesy of the Federal Corrections Institute.

Copyright

Cataloging in Publication Data
Main entry under title: Annual Editions: Corrections. 2001/2002.

1. Corrections—United States. 2. Criminal justice, Administration of—United States. 3. Prisons—United States.
I. Leone, Matthew, *comp.* II. Title: Corrections.
ISBN 0–07–240432–9   365.973   80–643193   ISSN 1530-3691

© 2001 by McGraw-Hill/Dushkin, Guilford, CT 06437, A Division of The McGraw-Hill Companies.

Copyright law prohibits the reproduction, storage, or transmission in any form by any means of any portion of this publication without the express written permission of McGraw-Hill/Dushkin, and of the copyright holder (if different) of the part of the publication to be reproduced. The Guidelines for Classroom Copying endorsed by Congress explicitly state that unauthorized copying may not be used to create, to replace, or to substitute for anthologies, compilations, or collective works.

Annual Editions® is a Registered Trademark of McGraw-Hill/Dushkin, A Division of The McGraw-Hill Companies.

First Edition

Cover image © 2001 PhotoDisc, Inc.

Printed in the United States of America   1234567890BAHBAH54321   Printed on Recycled Paper

Editors/Advisory Board

Members of the Advisory Board are instrumental in the final selection of articles for each edition of ANNUAL EDITIONS. Their review of articles for content, level, currentness, and appropriateness provides critical direction to the editor and staff. We think that you will find their careful consideration well reflected in this volume.

EDITOR

Matthew C. Leone
University of Nevada
Reno

ADVISORY BOARD

Gordon Bazemore
Florida Atlantic University

Cecil Canton
California State University
Sacramento

Colleen Ann Dell
Carleton University

Preston Elrod
Eastern Kentucky University

Mark Fleisher
Illinois State University

Elizabeth Foley
Lake Superior State University

Randy Gainey
Old Dominion University

Craig Hemmens
Boise State University

Greg Howard
Western Michigan University

Ken Kerle
American Jail Association

Patrick Kinkade
Texas Christian University

John Klofas
Rochester Institute of Technology

Richard Lawrence
St. Cloud State University

Celia Lo
University of Akron

Thomas Mahoney
Santa Barbara City College

G. Larry Mays
New Mexico State University

Marilyn McShane
Northern Arizona University

Alida Merlo
Indiana University of Pennsylvania

Merry Morash
Michigan State University

Barbara Owen
California State University
Fresno

Lawrence Salinger
Arkansas State University

Judith Sgarzi
Mount Ida College

K. Gary Sherman
University of Wyoming

Robert A. Taylor
Ohio State University

Wayne Welsh
Temple University

John Wooldredge
University of Cincinnati

Staff

EDITORIAL STAFF

Ian A. Nielsen, Publisher
Roberta Monaco, Senior Developmental Editor
Dorothy Fink, Associate Developmental Editor
Addie Raucci, Senior Administrative Editor
Cheryl Greenleaf, Permissions Editor
Joseph Offredi, Permissions/Editorial Assistant
Diane Barker, Proofreader
Lisa Holmes-Doebrick, Senior Program Coordinator

TECHNOLOGY STAFF

Richard Tietjen, Senior Publishing Technologist
Jonathan Stowe, Director of Technology
Janice Ward, Technology Editorial Assistant

PRODUCTION STAFF

Brenda S. Filley, Director of Production
Charles Vitelli, Designer
Laura Levine, Graphics
Mike Campbell, Graphics
Tom Goddard, Graphics
Eldis Lima, Graphics
Nancy Norton, Graphics
Juliana Arbo, Typesetting Supervisor
Marie Lazauskas, Typesetter
Karen Roberts, Typesetter
Larry Killian, Copier Coordinator

iii

To the Reader

In publishing ANNUAL EDITIONS we recognize the enormous role played by the magazines, newspapers, and journals of the public press in providing current, first-rate educational information in a broad spectrum of interest areas. Many of these articles are appropriate for students, researchers, and professionals seeking accurate, current material to help bridge the gap between principles and theories and the real world. These articles, however, become more useful for study when those of lasting value are carefully collected, organized, indexed, and reproduced in a low-cost format, which provides easy and permanent access when the material is needed. That is the role played by ANNUAL EDITIONS.

New to ANNUAL EDITIONS is the inclusion of related World Wide Web sites. These sites have been selected by our editorial staff to represent some of the best resources found on the World Wide Web today. Through our carefully developed topic guide, we have linked these Web resources to the articles covered in this ANNUAL EDITIONS reader. We think that you will find this volume useful, and we hope that you will take a moment to visit us on the Web at *http://www.dushkin.com* to tell us what you think.

The goal of the corrections system, unlike policing and law, changes over both time and place. Policing, driven by the Constitution and the policy of "accepted" practice, often varies little from jurisdiction to jurisdiction. Similarly, the practice of law, driven by due process and case law, also has little latitude for interpretation among jurisdictions. But correctional practices are able to change, and the goals and policies of different state-level facilities may be unique to their respective states and based on the beliefs of the current political base and prison administration; elements that could change at any given time. Correctional administrators, recognizing that these "new" goals are probably temporary, may be unwilling or unable to meet these goals, so they revert to the simple and constant goals of care and custody. While these are admirable goals, in that they seek to ensure that the offender is safe within the institution and that the society is safe from the offender, they do little to change the behaviors that placed the offender in the hands of the criminal justice system in the first place. Furthermore, the rare administrator who recognizes the various causes of crime and seeks to address these causes therapeutically within the custodial institution is usually met with limited resources and often suspicion or scorn from the taxpaying public. To many, rehabilitation seems "soft" on crime.

Add to this quagmire the problem of getting research information to the practitioner in a timely and understandable manner, and you create a justice system that supports the status quo, and a corrections system that typically offers the lowest form of care allowable by law. Is it any wonder that recidivism rates are as high as they are?

Annual Editions: Corrections 01/02 is a small step toward correcting these problems for future generations. Many of you, the readers of this collection of articles, will eventually assume leadership roles in the criminal justice system. You will be asked to both create policy and institute change. It is my sincere hope that exposure to this material will both educate and enlighten, and break down the stereotypes and misinformation that plague the criminal justice and correctional systems.

The articles included in *Annual Editions: Corrections 01/02* were selected for their timeliness and their perspective. The practice of corrections changes so rapidly that most anthologies are out of date before they hit the shelves in college bookstores. The Annual Editions format offers assurance that you will be exposed to current problems, perspectives, and information. If used properly, this reader will help you to understand how change occurs within the corrections system, how these changes may produce unintended and negative consequences, and how these consequences fit into a classic and historical perspective. From this interaction, a better perspective can be achieved and learning can be enhanced.

Annual Editions: Corrections 01/02 may be used in two ways: As an accompaniment to a more traditional corrections text (which is its primary purpose), it can be used to examine in greater depth the "hot" issues in corrections. To achieve this end I suggest that the articles be selected and scheduled based on their appropriateness for each of the sections in the primary text. Another way to use this anthology could be as the primary text in an advanced corrections class, where the students have already been exposed to the traditional information, and are more prepared and motivated to engage in in-depth discussions of timely issues in corrections. In either case, *Annual Editions: Corrections 01/02* represents current and classic issues in corrections, and it will continue to do so in each of its upcoming editions. We are interested in your thoughts about the selections contained in this edition. Please fill out the postage-paid *article rating form* on the last page and let us know your opinions. We endeavor to improve each edition annually, and with your help, we will.

Matthew Leone
Editor

Contents

To the Reader — iv
Topic Guide — 2
● Selected World Wide Web Sites — 4

Overview — 6

1. **American Criminal Justice Philosophy: What's Old—What's New?** Curtis R. Blakely and Vic W. Bumphus, *Federal Probation*, June 1999. — 8
   Curtis Blakely and Vic Bumphus show how **public interest and social change** affect the operations of the various agencies of the criminal justice system. The authors provide a comparison among the current police philosophies and examine how they could be applied to the corrections system.

2. **Prisoners in 1998,** Allen J. Beck and Christopher J. Mumola, *Bureau of Justice Statistics Bulletin, U.S. Department of Justice,* August 1999. — 13
   The Department of Justice releases a report approximately every 2 years that chronicles the changes in the nation's prison population. In this report, Allen Beck and Christopher Mumola highlight the **changes in inmate demographics and incarceration rates** nationwide.

3. **Prior Abuse Reported by Inmates and Probationers,** Caroline Wolf Harlow, *Bureau of Justice Statistics: Selected Findings,* April 1999. — 27
   Anecdotal data have long argued a **relationship between childhood abuse and later criminal behavior.** This federal report compares inmates' personal histories of abuse with their placement at different levels of control within the correctional system. The links between prior abuse and later alcohol/drug use are also examined.

4. **Drug Use History and Criminal Behavior among 133 Incarcerated Men,** Elena M. Kouri, Harrison G. Pope Jr., Kenneth F. Powell, Paul S. Oliva, and Corbett Campbell, *American Journal of Drug and Alcohol Abuse,* August 1997. — 31
   This article further examines the **relationship between substance abuse and crime** in a sample of 133 incarcerated males. While the sample is narrow, it still provides compelling evidence of the relationship between crime, incarceration, and clinical substance dependence.

5. **Drugs, Crime, Prison, and Treatment,** Charles Blanchard, *Spectrum,* Winter 1999. — 34
   Charles Blanchard states that there is a close connection between **crime and substance abuse.** He examines this **linkage** to support the idea of treatment programs in prison and the use of specialized areas of the justice system to support the substance-abusing criminal.

6. **The Forgotten Offender,** Meda Chesney-Lind, *Corrections Today,* December 1998. — 37
   Female offenders have been, for most of the past decade, the fastest-growing segment of the correctional population. In this article, Meda Chesney-Lind examines the reasons for this change. Issues discussed include how the drive for equality helped to create this situation and how we could help to correct some of these new problems by **changing our imprisonment philosophy** and recognizing the **differences between male and female inmates.**

UNIT 1

Who Are the Prisoners?

The six selections in this section examine the makeup of the current U.S. prison population.

The concepts in bold italics are developed in the article. For further expansion please refer to the Topic Guide and the Index.

UNIT 2
Prison Life

This unit's eleven articles look at what being a prisoner or a corrections officer is like in today's correctional institutions.

Overview   42

7. **Coping with Incarceration—From the Other Side of the Bars,** Mary Dallao, *Corrections Today,* October 1997.   44
   Often forgotten in the debate on imprisonment and sentencing are the ***families of the inmates.*** This article provides a feel for what others experience when a loved one is sentenced to prison. It offers corrections professionals some suggestions to help mitigate the impact on families.

8. **Behind Bars: We've Built the Largest Prison System in the World. Here's a Look Inside,** Wray Herbert, *U.S. News & World Report,* March 23, 1998.   46
   With the rapid and seemingly uncontrollable increases in prison populations, it is helpful to take a look inside and see what the day-to-day experience of imprisonment looks like. This is a photographic essay on ***life inside various incarcerative institutions.***

9. **Behind Bars: Substance Abuse and America's Prison Population,** *Spectrum,* Winter 1999.   50
   Substance abuse and ***addiction*** have fundamentally changed the nature of America's ***prison population.*** Crime and substance abuse are joined at the hip.

10. **Inside the New Alcatraz,** Peter Annin, *Newsweek,* July 13, 1998.   55
    As prisons continue to grow in size and to house more serious and dangerous inmates, places need to be constructed to keep those inmates who are too dangerous for the general population. This is a brief description of the operation and design of the newest ***Administrative Maximum Federal Prison.***

11. **Life on the Inside: The Jailers,** Andrew Metz, *Newsday,* March 21, 1999.   56
    At the ***Nassau County Correctional Center,*** one of the largest ***jails*** in the country, correction officers battle tension, fear, and stereotypes. Many ***officers*** believe that they are seen as brutes, only a shade better than the people behind bars.

12. **Prison Crime in New York State,** David R. Eichenthal and Laurel Blatchford, *The Prison Journal,* December 1997.   62
    As noted earlier, crime in the streets seems to be decreasing, but inmate populations seem to be increasing. What are all these inmates doing while they are in prison? This article examines ***the prevalence of crime in prisons,*** discusses some of the social, political, and practical reasons for the increase in prison crime, and offers ways for states to combat this problem.

13. **Stopping Abuse in Prison,** Nina Siegal, *The Progressive,* April 1999.   67
    Nina Siegal makes the argument that abuse of inmates by correctional staff is widespread (a position not wholly supported by other researchers) and offers case studies to support that position. Included in the article are some perspectives of governmental and private groups, and an explanation of how suggested legislation and ***training may better control staff behavior.***

14. **A Day in the Life,** Gabrielle deGroot, *Corrections Today,* December 1998.   70
    This article looks at both the ***emotional*** and ***physical experience*** of being an ***inmate in a female prison.*** In the course of this article, four female inmates discuss the life on the inside, the situations on the outside that preceeded their crimes, and the mechanisms that they employ to attempt to create an improved quality of life in prison.

The concepts in bold italics are developed in the article. For further expansion please refer to the Topic Guide and the Index.

15. The Gangs behind Bars, Tiffany Danitz, *Insight*, September 28/October 5, 1998.   74

Male inmates, as a rule, differ from female inmates in the ways that they cope with incarceration. This brief article shows **how prevalent gangs are in prison,** and the many reasons why inmates **join or create prison gangs.**

16. The Effects of the Duran Consent Decree, Curtis R. Blakely, *Corrections Today*, February 1997.   76

During the New Mexico State Prison Riot, prison officials made promises to the inmates who helped **to quell the riot** and who eventually allowed the prison to be retaken with minimal resistance. For over a decade the promises of the prison officials and the suggestions of other governmental agencies have been ignored. In this article Curtis Blakely examines the decree, and assesses the impact of the decree on the prison system of New Mexico.

17. The Constitution and the Federal District Judge, Frank M. Johnson, *Texas Law Review*, Volume 903, 1976.   78

Based on the number of suits filed by inmates, it can be easily suggested that **prisons violate the constitutional rights of inmates** on a regular basis. Why then the lack of federal case law to control prison behavior? In this classic article the self-defined role of a federal court judge is discussed by an active federal judge.

Overview   84

18. Like Mother, Like Daughter: Why More Young Women Follow Their Moms into Lives of Crime, Toni Locy, *U.S. News & World Report*, October 4, 1999.   86

In this brief but important view of **the relationship between mothers and daughters** when the mother is a criminal and an inmate, Toni Locy provides insight into the mother's desire for her daughter to lead a different life, and the daughter's perspective of the mother as a role model.

19. Percentage of Women on Probation and Parole Rising, *U.S. Justice Department*, 1997   89

In this short report, Justice Department data are used to support the idea that **some types of female crime** are increasing sharply, and that these increases are resulting in more females coming under the control of the corrections system.

20. Addressing the Needs of Elderly Offenders, Connie L. Neeley, Laura Addison, and Delores Craig-Moreland, *Corrections Today*, August 1997.   90

As sentences increase and parole becomes more difficult to obtain, the predicted outcome will be more **inmates living in prison as senior citizens.** This article outlines some of the changes that will need to be made to both prison structure and operations to accommodate these aging inmates.

21. Elder Care: Louisiana Initiates Program to Meet **Needs of Aging Inmate Population,** Jean Wall, *Corrections Today*, April 1998.   93

Jean Wall describes a pilot program that was initiated to better and more effectively deal with aging and aged inmates in Louisiana. Included are programs designed to keep **aging inmates** healthy, with the idea of both improving their quality of life and decreasing medical costs for the facility.

22. Chaser: A Medication Addict, Victor Hassine, from *Life without Parole*, Roxbury Publishers, Los Angeles, CA, 1999.   96

In this chapter excerpt from Victor Hassine's book, the life and crimes of an inmate called Chaser are discussed. An image emerges of a prison system that seeks to **control needy inmates with medication** rather than with more substantial and effective long-term therapy.

UNIT 3

Unusual Problems and Unusual Populations

Eight selections examine some of the problems faced by prisoners who are somewhat unique: young women, the elderly, the mentally impaired, and juveniles.

The concepts in bold italics are developed in the article. For further expansion please refer to the Topic Guide and the Index.

23. Mental Health and Treatment of Inmates and Probationers, Paula M. Ditton, *Bureau of Justice Statistics Special Report*, July 1999. **100**

In this Bureau of Justice Statistics report, **causes of criminal behavior** are examined and the mental health of the inmate population is assessed. Linkages are examined between physical/substance abuse and criminality. In addition, treatment programs are evaluated in terms of their availability to mentally ill inmates.

24. Juveniles in Federal Prison, Jack Kresnak, *The Education Digest*, February 1999. **111**

As the federal government takes a greater interest in crime and, predictably, creates more federal legislation to control crime, the outcome will be an increased need for federal prison beds to house these criminals. When this situation is applied to the juvenile population, the expected outcome will be increases in the federal juvenile population. This article outlines what happens in **a federal juvenile facility** with a burgeoning population of Native American juvenile offenders.

25. Re-Forming Juvenile Justice: The New Zealand Experiment, Allison Morris and Gabrielle Maxwell, *The Prison Journal*, June 1997. **115**

The United States is not the only place experiencing **increases in juvenile correctional populations.** This article examines the impact of the Children, Young Persons, and Their Families Act of 1989 in New Zealand. Included in this act are some of the same strategies that are being used in some U.S. cities.

UNIT 4

Dying on the Inside: The Death Penalty

Five selections look at the death penalty issue in U.S. prisons.

Overview **120**

26. A House without a Blueprint, Ted Gest, *U.S. News & World Report*, July 8, 1996. **122**

Ted Gest examines the case of Gary Burris and uses it as an example of some of the enduring problems with the process of **the death penalty.** The article ends with an examination of the data that shows the impact that race and geography can have on the potential for execution.

27. Facts and Figures: A Costly Matter of Life or Death, Bevolyn Williams-Harold, *Black Enterprise*, September 1998. **124**

The death penalty requires extraordinary levels of due process to ensure the guilt and the level of guilt of the accused. This brief article outlines **the costs of this "super" due process.**

28. Stolen Lives: Men and Women Wrongfully Sentenced to Death Row, Jenny Allen and Lori Grinker, *Life*, October 1994. **125**

One of the most compelling **arguments against execution** is its irreversibility. This article shows how often innocent people end up on death row, and the devastating consequences for them and their families.

29. Death Row Justice Derailed, Ken Armstrong and Steve Mills, *Chicago Tribune*, November 14, 1999. **129**

While the court process is often less than perfect, the authors of this article show us how particularly imperfect the system was in Illinois. This article, through the use of court records and offender interviews, shows how this system, which lacked the checks and balances that we all take for granted, could convict innocent individuals and place them on death row.

30. **The Death Penalty Brings Justice,** Gov. George E. Pataki, 135
and **Death at Midnight . . . Hope at Sunrise,** Steven Hawkins, *Corrections Today,* August 1996.
Two perspectives on the death penalty are advanced in these two articles. For Governor George Pataki, execution is seen as the ultimate justice for society and the family of the victim. Steven Hawkins considers the legal process, which is more affected by the economic condition of the offender and the race of the offender and the victim, rather than by the guilt or innocence of the offender.

Overview 138

31. Correctional Treatment: Some Recommendations **for Effective Intervention,** Paul Gendreau and Robert R. Ross, *Juvenile and Family Court Journal,* Winter 1983–1984. 140
In this article, Paul Gendreau and Robert Ross show the potential value of **treatment programs** and discuss the reasons why many have failed, and why society seems to want to punish rather than to treat the offender, even though effective treatment is possible.

32. Habilitation, Not Rehabilitation, Dyan Machan, *Forbes,* November 2, 1998. 146
Sometimes the truth is stranger than fiction. In this article the judge who was immortalized in the book and movie *The Bonfire of the Vanities* is interviewed regarding his beliefs about the **function of the criminal justice system.** He offers some insights and suggestions for making the legal and correctional processes more effective.

33. A Decade of Experimenting with Intermediate Sanctions: What Have We Learned? Joan Petersilia, *Federal Probation,* December 1998. 148
Intermediate sanctions, those **sentencing options** that exist between full incarceration and complete release, have been in use for over a century. More modern, intermediate sanctions have been in use for a little over a decade. In this article, Joan Petersilia discusses the practical and political problems that have afflicted the system of intermediate sanctions, and she shows some locations where some **new ideas seem to be working.**

34. Eliminating Parole Boards Isn't a Cure-All, Experts **Say,** Fox Butterfield, *New York Times,* January 10, 1999. 155
Parole has been abolished or severely restricted in nearly 20 states, yet **the reasons for abolishing parole** and the impacts of this action are unclear. In this brief article, Fox Butterfield discusses the views of practitioners and predicts some of the dire consequences of this action.

35. Job Placement for Offenders: A Promising Ap**proach to Reducing Recidivism and Correctional Costs,** Peter Finn, *National Institute of Justice Journal,* July 1999. 157
One method of controlling prison populations is to reduce the high rate of **recidivism** among **ex-offenders.** Programs described here aim to help large numbers of ex-offenders to remain employed in order to avoid reincarceration.

36. Young Probation/Parole Officer Toughens with **Experience,** Susan Clayton, *Corrections Today,* June 1996. 165
Similar to improving athletic skills, the process of **becoming a "seasoned" probation/parole officer** is not without pain. In this article, the day-to-day actions and challenges of Baltimore Home Detention Agent Rachelle White are detailed. The process of electronic home detention is presented, along with the problems encountered in running such a unit.

Overview 168

UNIT 5

Living on the Outside: Intermediate Sanctions

The six articles in this unit consider the programs and treatments that follow the paroled prisoner.

The concepts in bold italics are developed in the article. For further expansion please refer to the Topic Guide and the Index.

UNIT 6

Future Issues in Corrections

Twelve selections examine some of the issues that those involved with corrections will face in the future: the "three strikes" law, the role of education, privatization, chain gangs, mental and physical health, and youth courts.

37. **New Bedlam: Jails—Not Psychiatric Hospitals—Now Care for the Indigent Mentally Ill,** Spencer P. M. Harrington, *The Humanist,* May 1999. **170**

Jails, which have always been at the center of the ***criminal justice system,*** and have always been negatively impacted by changes in law enforcement, courts, or prisons, now have a new problem. The ***lack of sufficient space in mental hospitals*** for the indigent mentally ill has forced the criminal justice system into holding and processing this population. The author shows how jails are ill-equipped to do so and points out that ***inmate suicides*** may be the result of this unfortunate mix of person and place.

38. **A Get-Tough Policy That Failed,** John Cloud, *Time,* February 1, 1999. **175**

The ***punishment philosophy of deterrence*** depends on the criminal making a thoughtful calculation of the punishments and the gains. It requires that the potential repeat offender be aware of the level and probability of punishment and whether the severity of the punishment outweighs the pleasure of the crime. This article examines the negative consequences of the "three strikes" model of deterrence for repeat offenders.

39. **The Deterrent Effect of the Three Strikes Law,** John R. Schafer, *FBI Law Enforcement Bulletin,* April 1999. **177**

In this article, proponents of ***the three strikes laws*** are given the opportunity to show that the laws may be having positive social consequences, and that society may be better off because of the legislation. Also included in the article is an analysis of offender attitudes that indicates which offender types the three strikes legislation is most likely to control.

40. **"Lock 'em Up and Throw Away the Key": A Policy That Won't Work,** William H. Rentschler, *USA Today Magazine (Society for the Advancement of Education),* November 1997. **181**

The punishment philosophy that was espoused in the 1980s did not arise from a vacuum but was rather the result of political pressures and social concerns, the roots of which were created in the 1970s. In this article William Rentschler discusses both the ***causes and consequences of the imprisonment binge.*** He includes the politics of reelection and the perception of a society that paints those who oppose prison building for fiscal reasons as being "soft on crime."

41. **Education As Crime Prevention: Providing Education to Prisoners,** *Research Brief (The Center on Crime, Communities & Culture),* September 1997. **184**

This research brief presents recent data on the impact of ***education*** on crime and crime prevention, and examines the debate on providing higher education to inmates.

42. **Probation Department in Michigan Finds Volunteers Make Fine Officers,** Brian M. Smith, *Corrections Today,* August 1993. **190**

As the costs of operating probation departments increases, due to both increasing wages and increased numbers of officers and offenders, society is going to have to be inventive in finding solutions. One proposed idea, which has been tried in other countries, is ***the use of volunteers*** to supervise low-level offenders in the community. This article is an analysis and evaluation of one such program in Michigan.

The concepts in bold italics are developed in the article. For further expansion please refer to the Topic Guide and the Index.

43. Correctional Privatization: Defining the Issues and **Searching for Answers,** G. Larry Mays, from *Privatization and the Provision of Correctional Services: Context and Consequences*, ACJS/Anderson Monograph Service, January 1996.   **192**

Another creative solution to **the cost of building and operating correctional facilities** involves partnerships with the private sector. These partnerships, while financially attractive, are not without risk. In this article, Larry Mays discusses the idea of privatization in corrections and defines some of the issues which must be considered when making the decision to privatize.

44. Chain Gangs Are Right for Florida, Charlie Crist, and **Chain Gangs Are Cruel and Unusual Punishment,** Rhonda Brownstein, *Corrections Today*, April 1996.   **196**

As society and politicians seek to increase punishments in order to achieve deterrence, they also increase the **operating costs of the criminal justice system.** One solution has been to **put inmates back to work outside the prison.** Here are opposing views on the use of chain gangs as a way to ensure the safety of the public.

45. Restorative Justice: The Concept, Howard Zehr, *Corrections Today*, December 1997.   **199**

When the criminal justice system punishes an offender for the violation of a law that has harmed another individual, often **the person who is harmed is left unrestored.** The current philosophy for dealing with offenders—restorative justice—promotes not just the punishment of the offender but also (and sometimes only) the restoration of the person harmed by the offender's actions.

46. Rough Justice in the Youth Courts, Kirsty Milne, *New Statesmen*, January 30, 1998.   **203**

Criminal justice issues are the motivation for campaign promises in other countries as well as in the United States. In this article, the perspectives and promises of the Labour party in England are contrasted with the reality, both political and economic, of the nation. What emerges is a system and a situation that is very similar to what has emerged in the United States over the past 10 years.

47. HIV/AIDS Education and Prevention Programs for Adults in Prisons and Jails and Juveniles in Confinement Facilities, *Journal of the American Medical Association*, May 1, 1996.   **206**

As correctional populations rise and supervision becomes less absolute, it is inevitable that sexual contact will occur between inmates in both adult and juvenile facilities. This report argues that programs that seek to decrease the spread of **sexually transmitted diseases in correctional settings** can be successful and should be promoted more aggressively in institutions nationwide.

48. It's Time to Open the Doors of Our Prisons, Rufus King, *Newsweek*, April 19, 1999.   **208**

In this brief article, Rufus King makes the argument that society has responded to crime with hysteria, which has resulted in the creation of **a justice system with little flexibility** and even less compassion. He suggests that the low-level offender would be better served by programs outside of the prison, and he suggests that the government should immediately review all sentences and release those who have served excessive amounts of time for seemingly minimal offenses.

Index   **209**
Article Review Form   **212**
Article Rating Form   **213**

The concepts in bold italics are developed in the article. For further expansion please refer to the Topic Guide and the Index.

Topic Guide

This topic guide suggests how the selections and World Wide Web sites found in the next section of this book relate to topics of traditional concern to students and professionals in the study of corrections. It is useful for locating interrelated articles and Web sites for reading and research. The guide is arranged alphabetically according to topic.

The relevant Web sites, which are numbered and annotated on pages 4 and 5, are easily identified by the Web icon (◉) under the topic articles. By linking the articles and the Web sites by topic, this ANNUAL EDITIONS reader becomes a powerful learning and research tool.

TOPIC AREA	TREATED IN	TOPIC AREA	TREATED IN
Addictions	6. Forgotten Offender 14. Day in the Life 31. Correctional Treatment 32. Habilation, Not Rehabilitation 37. New Bedlam ◉ 4, 5, 7, 11, 13		38. Get-Tough Policy That Failed 39. Deterrent Effect of the Three Strikes Law 46. Rough Justice in the Youth Courts ◉ 7, 13, 14, 21, 27, 28, 30, 31, 32, 33
Aging	20. Addressing the Needs of Elderly Offenders ◉ 4, 20	Drug Treatment	5. Drugs, Crime, Prison, and Treatment 31. Correctional Treatment 33. Decade of Experimenting with Intermediate Sanctions 37. New Bedlam 40. "Lock 'em Up and Throw Away the Key" ◉ 4, 5, 7, 11, 13
AIDS/HIV	47. HIV/AIDS Education and Prevention Programs ◉ 7, 11		
Behavioral Change	8. Behind Bars: We've Built the Largest Prison System 12. Prison Crime in New York State 33. Decade of Experimenting with Intermediate Sanctions 37. New Bedlam ◉ 4, 7, 8, 12, 19, 28, 30	Drugs and Crime	4. Drug Use History and Criminal Behavior 5. Drugs, Crime, Prison, and Treatment 14. Day in the Life 15. Gangs behind Bars ◉ 4, 5, 7, 11, 13
Chain Gangs	44. Chain Gangs		
Cost of Prison Operations	27. Facts and Figures 28. Stolen Lives 31. Correctional Treatment 33. Decade of Experimenting with Intermediate Sanctions 38. Get-Tough Policy That Failed 40. "Lock 'em Up and Throw Away the Key" ◉ 3, 5, 6, 13, 32, 33	Family Issues	6. Forgotten Offender 7. Coping with Incarceration 14. Day in the Life 18. Like Mother, Like Daughter ◉ 4, 7, 13, 15, 20, 27
		Federal Bureau of Prisons	10. Inside the New Alcatraz 24. Juveniles in Federal Prison 37. New Bedlam
Crime Causation	4. Drug Use History and Criminal Behavior 9. Behind Bars: Substance Abuse 15. Gangs behind Bars 37. New Bedlam 39. Deterrent Effect of the Three Strikes Law 40. "Lock 'em Up and Throw Away the Key" ◉ 1, 2, 3, 4, 7, 8, 10, 12, 30, 31	Gender Factors	6. Forgotten Offender 7. Coping with Incarceration 14. Day in the Life 18. Like Mother, Like Daughter 19. Percentage of Women on Probation and Parole Rising ◉ 15
		History of the Correctional System	1. American Criminal Justice Philosophy 38. Get-Tough Policy That Failed ◉ 2, 6, 11
Crime Changes	2. Prisoners in 1998 12. Prison Crime in New York State 37. New Bedlam 45. Restorative Justice: The Concept ◉ 5, 9, 11, 25, 30, 31	History of the Criminal Justice System	1. American Criminal Justice Philosophy 2. Prisoners in 1998 6. Forgotten Offender ◉ 2, 3, 11
Death Penalty	26. House without a Blueprint 27. Facts and Figures 28. Stolen Lives 29. Death Row Justice Derailed 30. Death Penalty ◉ 4, 7, 24, 25, 26	Home Detention/Electronic Surveillance	36. Young Probation/Parole Officer Toughens with Experience ◉ 27
Deterrence/ Three Strikes	8. Behind Bars: We've Built the Largest Prison System 32. Habilation, Not Rehabilitation 33. Decade of Experimenting with Intermediate Sanctions	Inmate History	2. Prisoners in 1998 3. Prior Abuse Reported by Inmates and Probationers 6. Forgotten Offender 15. Gangs behind Bars

TOPIC AREA	TREATED IN	TOPIC AREA	TREATED IN
	37. New Bedlam 38. Get-Tough Policy That Failed ● **3, 4, 5, 6, 7, 9, 11, 12, 20**		15. Gangs behind Bars 32. Habilitation, Not Rehabilitation ● **5, 6, 7, 8, 11, 13**
Inmate Riots	15. Gangs behind Bars 16. Effects of the Duran Consent Decree	Prison Design	10. Inside the New Alcatraz 37. New Bedlam
Inmate Suits	16. Effects of the Duran Consent Decree 17. Constitution and the Federal District Judge ● **26**	Prison Labor	6. Forgotten Offender 33. Decade of Experimenting with Intermediate Sanctions 44. Chain Gangs
Jail Problems	2. Prisoners in 1998 37. New Bedlam ● **17, 18, 20**	Privatizing Prisons	36. Young Probation/Parole Officer Toughens with Experience 42. Probation Department in Michigan ● **32**
Judicial Authority	16. Effects of the Duran Consent Decree 17. Constitution and the Federal District Judge ● **2, 6, 24, 25, 26**	Race Factors	15. Gangs behind Bars 18. Like Mother, Like Daughter 23. Mental Health and Treatment of Inmates and Probationers 29. Death Row Justice Derailed 48. It's Time to Open the Doors of Our Prisons ● **4**
Juveniles	14. Day in the Life 23. Mental Health and Treatment of Inmates and Probationers 24. Juveniles in Federal Prison 25. Re-Forming Juvenile Justice 39. Deterrent Effect of the Three Strikes Law 42. Probation Department in Michigan ● **7, 12, 19, 22, 23**	Rape/Sex in Prison	6. Forgotten Offender 13. Stopping Abuse in Prison 14. Day in the Life 15. Gangs behind Bars 47. HIV/AIDS Education and Prevention Programs ● **18**
Mental Illness	6. Forgotten Offender 23. Mental Health and Treatment of Inmates and Probationers 33. Decade of Experimenting with Intermediate Sanctions 37. New Bedlam ● **4, 9, 10, 12**	Restorative Justice	33. Decade of Experimenting with Intermediate Sanctions 45. Restorative Justice: The Concept ● **30**
Parole Boards	34. Eliminating Parole Boards Isn't a Cure-All ● **27**	Substance Abuse	4. Drug Use History and Criminal Behavior 5. Drugs, Crime, Prison, and Treatment 15. Gangs behind Bars 22. Chaser ● **4, 5, 7, 11, 13**
Prison Crime	6. Forgotten Offender 12. Prison Crime in New York State 13. Stopping Abuse in Prison 14. Day in the Life 15. Gangs behind Bars 16. Effects of the Duran Consent Decree ● **18**	Victims' Rights/ Restoration	33. Decade of Experimenting with Intermediate Sanctions 45. Restorative Justice: The Concept ● **30**
Prison Demographics	2. Prisoners in 1998 6. Forgotten Offender 14. Day in the Life	Volunteers in Probation	42. Probation Department in Michigan ● **28**

AE: Corrections

The following World Wide Web sites have been carefully researched and selected to support the articles found in this reader. If you are interested in learning more about specific topics found in this book, these Web sites are a good place to start. The sites are cross-referenced by number and appear in the topic guide on the previous two pages. Also, you can link to these Web sites through our DUSHKIN ONLINE support site at *http://www.dushkin.com/online/*.

The following sites were available at the time of publication. Visit our Web site—we update DUSHKIN ONLINE regularly to reflect any changes.

General Sources

1. American Society of Criminology
http://www.bsos.umd.edu/asc/four.html
This is an excellent starting place for studying all aspects of corrections, criminal justice, and criminology, with links to international sources, court information, police, and so on.

2. Introduction to American Justice
http://www.uaa.alaska.edu/just/just110/home.html
Here is an excellent outline of the causes of crime, including major theories, prepared by Professor Darryl Wood of the Justice Center at the University of Alaska at Anchorage. It provides an introduction to crime, law, corrections, police and policing, and more.

3. National Archive of Criminal Justice Data (NACJD)
http://www.icpsr.umich.edu/NACJD/index.html
NACJD holds more than 500 data collections relating to criminal justice, most of which can be accessed from this site.

4. SOSIG: Sociology of Law and Crime
http://sosig.esrc.bris.ac.uk/roads/subject-listing/World-cat/sociolaw.html
This international site offers articles, papers and reports, government publications, research projects, and much more. Information covered includes aging inmates, American Indians and crime, and the death penalty.

5. Sourcebook of Criminal Justice Statistics Online
http://www.albany.edu/sourcebook/
Data about all aspects of criminal justice in the United States is available at this site, which includes more than 600 tables from dozens of sources and search features.

6. U.S. Department of Justice
http://www.usdoj.gov
The DOJ represents the American people in enforcing the law in the public interest. This site provides U.S. judicial system information and links to federal government Web servers, topics of interest related to the justice system, documents and resources, and a topical index.

7. Yahoo! Society and Culture: Crime: Correction and Rehabilitation
http://dir.yahoo.com/Society_and_Culture/Crime/Correction_and_Rehabilitation/
Yahoo!'s large site includes sections on AIDS/HIV, Correctional issues, Death Penalty, Inmates, Juvenile Detention Centers, Prison History, Sentencing, and much more.

Who Are the Prisoners?

8. Crime Times
http://www.crime-times.org/titles.htm
This site on crime presents research reviews and other information regarding biological causes of criminal, violent, and psychopathic behavior. It consists of many articles that are listed by title.

9. David Willshire's Forensic Psychology & Psychiatry Links
http://www.ozemail.com.au/~dwillsh/
A number of links to professional journals and associations are offered on this site. It is a valuable resource for the study of possible connections between violence and mental disorders. Topics include serial killers, sex offenders, and trauma.

10. Explanations of Criminal Behavior
http://www.uaa.alaska.edu/just/just110/crime2.html
Prepared by Darryl Wood at the University of Alaska, this outline examines the causes of crime, including major theories.

11. Justice Information Center (JIC)
http://www.ncjrs.org
Provided by the National Criminal Justice Reference Service, the JIC site connects to information about corrections, courts, crime prevention, criminal justice, statistics, drugs and crime, law enforcement, victims, and other topics. News and current highlights are also presented.

12. Victims of Childhood Sexual Abuse—Later Criminal Consequences
http://www.ncjrs.org/txtfiles/abuse.txt
This interesting article investigates earlier evidence of a circle of violence—people who are abused become abusers later in life—and comes up with somewhat different results.

Prison Life

13. Accommodating Prison Population Growth
http://www.lao.ca.gov/sc010695a.html
In this 1995 report, the California Board of Corrections had predicted that, because of the "Three Strikes and You're Out" legislation, the prison population would grow by almost 70 percent. This report discusses this issue and what can be done.

14. The Corrections Connection Network
http://www.corrections.com
This site is the largest online network providing news and information for corrections professionals. See also the American Correctional Association at *http://www.corrections.com/aca/* and the American Jail Association at *http://www.corrections.com/aja/*.

15. The Farm: Life Inside a Women's Prison
http://www.igc.org/thefarm/links.htm
Follow the links at this site for information about the issues of women in prison: pregnant women, sexual abuse of incarcerated women, and African American women.

16. Oregon Department of Corrections
http://www.doc.state.or.us/links/welcome.htm
Resources in such areas as crime and law enforcement as well as links to U.S. state corrections departments are available at this site.

17. Prison Life
http://www.hmprisonservice.gov.uk/life/
Aspects of life in prison are covered at this site from the UK, including what a "life" sentence means.

18. Stop Prisoner Rape, Inc.
http://www.spr.org/spr.html
Access the materials available through this site to gain an understanding into the social relationships that may develop in incarceration facilities.

Unusual Problems and Unusual Populations

19. Basics of Juvenile Justice
http://www.uaa.alaska.edu/just/just110/intro2.html
A list of similarities and differences between juvenile and adult justice systems is available at this site. Also listed by time periods are changes in the philosophy of juvenile justice.

20. Behind Bars: Aging Prison Population Challenges Correctional Health Systems
http://www.nurseweek.com/features/99-7/prison.html
In this article from *Nurse Week*, Chris Schreiber discusses the growth of an elderly population in prison and the health-delivery problems that the over 2 million aging inmates will create.

21. Center for Rational Correctional Policy
http://pierce.simplenet.com
Data on courts and sentencing, with many additional links to a variety of criminal justice sources, may be accessed here.

22. Institute for Intergovernmental Research (IIR)
http://www.iir.com
The IIR is a research organization that specializes in law enforcement, juvenile justice, and criminal justice issues. Explore the projects, links, and search engines from this home page. Topics include youth gangs and white-collar criminals.

23. Juvenile Justice Documents: Corrections
http://www.ncjrs.org/jjcorr.htm
This extensive site, sponsored by the National Criminal Justice Reference Service, includes more than 30 news articles, plus fact sheets on a wide variety of juvenile corrections issues.

Dying on the Inside: The Death Penalty

24. ACLU Criminal Justice Home Page
http://aclu.org/issues/criminal/hmcj.html
This Criminal Justice page of the ACLU (American Civil Liberties Union) Web site highlights recent events, lists important resources, and contains a search mechanism.

25. Critical Criminology Division of the ASC
http://sun.soci.niu.edu/~critcrim
Provided by the American Society of Criminology, this site provides basic criminology and related government resources as well as other useful links. Restorative justice and the death penalty are discussed.

26. Prison Law Page
http://www.wco.com/~aerick/prison.htm
This site contains resources on prisons and on the death penalty debate.

Living on the Outside: Intermediate Sanctions

27. American Probation and Parole Association (APPA)
http://www.appa-net.org
Open the APPA site to find information and resources related to probation and parole issues, position papers, the APPA code of ethics, and research and training programs and opportunities.

28. VIP: Volunteers in Prevention, Probation, and Prisons, Inc.
http://comnet.org/vip/
A description of volunteers in prevention, prison, and probation may be accessed here along with data on VIP training, research library facilities, and the Partners against Crime Mentoring Program. Professional links are also offered.

Future Issues in Corrections

29. ACLU: Corrections: News
http://aclu.org/issues/criminal/hmcj.html
The latest news releases in the field of corrections at any given moment, culled from all over the United States, are available here.

30. Campaign for Equity-Restorative Justice (CERJ)
http://www.cerj.org
This is the home page of CERJ, which sees monumental problems in justice systems and the need for reform. Examine this site and its links for information about the restorative justice movement.

31. National Center for Policy Analysis (NCPA)
http://www.public-policy.org/~ncpa/pd/law/index3.html
Through the NCPA's "Idea House" click onto links to read discussions on an array of topics that are of major interest in the study of the American judicial system. Available are sections on the courts, judges, lawyers, and other aspects of the legal system and resulting corrections.

32. National Institute of Corrections (NIC)
http://www.nicic.org/inst/
The NIC is a small agency of correctional learning and experience, and it is part of the Department of Justice. NIC advances and shapes effective correctional practice and public policy through collaboration and leadership, and it provides assistance, information, education, and training in the field of corrections. Visit also NIC's Community Corrections Division, which is involved in a national initiative to update the Interstate Compact for the Supervision of Parolees and Probationers, at *http://www.nicic.org/inst/nicccd.htm*.

33. National Institute of Justice (NIJ)
http://www.ojp.usdoj.gov/nij/lawedocs.htm
The NIJ sponsors projects and conveys research findings to practitioners in the field of criminal justice and corrections. Through this site you can access the initiatives of the 1994 Violent Crime Control and Law Enforcement Act, monitor international criminal activity, learn the latest about policing techniques and issues, and more.

We highly recommend that you review our Web site for expanded information and our other product lines. We are continually updating and adding links to our Web site in order to offer you the most usable and useful information that will support and expand the value of your Annual Editions. You can reach us at:
http://www.dushkin.com/annualeditions/.

Unit 1

Unit Selections

1. **American Criminal Justice Philosophy: What's Old—What's New?** Curtis R. Blakely and Vic W. Bumphus
2. **Prisoners in 1998,** Allen J. Beck and Christopher J. Mumola
3. **Prior Abuse Reported by Inmates and Probationers,** Caroline Wolf Harlow
4. **Drug Use History and Criminal Behavior among 133 Incarcerated Men,** Elena M. Kouri, Harrison G. Pope Jr., Kenneth F. Powell, Paul S. Oliva, and Corbett Campbell
5. **Drugs, Crime, Prison, and Treatment,** Charles Blanchard
6. **The Forgotten Offender,** Meda Chesney-Lind

Key Points to Consider

❖ What are some of the common background variables we see within the inmate population? Which background variables are linked to which types of crime? What does this suggest about the causes of crime?

❖ How could prisons change to become more effective in controlling crime?

❖ How has social change affected the criminal justice system?

❖ How could substance abuse programs in prison be combined with changes in sentencing to encourage inmates to participate in these programs?

❖ In which specific areas of behaviors have laws changed to reflect changing social interests?

❖ How have these social changes affected the social perception of the female offender and contributed to the increases in female incarceration rates?

 **Links**   www.dushkin.com/online/

8. **Crime Times**
   http://www.crime-times.org/titles.htm
9. **David Willshire's Forensic Psychology & Psychiatry Links**
   http://www.ozemail.com.au/~dwillsh/
10. **Explanations of Criminal Behavior**
    http://www.uaa.alaska.edu/just/just110/crime2.html
11. **Justice Information Center (JIC)**
    http://www.ncjrs.org
12. **Victims of Childhood Sexual Abuse—Later Criminal Consequences**
    http://www.ncjrs.org/txtfiles/abuse.txt

These sites are annotated on pages 4 and 5.

Who Are the Prisoners?

As we begin our study of the corrections system, we examine the makeup of the current prison population in the context of both the criminal justice system and the needs and opinions of society. In the first article, "American Criminal Justice Philosophy: What's Old—What's New?" we see how the philosophies of each component of the justice system drive the behavior of that specific agency. Curtis Blakely and Vic Bumphus provide a comparison among current police philosophies and examine how to apply them to corrections. The next article, "Prisoners in 1998," follows that theme and shows how some of these system changes and social transformations have affected the composition of the prison system. Allen Beck and Christopher Mumola include tables that show changes in inmate demographics and incarceration rates nationwide.

The next three articles in the unit discusses the makeup of the current prison population. The various backgrounds of the prisoners and causal links are forged to help explain the reasons why some end up in prison while others with similar backgrounds do not. The first article links early child abuse to later criminal behavior, while the next two articles explore the relationship between substance abuse and criminal behavior. These articles support the data presented previously in unit 1, and offer suggestions based on these data. If taken as a singular set of information, these articles can be used to strongly support the idea of treatment programs for addicted offenders.

Lastly, this unit looks at female or "forgotten" offenders, who have been increasing their presence in the correctional system over the past two decades. While their numbers have increased, they still make up a small percentage of the overall prisoner population. Meda Chesney-Lind's article offers some explanations as to why these offenders have remained forgotten, and how the system could adapt to better provide for their needs and their rehabilitation.

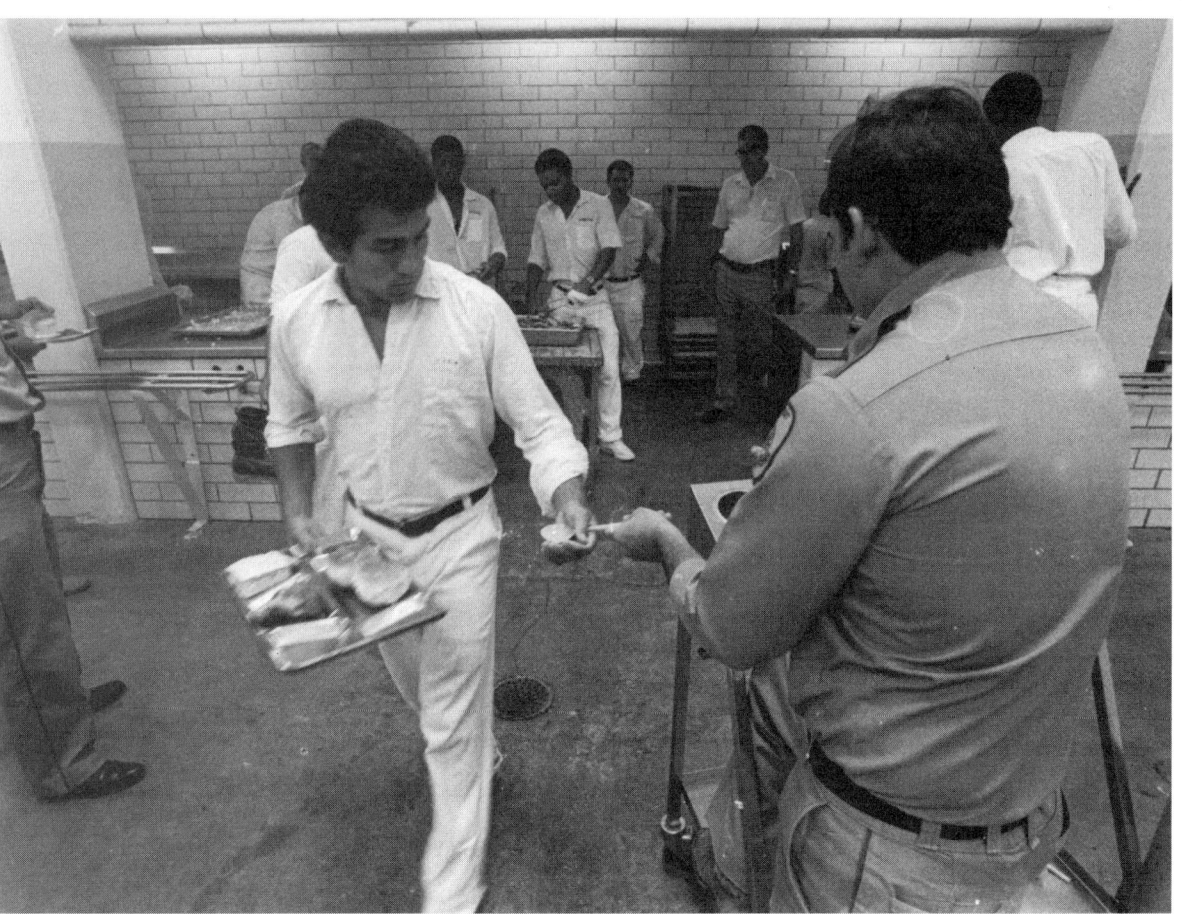

# Article 1

American Criminal Justice Philosophy: What's Old—What's New?

BY CURTIS R. BLAKELY AND VIC W. BUMPHUS*

Introduction

Contemporary movements in criminal justice, such as community-oriented policing and certain community corrections strategies, have been portrayed as new innovations, having little historical precedent. While specific programs are genuinely original, criminologists have advocated the importance of proactive and preventive programming for decades. Toward that end, the criminal justice system is currently integrating its adversarial approach to the identification, apprehension, and correction of offenders with an increased service orientation by emphasizing community involvement. As such, criminal justice scholars and activists are encouraging officials to cultivate community partnerships to solicit citizen input.

The following review of literature explores the idea that the underlying objectives of the early American criminal justice system remain largely unaltered. What has changed is public attitudes about crime, police organization, police and public perceptions about each other, and the complex relationship between politics and justice initiatives. Community policing and restorative justice paradigms are briefly discussed. The specifics are less important than the guiding philosophy behind their growing popularity. While the political rhetoric surrounding these "new" programs envisions them as novel approaches, a review of the extant literature suggests that they are nothing more than modem adaptations to earlier innovations. The authors do not intend an exhaustive historical account of either policing or corrections. Instead, they hope to provoke more comprehensive thought by briefly examining criminal justice change from a socio-historical perspective.

Police: A historical review

The impact of European ideals upon early American policing is evident (Uchida, 1993; Walker, 1980; Carter & Radelet, 1999); however, unlike English protocol, original attempts at policing within America were characterized by direct citizen participation. This may be due to philosophical beliefs regarding governmental intervention and the slow, often hesitant, establishment of colonial law enforcemerit agencies. Colonists were attempting to escape a strong, often tyrannical government; therefore, they naturally valued individual freedom, discretion, and participation. Due to this vacuum in official authority, individuals participated directly in criminal justice activities (Walker, 1980). Uchida (1993: 20) notes that an organized police force was viewed with suspicion due to its potential for "despotic control over citizens and subjects." However, as the colonies became more permanent and socially complex, the need for a more organized style of policing developed.

An early forerunner of contemporary policing was the night watch system, and as the name suggests, it was nothing more than night-time patrol. New York began experimenting with a night watch as early as 1684 (Walker, 1980; Uchida, 1993; Carter & Radelet, 1999; Lyman, 1999). These sentry men were primarily charged

---

*Both authors are members of the Department of Police Studies at Eastern Kentucky University. Mr. Blakely is a Training Specialist and Adjunct Professor, and Mr. Bumphus is an Assistant Professor.

with patrolling the city for fires, suspicious individuals, riots, or other incidents requiring immediate intervention. This system was eventually modified to include a day watch component. Thus, the first forerunner of the modern police force emerged. Walker (1980:59) credits these early attempts with engaging in "preventive patrol,"—arguably, the first attempt at proactive policing within America. Another example of early policing can be found in the use of "frank pledges" which compelled all males twelve years of age and older to serve in a quasipolice role. These were small groups of citizens that vowed to deliver to court any group member committing an unlawful act. According to Uchida (1993: 17), this style of community policing became increasingly popular in England after 1066.

While these two approaches were primarily designed to prevent and control crime, they also served to reinforce the value of community involvement in law enforcement activities. Likewise, when reviewing the early epoch of American policing, it can be seen that police were involved in a wide variety of social service tasks including providing food to the hungry and shelter to the homeless (Uchida, 1993: 22; Kelling & Moore, 1995: 7).

It was during the reform era (beginning in the 1930s), under the direct tutelage of the Federal Bureau of Investigation, that professionalism and technology began to become paramount. The Wickersham Commission, under President Hoover, also advocated changes in policing envisioned as efforts to professionalize law enforcement (Carter & Radelet, 1999; Lyman, 1999). Departments nationwide followed suit and began to adopt a "professional" style of policing. This movement was characterized by a reduction of the social service role and an official emphasis upon crime control and offender apprehension. Therefore, police began to rely upon arrests and percentages of crimes cleared to measure effectiveness (Walker, 1980: 191; Kelling & Moore, 1995: 14). This shifted the human approach to a much lesser profile in formalized policing (Keliing & Moore, 1995:12). Walker (1980:135) states that this model remained dominant and unchallenged until the 1970s. However, he has also noted (1980:189), that "while the police role was redefined toward crime fighting, day to day police work increasingly involved miscellaneous services to the public." Reiss (1971) and Walker (1980) both conclude that during the l960s, as much as 80 percent of police work was consumed by noncriminal matters. This suggests that even during an era characterized by growing police professionalism and isolation, delivery of informal policing tasks remained the norm.

Contemporary policing issues

Those familiar with the history of American policing are aware of the many challenges inhibiting the effective application of law enforcement. These include organizational (fiscal restraints, staffing problems, and large patrol districts), ethical, and socio-legal problems. Increasingly, police have been placed under closer scrutiny due to high-profile incidents such as the Rodney King beating, the Los Angeles riots, and more recently the flurry of misconduct complaints landing on the New York City Police Department. Substantial criticism has involved the treatment of the young, poor, and those of minority status. These various problems have subjected nearly all police agencies to critical examination in areas of public relations and citizen contact. Likewise, police administrators across America are currently concerned with managing public relations, often accompanied by some degree of community-oriented policing.

The 1970s marked a time in which the public, somewhat dissatisfied with police services, increasingly demanded that the police take a proactive and personal approach toward community issues. This desire is summarized by Meese (1993), who proposes that the police should be more than merely reactive, responding to crimes already committed. It is important that law enforcement develop a proactive posture toward community disorder, social problems, and quality of life issues.

In response, police establishments began to abandon a strict "law enforcement" approach, replacing it with a greater "peace and service" orientation. The latter, of course, embraces a more social service and holistic approach to policing. This shift away from a strict crime control approach to one that encourages citizen involvement in police operations, and police involvement in community activities, has been referred to as strategic, problem solving, and neighborhood oriented policing (Meese, 1993). Kelling and Moore (1995) have noted that this movement signifies a new era, distinguishable from the political and reform eras.

Central to community policing is a belief that the police can more effectively achieve their basic goals of crime prevention and control through the assistance and support of the community (Meese, 1993). By establishing partnerships with other institutions like families, schools, churches, and neighborhood associations, police potentially widen their ability to identify and solve community problems. This approach envisions the importance of peace-keeping and social service tasks as equal to enforcement activities.

Corrections: A historical review

Many of the major shifts in correctional ideology parallel changes in approaches to law enforcement. Beginning in the 16th century, "workhouses, or houses of correction," spread widely over northwestern Europe (Shichor, 1995: 23). While little is known about these early institutions and their practices, anecdotal accounts present them as an attempt systematically to address and rectify increasing crime and disorder problems. Walker (1980: 16) adds that these institutions resembled modern prisons in their attempts to rehabilitate the offender and make him or her a productive member of society. Then

1 ❖ WHO ARE THE PRISONERS?

in 1576, the English Parliament passed an act providing for the establishment of the "bride well" (Shichor, 1995). These institutions were places where vagrants, prostitutes, and offenders were instilled with rehabilitative rationale and provided rudimentary skills training (Welch, 1996: 44). Shichor (1995: 24) identifies these institutions as early forerunners to reformatories and prisons. Likewise, Welch (1996: 44) recounts that these institutions formed the basis for rehabilitative rationale and the work ethic. Philosophical statements like, "It is of little advantage to restrain the bad by punishment, unless you render them good by discipline," reverberated this sentiment (Walker, 1980: 42). According to Walker (1980: 66), incarceration was meant to rehabilitate the offender through "creating a better environment, separating the individual from harmful influences and subjecting him to a corrective prison discipline of solitude, hard work, and religious study." Morris (1998: 32) concludes that the penitentiary was intended to reform criminals by "isolating them from each other and other infectious diseases." Thomas (1987: 60) states that this rehabilitative ideal began to take root in Europe long before the 17th century and the colonization of America. Likewise, he states that an "argument can be made that enthusiasm for rehabilitation as a major objective of penal sanctions dates back to the time of Plato or before" (Thomas, 1987: 91).

Colonial America adopted many of the same European philosophies and practices. However, Walker (1980:12) notes that colonial criminal codes were often more lenient in their punishments than were their English counterparts. This comparative leniency may indicate an early philosophical difference existing between the colonists and England: a perception that English sanctions were more punitive than corrective. Thomas (1987: 66) recognizes this and states that well before the Civil War, sanctions were being applied within America's prisons with the conviction that they could serve the goal of crime prevention. Toward the end of the 18th century, the penitentiary arose (Shichor, 1995: 26). As the name implies, the penitentiary had as its main objectives repentance, penitence, and rehabilitation (Shichor, 1995: 26; Walker, 1980: 65).

Much like the blind men of Hindustan who gave despairingly divergent descriptions of an elephant, penologists also maintain individualistic ideals regarding correctional objectives. Most researchers, however, have consistently identified four goals. For example, Barak (1998: 75) lists these goals as revenge, deterrence, incapacitation, and rehabilitation. Shichor (1995: 65) identifies these same four goals but substitutes retribution for revenge. Wilkinson (1997) identifies the same four, but substitutes vengeance for retribution. Thomas (1987: 51) reduces the number of correctional goals to three, including retribution, crime prevention, and rehabilitation. The designation of correctional objectives suggests only a slight difference in semantics, not in overall philosophy.

Morris (1998) notes that whether prisons are considered tools of retribution or rehabilitation, most people believe that they fail to achieve either goal. He states:

> Instead, the institution has unintentionally spawned a subculture that is antithetical to both goals—and it has become clear that the beliefs and behavior of inmates are far more likely to be shaped by this subculture than by prison and its programs (Morris, 1998: 8).

Thomas (1987: 85) notes that the life and death struggle of rehabilitative efforts may be the single most pervasive issue that has occurred in corrections over the past decade.

As already observed, one objective of the American correctional system has traditionally been rehabilitation. Historically, a belief in the innate goodness of humanity and one's ability to change have been valued in American correctional policies. This can be seen in the implementation of indeterminate sentencing, probation, and parole (Thomas, 1987: 93). Rehabilitation was strongly emphasized until the early 1970s when the United States began to experience unparalleled increases in crime rates and prison commitments (Shichor, 1995: 9; Blakely, 1997). Morris (1998: 8) observes that, due to overcrowding, correctional facilities are increasingly de-emphasizing their original mandate of offender rehabilitation, focusing instead on maintaining facility control. To manage the ever-increasing inmate population, rehabilitative efforts—which provide ample opportunity for inmate conflict, divert fiscal and personnel resources, and are labor intensive—increasingly become secondary to the orderly operation of the facility (Cullen, Latessa, Burton, & Lombardo, 1993; Thomas, 1995). Conditions associated with overcrowding and the violence that it spawns (Montgomery & Crews, 1998), are increasingly convincing prison officials that a strict model of incapacitation might be necessary. Contemporary correctional efforts appear less concerned with initiating inmate change and more interested in maintaining facility control by limiting opportunities for inmate misconduct. However, amidst the emergence of punitive, crime-control ideology, inmate enhancement and life skills programming remain central to correctional practices.

In the recent past, it appears that, much like the police, corrections has been guided by a strict crime control mandate. This is reflected in that large segment of society that values incarceration of offenders over the remaining three goals (Blakely, 1997; Briscoe, 1997; Wittenberg, 1997). The current "get tough" response to crime is resulting in a growing reliance upon confinement strictly as a punitive measure (Cullen, Latessa, Burton, & Lombardo, 1993; Blakely, 1997; Briscoe, 1997; Wittenberg, 1997; Montgomery & Crews, 1998). The Congress' "Safe Streets" and "3-Strikes You're Out" bills as well as the President's "War on Crime" and "Get Tough" campaigns clearly indicate a more punitive ideology (Blakely, 1998;

Montgomery & Crews, 1998). Additionally, the popularity of "Truth in Sentencing" laws requires offenders to serve increasingly longer terms of confinement (Cowley, 1998; Montgomery & Crews, 1998). In a recent study conducted by Cullen, Latessa, Burton, and Lombardo (1993), rehabilitation was ranked as a secondary goal by a large percentage of prison administrators. Wittenberg (1996: 46) reports that a substantial number of Americans currently prefer punishment to rehabilitation. Thomas (1987: 99) notes that this "get tough" response is culminating in an organized "anti-rehabilitation" trend, emphasizing the protection of society through incapacitation (Shichor, 1995: 10; Montgomery & Crews, 1998).

This apparent shift in goals has prompted Albanese (1996: 558) to state, "We just can't seem to punish enough." Wilkinson (1997: 100) observes that this approach has often been at the expense of both the offender and community. Shichor (1995: 10) states that this movement has culminated in an organized "anti-rehabilitation" trend emphasizing the protection of society through incapacitation. These scholars concur that the current punitive approach within corrections lacks any identifiable objective, other than punishment itself.

Contemporary correctional issues

A new paradigm in criminal justice has recently emerged. The restorative justice paradigm envisions a more proactive criminal justice system emphasizing preventing crime in the early stages, protecting society, and relying on incarceration as a last resort (Hahn, 1998; Bazemore & Umbreit, 1997). This philosophy advocates a more integrated approach to justice, encouraging community, victim, and offender participation. Restorative justice involves long-term commitment to systemic changes (Umbreit, 1995) and builds on existing programs like victim-offender mediation, restitution, community service, and police-community partnerships (Bazemore & Umbreit, 1997; Hahn, 1998).

To pursue rehabilitation again, corrections is currently experimenting with a number of restorative justice programs. At the nucleus of this movement is a belief in an offender's ability to change, and an expectation that offenders will accept responsibility for their actions. In a recent study conducted in Vermont, Gorczyk and Perry (1997: 79) report that 93 percent of that state's population wanted violent offenders to serve their entire sentences with no opportunity for early release. But these same researchers also found that Vermonters expect the system to operate with specific concern for future behavior. While these findings cannot be generalized nationwide, they may indicate a desire by many for proactive and rehabilitative measures. Maryland, too, has implemented a restorative justice approach to its juvenile justice system. This program has the expressed objectives of increasing "public safety," and offender "accountability," while initiating "rehabilitative" measures (Simms, 1997).

A comparison of proactive policing and proactive corrections

After reviewing the historical objectives of policing and corrections, and current attempts to implement community policing and restorative justice programs, the question persists whether these philosophical approaches are new, or an attempt to return to earlier criminal justice pursuits. While it may initially appear unnecessary to make this determination, there are two compelling reasons to do so. First, a strong grounding in historical precedent is essential for the application of criminal justice and permits contemporary practitioners to make intelligent and informed decisions about crime control strategies and tactics. Secondly, this determination permits contemporary practitioners to further refine their approach to the ever-changing nature of criminal justice. This, in turn, allows for a more informed perspective on the evolution of correctional ideologies.

It appears that the early criminal justice system was originally more forward-looking than its contemporary counterpart. This is evidenced in the early establishment of peacekeeping and rehabilitative goals. While we are less interested in the methods of early justice than in the philosophical basis for their implementation, evidence indicates that early practitioners wished to cultivate a strong interpersonal relationship with society.

Likewise, with the advent of community policing, it appears that American policing is attempting to return to its original functions of public service and crime control. Faced with increasing crime rates during the reform era, police were largely unprepared to address social problems effectively. Therefore, police agencies adopted a defensive position of quick response times and the ready application of force. Rising crime rates also began to drive a wedge between the police and community. Increasingly, the police were being relegated to responding to incidents rather than intervening proactively. This encouraged society to view police efforts as unproductive and uncaring, and police to view communities as uncaring and nonsupportive.

Increasing crime rates and a defensive orientation readily lent itself to an adoption of military-style structuring. As can be expected, this further weakened the peacekeeping mandate of police agencies. Meese (1993) and Walker (1980) have noted the general negative impact of the military structure upon police agencies. Further, the inherent nature of military structuring stifled individual discretion and creative problem-solving techniques. Police departments began to departmentalize, and internalize operations. Society also began to view government apprehensively. With growing discontent with government and police services, anti-government public sentiment emerged. This was compounded by the unpopularity of the Vietnam war and skyrocketing claims of police brutality.

The increased reliance by police agencies on the automobile also took its toll. Walker (1980) credits the introduction of the automobile with isolating the police officer from the community and ultimately increasing the officer's adversarial relationship with new segments of society. While the car allowed a rapid response to calls for service, it ultimately removed officers from the neighborhood, relegating them to the confines of the cruiser. Motorized patrol demanded that an officer be reactive rather than proactive. Along with the automobile came new forms of communication, which inhibited personalized contact with the public, and instead, encouraged a reliance on other police personnel such as the dispatcher. The dispatcher became the source of information for police personnel and effectively replaced face to face contact with citizenry.

Likewise, corrections, which was largely a victim in this crime control approach, increasingly emphasized incapacitation. With increases in arrests, convictions, and imprisonments, they too were unprepared to continue emphasizing service through treatment programs. Morris (1998: 8) observes, "Instead of concerning themselves with the original purpose of the institution, prison officials are forced to focus almost exclusively on simply keeping control over their wards." Between 1970 and 1995, the number of inmates being housed in state and federal prison more than quintupled (Morris, 1998: 7). This "explosion" led Morris to state: "America's prison populations have been growing at such a rate that prison authorities may soon be forced to post 'no vacancy' signs outside their gates." In an attempt to "tread water," efforts to impart skills and increase education became secondary to the safe management of large inmate populations (Morris, 1998: 8). Because of overcrowding and increases in prison violence, correctional officials increasingly limited or eliminated activities not seen as absolutely necessary. The 1970s and early 1980s became known for prison riots like those that ravaged Attica and the Penitentiary of New Mexico. These and similar events convinced prison officials that a strict model of incapacitation might best suit criminal justice policy. And yet, through all these changes, America's penal system did not totally abandon its original intent, and increasingly began to use terms like "correctional officer," "correctional center," and "departments of corrections." While many argue, like Thomas (1987: 96) that a change in terminology does not necessarily imply a change in practice, this change may indicate an attempt to identify with an overall objective.

Conclusion

The historical record does not support community policing and restorative justice as contemporary innovations, but as attempts to return to an earlier model of justice emphasizing people, discretion, and a belief in the inherent goodness of humanity. Though criminal justice perspectives have gained and lost momentum due to social change, the symbiotic relationship between the various objectives ensures a criminal justice system that places emphasis on both reactive and proactive strategies. Therefore, contemporary proactive justice is part and parcel of the larger philosophical basis of the modern criminal justice system. In sum, it is the various interpretations of historical events in criminal justice that suggests that what is old (proactive or reactive) will eventually become new, again and again.

REFERENCES

Albanese, J. (1996). Five fundamental mistakes of criminal justice. *Justice Quarterly*, 13(4): 551–565.

Barak, G. (1998). *Integrating criminologies*. Boston, MA: Allyn and Bacon.

Bazemore, G. & Umbreit, M. (1997). *Balanced and restorative justice for juveniles: a framework for juvenile justice in the 21st century*. Washington DC: Office of Juvenile Justice and Delinquency Prevention.

Blakely, C. (1998). The rehabilitative benefits of education. *The (British) Prison Service Journal* (120): 29.

Blakely, C. (1997). Offender rehabilitation: A worthy goal. *Corrections Compendium*. 22(5): 1–2.

Bloomer, K. (1997). America's newest growth industry. *In These Times* (March).

Briscoe, J. (1997). Breaking the cycle of violence: A rational approach to at-risk youth. *Federal Probation*, 51(3): 3.

Carter, D., & Radelet, L. (1999). *The police and the community* (6th edition). Upper Saddle River, NJ: Prentice Hall.

Cowley, J. (1998). Changing public opinion. *Corrections Today* (February).

Cullen, F., Latessa, E., Burton, V., & Lombardo, L. (1993). Prison wardens: Is the rehabilitative ideal supported. *Criminology*, 31(1): 69–87.

Gorczyk, J., & Perry, J. (1997). What the public wants. *Corrections Today* (December).

Hahn, P. (1998). *Emerging criminal justice: three pillars for proactive justice system*. Thousand Oaks, CA: Sage Publications.

Johnson, B.R., & Ross, P.P. (1990). The privatization of correctional management: A review. *Journal of Criminal Justice*, 18: 351–355.

Kelling, G. and Moore, M. (1995). The evolving strategy of policing. In Kappeler's *The police and society: Touchstone Readings*. Prospect Heights, IL: Waveland Press, Inc.

Lyman, M. (1999). *The police: an introduction*. Upper Saddle River, NJ: Prentice Hall.

Meese III, E. (1993). *Community policing and the police officer*. Washington DC: U.S. Dept. of Justice.

Montgomery, Jr., Reid, & Crews, G. (1998). *A history of correctional violence: An examination of reported causes of riots and disturbance*. Lanham, MD: American Correctional Association.

Morris, J. (1998). *Jailhouse Journalism: The Fourth Estate Behind Bars*. Jefferson, NC: McFarland and Company, Inc.

Reiss, A. (1971). *The police and the public*. New Haven: Yale University Press.

Rothman, D. (1971). *The discovery of the asylum*. Boston: Little, Brown.

Shichor, D. (1995). *Punishment for profit*. Thousand Oaks, CA: Sage Publications.

Simms, S. (1997). Restorative juvenile justice. *Corrections Today* (December).

Thomas, J. (1995). The ironies of prison education. In Davidson's *Schooling in a Total Institution*, Westport, CT: Bergin and Garvey.

Thomas, C. (1987). *Corrections in America—Problems of the past and the present*. Thousand Oaks, CA. Sage Publications.

Uchida, C. (1993). The development of two American police: An historical overview. In Dunham and Alpert's *Critical issues in policing*. Prospect Heights, IL: Waveland Press, Inc.

UC Research (1993/94). *Punishment vs. rehabilitation*. Cincinnati: University of Cincinnati.

Umbreit, M. (1995). Holding juvenile offenders accountable: a restorative justice perspective. *Juvenile and Family Court Journal*, 42(2):31–42.

Walker, S. (1980). *Popular justice: A history of American criminal justice*. New York: Oxford University Press.

Welch, M. (1996). *Corrections: a critical approach*. New York: McGraw-Hill.

Wilkinson, R. (1997). Community justice in Ohio. *Corrections Today* (December).

Wittenberg, P. (1997). Leadership and the management of agency image. *Federal Probation*, 61(3): 46.

Wittenberg, P. (1996). Power, influence and the development of correctional policy. *Federal Probation*, 60(2): 43.

Article 2

Prisoners in 1998

By Allen J. Beck, Ph.D., BJS Statistician, and
Christopher J. Mumola, BJS Policy Analyst

The total number of prisoners under the jurisdiction of Federal or State adult correctional authorities was 1,302,019 at yearend 1998. During the year the States and the District of Columbia added 49,798 prisoners, and the Federal prison system added 10,068 prisoners. Overall, the Nation's prison population grew 4.8%, which was less than the average annual growth of 6.7% since 1990. In absolute numbers, prison growth during 1998 was equivalent to 1,151 more inmates per week, up from 1,130 per week in 1997.

At yearend 1998, more than 1,825,000 U.S. residents were in either jail or prison. State and Federal prisons housed two-thirds of the incarcerated population. Jails, which are locally operated and typically hold persons awaiting trial and those with sentences of a year or less, held the other third (592,462).

Relative to the number of U.S. residents, the rate of incarceration in prisons at yearend 1998 was 461 sentenced inmates per 100,000 residents—up from 292 in 1990. On December 31, 1998, 1 in every 113 men and 1 in every 1,754 women were sentenced prisoners under the jurisdiction of State or Federal authorities.

U.S. prison population rose 4.8% during 1998—the smallest annual growth rate since 1979

The 1998 prison growth rate of 4.8% was slightly smaller than the percentage increase recorded during 1997 (5.0%) (table 2). The total prison population increased by 59,866 inmates during 1998, slightly higher than in 1997 (up 58,785). Since 1990 the total prison population has grown an average of 63,144 per year, for an overall increase of 528,100 in 8 years.

Prisoners with sentences of more than 1 year ("sentenced prisoners") represented 96% of the total prison population at yearend 1998. During the 12-month period, the sentenced prison population grew 4.8% (table 3). The remaining prisoners had sentences of a year or less or were currently unsentenced (that is, awaiting trial in States with combined prison-jail systems).

The sentenced Federal prison population grew at over twice the rate of the sentenced State prison population during 1998 (9.2% compared to 4.4%). The sentenced Federal population grew faster than in 1997 (6.9%), while growth in the sentenced State population was down from 1997 (4.8%).

Highlights

December 31	Number of inmates		Sentenced prisoners per 100,000 resident population		Population housed as a percent of highest capacity	
	Federal	State	Federal	State	Federal	State
1990	65,526	708,393	20	272	151%	115%
1995	100,250	1,025,624	32	379	126	114
1996	105,544	1,077,824	33	394	125	116
1997	112,973	1,129,180	35	410	119	115
1998	123,041	1,178,978	38	423	127	113

- During 1998 the number of female prisoners rose by 6.5%, greater than the increase in male prisoners (4.7%). At yearend 1998, 84,427 women were in State or Federal prisons—6.5% of all prison inmates.

- On December 31, 1998, State prisons were operating at between 13% and 22% above capacity, while Federal prisons were operating at 27% above capacity.

- California (161,904), Texas (144,510), and the Federal system (123,041) together held 1 in every 3 prisoners in the Nation. Fifteen States, each holding fewer than 5,000 inmates, together held less than 4% of the Nation's prisoners.

- Seven jurisdictions had increases of at least 10% in 1998, led by Mississippi (16.7%) and North Dakota (14.8%). Four jurisdictions—Alaska (down 1.6%), Hawaii (-1.1%), Massachusetts (-1.0%), and Maine (-0.5%)—experienced decreases.

- Eighteen States housed inmates in other State or Federal facilities in 1998. Wisconsin had the most inmates in other States (3,028).

- Factors underlying the growth in the State prison population between 1990 and 1997 included—
  —a 39% rise in the number of parole violators returned to prison and a 4% increase in new court commitments.
  —a drop in annual release rates of inmates from 37% in 1990 to 31% in 1997.
  —an increase in the average time served in prison by released inmates (from 22 months in 1990 to 27 months in 1997) and in the time expected to be served by those entering prison (from 38 months to 43 months).
  —a small but growing number (10%) of inmates who will serve 20 or more years in prison before release and 5% who will never be released.

- Analyses of imprisonment rates from 1990 to 1997 reveal—
  —a 49% increase among males and a 71% increase among females in the number of sentenced prisoners per 100,000 residents.
  —widespread disparities by race and Hispanic origin. In 1997 the rate among black males in their late twenties reached 8,630 prisoners per 100,000 residents compared to 2,703 among Hispanic males and 868 among white males.

From *Bureau of Justice Statistics Bulletin,* August 1999, pp. 1-15. © 1999 by the U.S. Department of Justice. Reprinted by permission.

1 ❖ WHO ARE THE PRISONERS?

Table 1. Number of persons held in State or Federal prisons or in local jails, 1990–98.

Year	Total inmates in custody	Jurisdiction[a]	Custody	Inmates in local jails on June 30	Incarceration rate[b]
1990	1,148,702	773,919	743,382	405,320	461
1991	1,219,014	825,559	792,535	426,479	483
1992	1,295,150	882,500	850,566	444,584	508
1993	1,369,185	970,444	909,381	459,804	531
1994	1,476,621	1,054,702	990,147	486,474	567
1995	1,585,589	1,125,874	1,078,542	507,044	601
1996	1,646,020	1,183,368	1,127,528	518,492	618
1997	1,744,001	1,242,153	1,176,922	567,079	649
1998[c]	1,825,400	1,302,019	1,232,900	592,462	672
Average annual increase, 1990–98	6.0%	6.7%	6.5%	4.9%	

Note: Jail counts for 1994–98 exclude persons supervised outside of a jail facility.
[a] Includes prisoners held in local jails because of prison crowding.
[b] Number of prison and jail inmates per 100,000 U.S. residents at yearend.
[c] The 1998 prison custody count was estimated and rounded to nearest 100.

From yearend 1990 to yearend 1998—

- The Nation's incarcerated population rose by nearly 676,700 inmates, increasing at an average annual rate of 6.0%.
- State, Federal, and local governments had to accommodate an additional 84,587 inmates per year (or the equivalent of 1,627 new inmates per week).
- The rate of incarceration increased from 1 in every 217 U.S. residents to 1 in every 149.
- The Nation's prison and local jail facilities added space for about 675,270 inmates. By 1998 State prisons were 13% above their highest capacity; Federal prisons 27% above their rated capacity; and local jails 3% below their rated capacity.

On December 31, 1998, the number of sentenced prisoners per 100,000 U.S. residents was 461. Of the 11 States with rates greater than that for the Nation, 7 were in the South, 3 were in the West, and 1 was in the Midwest. Three States—Minnesota (117), Maine (125), and North Dakota (128)—had rates that were less than a third of the national rate. The District of Columbia, a wholly urban jurisdiction, held 1,913 sentenced prisoners per 100,000 residents.

Since 1990 the number of sentenced prisoners per 100,000 residents has risen from 292 to 461. During this period, incarceration rates rose most in the South (from 316 to 520) and West (from 277 to 417). The rate in the Midwest rose from 239 to 360, and the rate in the Northeast grew from 232 to 328. The number of sentenced Federal prisoners per 100,000 U.S. residents increased from 20 to 38.

Seven States reported increases of at least 10% during 1998

Between January 1 and December 31, Mississippi experienced the largest increase (up 16.7%), followed by North Dakota (14.8%), Wisconsin (13.4%), Vermont (12.3%), Oregon (11.6%), West Virginia (10.5%), and Louisiana (10.1%). Four States experienced a decline in prison populations. Alaska had the largest decline (down 1.6%), followed by Hawaii (down 1.1%), Massachusetts (down 1.0%), and Maine (down 0.5%).

In absolute numbers of inmates, 11 jurisdictions grew by at least 2,000. The Federal system (up 10,068 inmates), experienced the largest growth, followed by California (up 6,114), Texas (up 4,159), Louisiana (up 2,962), and New Jersey (up 2,760). These five jurisdictions, which incarcerated nearly 40% of all prisoners, accounted for 44% of the total growth during 1997.

Growth in sentenced State prisoners showed little regional variation

During 1998 the number of sentenced State and Federal prisoners grew by an additional 1,102 inmates per week. The 1998 average weekly increase was 15 inmates greater than the weekly increase in 1997 and 71 greater than in 1996.

Unlike recent years, there was little regional variation in the growth of the sentenced State prison population during 1998. The Western States had the highest percentage increase, with a gain of 5.1% in the number of sentenced prisoners, followed closely by the Midwest and Northeast (both rose 4.3%), and the South (4.2%).

Twenty-three States recorded higher growth rates of sentenced prisoners in 1998 than in 1997. Of these, four recorded growth rates over 10% in 1998: Vermont (34.1%), Mississippi (15.9%), North Dakota (13.8%), and Louisiana (10.1%). Five States reported increases of less than 2% during 1998, including New Hampshire, which reported an increase of one sentenced inmate. Delaware (−1.6%), North Carolina (−1.4%), Alaska and Virginia (both −1.2%), and Massachusetts (−1.0%) experienced declines.

Since 1990 the sentenced inmate population in State prisons has grown 64.9% (table 4). During this period 14 States reported increases of at least 75%, led by Texas (up 155%) and West Virginia (up 122%). Maine was the only State to report an increase of less than 10% (up 5.5%). During this time the Federal system reported an increase of 106%—53,279 additional inmates with sentences of more than 1 year.

Among States, Louisiana had the highest incarceration rate; Minnesota, the lowest

At yearend 1998 the 10 jurisdictions with the largest prison populations had under their jurisdiction 782,326 inmates, or 60% of the Nation's total prison population (table 5). California (161,904), Texas (144,510), and the Federal system (123,041) accounted for a third of the population. The 10 States with the smallest prison populations each held fewer than 4,000 inmates. Collectively, these States held only 1.8% of the Nation's total prison population.

Louisiana had the highest prison incarceration rate (736 sentenced inmates per 100,000 residents), followed by Texas (724), Oklahoma (622), Mississippi (574), and South Carolina (550). Six States had prison incarceration rates below 200, led by Minnesota (117), Maine (125), and North Dakota (128).

Since 1990 three States had average annual prison population increases of at least 10%: Texas (12.4%), West Virginia (10.5%), and Hawaii (10.0%). Seven States had average annual growth rates

2. Prisoners in 1998

Prisoners under military jurisdiction, by branch of service, yearend 1997 and 1998

Branch of service	Number 1998	Number 1997	Percent change, 1997–98	Percent of prisoners, 1998
To which prisoners belonged				
Total	2,426	2,772	−12.5%	100.0%
Air Force	484	575	−15.8	20.0
Army	862	1,063	−18.9	35.3
Marine Corps	682	628	8.6	28.1
Navy	389	490	−20.6	16.0
Coast Guard	9	16	−43.8	0.4
Holding prisoners				
Total	2,426	2,772	−12.5%	100.0%
Air Force	128	103	24.3	5.3
Army	1,115	1,494	−22.7	47.6
Marine Corps	617	571	8.1	25.4
Navy	526	604	−12.9	21.7

Note: Detail may not add to total because of rounding.

At yearend 1998 U.S. military authorities held 2,426 prisoners in 69 facilities

About 84% of prisoners held by the Army, Air Force, Navy, and Marine Corps were convicted inmates; 16% were unconvicted persons whose cases had not been tried. Fifty-seven percent of the prisoners (1,377) had sentences of 1 year or more.

At yearend 1998 the Army's Disciplinary Barracks, Fort Leavenworth, Kansas, and five other local or regional Army facilities held almost half (48%) of all inmates under military jurisdiction. The 7 Marine Corps facilities held 25% of all inmates; the 11 Navy facilities, 22% of all inmates; and the 45 Air Force facilities held 5% of all inmates.

The operational capacity of the 69 military confinement facilities totaled 4,588. At yearend 1998 these facilities were operating at 53% of their operational capacity.

of less than 4%, led by Maine (0.7%), Maryland (3.2%), and South Carolina (3.4%).

Female prisoner population nearly doubled since 1990

During 1998 the number of women under the jurisdiction of State or Federal prison authorities increased 6.5%, from 79,268 to 84,427, outpacing the rise in the number of men for the third consecutive year (table 6). The number of men grew from 1,162,885 to 1,217,592, an increase of 4.7%.

Since 1990 the annual rate of growth of the female inmate population has averaged 8.5%, higher than the 6.6% average increase in the number of male inmates. While the total number of male prisoners has grown 67% since 1990, the number of female prisoners has increased 92%. By yearend 1998 women accounted for 6.5% of all prisoners nationwide, up from 5.7% in 1990.

Relative to their number in the U.S. resident population, men were 16 times more likely than women to be incarcerated in a State or Federal prison. At yearend 1998 there were 57 sentenced female inmates per 100,000 women in the United States, compared to 885 sentenced male inmates per 100,000 men.

Over a third of all female prisoners were held in the three largest jurisdictions: California (11,694), Texas (10,343), and the Federal system (9,186) (table 7). Oklahoma (with 122 sentenced female inmates per 100,000 female State residents) and Texas (with 102) had the highest female incarceration rates. Maine and Vermont (both with 9 sentenced female prisoners per 100,000 female residents) had the lowest incarceration rates.

Since 1990 the female prisoner population grew at annual average rate of at least 10% in 18 States. North Dakota reported the highest average annual increase in female prisoners (16.7%), while the District of Columbia was the only jurisdiction to report fewer female prisoners since 1990, averaging a 2.9% annual decline.

Local jails held over 24,000 State prisoners because of crowding

At the end of 1998, 30 States reported a total of 24,925 State prisoners held in local jails or other facilities because of crowding in State facilities (table 8). These inmates held in local jails represent 2.1% of all State prisoners, up slightly from 2.0% in 1997.

New Mexico and West Virginia had the largest percentage of their inmate population housed in local jails, 24.7% and 18.7% respectively. Three other States—Utah (17.7%), New Jersey (12.2%), and Tennessee (11.9%)—had at least 10% of their population housed in local jail facilities.

In addition to housing inmates in local jails, 18 States eased prison crowding by placing inmates in other States or in Federal facilities. On December 31, 1998, 11,105 prisoners nationwide were held under such arrangements—representing about 1% of all State prisoners. Wisconsin placed the most inmates (3,028), followed by the District of Columbia (2,660) and Michigan (1,317). The District of Columbia (26.7%), Hawaii (23.8%), and Arkansas (21.6%) had more than 20% of their prison population housed in facilities of other States or the Federal system.

Prison capacity measures vary

The extent of prison crowding is difficult to determine because of the absence of

Table 2. Change in the State and Federal prison populations, 1990–98

		Annual increase	
Year	Number of inmates	Number	Annual percent change
1990	773,919		
1991	825,559	51,640	6.7%
1992	882,500	56,941	6.9
1993*	970,444	64,992	7.4
1994	1,054,702	84,258	8.7
1995	1,125,874	71,172	6.7
1996	1,183,368	57,494	5.1
1997	1,242,153	58,785	5.0
1998	1,302,019	59,866	4.8
Average annual increase, 1990–98		63,144	6.7%

Note: All counts are for December 31 of each year and may reflect revisions of previously reported numbers.

*Includes the jurisdiction populations in Massachusetts and Texas for the first time. The 1993 count (947,492), excluding the noncustody population in Texas and Massachusetts, may be used for comparisons.

1 ❖ WHO ARE THE PRISONERS?

Table 3. Prisoners under the jurisdiction of State or Federal correctional authorities, by region and jurisdiction, yearend 1997 and 1998

	Total			Sentenced to more than 1 year			
Region and jurisdiction	Advance 1998	1997	Percent change, 1997–98	Advance 1998	1997	Percent change, 1997–98	Incarceration, rate, 1998a
U.S. total	1,302,019	1,242,153	4.8%	1,252,830	1,195,498	4.8%	461
Federal	123,041	112,973	8.9	103,682	94,987	9.2	38
State	1,178,978	1,129,180	4.4	1,149,148	1,100,511	4.4	423
Northeast	178,225	171,237	4.1	169,731	162,744	4.3	328
Connecticut[b]	17,605	17,241	2.1	12,193	11,920	2.3	372
Maine	1,612	1,620	−0.5	1,562	1,542	1.3	125
Massachusetts[c]	11,832	11,947	−1.0	10,739	10,847	−1.0	275
New Hampshire	2,169	2,168	0.0	2,169	2,168	0.0	182
New Jersey[e]	31,121	28,361	9.7	31,121	28,361	9.7	382
New York	72,638	70,295	3.3	72,289	70,021	3.2	397
Pennsylvania	36,377	34,964	4.0	36,373	34,957	4.1	303
Rhode Island[b]	3,445	3,371	2.2	2,175	2,100	3.6	220
Vermont[b]	1,426	1,270	12.3	1,110	828	34.1	188
Midwest	228,177	218,369	4.5%	226,788	217,383	4.3%	360
Illinois[d,e]	43,051	40,788	5.5	43,051	40,788	5.5	357
Indiana	19,197	17,903	7.2	19,016	17,730	7.3	321
Iowa[d,e]	7,394	6,938	6.6	7,394	6,938	6.6	258
Kansas[e]	8,183	7,911	3.4	8,183	7,911	3.4	310
Michigan	45,879	44,771	2.5	45,879	44,771	2.5	466
Minnesota	5,572	5,326	4.6	5,557	5,306	4.7	117
Missouri	24,974	23,998	4.1	24,949	23,998	4.0	457
Nebraska	3,676	3,402	8.1	3,588	3,329	7.8	215
North Dakota	915	797	14.8	814	715	13.8	128
Ohio[e]	48,450	48,016	0.9	48,450	48,016	0.9	432
South Dakota	2,435	2,242	8.6	2,430	2,242	8.4	329
Wisconsin	18,451	16,277	13.4	17,477	15,639	11.8	334
South	511,525	490,493	4.3%	499,184	479,278	4.2%	520
Alabama	23,326	22,290	4.6	22,655	21,680	4.5	519
Arkansas	10,638	10,021	6.2	10,561	9,936	6.3	415
Delaware[b]	5,558	5,435	2.3	3,211	3,264	−1.6	429
Dist. of Col.[b]	9,949	9,353	6.4	9,949	9,353	6.4	1,913
Florida[d]	67,224	64,626	4.0	67,193	64,574	4.1	447
Georgia[d]	39,262	36,505	7.6	38,758	35,787	8.3	502
Kentucky	14,987	14,600	2.7	14,987	14,600	2.7	379
Louisiana	32,227	29,265	10.1	32,227	29,265	10.1	736
Maryland	22,572	222,32	1.5	21,540	21,088	2.1	418
Mississippi	16,678	14,296	16.7	15,855	13,676	15.9	574
North Carolina	31,811	31,612	0.6	27,193	27,567	−1.4	358
Oklahoma[e]	20,892	20,542	1.7	20,892	20,542	1.7	622
South Carolina	22,115	21,173	4.4	21,236	20,264	4.8	550
Tennessee[e]	17,738	16,659	6.5	17,738	16,659	6.5	325
Texas[e]	144,510	140,351	3.0	144,510	140,351	3.0	724
Virginia	28,560	28,385	0.6	27,191	27,524	−1.2	399
West Virginia	3,478	3,148	10.5	3,478	3,148	10.5	192
West	261,051	249,081	4.8%	253,445	241,106	5.1%	417
Alaska[b]	4,097	4,165	−1.6	2,541	2,571	−1.2	413
Arizona[d]	25,311	23,484	7.8	23,955	22,353	7.2	507
California	161,904	155,790	3.9	159,109	152,739	4.2	483
Colorado	14,312	13,461	6.3	14,312	13,461	6.3	357
Hawaii[b]	4,924	4,978	−1.1	3,670	3,448	6.4	307
Idaho	4,083	3,911	4.4	4,083	3,911	4.4	330
Montana	2,734	2,517	8.6	2,734	2,517	8.6	310
Nevada	9,651	9,024	6.9	9,651	9,024	6.9	542
New Mexico	4,985	4,688	6.3	4,732	4,450	6.3	271
Oregon	8,927	7,999	11.6	8,596	7,589	13.3	260
Utah	4,391	4,301	2.1	4,337	4,280	1.3	205
Washington	14,161	13,214	7.2	14,154	13,214	7.1	247
Wyoming	1,571	1,549	1.4	1,571	1,549	1.4	327

[a]The number of prisoners with sentences of more than 1 year per 100,000 U.S. residents.
[b]Prisons and jails form one integrated system. Data include total jail and prison population.
[c]The incarceration rate includes an estimated 6,200 inmates sentenced to more than 1 year but held in local jails or houses of corrections.
[d]Population figures are based on custody counts.
[e]"Sentenced to more than 1 year" includes some inmates "sentenced to 1 year or less."

2. Prisoners in 1998

Table 4. Change in the number of sentenced prisoners under the jurisdiction of State or Federal correctional authorities, 1990–98.

Region and jurisdiction	Population difference	Percent change	Average annual percent change
U.S. total	505,712	67.7%	6.7%
Federal	53,279	105.7%	9.4%
State	452,433	64.9	6.5
Northeast	50,668	42.6%	4.5%
Connecticut	4,422	56.9	5.8
Maine	82	5.5	0.7
Massachusetts[a]	2,840	36.0	3.9
New Hampshire	827	61.6	6.2
New Jersey	9,993	47.3	5.0
New York	17,394	31.7	3.5
Pennsylvania	14,092	63.2	6.3
Rhode Island	589	37.1	4.0
Vermont	429	63.0	6.3
Midwest	81,207	55.8%	5.7%
Illinois	15,535	56.6	5.8
Indiana[a]	6,401	50.7	5.3
Iowa	3,427	86.4	8.1
Kansas	2,408	41.7	4.5
Michigan[a]	11,612	33.9	3.7
Minnesota	2,381	75.0	7.2
Missouri	10,006	67.0	6.6
Nebraska	1,302	57.0	5.8
North Dakota	379	87.1	8.1
Ohio	16,628	52.3	5.4
South Dakota	1,089	81.2	7.7
Wisconsin	10,039	—	—
South	216,593	76.6	7.4
Alabama	7,290	47.4	5.0
Arkansas	3,287	45.2	4.8
Delaware	970	43.3	4.6
Dist. of Col.[a]	3,151	46.4	4.9
Florida	22,813	51.4	5.3
Georgia	17,087	78.8	7.5
Kentucky	5,964	66.1	6.5
Louisiana	13,628	73.3	7.1
Maryland	4,806	28.7	3.2
Mississippi	7,771	96.1	8.8
North Carolina[a]	9,429	53.1	5.5
Oklahoma	8,607	70.1	6.9
South Carolina	5,028	31.0	3.4
Tennessee	7,350	70.8	6.9
Texas[b]	87,726	154.5	12.4
Virginia	9,773	56.1	5.7
West Virginia	1,913	122.2	10.5
West	103,965	69.6%	6.8%
Alaska	690	37.3	4.0
Arizona	10,174	73.8	7.2
California[a]	64,987	69.0	6.8
Colorado	6,641	86.6	8.1
Hawaii	1,962	114.9	10.0
Idaho	2,122	108.2	9.6
Montana	1,309	91.9	8.5
Nevada	3,828	65.7	6.5
New Mexico	1,665	54.3	5.6
Oregon	2,104	32.4	3.6
Utah	1,863	75.3	7.3
Washington	6,159	77.0	7.4
Wyoming[a]	461	41.5	4.4

—Not calculated because of changes in reporting procedures
[a]Growth may be slightly overestimated due to a change in reporting from custody to jurisdiction counts
[b]Includes 6,742 "paper-ready" State inmates held in local jails in 1990.

Prisoners held in other States or Federal facilities

States housing prisoners in other States or Federal facilities	Number	As a percent of all State prisoners
U.S. total	11,105	0.9%
Wisconsin	3,028	16.4
Dist. of Col.	2,660	26.7
Michigan	1,317	2.9
Hawaii	1,174	23.8
Arkansas	887	21.6
Montana	394	14.4
Delaware	300	5.4
Vermont	247	17.3
Idaho	200	4.9
Indiana	184	1.0
Massachusetts	173	1.5
Alabama	114	0.5
Iowa	100	1.3
Wyoming	100	1.3
Oregon	80	0.9
New Hampshire	79	3.6
North Dakota	50	5.5
Colorado	18	0.1

uniform measures for defining capacity. Jurisdictions apply a variety of capacity measures to reflect both the available space to house inmates and the ability to staff and operate an institution. To estimate the capacity of their prisons, jurisdictions were asked to supply three measures for yearend 1998: rated, operational, and design capacities. These measures were defined as follows:

Rated capacity is the number of beds or inmates assigned by a rating official to institutions within the jurisdiction.

Operational capacity is the number of inmates that can be accommodated, based on a facility's staff, existing programs, and services.

Design capacity is the number of inmates that planners or architects intended for the facility.

Of the 52 reporting jurisdictions, 30 supplied a rated capacity; 43, an operational capacity; and 35, a design capacity (table 9). Twenty-two jurisdictions provided only 1 measure or the same figure for each measure they reported. For the 30 jurisdictions with more than 1 reported type of capacity, estimates of population as a percent of capacity are based on the highest and lowest figures provided.

Most jurisdictions were operating above capacity

Prisons generally require reserve capacity to operate efficiently. Dormitories and cells need to be maintained and repaired periodically, special housing is needed for protective custody and disciplinary

1 ❖ WHO ARE THE PRISONERS?

Table 5. The 10 highest and lowest jurisdictions for selected characteristics of the prison population, yearend 1998

Prison Population	Number of inmates	Incarceration rates, 1998	Rate per 100,000 State residents[a]	1-year growth, 1997–98	Percent change	Growth since 1990	Average percent change[b]
10 highest:							
California	161,904	Louisiana	736	Mississippi	16.7%	Texas	12.4%
Texas	144,510	Texas	724	North Dakota	14.8	West Virginia	10.5
Federal	123,041	Oklahoma	622	Wisconsin	13.4	Hawaii	10.0
New York	72,638	Mississippi	574	Vermont	12.3	Idaho	9.6
Florida	67,224	South Carolina	550	Oregon	11.6	Federal	9.4
Ohio	48,450	Nevada	542	West Virginia	10.5	Mississippi	8.8
Michigan	45,879	Alabama	519	Louisiana	10.1	Montana	8.5
Illinois	43,051	Arizona	507	New Jersey	9.7	North Dakota	8.1
Georgia	39,252	Georgia	502	Federal	8.9	Colorado	8.1
Pennsylvania	36,377	California	483	South Dakota	8.6	Iowa	8.1
10 lowest:							
North Dakota	915	Minnesota	117	Alaska	451.6%	Maine	0.7%
Vermont	1,426	Maine	125	Hawaii	−1.1	Maryland	3.2
Wyoming	1,571	North Dakota	128	Massachusetts	−1.0	South Carolina	3.2
Maine	1,612	New Hampshire	182	Maine	−0.5	New York	3.5
New Hampshire	2,169	Vermont	188	New Hampshire	0.0	Oregon	3.6
South Dakota	2,435	West Virginia	192	North Carolina	0.6	Michigan	3.7
Montana	2,734	Utah	205	Virginia	0.6	Massachusetts	3.95
West Virginia	3,445	Nebraska	215	Ohio	0.9	Rhode Island	4.0
Rhode Island	3,478	Rhode Island	220	Wyoming	1.4	Alaska	4.0
Nebraska	3,676	Washington	247	Mississippi	1.5	Wyoming	4.4

[a]The number of prisoners with a sentence of more than 1 year per 100,000 residents in the State population. The Federal Bureau of Prisons and the District of Columbia are excluded.
[b]The average annual percent change from 1990 to 1998.

cases, and space may be needed for protective custody and disciplinary cases, and space may be needed to copy with emergencies.

At yearend 1998, 16 States and the District of Columbia reported that they were operating at or below 99% of their highest capacity. Thirty-seven States, the District of Columbia, and the Federal prison system reported operating at 100% or more of their lowest capacity. Utah, which was operating at 84% of its lowest capacity, had the least crowded prison system. California, operating at over twice its highest reported capacity (203%), had the most crowded system.

By yearend 1998 the Federal prison system was estimated to be operating at 27% over capacity, increasing since yearend 1997 (19%). Overall, State prisons were estimated to be operating at 13% above their highest capacity, down from the 15% for last year (table 10). Based on the lowest capacity figures, State prisons were operating at 22% over capacity at yearend 1998, continuing the steady decline from 31% in 1992.

Between 1990 and 1997 the number of prisoners with sentences of more than 1 year rose by more than 455,500—or 62% (table 11). The number of white males increased by 54%, the number of black males by 61%, the number of white females and black females by 80%. At yearend 1997 (the latest available data), there were more black males in State or Federal prisons (548,900) than white males (541,700).

Relative to the number of U.S. residents, the number of sentenced prisoners rose by 50% (from 297 prisoners per 100,000 residents in 1990 to 445 per 100,000 residents in 1997) (table 12). Blacks were at least 6 times more likely than whites to be in State or Federal prison at yearend 1997, unchanged from 1990.

Hispanic inmates, who may be of any race, totaled an estimated 213,100 at yearend 1997—increasing 64% from 1990 (table 13). The number of Hispanic males rose 62%, while the number of Hispanic females rose 97%. During the

An increasing percentage of prisoners are black or Hispanic

	Percent of prisoners under State or Federal jurisdiction*	
	1990	1997
Total	100.0%	100.0%
White	50.1	47.9
Black	48.6	49.4
American Indian/Alaska Native	0.9	1.8
Asian/Pacific Islander	0.4	0.8

*Based on adjusted NPS counts.

Table 6. Prisoners under the jurisdiction of State or Federal correctional authorities, by gender, yearend 1990, 1997, and 1998

	Men	Women
All inmates		
Advance 1998	1,217,592	84,427
Final 1997	1,162,885	79,268
Final 1990	729,840	44,065
Percent change, 1997–98	4.7%	6.5%
Average annual 1990–98	6.6	8.5
Sentenced to more than 1 year		
Advance 1998	1,174,124	78,706
Final 1997	1,121,663	73,835
Percent change, 1997–98	4.7%	6.6%
Incarceration rate*		
1998	885	57
1990	572	32

*The number of prisoners with sentences of more than 1 year per 100,000 residents on December 31.

2. Prisoners in 1998

Table 7. Women under the jurisdiction of State or Federal correctional authorities, 1990-98

	Number of female inmates 1998	Number of female inmates 1990	Percent change 1997-98	Percent change Average, 1990-98[a]	Incarceration rate, 1998[b]
U.S. total	84,427	44,065	6.5%	8.5%	57
Federal	9,186	5,011	10.6%	7.9%	5
State	75,241	39,054	6.0	8.5	51
Northeast	9,367	6,293	3.6%	5.1%	31
Connecticut	1,357	683	-3.1	9.0	43
Maine	63	44	1.6	4.6	9
Massachusetts[c]	750	582	2.3	3.2	13
New Hampshire	116	44	6.4	12.9	19
New Jersey	1,653	1,041	17.7	6.0	39
New York	3,631	2,691	-0.3	3.8	38
Pennsylvania	1,517	1,006	6.5	5.3	24
Rhode Island	235	166	10.3	4.4	18
Vermont	45	36	-15.1	2.8	9
Midwest	13,684	7,521	7.0%	7.8%	42
Illinois	2,646	1,183	8.9	10.6	43
Indiana[c]	1,198	681	11.9	7.3	39
Iowa	491	212	-7.0	11.1	33
Kansas	523	284	9.9	7.9	39
Michigan[c]	2,052	1,688	-0.2	2.5	41
Minnesota	288	159	11.6	7.7	12
Missouri	1,880	777	11.0	11.7	67
Nebraska	254	145	14.4	7.3	28
North Dakota	69	20	11.3	16.7	19
Ohio	2,912	1,947	2.5	5.2	50
South Dakota	202	77	19.5	12.8	54
Wisconsin	1,169	348	18.4	Σ	42
South	33,345	15,366	5.3%	10.2%	65
Alabama	1,525	955	12.1	6.0	64
Arkansas	696	435	13.9	6.1	52
Delaware	440	226	14.9	8.7	51
District of Col.[c]	478	606	17.4	-2.9	173
Florida	3,526	2,664	3.1	3.6	45
Georgia	2,474	1,243	8.4	9.0	61
Kentucky	1,046	479	-0.6	10.3	51
Louisiana	2,126	775	13.8	13.4	94
Maryland	1,140	877	2.9	3.3	39
Mississippi	1,213	448	26.1	13.3	77
North Carolina[c]	1,932	945	3.9	9.4	35
Oklahoma	2,091	1,071	1.9	8.7	122
South Carolina	1,412	1,053	8.4	3.7	63
Tennessee	886	390	11.0	10.8	31
Texas[d]	10,343	2,196	0.4	Σ	102
Virginia	1,806	927	5.6	8.7	47
West Virginia	211	76	13.4	13.6	23
West	18,845	9,874	7.9%	8.4%	58
Alaska	302	128	-0.7	11.3	54
Arizona	1,780	835	14.1	9.9	66
California[c]	11,694	6,502	7.1	7.6	67
Colorado	1,070	433	12.8	12.0	53
Hawaii	430	171	-17.0	12.2	60
Idaho	321	120	22.1	13.1	52
Montana	248	76	48.5	15.9	56
Nevada	743	406	6.9	7.8	85
New Mexico	315	193	-15.8	6.3	32
Oregon	523	362	16.2	4.7	29
Utah	270	125	26.8	10.1	25
Washington	1,018	435	10.2	11.2	35
Wyoming[c]	131	88	-3.7	5.1	55

ΣNot calculated because of changes in reporting procedures.
[a]The average annual percentage increase from 1990 to 1998.
[b]The number of female prisoners with sentences of more than 1 year per 100,000 U.S. residents.
[c]Growth from 1990 to 1998 may be slightly overestimated due to a change in reporting from custody to jurisdiction counts.
[d]Excludes an unknown number of female inmates in 1990 who were "paper-ready" State inmates held in local jails.

Table 8. State prisoners held in local jails because of prison crowding, by State, yearend 1997 and 1998

	State prisoners held in local jails Number 1998	Number 1997	As a percent of State inmates 1998	1997
U.S. total	24,925	22,941	2.1%	2.0%
New Jersey	3,811	2,864	12.2%	10.1%
Colorado	2,716	1,886	19.0	14.0
New York	2,288	918	3.1	1.3
Virginia	2,169	3,753	7.6	13.2
Tennessee	2,119	1,428	11.9	8.6
Mississippi	1,639	1,463	9.8	9.5
Indiana	1,408	1,323	7.3	7.4
Alabama	1,403	1,824	6.0	8.2
New Mexico	1,230	557	24.7	11.9
Kentucky	1,073	1,144	7.2	7.8
Oklahoma	920	802	4.4%	3.9%
Utah	779	348	17.7	8.1
West Virginia	651	775	18.7	24.2
Massachusetts	509	484	4.3	4.1
Arkansas	432	1,376	4.1	13.7
South Carolina	377	400	1.7	1.9
Wisconsin	296	284	1.6	1.9
North Carolina	255	282	0.8	0.9
Michigan*	208	151	0.5	0.3
Arizona*	197	211	0.8	0.9
Montana	144	217	5.3%	9.7%
Idaho	77	31	1.9	0.8
Minnesota	67	50	1.2	0.9
New Hampshire	54	66	2.5	3.0
Wyoming	41	29	2.6	1.9
Pennsylvania	27	25	0.1	0.1
North Dakota	21	68	2.3	8.5
Oregon	14	72	0.2	0.9
Missouri	0	55	—	0.2
Alaska	0	55	—	1.3

Note: Excludes 10,795 Louisiana inmates at yearend 1997 and 13,211 inmates at yearend 1998 held in local jails as a result of a partnership with local authorities. See *Jurisdiction notes*.
—Not calculated.
*In States without jail backups in the count, the percentage is based on the total of State inmates in jail and prison.

7-year period, the Hispanic female incarceration rate rose 55% (from 56 sentenced prisoners per 100,000 Hispanic female residents to 87), while the Hispanic male rate rose 25% (from 1,016 to 1,272).

Nearly 12,000 American Indians were held in State or Federal prisons on December 31, 1997 (table 14). Excluding inmates held in 69 Indian Country detention facilities, run by the Bureau of Indian Affairs or tribal authorities, there

1 ❖ WHO ARE THE PRISONERS?

Prisoners in custody of correctional authorities in the U.S. Territories, yearend 1997 and 1998

	Total			Sentenced to more than 1 year			Incarceration rate 1998*
	Advance 1998	Final 1997	Percent change, 1997–98	Advance 1998	Final 1997	Percent change, 1997–98	
Total	17,824	15,762	13.1%	13,406	11,790	13.7%	315
American Samoa	112	102	9.8	95	92	3.3	153
Guam	629	464	35.6	272	301	–9.6	182
Commonwealth of the Northern Mariana Islands	112	63	77.8	52	63	–17.5	78
Commonwealth of Puerto Rico	16,524	14,716	12.3	12,747	11,097	14.9	330
U.S. Virgin Islands	447	417	7.2	240	237	1.3	203

*The number of prisoners with a sentence of more than 1 year per 100,000 persons in the resident population. Midyear population estimates were provided by the U.S. Bureau of the Census, International Data Base.

U.S. Territories held nearly 18,000 inmates in 1998

The U.S. Territories and Commonwealths—American Samoa, Guam, Northern Mariana Islands, Puerto Rico, and Virgin Islands—reported 17,824 inmates under the jurisdiction of their prison systems at yearend 1998—an increase of 13.1% since 1997.

Prisoners with a sentence of more than 1 year totaled 13,406 (or three-quarters of the total territorial prison population). Since 1995, the number of sentenced prisoners held in U.S. Territories has grown 40%, compared to the 15% increase in the number of sentenced State prisoners.

Relative to the resident populations in the Territories, the rate of incarceration was 315 prisoners per 100,000 residents—over two-thirds of the combined rate of the 50 States and the District of Columbia. Of the 5 Territories, the Northern Mariana Islands had the lowest prison incarceration rate (78 inmates per 100,000 residents), while Puerto Rico (with 330) had the highest rate.

Puerto Rico, the largest of the Territories, had the most sentenced prisoners (12,747 at yearend 1998), up from 11,097 in 1997. In 1998, 24 States and the District of Columbia had fewer sentenced inmates than Puerto Rico; 23 States had equal or lower incarceration rates.

were 492 sentenced inmates per 100,000 American Indians. Among Indian women the incarceration rate was 80 per 100,000, 2 1/2 times the rate among white women.

Middle-aged inmates comprise a growing part of the Nation's prison populations

The Nation's prison population is aging. Based on data from the 1997 surveys of State and Federal prison inmates, 30% were between the ages of 35 and 44, compared with 23% in 1991. This rise was offset by a decline in the percentage of inmates 18 to 34. The percentage of inmates age 55 or older did not change—about 3% in both years. Nearly half of 1% were under age 18 in 1997, unchanged from 1991.

	Percent of inmates held in State or Federal prison*	
	1991	1997
Total	100.0%	100.0%
17 or younger	0.6	0.4
18–19	2.9	2.6
20–24	17.4	15.8
25–29	23.6	18.7
30–34	21.3	19.3
35–39	14.4	17.5
40–44	9.1	12.0
45–54	7.2	10.3
55 or older	3.4	3.3

*Based on data from the 1991 and 1997 surveys of State and Federal prison inmates.

An estimated 7% of black males in their twenties and thirties were in prison in 1997

When incarceration rates are estimated separately by age group, black males in their twenties and thirties are found to have very high rates relative to other groups (table 15). Expressed in terms of percentages, 8.6% of black non-Hispanic males age 25 to 29 were in prison in 1997, compared to 2.7% of Hispanic males and about 0.9% of white males in the same age group. Although incarceration rates drop with age, the percentage of black males age 45 to 54 in prison in 1997 was still nearly 2.8% —larger than the highest rate among Hispanic males (age 25 to 29) and nearly 3 times larger than the highest rate (0.9%) among white males (age 30 to 34).

Female incarceration rates, though substantially lower than male incarceration rates at every age, reveal similar racial and ethnic disparities. Black non-Hispanic females (with an incarceration rate of 200 per 100,000) were more than twice as likely as Hispanic females (87 per 100,000) and 8 times more likely than white non-Hispanic females (25 per 100,000) to be in prison in 1997. These differences among white, black, and Hispanic females were consistent across all age groups.

Growth linked to increasing number of inmates in State prison for violent and drug offenses

Between 1990 and 1997 the distribution of the four major offense categories—violent, property, drug, and public-order offenses—changed slightly among State prisoners. The percent held for property and drug offenses dropped while the percent held for public-order offenses rose.

	Percent of sentenced State inmates	
	1990	1997
Total	100%	100%
Violent	46	47
Property	25	22
Drug	22	21
Public-order	7	10

In absolute numbers, an estimated 519,800 inmates in State prison at yearend 1997 were held for violent offenses, 155,600 for robbery, 128,700 for murder, 102,900 for assault, and 94,000 for rape and other sexual assaults (table 16). In addition, 241,900 inmates were held for property offenses, 227,400 for drug offenses and 108,700 for public-order offenses.

Overall, the largest growth in State inmates between 1990 and 1997 was among violent offenders. During the 7-year period, the number of violent

2. Prisoners in 1998

offenders grew 203,900, while the number of drug offenders grew 77,700 (table 17). As a percentage of the total growth, violent offenders accounted for 50% of the total growth, drug offenders 19%, property offenders 16%, and public-order offenders 15%.

Sources of population growth differ among men and women and among white, black, and Hispanic inmates

Detailed estimates of the State inmates at yearend 1990 and 1997 reveal differences in the sources of growth among male and female inmates. During this period the number of female inmates serving time for drug offenses nearly doubled, while the number of male inmates in for drug offenses rose 48%. The number serving time for violent offenses, however, rose at about the same pace (up 64% for men and 68% for women).

The increasing number of violent offenders accounted for the 52% of the total growth among male inmates and

Table 9. Reported Federal and State prison capacities, yearend 1998

Region and jurisdiction	Rated	Operational	Design	Highest capacity[a]	Lowest capacity[a]
Federal[a]	86,315	...	...	127%	127%
Northeast					
Connecticut[c]	...	...	...	...	...
Maine	1,460	1,629	1,460	99%	110%
Massachusetts	...	...	9,162	122	122
New Hampshire	1,841	1,864	1,744	109	117
New Jersey[b]	...	...	17,282	158	158
New York	60,879	65,717	53,409	107	132
Pennsylvania[b]	24,247	30,992	24,247	117	150
Rhode Island	3,858	3,858	3,858	89	89
Vermont	1,140	1,140	1,023	103	115
Midwest					
Illinois	32,062	32,062	27,342	134%	157%
Indiana	13,983	17,119	...	101	123
Iowa	5,701	5,701	5,701	130	130
Kansas	8,189	...	...	100	100
Michigan[b]	...	44,804	...	99	99
Minnesota[b]	5,567	5,724	5,724	96	99
Missouri[b]	...	26,302	...	95	95
Nebraska[b]	...	2,963	2,371	124	155
North Dakota[b]	1,005	952	1,005	84	89
Ohio	37,245	...	...	130	130
South Dakota[b]	...	2,470	...	99	99
Wisconsin[b]	...	11,136	...	136	136
South					
Alabama	21,800	21,800	21,800	100%	100%
Arkansas[b]	10,208	10,208	10,208	100	100
Delaware[b]	...	4,206	3,192	125	165
District of Columbia[d]	7,973	7,289	...	91	100
Florida[b]	77,370	70,785	52,407	87	128
Georgia[b]	...	39,320	...	100	100
Kentucky	11,428	11,180	7,421	122	187
Louisiana[b]	19,016	18,975	...	100	100
Maryland[b]	...	22,688	...	99	99
Mississippi[b]	...	13,916	14,649	103	108
North Carolina[b]	27,866	...	27,866	113	113
Oklahoma	...	21,578	...	93	93
South Carolina[b]	...	22,595	21,265	96	102
Tennessee[b]	16,130	15,778	...	97	99
Texas	148,756	148,756	151,430	95	97
Virginia[b]	29,171	29,171	29,171	90	90
West Virginia	2,698	2,827	2,695	100	105
West					
Alaska	2,603	2,691	2,603	119%	123%
Arizona	...	23,036	23,036	110	110
California	...	...	79,875	203	203
Colorado[b]	...	9,842	8,037	118	144
Hawaii	...	3,122	2,197	120	171
Idaho[b]	3,167	3,991	3,167	95	120
Montana	...	1,748	1,244	126	178
Nevada[b]	9,251	...	6,820	104	142
New Mexico	...	3,447	...	109	109
Oregon[b]	...	8,646	...	102	102
Utah	...	4,280	4,462	81	84
Washington[b]	8,902	11,575	11,575	122	159
Wyoming	1,231	1,243	1,047	115	137

... Data not available.
[a]Population counts exclude jail backups and inmates held in other States.
[b]See NPS jurisdiction notes.
[c]Connecticut no longer reports capacity because of a law passed in 1995.
[d]Excludes DC inmates held in State or Federal facilities.

Table 10. State prison population as a percent of capacity, yearend 1998

	State prisons[a]
Highest capacity	1,007,153
Lowest capacity	933,478
Net change in capacity, 1997–98	
Highest	59,403
Lowest	58,686
Population as a percent of capacity[b]	
Highest	
1990	115
1995	114
1996	116
1997	115
1998	113
Lowest	
1990	127
1995	125
1996	124
1997	124
1998	122

Note: States were asked to report their rated, operational, and design capacities. Data reflect the highest and lowest of the three capacities.

[a]Data include estimated capacity figures for Connecticut at yearend 1995-98.

[b]Excludes inmates sentenced to prison but held in local jails because of crowding.

1 ❖ WHO ARE THE PRISONERS?

Table 11. Number of sentenced prisoners under State or Federal jurisdiction, by gender and race, 1990, 1995–97

Year	Total	Male All[a]	Male White[b]	Male Black[b]	Female All[a]	Female White[b]	Female Black[b]
1990	739,980	699,416	350,700	340,300	40,564	20,200	19,700
1995	1,085,022	1,021,059	487,400	509,800	63,963	30,500	31,900
1996	1,137,722	1,068,123	511,300	528,600	69,599	33,800	34,000
1997	1,195,498	1,121,663	541,700	548,900	73,835	36,300	35,500

Note: Previous estimates for 1996 by gender and race have been revised. Sentenced prisoners are those with a sentence of more than 1 year.
[a]Includes Asians, Pacific Islanders, American Indians, Alask Natives, and other racial groups.
[b]The numbers for gender and race were estimated and rounded to the nearest 100.

Table 12. Number of sentenced prisoners under State or Federal jurisdiction, per 100,000 residents, by gender and race, 1990, 1995–97

Year	Total	Male All*	Male White	Male Black	Female All*	Female White	Female Black
1990	297	564	338	2,234	31	19	117
1995	411	781	449	3,095	47	27	176
1996	427	810	468	3,164	51	30	185
1997	445	841	491	3,253	53	32	192

Note: Based on estimates of the U.S. resident population on July 1 of each year and adjusted for the census undercount. See *Methodology* for further details.
*Includes Asians, Pacific Islanders, American Indians, Alaska Natives, and other racial groups.

Table 13. Number of sentenced Hispanic prisoners under State or Federal jurisdiction, by gender, 1990, 1995–97

Year	Number of sentenced Hispanic prisoners Total	Male	Female	Sentenced prisoners per 100,000 Hispanic residents Total	Male	Female
1990	130,000	123,500	6,500	548	1,016	56
1995	190,000	181,300	8,800	675	1,264	64
1996	200,400	189,300	11,100	688	1,279	78
1997	213,100	200,300	12,800	698	1,272	87

Note: Sentenced prisoners are those with a sentence of more than 1 year. The total number of Hispanic inmates was estimated in each year by multiplying the percent identifying as Hispanic in 1991 and 1997 surveys by the NPS sentenced inmate counts. Estimates have been rounded to the nearest 100.

25% among female inmates. Drug offenders accounted for the largest source of the total growth among female inmates (38%), compared to 17% among male inmates. The increasing number of property offenses accounted for a slightly higher percent of the growth among female inmates (20%) than among male inmates (16%). Although the number of public-order offenders rose sharply, they account for only 15% of the total growth among male inmates and 17% of the growth among female inmates.

The sources of population growth also differed among white, black, and Hispanic prisoners. Between 1990 and 1997 the number of black inmates serving time for drug offenses increased by 60%, while the number of white inmates increased by 46% and the number of Hispanic inmates by 32%. The number of violent offenders also rose more sharply among black inmates (up 69%) and Hispanic inmates (up 86%) than among white inmates (up 47%).

Percent change in number of State inmates, 1990–97*			
	White	Black	Hispanic
Total	51%	64%	62%
Violent	47	69	86
Property	38	38	42
Drug	46	60	32
Public-order	138	129	132

*Based on State inmates with a sentence of more than 1 year.

Percent change in number of State inmates, 1990–97*		
	Male	Female
Total	58%	83%
Violent	64	68
Property	37	53
Drug	48	99
Public-order	131	274

*Based on State inmates with a sentence of more than 1 year.

Overall, the increasing number of drug offenses accounted for 24% of the total growth among black inmates, 18% of the total growth among Hispanic inmates, and 11% of the growth among white inmates (table 18). Violent offenders accounted for the largest source of growth for all groups—among white State inmates (44%), black inmates (51%), and Hispanic inmates (53%).

Rise in State prison population linked to increasing numbers of parole violators returned to prison

Underlying the growth in the State prison population between 1990 and 1997 has been a 39% increase in the number of offenders returned to prison for parole violations (table 19). In 1997, 186,659 of the offenders entering State prison had violated the conditions of their release, up from 133,870 in 1990. These offenders had been released to parole either by decision of a parole board or by provision of the statute under which they were sentenced. While on parole, they had been arrested for or convicted of a new offense or had violated a condition of their release (such as failing a drug test, absconding, or failing to meet financial obligations imposed by a court). (For reasons for imprisoning violators, see *Probation and Parole Violators in State Prison, 1991*, August 1995, NCJ 149076.)

In contrast, the number of new court commitments to State prison remained nearly unchanged, totaling approximately 334,500 in 1997. Though the number admitted in 1997 was 3.5% larger than the number in 1990, the number of new court commitments has fluctuated during the 7-year period.

2. Prisoners in 1998

Table 14. Number of sentenced American Indian prisoners under State or Federal jurisdiction, by gender, 1990, 1995-97

Year	Number of sentenced American Indian prisoners Total	Male	Female	Sentenced prisoners per 100,000 American Indian residents Total	Male	Female
1990	6,000	5,600	400	275	516	35
1995	9,800	9,000	800	419	769	72
1996	11,000	10,100	900	462	850	77
1997	11,900	10,900	1,000	492	905	80

Note: The number of American Indian inmates was based on reports in NPS, which exclude those held in detention facilities in Indian country. The number with sentences of more than 1 year have been estimated and rounded to the nearest 100.

State prison growth the result of declining release rates and increasing time served

While the actual number of prisoners released each year grew between 1990 and 1997, the rate of release (or the number released relative to the number of inmates in prison) dropped sharply. In 1997 nearly 490,000 offenders were released from prison, up from 405,374 in 1990 (table 20). However, the release rate dropped from 37 per 100 State prisoners in 1990 to 31 per 100 in 1997.

A major source of prison growth is increasing time served. Among inmates released from prison for the first time on their current offense (that is, first releases) the average time served has increased from 22 months in 1990 to 27 months in 1997. Among those entering prison, the average time expected to be served before first release rose from 38 months to 43 months.

	New court commitments to State prison* Mean sentence	Mean minimum time to be served
1990	70 mos.	38 mos.
1995	72	42
1997	65	43

*Based on inmates with sentences of more than 1 year.

Current inmates have served longer; however, 40% expect to be released in next 12 months

Consistent with recent changes in sentencing and release policies, State prisoners report having served more time since admission than inmates in the past. Based on the 1991 and 1997 Surveys of Inmates in State Correctional Facilities, an estimated 53% of State inmates in 1997 had served less than 3 years, down from 71% in 1991 (table 21). Nearly 10% had served 10 years or more in 1997, up from 4% in 1991.

Though their average length of stay in prison had increased, 40% of inmates in 1997 said they expected to be released within the next 12 months, compared to 42% of the inmates in 1991. Most of the increase in time served was due to a sharp drop in the percentage of inmates who expected to serve less than 2 years (18% in 1997 down from 26% in 1991).

In both years, about 95% of inmates were expected to be released from prison at some time. An estimated 3.2% of inmates in 1997 said they expected to never be released. In addition, based on the sentence length, another 2% (of the 5.9% who said they didn't know when they would be released) may never be released.

Methodology

National Prisoner Statistics

The Bureau of Justice Statistics (BJS), with the U.S. Bureau of the Census as its collection agent, obtains yearend and midyear counts of prisoners from departments of correction in each of the 50 States, the District of Columbia, and the Federal Bureau of Prisons. In an effort to collect comparable data from all jurisdictions, National Prisoner Statistics (NPS) distinguishes prisoners in custody from those under jurisdiction. To have custody of a prisoner, a State must hold that person in one of its facilities. To have jurisdiction means that a State has legal authority over the prisoner. Prisoners under a State=s jurisdiction may be in the custody of a local jail, another State=s prison, or other correctional facility. Some States are unable to provide both custody and jurisdiction counts. (*See NPS jurisdiction notes.*)

Excluded from NPS counts are persons confined in locally administered confinement facilities who are under the

Table 15. Number of sentenced prisoners under State or Federal jurisdiction per 100,000 residents, by gender, race, Hispanic origin, and age, 1997

	Number of sentenced prisoners per 100,000 residents of each group							
	Male				Female			
Age	Total[a]	White[c]	Black[b]	Hispanic	Total[a]	White[b]	Black[b]	Hispanic
Total	841	386	3,209	1,273	53	25	200	87
18-19	776	274	2,587	1,184	28	17	83	30
20-24	1,956	789	6,999	2,603	78	41	215	128
25-29	2,143	868	8,630	2,703	134	58	452	210
30-34	2,002	950	7,485	2,587	176	83	650	253
35-39	1,682	806	6,814	2,207	141	66	546	213
40-44	1,257	615	4,841	2,217	82	37	337	131
45-54	700	394	2,775	1,263	42	21	154	99
55 or older	155	100	509	394	5	4	20	10

Note: Based on estimates of the U.S. resident population on July 1, 1997, and adjusted for the 1990 census undercount.
[a]Includes Asians, Pacific Islanders, American Indians, Alaska Natives, and other racial groups.
[b]Excludes Hispanics.

jurisdiction of local authorities. NPS counts include all inmates in State-operated facilities in Alaska, Connecticut, Delaware, Hawaii, Rhode Island, and Vermont, which have combined jail-prison systems.

Military Corrections Statistics

BJS obtains yearend counts of prisoners in the custody of U.S. military authorities from the Department of Defense Corrections Council. In 1994 the council, comprised of representatives from each branch of military service, adopted a standardized report (DD Form 2720) with a common set of items and definitions. This report provides information on persons held in U.S. military confinement facilities inside and outside the continental United States, by branch of service, sex, race, Hispanic origin, conviction status, sentence length, and offense. It also includes data on the number of fa-

1 ❖ WHO ARE THE PRISONERS?

Table 16. Estimated number of sentenced prisoners under State jurisdiction, by offense, gender, race, and Hispanic origin, 1997

Offenses	All	Male	Female	White	Black	Hispanic
Total	1,100,500	1,033,200	67,300	366,500	511,700	186,900
Violent offenses	519,800	501,100	18,700	172,300	246,000	81,400
Murder[a]	128,700	123,100	5,600	41,200	63,900	20,000
Manslaughter	17,400	15,700	1,700	6,100	7,200	3,300
Rape	28,200	27,900	300	12,800	11,700	2,200
Other sexual assault	65,800	65,200	600	38,900	16,100	8,200
Robbery	155,600	150,900	4,700	32,200	94,500	24,000
Assault	102,900	98,400	4,500	31,800	46,100	20,300
Other violent	21,200	19,900	1,300	9,300	7,600	3,400
Property offenses	241,900	224,000	17,900	103,700	97,600	34,400
Burglary	117,600	114,300	3,300	49,900	48,100	16,600
Larceny	46,200	40,300	5,900	17,500	20,700	6,400
Motor vehicle theft	20,300	19,500	800	7,900	7,300	4,600
Fraud	29,500	22,600	6,900	15,400	10,800	2,800
Other property	28,300	27,300	1,000	13,000	10,700	3,900
Drug offenses	227,400	203,900	23,500	43,200	127,700	51,200
Public-order offenses[b]	108,700	101,600	7,100	46,800	38,000	19,300
Other/unspecified[c]	2,700	2,600	100	500	1,400	600

Note: Data are for inmates with a sentence of more than 1 year under the jurisdiction of State correctional authorities. The number of inmates by offense were estimated using 1997 Survey of Inmates in State Correctional Facilities and rounded to the nearest 100.
[a] Includes nonnegligent manslaughter.
[b] Includes weapons, drunk driving, court offenses, commercialized vice, morals and decency charges, liquor law violations, and other public-order offenses.
[c] Includes juvenile offenses and unspecified felonies.

Table 17. Partitioning the total growth of sentenced prisoners under State jurisdiction, by offense and gender, 1990–97

	Total Increase, 1990–97	Percent of total	Male Increase, 1990–97	Percent of total	Female Increase, 1990–97	Percent of total
Total	410,900	100%	380,400	100%	30,600	100%
Violent	203,900	50	196,300	52	7,600	25
Property	66,900	16	60,700	16	6,200	20
Drug	77,700	19	66,000	17	11,700	38
Public-order	62,900	15	57,700	15	5,200	17

Table 18. Partitioning the total growth of sentenced prisoners under State jurisdiction, by offense, gender, race, and Hispanic origin, 1990–97

	White Increase, 1990–97	Percent of total	Black Increase, 1990–97	Percent of total	Hispanic Increase, 1990–97	Percent of total
Total	123,100	100%	197,000	100%	71,600	100%
Violent	54,700	44	100,800	51	37,700	53
Property	28,500	23	26,700	14	10,200	14
Drug	13,600	11	47,900	24	12,500	18
Public-order	27,100	22	21,400	11	11,000	15

cilities, and their design and rated capacities.

Surveys of Inmates in State and Federal Correctional Facilities

The Surveys of Inmates in State and Federal Correctional Facilities, which BJS conducts regularly every 5 to 6 years, provide detailed data on individual characteristics of prison inmates. Based on scientifically selected samples of facilities and of inmates held in them, these surveys provide detailed information unavailable from any other source. (See Substance Abuse and Treatment, State and Federal Prisoners, 1997, NCJ 172871, for a description of the 1997 surveys, sample designs, and accuracy.)

For this report, information on sex, race/Hispanic origin, age, offense, sentence length, time served since admission and remaining time to be served was drawn from the 1991 and 1997 surveys. Because the data are restricted to persons in prison, they may overstate the average sentence and time to be served by those entering prison. Person[s] with shorter sentences leave prison more quickly, resulting in longer average sentences among persons in the inmate surveys.

National Corrections Reporting Program

BJS obtains data on time served by released State prisoners from the National Corrections Reporting Program (NCRP). The data cover persons released from custody regardless of the jurisdiction where the prisoner was sentenced. The number of jurisdictions reporting data varies for year to year. In 1997, 36 States reported data on releases. While NCRP collects individual level data on all offenders, time served calculations in this report were restricted to prisoners with sentences of more than 1 year.

Estimating age-specific incarceration rates

The number of sentenced prisoners within each age group was estimated for men, women, whites, blacks, and Hispanics. Estimates for 1990 and 1997 were produced by combining data from NPS and from the State and Federal prison inmate surveys. The following procedures were used:
1. To obtain estimates of the number of sentenced State and Federal inmates by sex, race, and Hispanic origin in each year, NPS custody counts for men and women were used. These counts of State and Federal inmates were multi-

2. Prisoners in 1998

Table 19. Number of sentenced inmates admitted to State prisons, by type of admission, 1990–97

Year	All admissions	New court commitments	Parole violators
1990	460,739	323,069	133,870
1991	466,286	317,237	142,100
1992	480,676	334,301	141,961
1993	475,100	318,069	146,366
1994	498,919	322,141	168,383
1995	521,970	337,492	175,726
1996	512,618	326,547	172,633
1997	538,375	334,525	186,659
Percent change, 1990–97	16.9%	3.5%	39.4%

Note: Sentenced inmates are those with a sentence of more than 1 year. Admissions exclude returned escapees and AWOL's and transfers from other jurisdictions. Admissions for Alaska were estimated for 1994.

Table 20. Trends in State prison releases, release rates, and time served by first releases, 1990–97

Year	Number of releases	Release rate[b]	Time served by first releases[a] Mean	Percent 6 months or less	Percent 10 years or more
1990	405,374	37.0%	22 mos.	26.5%	1.4%
1991	421,687	36.5	22	24.1	1.4
1992	430,198	35.5	22	26.2	1.4
1993	417,838	33.3	21	29.0	1.3
1994	418,372	30.8	22	26.1	1.3
1995	455,140	31.2	23	21.0	1.3
1996	467,193	30.8	25	18.1	1.4
1997	489,914	30.8	27	16.5	1.7

Note: All data are limited to inmates with sentences of more than 1 year and exclude escapees, AWOLs, and transfers.
[a]Includes all inmates released for the first time on the current sentence. Time served is based on prison time only and excludes jail time credits.
[b]The number of releases per 100 sentenced prisoners at the beginning of each year, plus the number admitted during the year.

plied by the proportion white, black, Hispanic, or other race as estimated from the State and Federal inmate surveys in each year. The estimates were then adjusted to equal the number of sentenced inmates by sex in State and Federal prisons as reported in NPS for yearend 1990 and 1997.

2. To obtain estimates by age in each year, age distributions for each demographic group were drawn from the State and Federal prison inmate surveys. These percentages were then multiplied by the number of sentenced inmates for each group defined by sex, race, and Hispanic origin.

3. Estimates of the U.S. resident population for July 1, 1990, and 1997, were obtained from the U.S. Bureau of the Census. (See U.S. Population Estimates, by Age, Sex, Race, and Hispanic Origin: 1990 to 1995, PPL-41, and updates for 1996 and 1997.) These data were then adjusted for the 1990 decennial census, using the 1990 Post Enumeration Survey.

4. Age-specific rates of incarceration for each demographic group were calculated by dividing the estimated number of sentenced prisoners in each age group by the number of U.S. residents in each age group and then multiplying by 100,000.

NPS jurisdiction notes

Alabama—Capacity figures exclude community programs.

Alaska—Prisons and jails form one integrated system. All NPS data include jail and prison populations.

Arizona—Population counts are based on custody data. Operational capacity excludes temporary beds and double bunks used in situations of crowding.

Arkansas—Only one type of capacity, set by the Board of Corrections and Community Punishment, is reported.

Colorado—Capacity figures exclude Bent County Correctional Center, Huerfano Correctional Center, Crowley County Correctional Center, and facilities under contract in Minnesota.

Connecticut—Prisons and jails form one integrated system. All NPS data include jail and prison populations.

Legislation in 1995 abolished the capacity law so that prisons no longer have a rated or operational capacity. Design capacity is recorded separately in each facility.

Population counts for 1997 were revised.

Delaware—Prisons and jails form one integrated system. All NPS data include jail and prison populations.

Capacity counts include Department of Correction halfway houses.

District of Columbia—Prisons and jails form one integrated system. All NPS data include jail and prison populations.

Design capacity is no longer meaningful because of the prison closure program.

Federal—Rated capacity excludes contract beds.

Florida—Population counts are based on custody data.

Rated capacity is the maximum safe capacity, and operational capacity has been redefined as total capacity.

Georgia—Population counts are based on custody data.

Facilities in Georgia are not given rated or design capacities.

Hawaii—Prisons and jails form one integrated system. All NPS data include jail and prison populations.

Idaho—Operational capacity is the emergency maximum capacity.

Illinois—Population counts are based on custody data.

Population counts of inmates with a sentence of more than 1 year include an undetermined number with a sentence of 1 year or less.

Capacity figures include 721 inmates on electronic detention.

Iowa—Population counts are based on custody data.

Population counts of inmates with a sentence of more than 1 year include an undetermined number with a sentence of 1 year or less.

Kansas—Population counts of inmates with a sentence of more than 1 year include an undetermined number with a sentence of 1 year or less.

Louisiana—Operational capacity is based on day-to-day operations. Rated and operational capacities include contractual work release facilities.

Population counts include 12,018 males and 1,193 females housed in local jails as a results of a partnership with the Louisiana Sheriff's Association and local authorities.

Maryland—Design capacity is no longer reported because of renovations and other changes. Operational capacity was estimated by applying a percentage to the population count on December 31, 1998.

Massachusetts—Population counts are for December 28, 1998.

By law, offenders may be sentenced to terms of up to 2 years in locally operated jails. Such offenders are included in counts and rates for local jails. About 6,200 inmates with sentences of more than 1 year were held in local jails in 1998.

Michigan—Population counts are based on jurisdiction data, excluding inmates held in local jails. Counts include adults housed in institutions, camps, community correction centers, out of state, and on electronic monitoring.

1 ❖ WHO ARE THE PRISONERS?

Table 21. Time served since admission and time expected to be served until release, by inmates held in State prison, 1991 and 1997

	1997	1991
Time served since admission[a]		
Total	100%	100%
Less than 12 months	18.8	31.0
12 to 35	33.9	40.1
36 to 59	19.3	13.1
60 to 119	18.7	11.6
120 to 179	5.6	3.2
180 to 239	2.7	0.9
240 or more	1.1	0.2
Remaining time expected to be served until release[b]		
Total	100%	100%
Less than 6 months	21.9	24.1
6 to 12	17.8	17.4
13 to 59	33.5	33.0
60 to 119	9.6	8.1
120 to 239	5.5	4.3
240 or more	2.7	2.0
Life	3.2	2.3
Don't know	5.8	8.8
Estimated total time expected to be served on current sentence[c]		
Total	100%	100%
Less than 24 months	17.5	25.8
24 to 47	20.6	23.5
48 to 71	15.1	12.7
72 to 119	16.4	12.5
120 to 179	9.3	7.4
180 to 239	5.0	3.5
240 or more	7.0	4.0
Life	3.2	2.2
Don't know	5.9	8.4

Note: Data are based on the 1991 and 1997 Survey of Inmates in State Correctional Facilities.
[a] Includes time served in local jails that was credited to the prison sentence prior prison time served by returned parole violators.
[b] Based on the time served from date of interview to the expected date of release by each inmate.
[c] Based on the time served when interviewed plus time to be served until the expected date of release.

Rated capacity is no longer kept. Operational capacity includes institution and camp net capacities and populations in community programs.

Minnesota—Capacity is defined as the total beds minus 10% of the segregation beds and 2% of the remaining beds which are reserved for maintenance.

Mississippi—Operation and design capacities include private prison capacities.

Missouri—Design capacities are not available for older prisons. Operational capacity is defined as the number of beds.

Nebraska—Operational capacity is defined as stress capacity (or 125% of design capacity), which is ordered by the governor and set by the Department of Corrections.

Nevada—Rated capacity is defined as emergency capacity.

Design capacity is defined as one bed per cell. Capacity figures include 500 beds in a private facility.

New Jersey—Rated and operational capacity figures are not maintained.

Population counts of inmates with a sentence of more than 1 year include an undetermined number with a sentence of 1 year or less.

North Carolina—Operational capacity has been eliminated due to a legislative cap.

North Dakota—Capacity figures include a new facility opened in 1998 and double bunking in the State Penitentiary.

Ohio—Population counts of inmates with a sentence of more than 1 year include an undetermined number with a sentence of 1 year or less.

Oklahoma—Population counts of inmates with a sentence of more than 1 year include an undetermined number with a sentence of 1 year or less.

Oregon—Under a new law, inmates with under a 1 year maximum sentence remain under the control of local counties.

Rated and design capacities are not recognized.

Pennsylvania—Reported capacities are single-cell capacities. Operational capacity is based on multiple occupancy.

Rhode Island—Prisons and jails form one integrated system. All NPS data include jail and prison populations.

South Carolina—Population counts include unsentenced inmates on Youthful Offender Act observation status.

Operational capacity includes triple cell beds and excludes administrative segregation, infirmary/hospital, and mental health beds. Design capacity also excludes triple cell beds.

South Dakota—Operational capacity is planned capacity. Rated and design capacities are not recognized.

Tennessee—Rated capacity is the total beds available based on the original design plus any modifications. Operational capacity is the percent of total beds deemed appropriate by the Department of Corrections.

Population counts of inmates with a sentence of more than 1 year include an undetermined number with a sentence of 1 year or less.

Texas—Population counts of inmates with a sentence of more than 1 year include an undetermined number with a sentence of 1 year or less.

Vermont—Prisons and jails form one integrated system. All NPS data include jail and prison populations.

Population counts are jurisdiction counts that include inmates housed in other States but exclude inmates on furlough or intermediate sanctions.

Virginia—Population counts for inmates with a sentence of 1 year or less were affected by a new law on January 1, 1995, making the State responsible for felons with a sentence of 6 months or more, and a subsequent change, effective July 1, 1997, limiting responsibility to those with a sentence of 1 year or more.

Rated, operational, and design capacity are calculated using an operational capacity method in which all inmates housed in a cell are counted.

Washington—Reported capacities exclude work release and pre-release facilities because the facilities are not reserved specifically for State inmates.

Wisconsin—Counts exclude temporary probation or parole placements and persons on escape status. Counts include Alternatives to Revocation (ATRs), adult inmates held in contract juvenile facilities, and inmates held in local jails or in out-of-State, private, and Federal prisons due to crowding.

Operational capacity excludes contracted local jails, Federal, other State, and private facilities.

Article 3

Bureau of Justice Statistics Selected Findings

Prior Abuse Reported by Inmates and Probationers

This [article] was revised 5/13/00 to be consistent with [original] printed report [April 1999.]

By Caroline Wolf Harlow, Ph.D.
BJS Statistician

In recent surveys completed by the Bureau of Justice Statistics, 19% of State prison inmates, 10% of Federal inmates, and 16% of those in local jails or on active probation told interviewers they had been physically or sexually abused before their current sentence. Just under half of the women in correctional populations and a tenth of the men indicated past abuse. The survey questions largely relied on respondents to define for themselves physical and sexual abuse.

For women, abuse as children more likely in correctional than general population

Between 6% and 14% of male offenders and between 23% and 37% of female offenders reported they had been physically or sexually abused before age 18. For the general U.S. population, prevalence estimates of child abuse vary, depending on definitions, types of questions, selection of study subjects, and response rates. A review of 16 studies estimated that for the general adult population 5% to 8% of males and 12% to 17% of females were abused as children. (See [last] page for Gorey-Leslie article reference.)

Sources of data

In four BJS surveys—the 1997 Surveys of Inmates in State or Federal Correctional Facilities, the 1996 Survey of Inmates in Local Jails, and the 1995 Survey of Adults on Probation—offenders selected through nationally representative samples responded to questions in hour-long interviews. These offenders reported past physical or sexual abuse, offense histories, drug and alcohol use, and personal and family characteristics. See [last] page for information on obtaining the survey methodologies.

Highlights

Prior abuse of correctional populations, by sex

		Percent experiencing abuse before sentence			
		Ever		Before 18	
	Total	Male	Female	Male	Female
Ever abused before admission					
State prison inmates	18.7%	16.1%	57.2%	14.4%	36.7%
Federal prison inmates	9.5	7.2	39.9	5.0	23.0
Jail inmates	16.4	12.9	47.6	11.9	36.6
Probationers	15.7	9.3	40.4	8.8	28.2
Physically abused					
State prison inmates	15.4%	13.4%	46.5%	11.9%	25.4%
Federal prison inmate	7.9	6.0	32.3	5.0	14.7
Jail inmates	13.3	10.7	37.3	—	—
Probationers	12.8	7.4	33.5	—	—
Sexually abused					
State prison inmates	7.9%	5.8%	39.0%	5.0%	25.5%
Federal prison inmates	3.7	2.2	22.8	1.9	14.5
Jail inmates	8.8	5.6	37.2	—	—
Probationers	8.4	4.1	25.2	—	—

- 19% of State prison inmates, 10% of Federal inmates, and 16% of those in local jails and on probation had been physically or sexually abused before their most recent admission to a correctional population.
- A third of women in State prison, a sixth in Federal prison, and a quarter in jail said they had been raped. Another 3-6% reported that someone had tried to rape them but had not succeeded.
- 9 in 10 knew their abuser.
- 9 in 10 abused men and women in State prison had used illegal drugs. 76% of the men and 80% of the women used them regularly.
- Two thirds had been injured in a fight or assault.

From *Bureau of Justice Statistics: Selected Findings*, April 1999. © 1999 by the U.S. Department of Justice. Reprinted by permission.

1 ❖ WHO ARE THE PRISONERS?

Table 1. Physical or sexual abuse before admission, by sex of inmate or probationer

Before admission	State inmates Male	State inmates Female	Federal inmates Male	Federal inmates Female	Jail inmates Male	Jail inmates Female	Probationers Male	Probationers Female
Ever abused	16.1%	57.2%	7.2%	39.9%	12.9%	47.6%	9.3%	40.4%
Physically[a]	13.4	46.5	6.0	32.3	10.7	37.3	7.4	33.5
Sexually[a]	5.8	39.0	2.2	22.8	5.6	37.2	4.1	25.2
Both	3.0	28.0	1.1	15.1	3.3	26.9	2.1	18.3
Age of victim at time of abuse								
17 or younger[b]	14.4%	36.7%	5.8%	23.0%	11.9%	36.6%	8.8%	28.2%
18 or older[b]	4.3	45.0	2.7	31.0	2.3	26.7	1.1	24.7
Both	2.5	24.7	1.3	14.2	1.3	15.8	0.5	12.5
Age of abuser								
Adult	15.0%	55.8%	6.9%	39.0%	12.1%	46.0%	8.5%	39.2%
Juvenile only	0.9	1.0	0.2	0.3	0.8	1.3	0.6	1.2
Rape before admission	4.0%	37.3%	1.4%	21.4%	3.9%	33.1%	—	—
Completed	3.1	32.8	1.0	17.9	3.0	26.6	—	—
Attempted	0.8	4.3	0.3	3.2	0.7	5.6	—	—

—Not available.
[a]Includes those both physically and sexually abused.
[b]Includes those abused in both age categories.

Abused males reported being mistreated as children, but females, as both children and adults

For all correctional populations, men who reported abuse generally had been age 17 or younger when they suffered the abuse.

Women, however, were abused as both juveniles and adults. Depending on the correctional population, a quarter to a third of women were abused as juveniles; a quarter to almost a half, as adults. Twenty-five percent of the female State prisoners were abused as both juveniles and adults, as were 16% of women in jail, 14% in Federal prison, and 13% on probation. If abused, almost all persons of both sexes were victimized by an adult rather than by a juvenile. Only 1% or less reported only being victimized by persons 17 or younger.

Abuse of men was by family members, but abuse of women by family members and intimates

About 9 in 10 of the surveyed persons who reported past abuse also said they had known at least 1 of their abusers (table 2).

Family members were the primary abusers of the men: a parent, guardian, or other relative was identified by 57% to 70%. Wives, ex-wives, and girlfriends were identified by 3% to 7%.

Female inmates and probationers were abused by both intimates and family members. Except for women in jail, most abused women reported their abusers to have been current or prior husbands or boyfriends: 61% of abused women in State prison, 66% in Federal prison, 57% on probation, and 43% in local jails. A parent, guardian, or other relative had abused about a third to a half of the reporting women.

Prisoners' prior abuse related to their family background

Prisoners reported higher levels of abuse if they grew up in foster care rather than with parents, if their parents were heavy users of alcohol or drugs, or if a family member had been in jail or prison.

Nonparental care. Forty-four percent of male prisoners and 87% of female prisoners who had spent their childhood in foster care or institutions reported abuse. Many of these inmates may have been removed from abusive homes. There is

Table 2. Relationship to abuser, by the inmate or probationer reporting abuse

Percent of those persons who reported experiencing physical or sexual abuse before admission

Relationship of victim to abuser	State inmates Male	State inmates Female	Federal inmates Male	Federal inmates Female	Jail inmates Male	Jail inmates Female	Probationers Male	Probationers Female
Knew abuser	89.5%	90.6%	86.3%	95.4%	87.9%	90.2%	93.9%	93.8%
Family	66.6	40.1	56.7	34.8	64.0	50.5	69.5	50.5
Parent or guardian	54.1	27.2	49.0	24.3	52.7	33.0	62.0	31.0
Other relative	22.0	21.0	15.1	15.4	18.9	28.1	11.9	23.5
Intimate	5.8	61.3	6.5	66.3	3.1	42.8	5.7	56.7
Spouse/ex-spouse	2.2	36.5	1.9	41.0	1.8	25.1	4.9	37.6
Boyfriend/girlfriend	4.4	36.0	4.8	36.0	1.4	26.2	1.7	24.9
Friend/acquaintance	22.6	26.2	24.4	17.2	19.0	23.7	17.8	10.1
Other	17.4	15.8	18.7	10.5	15.6	13.3	11.5	14.3
Knew none of abusers	10.5%	9.4%	13.7%	4.6%	12.1%	9.8%	6.1%	6.2%

Note: Detail does not add to totals because some were abused by more than 1 person.

3. Prior Abuse Reported by Inmates and Probationers

While growing up —	Percent of State inmates reporting abuse Male	Female
Prisoners lived with		
Both parents	14.0%	54.7%
One parent	16.4	57.3
Foster/agency/other	43.6	86.7
Parent abused alcohol or drugs	29.4%	75.7%
Did not abuse	10.0	45.9
At any time —		
Family* incarcerated	20.2%	63.9%
Not incarcerated	12.3	46.9

*Includes boyfriends or girlfriends with whom the inmate had lived before admission.

Table 3. Current and past violent offenses and past alcohol and drug use, by whether abused before admission to State prison, 1997

	Percent of State prison inmates					
	Reported being abused			Reported being not abused		
Offense history and drug and alcohol use	Total	Males	Females	Total	Males	Females
Current or past violent offense	70.4%	76.5%	45.0%	60.2%	61.2%	29.1%
Current violent offense	55.7%	61.0%	33.5%	45.3%	46.1%	20.9%
Homicide	15.9	16.3	13.9	12.7	12.8	7.3
Sexual assault	15.6	18.8	2.0	6.9	7.1	0.4
Robbery	12.5	13.5	7.8	14.5	14.7	6.1
Assault	9.5	9.9	7.6	9.3	9.4	5.7
Used an illegal drug						
Ever	88.6%	88.5%	88.9%	81.8%	81.9%	77.4%
Ever regularly	76.3	75.5	79.7	67.9	67.9	65.0
In month before offense	61.4	59.7	68.6	55.3	55.3	54.0
At time of offense	39.6	38.0	46.2	30.7	30.7	32.0
Drank alcohol						
Ever regularly	66.9%	69.1%	57.5%	59.0%	59.8%	38.2%
At time of offense	41.6	43.6	33.1	36.1	36.6	23.5

little difference in the percentage of abused inmates growing up with one parent and those with two.

Parental drinking. Of those who had grown up with a parent or guardian who drank heavily or used drugs regularly, 29% of the men and 76% of the women reported prior abuse.

Incarcerated relative. Abuse was reported for about 20% of male inmates and 64% of female inmates who had a family member (including boyfriend and girlfriend) who had ever served time.

Reported past abuse associated with violent crime

Abused State prisoners were more likely than those not abused to be serving a sentence for a violent crime.

Among State prisoners, 61% of abused men were serving a sentence for a violent offense, compared to 46% of those reporting no past mistreatment. Thirty-four percent of abused women and 21% of women not abused were in prison for a violent offense.

A past of abuse is specifically linked to sexual assault and homicide. Among men reporting abuse before prison, 19% were serving a sentence for sexual assault, including rape, compared to 7% of the men not abused. Higher percentages of prisoners had committed homicide if they reported abuse (men, 16%, and women, 14%) than if they reported no abuse (men, 13%, and women, 7%).

When the category of violent crime overall is broadened to include both current and past offenses, an association between abuse and violent offenses remains. Among male State prison inmates, 77% of those reporting past abuse and 61% of those without that history had ever been sentenced for a violent crime. About 45% of abused women in State prison and 29% of those not abused had served at least one sentence for a violent crime.

The reported use of illegal drugs and alcohol higher among abused

Illegal drug use and regular drinking were more common among abused State prison inmates than among those who said they were not abused. An estimated 76% of abused men and 80% of abused women had used illegal drugs regularly, compared to 68% of men and 65% of women who had not been abused. About 69% of abused men and 58% of abused women reported drinking regularly at some time in their lives, compared to 60% of men and 38% of women who were not abused.

Abused State inmates were more likely than those reporting no abuse to have been using alcohol or illegal drugs at the time of their offense. This pattern occurred especially among female inmates. Forty-six percent of the abused women committed their current offense under the influence of illegal drugs; 33% were drinking. Among women who were not abused, 32% committed their offense while on drugs and 24% while drinking.

Inmates and probationers answered surveys about their abuse

Data for this report were taken from four BJS surveys: the Surveys of Inmates in State and Federal Correctional Facilities, 1997; the Survey of Inmates in Local Jails, 1996; and the Survey of Adults on Probation, 1995. In all four surveys nationally representative samples of inmates or probationers were interviewed about their current offense and sentence, criminal history, personal and family background, and prior drug and alcohol use and treatment.

Descriptions of methodology, sample design, and standard error calculations can be found in the following:

Substance Abuse and Treatment of State and Federal Prisoners, 1997 (NCJ 172871); Profile of Jail Inmates, 1996 (NCJ 164620); and Substance Abuse and Treatment of Adults on Probation, 1995 (NCJ 166611).

In the probation and jail inmate surveys, past the interview's midpoint, each respondent was asked, "Have you ever been physically or sexually abused?" Inmates in the surveys in State and Federal correctional facilities were asked if "anyone ever pressured or forced you to have any sexual contact against your will, that is, touching of genitals" and for

1 ❖ WHO ARE THE PRISONERS?

Appendix table. Weighted totals of persons reporting in tables 1 and 2		
	Total number*	
	In population (table 1)	Reporting prior abuse (table 2)
State inmates		
Male	984,320	158,729
Female	65,425	37,391
Federal inmates		
Male	81,607	5,850
Female	6,347	2,530
Jail inmates		
Male	450,099	57,915
Female	50,298	23,777
Probationers		
Male	1,630,117	163,676
Female	428,644	176,454

*Missing data are excluded from totals.

females, "breast, or buttocks, or oral, anal, or vaginal sex?" and for males "or oral or anal sex?" In a separate question they were asked if they had "ever been physically abused?"

Question wording and respondent sensitivity affect level of reported abuse

The BJS survey questions rely on respondents to define abuse within the context of their own lives, to recall their pasts, and to report what they remember. Factors can intervene so that the reported experiences do not match the actual experiences. For example, respondents may be unwilling to admit that sensitive events occurred, may be reluctant to report abuse to others, may distrust interviewers or surveys, may forget, or may purposefully misrepresent.

In contrast, most studies of abuse in the general population have used a battery of questions listing specific kinds of experiences, some of which are then classified as abuse by the analyst. These questions elicit events respondents may not recognize as abuse and impose the analysts' definitions of abuse upon respondents' experiences. These differences in definition and measurement should be taken into account when comparing the results of various surveys.

Low response rates, as well as broad definitions, have been found to produce high estimates of abuse, while high response rates and narrow definitions produce low estimates. For a discussion of the effects of question wording and response rates on estimates of abuse in the general population, see Kevin M. Gooey and Donald R. Leslie, "The Prevalence of Child Sexual Abuse: Integrative Review Adjustment for Potential Response and Measurement Biases," *Child Abuse and Neglect,* 21, pp. 391–98, 1997.

Gallop Poll estimates of abuse for the general population are based on questions similar to those asked in the correctional population surveys. See the *Source Book of Criminal Justice Statistics,* 1990, 1993, and 1995, for tables from the poll. The following were general adult population responses about childhood experiences: 9%, raped by an older child or an adult; 5% of men and 10% of women, kicked, punched, or choked by a parent or guardian; and 13% of men and 10% of women, physically abused by their parents.

In recent surveys completed by the Bureau of Justice Statistics, 19% of State prison inmates, 10% of Federal inmates, and 16% of those in local jails or on active probation told interviewers they had been physically or sexually abused before their current sentence. Just under half of the women in correctional populations and a tenth of the men indicated past abuse. The survey questions largely relied on respondents to define for themselves physical and sexual abuse.

The Bureau of Justice Statistics is the statistical agency of the U.S. Department of Justice. Jan M. Chaiken, Ph.D. is director. ▼

BJS selected Findings present findings from diverse data series. This report was written by Caroline Wolf Harlow, under the supervision of Allen J. Beck. Thomas P. Bonczar assisted with analysis of the Survey of Adults on Probation and general statistical review. Tom Hester produced the report. Marilyn Marbrook administered final report production, assisted by Yvonne Boston.

April 1999, NCJ 172879

This report, as well as other reports and statistics, may be found at the Bureau of Justice Statistics World Wide Web site: http://www.ojp.usdoj.gov/bjs/

Data from the surveys can be obtained from the National Archive of Criminal Justice Data at the University of Michigan, 1-800-999-0960. The archive can be accessed through BJS Web site.

Drug use history and criminal behavior among 133 incarcerated men

Elena Kouri, Harrison G. Pope, Kenneth F. Powell, Paul S. Oliva and Corbett Campbell

INTRODUCTION

Most studies investigating the relationship between substance abuse and criminal behavior in the United States have focused primarily on heroin addiction (1–6). Only a few studies have examined substance abuse in general among arrested offenders (7, 8). In studies conducted by the National Institute of Justice Drug Use Forecasting System (8) in 22 major metropolitan areas, over 70% of inmates tested positive for at least one type of illicit drug at the time of incarceration. In particular, 60% of new arrestees tested positive for cocaine. Even though these kinds of studies provide information regarding drug use at the time of arrest, they do not provide information about past history of drug abuse among convicts. However, this latter information is important, given evidence that drug use is positively related to the number of felonies committed, such as burglary, robbery, and auto theft (3, 9).

The present study investigated the relationship between crime and substance abuse in a sample of 133 consecutively evaluated male prisoners. We assessed the prevalence of various forms of substance abuse in this population and attempted to judge whether substance abuse played a role in the index crime which had led to the present incarceration. Finally, we assessed whether there was a relationship between the nature of substance dependence and the type of crime committed, whether sexual, violent, or non-violent.

METHODS

The Massachusetts Correctional Institution in Concord (MCI-Concord) functions as a receiving facility for all newly incarcerated adult male prisoners in the Massachusetts state system. In addition, the prison houses a few inmates who are awaiting trial, and some men who have been transferred to Concord from elsewhere in the correctional system for various administrative reasons. Thus, the prison provides a virtually unselected sample of all men incarcerated for violations of state laws.

All new prisoners are required to undergo a psychological evaluation by the Corrections Mental Health Department upon arrival. These evaluations are scheduled for a fixed block of time on weekday afternoons. With the assistance of members of the Department, we invited all prisoners coming for evaluation to participate in a 15- to 30-minute interview regarding their history of "substance use." No compensation was offered for this interview. Approximately half of the inmates invited to participate agreed to the interview.

The interview was conducted by one of the investigators (HGP and/or KFP) who was blind to the criminal record of the subject. Subjects were asked basic demographic questions and were then administered the alcohol and substance abuse portions of the Structured Clinical Interview for DSM-III-R (10). In addition, subjects were asked whether they were intoxicated with or withdrawing from any substance at the time that they committed the index crime which had led to their present incarceration. Subjects who admitted to drug intoxication or withdrawal were then asked whether they felt that they would have committed their crime if they had not been under the influence of the drug.

Subsequently, another investigator (EMK), blind to the result of the subject interviews, examined the complete criminal records of all subjects. She recorded the dates and nature of all crimes for which the subject had been convicted. Crimes were classified as sexual if they involved rape or other sexual assault. The remaining crimes were classified as "violent" if they involved physical harm or the immediate threat of physical harm to another person; all other crimes were classified as non-violent.

RESULTS

A total of 133 men were interviewed. Their mean age ([+ or -] SD) was 30.7 ([+ or -] 7.6) years; their ages ranged from 17 to 47 years. Sixty-seven (50%) of the subjects were white, 31 (23%) were black and 27 (20%) were Hispanics. Ethnicity was not recorded for 8 (6%) men. Of the 133 prisoners, 95% (126 individuals) obtained a diagnosis of dependence on one or more substances. Figure 1 shows the number of individuals who obtained DSM-III-R diagnoses of various substance use disorders. Moreover, 77 (58%) of the inmates reported that they were acutely intoxicated with one or more substances at the time that they committed the index crime and an additional 8 (6%) were withdrawing from a substance at the time of the crime. Alcohol and cocaine were the two substances most commonly used at the time of the index offense.

We obtained detailed information on the index crimes for 129 of the 133 interviewed inmates. When we divided the types of crimes into violent, nonviolent, and sexual, 57 crimes out of the 129 (44%) were defined as violent, 54 (42%) were non-violent, and 18 (14%) were sexual. The violent crimes included offenses such as armed robbery, murder, manslaughter, and assault and battery by means of a deadly weapon. The non-violent crimes included offenses such as unarmed robbery, auto theft, breaking and entering, possession of a controlled substance with intent to distribute, and receiving stolen goods. The sexual crimes comprised rape, assault with intent to rape, and child pornography. There was no significant correlation between the type of substance abuse diagnosis and the type of crime committed. Similarly, there was no significant correlation between the number of individuals who reported they were intoxicated at the time of the offense and the type of crime committed.

DISCUSSION

The present study found that 95% of 133 interviewed state prison inmates reported at least one form of substance abuse or dependence by DSM-III-R criteria. Previous studies have reported incidence rates of substance dependence in jailed criminals between 61 and 83% (7, 11, 12). Our higher incidence rates may be due in part to the fact that our study is the first investigation to use structured clinical interviews to assess the diagnoses of dependence. To our knowledge, all previous investigations have used either self-report questionnaires or unstructured interviews.

The extremely high prevalence of DSM-III-R substance abuse dependence in this population raises the question of whether there was a relationship between their substance dependence and their criminal activities. On interview, 53% (72 individuals) reported that their drug use played a significant role in their committing the crime for which they were incarcerated. It must be remembered, however, that we scored only the index crime for which the individual had been incarcerated at the time of our interview. Upon looking at the probation records of these men, in many cases they had been convicted of a series of 10 or 20 crimes over the course of a period of a decade or more. When we looked at these cases, we found that almost all of the remaining individuals had at least at some point been convicted of a drug-related crime. In summary, therefore, it appears that in virtually all cases, the use of illicit substances has contributed to a crime requiring incarceration at some point in the inmate's career.

Our data are subject to several methodological limitations. First, we interviewed a modest number of subjects at only one institution. It is not certain that this group would be entirely representative of the overall population of prisoners in Massachusetts. However, since MCI Concord represents a receiving facility for all prisons in the Massachusetts system, it seems unlikely that sequential prisoners interviewed at this site would differ greatly from the overall population of prisoners in the state.

A second and more serious possible source of selection bias was the fact that only about half of prisoners invited for an interview agreed to participate. It might be speculated that those who declined to participate were reluctant to be interviewed regarding their substance abuse histories. Thus, our finding of a history of substance abuse or dependence in 95% of prisoners may actually represent an underestimate of the true prevalence.

Information bias may also have caused us to underestimate the magnitude of substance abuse and dependence in this population, since subjects may have withheld information about some or all of their history of substance use. Since we possessed no method for checking the validity of subjects' responses on interview, the degree of this information bias cannot be accurately assessed.

Subjects' subjective assessments of the role of substance abuse in the commission of their crimes must also be regarded as subject to information bias. For example, subjects may have preferred to portray their crimes as drug-induced in order to minimize their own responsibility for their acts. Thus, this aspect of the data must be regarded only as a very approximate measure.

In any event, it seems clear that substance abuse and dependence is extraordinarily prevalent among men incarcerated for crimes in Massachusetts and, very likely, elsewhere in the United States. It seems unlikely that our methodology led to an overestimate of the prevalence of substance abuse; more likely, our figure of 95% represents an underestimate. Although it seems reasonable to expect a frequent history of substance abuse among male prisoners, the extraordinarily high rates exhibited in our sample suggest that this issue deserves more systematic exploration. It is not clear, at this point, whether substance abuse is a cause, an effect, or merely an associated phenomenon in the criminal histories of these men. It is critical to discriminate among these various hypotheses in order to formulate rational strategies for addressing the problem of substance use among criminal offenders.

REFERENCES

[1.] Nurco, D. N., Shaffer, J. W., Ball, J. C., et al., Trends in the commission of crime among narcotic addicts over successive periods of addiction and nonaddiction, Am. J. Drug Alcohol Abuse 10:481–489 (1984).

[2.] Nurco, D. N., Ball, J. C., Shaffer, J. W., et al., The criminality of narcotic addicts, J. Nerv. Ment. Dis. 173:94–102 (1985).

[3.] Nurco, D. N., Shaffer, J. W., Ball, J. C., et al., A comparison of ethnic group and city of the criminal activities of narcotic addicts, J. Nerv. Ment. Dis. 174:112–116 (1986).

[4.] Ball, J. C., Rosen, L., Flueck, J. A., et al., The criminality of heroin addicts: When addicted and when off opiates, in The Drugs-Crime Connection, (J. A. Inciardi Ed.) Sage Publications, Beverly Hills, CA, 1981 pp. 39–65.

[5.] Ball, J. C., Rosen, L., Flueck, J. A., et al., Lifetime criminality of heroin addicts in the United States, J. Drug Issues 12:225–239 (1982).

[6.] McGlothlin, W. H., Anglin, M. D., and Wilson, B. D., Narcotic addiction and crime, Criminology 16:293–315 (1978).

[7.] Peters, R. H., Kearns, W. D., Drug abuse history and treatment needs of jail inmates, Am. J. Drug Alcohol Abuse 18:355–366 (1992).

[8.] National Institute of Justice, NIJ Reports, 215, Washington, D.C. 1989.

[9.] Hanlon, T. E., Nurco, D. N., Kinlock, T. W., et al., Trends in criminal activity and drug use over an addiction career, Am. J. Drug Alcohol Abuse 16:223–238 (1990).

[10.] Spitzer, R. L., Williams, J. B. W., and Gibbon, M., Structured Clinical Interview for DSM-III-R (SCID), New York State Psychiatric Institute, Biometrics Research, New York, 1987.

[11.] Barton, W. I., Drug histories and criminality: Survey of inmates of state correctional facilities, January 1974, Int. J. Addictions 15:233–258 (1980).

[12.] Barton, W. I., Drug histories and criminality of inmates of local jails in the United States (1978): Implications for treatment and rehabilitation of the drug abusers in a jail setting, Int. J. Addictions 17:417–444 (1978).

PERSPECTIVES

Drugs, Crime, Prison and Treatment

by Charles Blanchard, chief counsel, White House Office of National Drug Control Policy (ONDCP); former Arizona state senator and CSG Toll Fellow, class of '91

Talk to any police officer, judge or probation officer, or visit any prison. One fact becomes abundantly clear: there is a clear link between crime and drug use. While no one factor can explain criminal behavior, it is undeniable that drug addiction is an important factor in explaining crime and violence. Study after study confirms this link:

• Over half of the crime in this country is committed by individuals under the influence of drugs. The National Institute of Justice's ADAM drug-testing program found that more than 60 percent of adult male arrestees tested positive for drugs. In most cities, over half of young male arrestees are under the influence of marijuana. Importantly, the majority of these crimes result from the effects of the drug—and do not result from the fact that drugs are illegal.

• According to a study by the National Center on Addiction and Substance Abuse (CASA) at Columbia University, 80 percent of the men and women behind bars—about 1.4 million inmates—are seriously involved with alcohol and other drug abuse.

• A study published in the *Journal of American Medical Association* last year indicated that nondrug users who live in households where drugs (including marijuana) are used are 11 times as likely to be killed as those living in drug-free households. Drug abuse in a home increased a women's risk of being killed by a close relative by 28 times.

Despite this strong link between drugs and crime, few probationers and inmates receive drug or alcohol treatment. While states estimate that 70 to 85 percent of their inmates need some substance abuse treatment, only 13 percent of these inmates received any treatment in 1996. Sadly, even in those state prisons that do offer quality treatment, only a relatively small percentage of offenders take advantage of it.

It is time for state and federal leaders to take a closer look at funding substance abuse treatment in criminal justice systems. And, it is time to become more creative in using the coercive power of the criminal justice system (a system with many opportunities for rewards and punishments) to induce offenders to seek and remain in treatment.

Fortunately, in recent years many state and local governments and the federal government have experimented with drug treatment programs in the criminal justice system.

5. Drugs, Crime, Prison, and Treatment

Thanks to the evaluations of these innovative programs, we now have good evidence that using the coercive power of the criminal justice system to force probationers and inmates into treatment is a cost-effective means of reducing crime. Recent evaluations of a myriad of criminal justice treatment programs—ranging from diversion programs such as drug courts and the Brooklyn Drug Treatment Alternative-to-Prison program, and institutional drug treatment programs such as those in Delaware and the Federal Bureau of Prisons—have found that drug treatment reduces crime. These studies show that quality treatment programs of sufficient length that include transition services in the community reduce drug use and future criminal behavior.

Among inmates who completed residential drug treatment, only 3.3 percent were rearrested in the first six months, compared with 12.1 percent of inmates who did not receive treatment.

As a result of the Violent Crime Control and Law Enforcement Act of 1994, the Federal Bureau of Prisons now provides drug treatment to all eligible inmates prior to their release from custody. Last Spring, the Bureau of Prisons announced its first analysis of the success of this program. It shows that institution-based drug treatment can make a difference. Among inmates who completed residential drug treatment, only 3.3 percent were rearrested in the first six months, compared with 12.1 percent of inmates who did not receive treatment. Similarly, the Delaware Department of Corrections conducts outstanding drug treatment programs. A study of the Delaware program found that those inmates who received both institutional drug treatment and transitional support services had far fewer arrests and far less drug use after release than those inmates who had no such treatment. Eighteen months after arrest, 71 percent of the treated inmates were arrest-free, and 76 percent were drug-free. In contrast, only 30 percent of those inmates who had no treatment were arrest-free and only 19 percent were drug-free.

Perhaps the most innovative treatment programs, however, have not been in institutional settings. Instead, thanks in large measure to the ideas of scholars such as Mark Kleiman, several state and local leaders have begun to build treatment programs for offenders outside the prison system that are based on the concept of coerced abstinence. The idea is a simple one: use the coercive power of the criminal justice system to induce nonviolent offenders into treatment. Sadly, even when treatment is available, only a small number of offenders enter and remain in treatment. To remedy this problem, coerced abstinence programs use a "carrot and stick" approach—using drug testing, graduated sanctions and treatment—to induce offenders to take treatment seriously.

Surprisingly to some, these coerced abstinence programs work just as well as voluntary treatment programs in reducing the drug use and criminal activity of their graduates. Importantly, however, these coerced abstinence programs are more successful than voluntary programs both in inducing offenders to participate in treatment and in retaining offenders in treatment. For example, Charles J. Hynes, the Kings County (Brooklyn) District Attorney, has built a coerced treatment program known as the Drug Treatment Alternative-to-Prison (DTAP) program. Evaluations of the DTAP program found that the overall retention rate for offenders in the DTAP program was 64 percent—at least two times higher than the retention rate for most residential treatment programs. Moreover, after one year, DTAP offenders had less than half the arrest rate of drug offenders sent to prison.

Similarly, preliminary evaluations of drug courts have been encouraging. There are now about 300 drug courts in operation, with drug courts located in virtually every state. Using drug testing, treatment, and graduated sanctions, drug courts offer non-violent offenders the hope of a dismissal of charges if they successfully complete drug treatment. During the program, graduated sanctions (such as jail time) are used to punish offenders who test positive for drugs or who otherwise fail to participate in treatment. Offenders who fail the program altogether face time in prison. This combination of positive and negative incentives appears to work. Studies of the drug court programs in Brooklyn, Maricopa

County (Arizona), the District of Columbia, Portland (Oregon), and Dade County (Florida) all found high retention rates, low re-arrest rates and lower drug use. Participants in these programs had arrest and drug use rates far lower than similar offenders who did not participate in the program.

Substance abuse treatment of offenders will pay for itself. Indeed, the CASA study concluded that if just ten percent of inmates given one year of residential treatment stay sober and work during the first year after release, prison-based drug treatment would more than pay for itself in one year. This is because the costs of continued drug use by released offenders is tremendously expensive to society. By ensuring the availability of treatment in the entire continuum of criminal sanctions—from diversion programs to probation to prison—states can reduce crime, reduce arrest and prosecution costs, reduce incarceration costs, reduce drug-related emergency room visits, and increase employment.

Of course, states must carefully construct quality treatment programs that are based on models—such as the Delaware prison treatment program and Brooklyn's DTAP program—that work. If they do so, however, there is every indication of a large payoff. By breaking the cycle of drugs and crime, we will have fewer victims, more productive citizens, and safer communities.

More information on criminal justice treatment programs can be found on the ONDCP web site: http://www.whitehousedrugpolicy.gov.

THE FORGOTTEN OFFENDER

Women in Prison:
From Partial Justice to Vengeful Equity

By Meda Chesney-Lind

Throughout most of our nation's history, women in prison have been correctional afterthoughts. Ignored because of their small numbers, female inmates tended to complain, not riot, making it even easier for institutions to overlook their unique needs. Perhaps as a consequence, the United States never developed a correctional system for women to replace the reformatory system that fell into disuse shortly before World War II. In fact, by the mid-70s, only about half of the states and territories had separate prisons for women, and many jurisdictions housed women inmates in male facilities or in women's facilities in other states.

Something dramatic happened to this picture in the 1980s: During that decade, the number of women in U.S. prisons jumped dramatically. In 1980, there were just over 12,000 women in U.S. state and federal prisons. By 1997, that number had increased to almost 80,000. In about a decade and a half, the number of women incarcerated in the nation's prisons had increased sixfold.

This astonishing increase should not be seen simply as a reflection of the increase in male incarceration during the same period. Women's "share" of total imprisonment has more than doubled in the past three decades, from 3 percent in 1970 to 6.4 percent in 1997.

The rate of growth in female imprisonment also has outpaced that of men; since 1985 the annual rate of growth in the number of female inmates has averaged 11.1 percent, higher than the 7.6 percent average increase in male inmates. In 1996 alone, the number of females grew at a rate nearly double that of males (9.5 percent, compared to 4.8 percent for males).

Similar patterns have been seen in adult jails: Women constituted 7 percent of the population in the mid-80s, but today they account for 11 percent of the population. Likewise, the rate of increase in female incarceration in local jails since 1985 has been 9.9 percent for women, compared to 6.4 percent for men.

Finally, the rate of women's imprisonment is at a historic high, increasing from a low of six sentenced female inmates per 100,000 U.S. women in 1925 to 54 per 100,000 in 1997. In 1997, California led the nation with 11,076 women in prison, followed by Texas with 10,549, New York with 3,584 and Florida with 3,404.

The correctional establishment, long used to forgetting about women, was taken almost completely by surprise when this change started. Initially, women inmates were housed virtually anywhere (remodeled hospitals, abandoned training schools and converted motels) as jurisdictions struggled to cope with the soaring increase in women's imprisonment. Increasingly, though, states have begun to open new units and facilities to house female inmates. Data collected by Nicole Rafter, author of *Partial Justice: Women, Prisons and Social Control,* document this clearly. Between 1930 and 1950, the United States opened approximately two to three facilities for women each decade, but during the 1980s alone, more than 34 were opened. By 1990, the nation had 71 female-only facilities; in 1995, the number of female facilities had jumped to 104—an increase of 46.5 percent.

What has caused this shift in the way that we respond to women's crime? What unique challenges have these women inmates produced? And what could we do better or differently, as we struggle to create a woman-oriented response to the current state of affairs?

Women's Criminal Activity

Is the dramatic increase in women's imprisonment a response to a women's crime problem spiraling out of control? Empirical indicators give little evidence of this. For example, the total number of arrests of adult women, which might be seen as a measure of women's criminal activity, increased by 31.4 percent between 1987 and 1996, while the number of women in prison increased by 159 percent.

> *Women's imprisonment is at a historic high.*

And despite media images of hyper-violent female offenders, the proportion of women doing time in state prisons for violent offenses has been declining steadily from about half (48.9 percent) in 1979 to just over a quarter (27.6 percent) in 1997. In states like California, which runs the two largest women's prisons in the nation, the decline is even sharper. In 1992, 16 percent of the women admitted to the California prison system were incarcerated for violent crimes, compared to 37.2 percent in 1982. What explains the increase? A recent study by the Bureau of Justice Statistics (BJS) indicates that growth in the number of violent offenders has been the major factor for male prison population growth, but for the female prison population, "drug offenders were the largest source of growth." One explanation, then, is that the "war on drugs" has become a largely unannounced war on women. In 1979, one in 10 women in prison was doing time for drugs. Today, drug offenders account for more than a third of the female prison population (37.4 percent). Finally, while the intent of "get tough" policies was to rid society of drug dealers and so-called drug kingpins, more than a third (35.9 percent) of the women serving time for drug offenses in state prisons are there on charges of possession.[1]

Policies Impacting Women's Imprisonment

Many observers suspect that the increase in women's imprisonment is due to an array of policy changes within the criminal justice system, rather than a change in the seriousness of women's crime.

Certainly, as data on the characteristics of women in prison indicate, the passage of increased penalties for drug offenses has been a major factor. Also important has been the implementation of a variety of sentencing reform initiatives which, while devoted to reducing class and race disparities in male sentencing, pay little attention to gender.[2]

The scant evidence we have suggests that sentencing reform has played a major role in the soaring increase of women in federal prisons. In 1988, before full implementation of sentencing guidelines, women comprised 6.5 percent of those in federal institutions; by 1992, that figure had jumped to 8 percent. The number of women in federal prisons climbed by 97.4 percent in the space of three years.

Data on the offense characteristics of women in federal institutions further confirm the role played by policy shifts in response to drug convictions. In 1989, 44.5 percent of the women incarcerated in federal institutions were being held for drug offenses. Two years later, this figure was up to 68 percent.[3] Twenty years ago, nearly two-thirds of the women convicted of federal felonies were granted probation, but in 1991, only 28 percent were given straight probation. The mean time to be served by female drug offenders increased from 27 months in July 1984 to 67 months in June 1990.

As a result of these pressures, the federal prison system holds 8,306 women, and the number of women incarcerated in federal facilities continues to increase at an even faster pace than that found in state prisons. Additionally, women comprise an even larger proportion of those incarcerated in federal prisons (7.4 percent, compared to 6.3 percent in state prisons).

Other less obvious policy changes also have played a role in increasing women's imprisonment. For example, look at new technologies for determining drug use (e.g., urinalysis). Many women are being returned to prison for technical parole violations because they fail to pass random drug tests. Of the 6,000 women incarcerated in California in 1993, approximately one-third (32 percent) were imprisoned on parole violations. In Hawaii, 55 percent of new admissions to the women's prison during a two-month period in 1991 had been returned to prison for parole violations (largely drug violations). Finally, in Oregon, during a one-year period from October 1992 to September 1993, only 16 percent of females admitted to institutions were incarcerated for new convictions; the rest were probation and parole violators.

The impact of gender-blind sentencing, coupled with what might be seen as increased policing of women's behavior while on probation or parole, have played major, though largely hidden, roles in the growth of women's imprisonment.

Vengeful Equity?

What has happened in the last few decades signals a major change in the way the country is responding to women's offending. Without much fanfare and certainly with little public discussion or debate, the male model of incarceration has been increasingly accessed in response to the soaring number of women inmates.

Some might argue that this pattern is simply the product of a lack of reflection or imagination on the part of those charged with administering the nation's prison systems. They are, after all, used to running prisons built around the male model of inmate. However, an additional theme also is emerging in modern correctional response to women inmates: vengeful equity. This is the dark side of the equity or parity model of justice—one which emphasizes treating women offenders as though they were men, particularly when the outcome is punitive, in the name of equal justice.

Perhaps the starkest expression of this impulse has been the creation of chain gangs for women. While these have surfaced in several states, the most publicized example comes from Arizona. There, a sheriff pronounced himself an "equal opportunity incarcerator" and encouraged women "now locked up with three or four others in dank, cramped disciplinary cells" to "volunteer" for a 15-woman chain gang. Defending his controversial move, he commented, "If women can fight for their country, and bless them for that, if they can walk a beat, if they can protect the people and arrest violators of the law, then they should have no problem with picking up trash in 120 degrees." Other examples of vengeful equity can be found in the creation of women's boot camps, and in the argument that women should be subjected to capital punishment at the same rate as men.

Female Offender Characteristics

But who are these women inmates, and does it make sense to treat women in prison as though they were men? BJS recently conducted a national survey of imprisoned women in the United States and found that women in prison have far higher rates of physical and sexual abuse than their male counterparts. Forty-three percent of the women surveyed "reported they had been abused at least once" before their current admission to prison; the comparable figure for men was 12.2 percent.

For about a third of all women in prison (31.7 percent), the abuse started when they were young girls, but continued as they became adults. A key gender difference emerges here. A number of imprisoned young men (10.7 percent) also report abuse as boys, but the abuse generally does not continue into adulthood. One in four women reported that the abuse started during adulthood, compared to just 3 percent of male offenders. Fully 33.5 percent of the women surveyed reported physical abuse, and a slightly higher number (33.9 percent) had been sexually abused either as girls or young women, compared to relatively small percentages of men (10 percent of boys and 5.3 percent of adult men in prison).

A look at the offenses for which women are incarcerated quickly puts to rest the notion of hyper-violent, nontraditional women offenders. Nearly half of all women in prison are serving sentences for nonviolent offenses and have been convicted in the past of only nonviolent offenses. By 1996, about two-thirds of women in the nation's prisons were serving time either for drug offenses or property offenses.

Even when women commit violent offenses, gender plays an important role. Research indicates, for example, that of women convicted of murder or manslaughter, many had killed husbands or boyfriends who had repeatedly and violently abused them. In New York, of the women committed to the state's prisons for homicide in 1986, 49 percent had been the victims of abuse at some point in their lives and 59 percent of the women who killed someone close to them were being abused at the time of the offense. For half of the women committed for homicide, it was their first and only offense.

As with previous studies of women in prison, the BJS survey found that two-thirds of the women had at least one child under 18, yet more than half had never received visits from their children. Most of the women who did receive visits from their children saw them once a month or less frequently. More women were able to phone or send mail to their children, but one in five never sent mail to or received mail from their children, and one in four never talked on the phone with them. This was despite the fact that many of these women, prior to their incarceration, were taking care of their children (unlike their male counterparts).

Just under three-quarters of the women had children who had lived with them before going to prison, compared to slightly more than half (52.9 percent) of incarcerated men. In most cases, the imprisoned women's mothers (the children's grandmothers) take care of their children, while male inmates are more likely to be able to count on the children's mothers (89.7 percent). These patterns are particularly pronounced among African-American and Hispanic women.

Most importantly, the BJS study, like those done before, clearly documents the number of women of color behind bars. The numbers indicate that nearly half of the women in the nation's prisons are African American (46 percent) and Hispanic (14.2 percent). These data begin to hint at another important theme: The surge in women's imprisonment, particularly in the area of drug offenses, has disproportionately hit women of color in the United States. Specifically, while the number of women in state prisons for drug sales has increased by 433 percent between 1986 and 1991, this increase is far steeper for African-American women (828 percent) and Hispanic women (328 percent) than for Caucasian women (241 percent).

Women in prison, then, have different personal histories than their male counterparts and less serious offense backgrounds. In particular, women's long histories of victimization, coupled with the relative nonviolence of their crimes, suggests that extensive reliance on imprisonment could easily be rethought without compromising public safety.

What Could We Do Differently?

Inattention to gender difference, willful or otherwise, has meant that many modern women's prisons have encountered serious, and unanticipated, difficulties in managing this population. Jails and prisons are generally unprepared for the large number of pregnant women in their custody (some estimates put this at one in 10). The sexual harassment of women inmates also is an increasingly well-documented problem that is receiving both national and international attention. Finally, procedures that have been routine in corrections for decades (strip searches) are now being understood as problematic in women's prisons (particularly when dealing with victims of past sexual traumas). To put it simply, gender matters in corrections, and a woman in prison is not, and never will be, identical to her male counterpart.

Given the backgrounds of women in prison, many would argue that they could be better served in the community due to the decreased seriousness of their crimes and the treatable antecedents to their criminality. Since the expansion of the female prison population has been fueled primarily by increased rates of incarceration for drug offenses, not by commitments for crimes of violence, women in prison seem to be obvious candidates for alternative, in-community sentencing. To make this shift requires both planning and focus—something that has been absent in U.S. corrections with reference to women in prison.

We could, though, look north to Canada, where a high-level Task Force on Federally Sentenced Women was convened by the prime minister to deal with the long-standing problems within that nation's federal facility, as well as to lay out a national plan for women's corrections in Canada. California also has convened the Commission on Female Inmate and Parolee Issues to examine the unique needs of women offenders in that state.

It is clear that the United States should consider a national initiative similar to the Canadian task force; the numbers alone argue for a more coherent and planned national strategy regarding women in jail and prison.

The United States now imprisons more people than at any time in its history, and it has the world's second highest incarceration rate (behind the newly created nation of Russia). Women's share of the nation's prison population, measured in either absolute or relative terms, has never been higher. All of this has occurred without serious planning, consideration or debate.

As a nation, we face a choice. We can continue to spend tax dollars on the costly incarceration of women guilty of petty drug and property crimes, or we can seek other solutions to the problems of drug-dependent women. Given the characteristics of the women in prison, it is clear that the decarceration of large numbers of women in prison would not jeopardize public safety. Further, the money saved could be reinvested in programs designed to meet women's needs, which would enrich not only their lives but the lives of many other women who are at risk for criminal involvement.

Clearly, any in-community or alternative sentencing programs should be crafted with women's needs at the center. For example, many traditional forms of in-community sentences involve home detention—clearly unworkable for women with abusive boyfriends or husbands, but also problematic for women who are drug-dependent and/or unemployed. Restitution also is not a viable choice for some women offenders for many of the same reasons.

Women's programs must, first and foremost, give participants strategies to deal with their profound substance abuse problems. They must also be gender-sensitive in additional ways: they must understand that most women take drugs as a form of self-medication (rather than for adventure or challenge), and they must be sensitive to women's unique circumstances (by providing such services as child care and transportation). Community programs must also deal with women's immediate needs for safe housing and stable employment.

By moving dollars from women's imprisonment to women's services in the community, we not only will help women—we also will help their children. In the process, we are helping to break the cycle of poverty, desperation, crime and imprisonment that burdens so many of these women and their families.

ENDNOTES

1. In 1979, 26 percent of women doing time in state prison for drug offenses were incarcerated solely for possession.
2. Myrna Raeder notes, for example, that judges are constrained by federal guidelines from considering family responsibilities, particularly pregnancy and motherhood, which in the past may have kept women out of prison. Yet the impact of these "neutral" guidelines is to eliminate from consideration the unique situation of mothers, especially single mothers, unless their situation can be established to be "extraordinary." Nearly 90 percent of male inmates report that their wives or girlfriends are taking care of their children; by contrast, only 22 percent of mothers in prison could count on the fathers of their children to care for them during imprisonment. This means that many women in prison, the majority of whom are mothers, face the potential, if not actual, loss of their children. This is not a penalty that men in prison experience.

3. The comparable male figure was 58 percent in 1993, up from 39.6 percent in 1989.

REFERENCES

Adams, Rukaiyah, David Onek and Alissa Riker. 1998. *Double jeopardy: An assessment of the felony drug provision of the Welfare Reform Act.* San Francisco: Justice Policy Institute.

Adelberg, Ellen and Claudia Currie. 1993. *In conflict with the law: Women and the Canadian criminal justice system.* Vancouver: Press Gang Publishers.

Bloom, Barbara and David Steinhart. 1993. *Why punish the children?* San Francisco: National Council on Crime and Delinquency.

Bloom, Barbara, Meda Chesney-Lind and Barbara Owen. 1994. *Women in prison in California: Hidden victims of the war on drugs.* San Francisco: Center on Juvenile and Criminal Justice.

Bureau of Justice Statistics. 1988. *Profile of state prison inmates, 1986.* Washington, D.C.: U.S. Department of Justice.

Bureau of Justice Statistics. 1989. *Prisoners in 1988.* Washington, D.C.: U.S. Department of Justice.

Bureau of Justice Statistics. 1993. *Prisoners in 1992.* Washington, D.C.: U.S. Department of Justice.

Bureau of Justice Statistics. 1994. *Women in Prison.* Washington, D.C.: U.S. Department of Justice.

Bureau of Justice Statistics, 1998a. *Prisoners in 1997.* Washington, D.C.: U.S. Department of Justice.

Bureau of Justice Statistics, 1998b. *Prison and jail inmates at mid-year 1997.* Washington, D.C.: U.S. Department of Justice.

Calahan, Margaret. 1986. *Historical corrections: Statistics in the United States, 1850–1984.* Washington, D.C.: Bureau of Justice Statistics.

Chesney-Lind, Meda. 1997. *The female offender: Girls, women and crime.* Thousand Oaks, Calif.: Sage Publications.

Federal Bureau of Investigation. 1997. *Crime in the United States: 1996 Uniform Crime Reports.* Washington, D.C.: U.S. Department of Justice.

Huling, Tracy. 1991. *Breaking the silence.* Correctional Association of New York, March 4, mimeo.

Immarigeon, Russ and Meda Chesney-Lind. 1992. *Women's prisons: Overcrowded and overused.* San Francisco: National Council on Crime and Delinquency.

Kim, E. 1996. Sheriff says he'll have chain gangs for women. *Tuscaloosa News* (August 16, p. A1).

Mauer, Marc. 1994. *Americans behind bars: The international use of incarceration, 1992–1993.* Washington, D.C.: The Sentencing Project (September).

Mauer, Marc and Tracy Huling. 1995. *Young black Americans and the criminal justice system: Five years later.* Washington, D.C.: The Sentencing Project.

O'Brien, Patricia. 1998. *Women in prison: Making it in the free world.* University of Illinois at Chicago: School of Social Work.

Raeder, Myrna. 1993. Gender and sentencing: Single moms, battered women and other sex-based anomalies in the gender-free world of the federal sentencing guidelines. *Pepperdine Law Review,* 20(3):905–990.

Rafter, Nicole Hahn. 1990. *Partial justice: Women, prisons and social control.* New Brunswick, N.J.: Transaction Books.

Singer, Linda R. 1973. Women and the correctional process. *American Criminal Law Review,* 11:295–308.

Snell, Tracy L. and Danielle C. Morton. 1994. *Women in prison.* Washington, D.C.: Bureau of Justice Statistics, Special Report.

Meda Chesney-Lind, Ph.D., is a professor in the Women's Studies Program at the University of Hawaii at Manoa. She also is the author of The Female Offender: Girls, Women and Crime, *published in 1997 by Sage Publications.*

Unit 2

Unit Selections

7. **Coping with Incarceration—From the Other Side of the Bars,** Mary Dallao
8. **Behind Bars: We've Built the Largest Prison System in the World. Here's a Look Inside,** Wray Herbert
9. **Behind Bars: Substance Abuse and America's Prison Population,** Spectrum
10. **Inside the New Alcatraz,** Peter Annin
11. **Life on the Inside: The Jailers,** Andrew Metz
12. **Prison Crime in New York State,** David R. Eichenthal and Laurel Blatchford
13. **Stopping Abuse in Prison,** Nina Siegal
14. **A Day in the Life,** Gabrielle deGroot
15. **The Gangs behind Bars,** Tiffany Danitz
16. **The Effects of the Duran Consent Decree,** Curtis R. Blakely
17. **The Constitution and the Federal District Judge,** Frank M. Johnson

Key Points to Consider

❖ Who gets caught up in the "ripple" effects of incarceration? How might these effects change the potential for future criminality among those affected by a family member or friend's imprisonment?

❖ Why have we continued to build more and stronger prisons?

❖ Do prison workers abuse inmates? Does this behavior seem understandable in light of the working conditions and the realities of prison operations? Defend your answer.

❖ What are some of the reasons why inmates create and support prison gangs? Is the proliferation of prison gangs and the increase in the membership of these gangs a reasonable response to the realities of prison life? What factors are working to create the increase in prison gangs and what might be changed to reduce the perceived need for gangs?

❖ How do the experiences of female inmates differ from the experiences of their male counterparts? Do their experiences reflect in any significant way their status as "forgotten" offenders? Explain.

❖ What are some of the reasons why the courts find it difficult to control the behavior of the prisons? Why do federal judges avoid making decisions that control state-level prisons? How do these judges define their role in the context of prison operations?

DUSHKIN ONLINE Links   www.dushkin.com/online/

13. **Accommodating Prison Population Growth**
    http://www.lao.ca.gov/sc010695a.html
14. **The Corrections Connection Network**
    http://www.corrections.com
15. **The Farm: Life Inside a Women's Prison**
    http://www.igc.org/thefarm/links.htm
16. **Oregon Department of Corrections**
    http://www.doc.state.or.us/links/welcome.htm
17. **Prison Life**
    http://www.hmprisonservice.gov.uk/life/
18. **Stop Prisoner Rape**
    http://www.spr.org/spr.html

These sites are annotated on pages 4 and 5.

Prison Life

In this unit we attempt to show what being a prisoner or corrections officer is like in today's correctional institutions. Perspectives on life in prison begin with understanding how imprisoning a person can create a "ripple" effect across the lives of the family and friends of the offender. In "Coping with Incarceration—From the Other Side of the Bars" Mary Dallao exposes us to the experiences and perceptions of the prisoner's family members. This information is bolstered by the photo essay offered in the second entry of unit 2, in which we see the visual realities of life behind bars.

Then, an article from *Spectrum* describes how substance abuse and addiction have fundamentally changed the nature of the prison population. Crime goes hand-in-hand with substance abuse.

Next, Peter Annin examines the problems inherent in a correctional system that is imposing longer sentences and consequently dealing with more hardened offenders. In "Inside the New Alcatraz," the Federal Bureau of Prison's response to this challenge—offering a level of control previously unavailable in the United States—is discussed.

Life on the inside also includes the jailers. Andrew Metz, in the next article, describes how correction officers battle fear, tension, and being stereotyped as brutes, in this case at one of the largest jails in the country, Nassau County Correctional Center.

As the numbers of inmates increase, and prisons become more crowded while sentences become longer, we can reasonably expect that the inmate population will respond to their resulting frustration with disorder and violence. In the article, "Prison Crime in New York State," David Eichenthal and Laurel Blatchford consider the prison system of New York state, and examine the prevalence of crime by inmates in what is a relatively typical state prison system. The article that follows deals with inmate abuse, which tends to be a common outcome of the situation of large numbers of frustrated inmates being controlled by a small number of guards. "Stopping Abuse in Prison," by Nina Siegal, examines the prevalence of crime behind bars and offers suggestions for how this problem could be better addressed.

In keeping with the theme of "prison life," the following two articles deal with some of the realities of life in prison. The first of these "A Day in the Life," by Gabrielle de Groot, deals with four female offenders and offers case studies of their day-to-day existence in a typical female prison. The second of these articles, "The Gang behind Bars," by Tiffany Danity, deals with one of the enduring issues in male prisons: gangs. In this article we see both the power of the gang and the problems faced by inmates who desire to avoid gang problems and gang membership while doing their time.

Lastly, the unit concludes with two articles, "The Effects of the Duran Consent Decree," and "The Constitution and the Federal District Judge," that provide an explanation of what happens when a prison's operations are challenged by the Federal Court, and what the judges who hear these cases are asked to deal with, both practically and politically.

Coping With Incarceration

–From the other side of the bars.

By Mary Dallao

When Margaret's son went to prison for second-degree manslaughter, she went to prison, too, although the instrument of her confinement was not made of concrete and steel. Instead, it was an edifice she and society had fashioned out of stereotypes, judgments and guilt, and the punishment and mental anguish inflicted proved just as real as an 80-square-foot cell without windows.

Her nightmare started one Saturday night when her 18-year-old son, John, ended up in the woods, partying, smoking and drinking with his high school buddies in their small hometown in upstate New York. The little guy in the group, he became angry when six football players swiped his money and started pushing him around. John whipped out a knife, stabbing and killing one of his antagonists.

"It was a total shock," Margaret says. "He was a good kid . . . he was the easiest of my three."

Overnight, Margaret's middle-class world was shattered. Her family had never been associated with crime before, but now the story was being splashed all over town, on every local TV news broadcast, across the front page of the daily paper.

"In such a small town, the media really played it up big," she says.

Margaret didn't leave the house for weeks. She couldn't answer the phone. Eighteen months passed before the case came to trial, and the sentencing took another two or three months. During this time, she awoke every morning with an upset stomach. Waiting for the sentence, she says, brought her feelings of dread and anxiety. Every time the phone rang, she expected the worst.

Ultimately, John was charged with second-degree manslaughter and sentenced to four to 12 years in prison, with parole eligibility after four years. He served six years of his sentence, and has since moved away from his small town to start a new life.

Although John survived his time in prison, and his family, thanks to counseling, also came out relatively intact, the pain that loved ones must face when a son, daughter, parent or spouse breaks the law cannot be denied.

"I assumed that everyone in town saw me as a failure as a parent," Margaret says. "For at least a year after John went to prison, I went to grocery stores out of town."

Margaret and her family visited John every week. Although visiting lasted only three hours, Margaret found other ways to spend time in her son's presence, and even if she couldn't physically enter the prison, she always stayed nearby.

"I'd drive to the prison parking lot and sit there for hours, just to feel close," she says. "I blasted the radio with his favorite music. I'd never been through something like this, and I didn't know how to act."

Families At-Risk

Crime touches the lives of families everywhere. Having a loved one in prison brings with it a scarlet letter of shame that family members wear to school, work, church and the supermarket—not to mention the anxiety and internal torment they face.

Ann Adalist-Estrin, director of the Parent Resource Association in Wyncote, Pa., and board member of the Family and Corrections Network (FCN), points out that as national incarceration rates rise, a greater number of families are seeing loved ones locked up. Three-strikes laws are landing more people in prison who weren't in prison before, and female offender increases are placing more children in the care of grandparents or in foster care. To make matters worse, larger segments of today's American families have been termed "at-risk"—that is, in danger of repeating criminal behaviors of the previous generation.

Children of Offenders

Approximately 80 percent of all women and 50 percent of all men in prison have children, says FCN President Jim Mustin. In raw numbers, statistics from Prison Fellowship Ministries state that more than 1.5 million minors have a parent behind bars. Forty-three percent of these children are under 7 years old, with 46 percent between the ages of 7 and 12. For these impressionable youngsters, the effects of their parents' crimes can alter and upset emotional development for years to come.

The closeness of a child's relationship with a parent does not necessarily determine the severity of incarceration's impact, Adalist-Estrin says. Children who have little contact with a parent prior to incarceration can be just as upset as those who lose their primary caregiver.

"If a child has a disconnected relationship with a parent, he or she still mourns losing the chance to become close when that parent goes to prison," she says. "Even children who have been disappointed by parents hope that they'll learn to be effective—that they'll be able to read them stories at night or pick them up after school."

Adalist-Estrin says her experiences in counseling at-risk families have taught her that many children are smarter than their parents think, and most are aware when parents have drug habits or criminal lifestyles. It generally is unwise to hide a parent's incarceration from children, she says. Some are told by caregivers that the incarcerated parent is in the Army, away at college or in the hospital. As time passes, children begin to ask questions, and it becomes more difficult to continue these deceptions. Lying to them often makes children more confused and upset than telling them the truth.

For instance, caregivers told one little boy Adalist-Estrin counseled that his father was away on a tuna boat.

"They told me my dad was on a tuna run, and I'm very worried about him," he told her. "He's been gone since my last birthday, and that boat isn't big enough to hold all those tuna."

"Sounds like you don't really think he's on a boat," she said.

"No. I think he was bad, and he got caught," the boy replied.

Having protective factors in their lives—through community support groups, churches or positive personal relationships—helps children cope better, Adalist-Estrin says. Perception of success and competence in school and peer relationships also helps, as does strong religious faith.

Spouses of Offenders

The effects of a parent's incarceration on a child can worsen if, in a two-parent household, the parents separate soon after the parent who was incarcerated comes home. Unfortunately, this is often what happens. Prison Fellowship estimates that only 15 percent of married couples survive the incarceration of one partner. Of the 15 percent who do stay together, only 3 to 5 percent last the first year after the inmate's release.

Barbara De Jong, a group leader for a women's support group sponsored by Prison Fellowship, says the spouses of offenders often face emotional, social and economic burdens. Most are wives who had participated in unhealthy, co-dependent relationships with their husbands prior to the husbands' incarcerations. Fewer women than men in prison have spouses or significant others waiting for them on the outside.

"I've found that, when women go to prison, the men in their lives tend to bail out and dump the children on the grandparents," De Jong says. "But wives and girlfriends are more loyal."

When men go to prison, their wives must financially support themselves and their children, and often are forced to make major household decisions without the support of their partners. Most of these women are not accustomed to taking on such leadership roles.

"It's a constant battle for these wives, especially those who have low incomes," De Jong says. "They have to deal with cars breaking down, paying bills and explaining everything to the children. When they feel they can't survive, and have no way of figuring out how to survive, the situation can seem hopeless."

Drawing by C.W., the 8 year-old child of an inmate.

Members of De Jong's support group encourage each other to become independent. They work on improving their resumes and getting more education. When one of the group's members accepts disrespectful treatment from her husband, the other women point it out.

For those marriages that do remain intact during incarceration, problems still can develop upon the inmate's return home. The formerly incarcerated spouses often have trouble coping with positive changes in their spouses' lives. The ones who have been on the outside have become accustomed to being in charge and independent, and often are reluctant to slip back into co-dependent, unhealthy situations.

"The husbands have to figure out where they fit back into their wives' lives," De Jong says. "Many of these men never had role models growing up, and they don't have a clue how to be husbands or fathers. These marriages have the best chance of survival if counselors can work with the husbands and wives together."

Corrections' Role

Corrections professionals—particularly correctional officers who deal with visiting families—can play a role in how family members cope just by being nice to them.

Margaret gratefully remembers that correctional officers were always helpful to her and her family when they visited John. "The correctional officers were really kind and cheerful," she says. "Not everybody gets that kind of treatment, though. Some treat the families like criminals, too, and don't seem to care."

Adalist-Estrin offers recommendations for prison administrators and correctional staff dealing with families of offenders:

1) Learn how to make family visits interactive within the parameters of security. Learn about child development, so you'll better understand why inmates can't always keep their 2-year-olds quiet when you ask.

2) Develop materials to give to families, such as tips on what to tell children before, during and after the visit. Providing such literature shows families that the correctional system cares, and makes them feel less uncomfortable.

3) Be consistent in the rules and regulations imposed during visiting. Predictability in visiting makes it easier for some families to cope. If one correctional officer lets children bring crayons to a visit, for example, then the person working the next time should not forbid it.

4) Start focusing on pre-release programming the minute an individual is incarcerated, and develop more programs to help parents or spouses in prison. Parenting courses in prison can be helpful to inmates, although prison staff should make sure that these programs are customized to meet the needs of specific cultural groups.

5) Try to help offenders maintain links to their families and their communities. School districts can work in partnership with facilities by mailing a child's report card to the parent in prison. They can involve incarcerated parents in parent-teacher conferences, either by visiting them in prison or talking with them on the phone. By working with agencies on the outside, case managers inside the prison can help keep family ties intact.

REFERENCES

Alist-Estrin, Ann. 1994. Family support and criminal justice. In *Putting families first: America's family support movement and the challenge of change*, eds. Sharon L. Kagan and Bernice Weissbourd, 161–179. San Francisco, Calif.: Jossey-Bass Inc.

Hostetter, Edwin C. and Dorthea T. Jinnah. 1993. *Families of adult offenders*. Prison Fellowship Ministries.

Mary Dallao is senior editor of Corrections Today.

Article 8

BEHIND BARS

We've built the largest prison system in the world. Here's a look inside

BY WRAY HERBERT

The United States has over the past 25 years built the largest prison system in the world, locking up more of its citizens than any other nation. More than 1.2 million convicted criminals are incarcerated in the country's 1,500 state and federal prisons, and an additional half-million inmates occupy the nation's 3,000 jails. That's 645 per 100,000 Americans in some kind of custody, second only to Russia. What's more, argues Elliot Currie, author of *Crime and Punishment in America,* America is tougher on criminals than most other industrialized nations, keeping them locked up longer for comparable crimes. Drug offenders, for instance, are three times as likely to draw long prison sentences here as in England.

In 1971 the prison population was only 200,000, where it had hovered since the 1940s. But a number of anticrime policies combined to balloon the incarceration rate. Mandatory-sentencing laws, "three strikes" laws, a nationwide crackdown on drugs and gang activity, the increasing tendency to treat youthful offenders as adults, the tightening of parole—these policies have not only increased the numbers of convicts but also changed the character of prison culture. In addition, many of the nation's seriously mentally ill released from state mental hospitals during the '70s and '80s have ended up in jails and prisons. An estimated 200,000 incarcerated Americans suffer from schizophrenia, clinical depression, or manic-depression. The Los Angeles County jail is said to be the nation's largest mental institution.

Whether or not these policies are responsible for the falling crime rates of recent years, they have without doubt created a new prison culture that is quite distinct from the prison culture of the past. Photographer Andrew Lichtenstein has spent more than two years exploring this new culture, visiting a dozen prisons and jails in several states. Here is a photographic report from behind bars.

From *U.S. News & World Report,* March 23, 1998, pp. 30-33, 36-38. © 1998 by U.S. News & World Report. Reprinted by permission.

8. Behind Bars: We've Built the Largest Prison System

Rank and file. New York is one of many states experimenting with military-style boot camps as an alternative to prison for those convicted of nonviolent crimes, mostly drug offenses. Many camps also have mandatory drug counseling. It's unclear whether the camps are any more effective than prison at rehabilitating offenders.

In Texas prisons, gang members are housed in a separate wing. They spend 23 hours a day in their cells and never leave without being handcuffed.

Jailhouse blues. Jails can be even more violent than prisons. People who have just been pulled in off the streets are often angry and high, an explosive combination that can lead to unpredictable behavior. This man has been restrained and hooded in his Arizona jail cell to prevent him from accosting and spitting at the jailers.

PHOTOGRAPHY BY ANDREW LICHTENSTEIN—SYGMA

2 ❖ PRISON LIFE

Working the land. The men in this Texas "hoe line" are not part of a chain gang. They are tilling the soil on a prison farm, where they will later plant and harvest cotton. While it's a productive farm, the labor serves another important purpose, keeping convicts exhausted and relieving tension in the cellblocks. Old-fashioned chain gangs have made a comeback in a few states, though critics dismiss them as tough-on-crime PR stunts.

Economy of cotton. Prison labor will turn the cotton on this Texas prison farm into clothing for the state's entire prison population. Armed guards—mostly white, and often second and third generation—patrol the fields on horseback. Black convicts called this prison "the plantation."

8. Behind Bars: We've Built the Largest Prison System

Race in play. Prisoners segregate themselves for every prison activity, including recreation. At this high-security rec yard at Hughes prison in Gatesville, Texas, whites play volleyball; blacks play basketball; Latinos, handball. The large black and Latino populations are further segregated by city or region, all factions vying for control over everything from cigarettes to drugs to TV.

Praying for rehab. Prisons have become an active recruiting ground for Muslim missionaries. And, after years of resistance, most prisons have acknowledged the role of Islam in the prisons, honoring dietary restrictions and providing space for worship and flexible scheduling to accommodate activities such as Ramadan prayers.

Family reunions. Everything is carrot and stick in the prison culture, and wardens hold all the power. Depending on a convict's behavior, he may be allowed contact visits or even conjugal "trailer visits"—the ultimate carrot. Prisoners who are considered security risks are separated from visitors by a glass plate and must talk by telephone. For the vast majority of convicts, the rules are irrelevant, since they receive no visitors anyway.

Messages in ink. Tattoos are prohibited in most prisons, but inmates tatoo themselves anyway as a way of openly defying "the man." The markings often identify gang affiliation, or in the case of many white inmates allegiance to a white supremacist faction. Gang members often end up at more violent prisons called "gladiator farms."

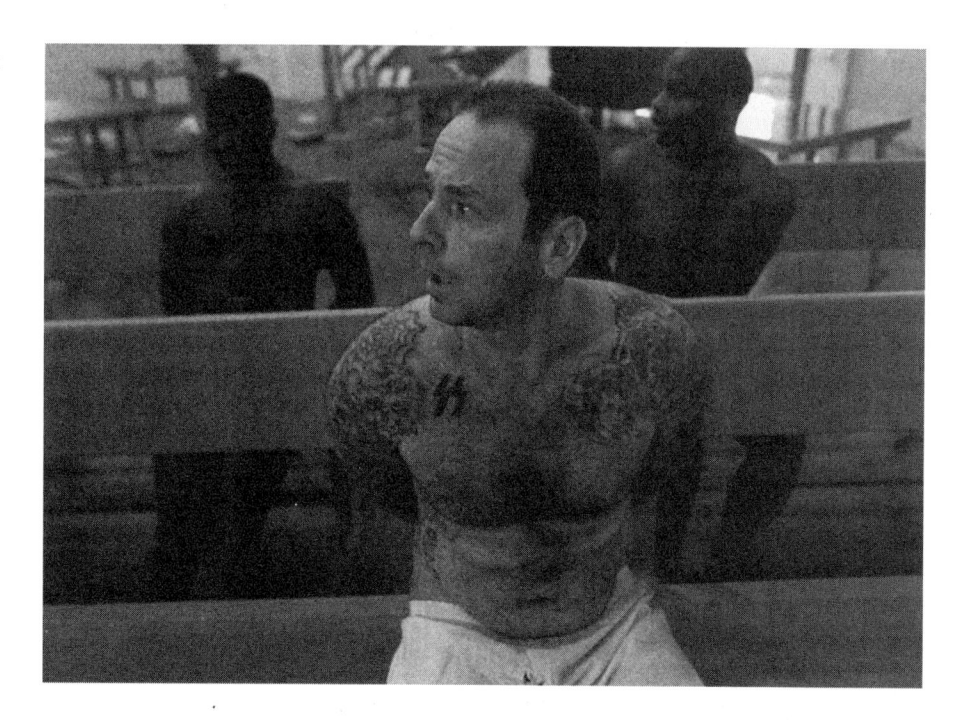

Behind Bars: Substance Abuse and America's Prison Population

The United States has the highest incarceration rate of any Western nation. The reason? Drugs. As America's crackdown on illegal drugs rolls along, prisons across the country hold more and more drug offenders. The National Center on Addiction and Substance Abuse at Columbia University looks at America's prison population in Behind Bars: Substance Abuse and America's Prison Population.

Substance abuse and addiction have fundamentally changed the nature of America's prison population. As America approaches the 21st century, state and federal prisons and local jails are bursting at the bars with drug abusers and addicts and those who sell illegal drugs. In America, crime and substance abuse are joined at the hip.

At the end of 1996, more than 1.7 million American adults were behind bars: 1,076,625 in state prisons, 105,544 in federal prisons and 518,492 in local jails—more than three times the number incarcerated just 15 years earlier. Of the 1.7 million inmates, only 130,430 or 7.7 percent are women, but the female prison population is growing at a faster rate than the male population. The surge in the number of Americans behind bars—now a population the size of Houston, Texas, the nation's fourth largest city—and the rapidly escalating costs of building and maintaining prisons are unprecedented. More and more Americans are becoming aware of this situation. What few understand is why.

State prisons generally hold inmates who have been convicted of felony offenses under state law and sentenced to at least one year of incarceration. Federal prisons hold inmates convicted of violating federal laws. Local jails generally house individuals convicted of misdemeanors and sentenced to less than one year in prison and individuals who are awaiting trial. Most offenses related to illegal drug selling are felonies, while possession of drugs may be either a felony or misdemeanor depending on state law and the amount of drugs. Possession of small amounts of marijuana is typically treated as a misdemeanor or a lesser, noncriminal infraction.

The estimate of 1,700,661 is based on the most recent data available: year-end 1996 for state (1,076,625) and federal prisoners (105,544), midyear 1996 for jail inmates (518,492). Throughout this report, different years may be cited for different types of data. This is because different data sets and publications are available for various types of criminal justice data, and not all data are available for the same year. The data used are the most recent available. Adults are defined as more than 17 years of age.

For three years, The National Center on Addiction and Substance Abuse at Columbia University (CASA) has been examining and probing all available data on the people in prison, surveying and interviewing state and federal corrections offi-

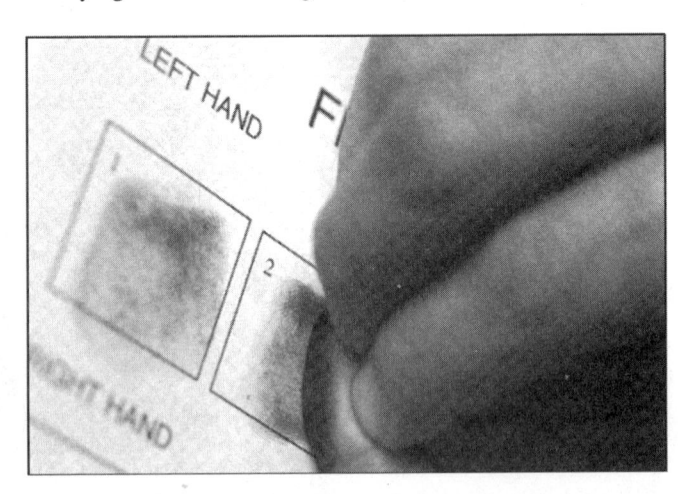

Four out of every five American inmates abuse drugs and alcohol.

cials, prosecutors and law enforcement officers, testing programs for substance-abusing offenders and reviewing relevant studies and literature in the most penetrating analysis ever attempted of the relationship of alcohol and drug abuse and addiction to the character and size of America's prison population.

The stunning finding of this analysis is that 80 percent of the men and women behind bars—some 1.4 million individuals—are seriously involved with drug and alcohol abuse and the crimes it spawns. These inmates number more than the individual populations of 12 of the 50 United States.' Among these 1.4 million inmates are the parents of 2.4 million children, many of them minors.

Substance-Involved Offenders

The overwhelming majority of those who have ever used drugs regularly used them in the month immediately before they entered prison—76 percent of state, 69 percent of federal and 70 percent of local jail inmates who have regularly used drugs. Alcohol and drug abuse and addiction are implicated in assaults, rapes and homicides. Thousands of individuals incarcerated for robbery and burglary stole to support drug habits. Thousands more are imprisoned for violations of laws prohibiting selling, trafficking, manufacturing or possessing illegal drugs like heroin and cocaine, driving while intoxicated and disorderly conduct while high or drunk. The bottom line is this: one of every 144 American adults is behind bars for a crime in which drugs and alcohol are involved.

The enormous prison population imposes a hefty financial burden on our nation. In 1996, America had more than 4,700 prisons—1,403 state, 82 federal and 3,304 local—to house an inmate population that is still growing. Americans paid $38 billion in taxes to build and operate these facilities: $35 billion for state prisons and local jails and $3 billion for federal prisons.

This report is an unprecedented effort to assess the relationship between drug and alcohol abuse and addiction and America's prison population and the implications of that relationship for our society—for public safety; state and federal criminal justice, public health and social service policies; taxes that Americans pay and the nation's economy. The first step in formulating sensible prison policies to protect the public safety in a cost-effective way is to understand the human, social and economic costs of substance abuse, crime and incarceration, how we got here and what we can do about it. The case for change is urgent and overwhelming: if rates of incarceration continue to rise at their current pace, one out of every 20 Americans born in 1997 will serve time in prison—one out of every 11 men, one of every four black men.

This CASA report targets America's prison and jail population. But prisons are the end game. Millions of children grow up in families wracked by drug and alcohol abuse and in neighborhoods and schools infested with illegal drugs and drug dealers—situations that General Colin Powell calls "training camps for America's prisons." There are 3.8 million individuals convicted of a crime who are on probation and parole, which brings the total to more than 5.5 million people currently under the supervision of state, federal and local criminal justice systems. That is a criminal population larger than the city of Los Angeles, the second largest city in the United States. The states monitor 3,146,062 individuals on probation and 645,576 on parole; the federal government, 34,301 on probation and 59,133 on parole. For most of these individuals, the road to prison, probation and parole is paved with alcohol and drug abuse.

How did America's prisons and jails come to be dominated by alcohol and drug abusers and those who deal drugs? Citizen concerns about crime and violence led federal, state and local officials to step up law enforcement, prosecution and punishment. As a result of such concern and the heroin epidemic of the 1970s and crack cocaine explosion in the 1980s state and federal legislatures enacted more criminal laws, especially with respect to selling illicit drugs and related activities such as money laundering; agents of the Federal Bureau of Investigation and Drug Enforcement Administration and state and local police made more arrests for all kinds of crime; prosecutors brought more charges and indictments; judges and juries convicted more defendants; and judges imposed more prison sentences authorized or mandated by law. While in prison, little attempt was made to deal with the underlying inmate drug and alcohol addiction that led to so much criminal activity. Inmates who are alcohol and drug abusers and addicts are the most likely to be reincarcerated —again and again— and sentences usually increase for repeat offenders. The result has been a steady and substantial rise in the nation's prison population over the past generation. Between 1980 and 1996, the number of inmates in state and federal prisons and local jails jumped 239 percent, from 501,886 to 1,700,661: the number of men from 477,706 to 1,570,231, a 229 percent increase; the number of women from 24,180 to 130,430, a 439 percent increase.

The Explosion of the Inmate Population is Drug- and Alcohol-Related

Most offenders, whatever their crime, have a drug or alcohol problem. Alcohol and drugs are implicated in the increased rate of arrest, conviction and imprisonment of

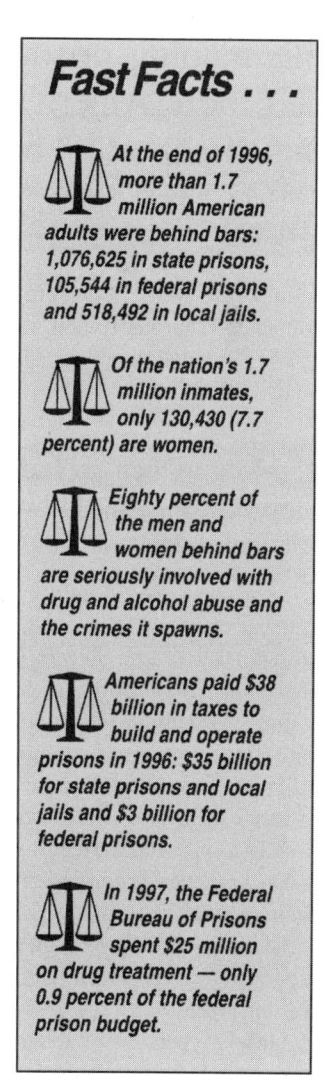

Fast Facts . . .

⚖ At the end of 1996, more than 1.7 million American adults were behind bars: 1,076,625 in state prisons, 105,544 in federal prisons and 518,492 in local jails.

⚖ Of the nation's 1.7 million inmates, only 130,430 (7.7 percent) are women.

⚖ Eighty percent of the men and women behind bars are seriously involved with drug and alcohol abuse and the crimes it spawns.

⚖ Americans paid $38 billion in taxes to build and operate prisons in 1996: $35 billion for state prisons and local jails and $3 billion for federal prisons.

⚖ In 1997, the Federal Bureau of Prisons spent $25 million on drug treatment — only 0.9 percent of the federal prison budget.

property, violent and drug law offenders, the three major groups of inmates.

Much of the growth in America's inmate population is due to incarceration of drug-law violators. From 1980 to 1995, drug law violators accounted for 30 percent of the total increase in the state prison population, and the proportion of offenders in state prisons convicted of drug-law violations rose from 6 percent to 23 percent. In federal prisons, drug law violators accounted for 68 percent of the total increase, driving the proportion of drug-law violators from 25 percent to 60 percent and making drug law violators by far the largest group of federal inmates. In local jails, drug law violators accounted for 41 percent of the increase in the total population between 1983 and 1989, and the proportion of drug-law violators rose from 9 percent to 23 percent. While the percentage of inmates convicted of property and violent crime declined, the number of such inmates increased, largely due to drug- and alcohol-related offenses.

> The surge in the number of Americans behind bars—now a population the size of Houston, Texas, the nation's fourth largest city—and the rapidly escalating costs of building and maintaining prisons are unprecedented. More and more Americans are becoming aware of this situation. What few understand is why.

The More Often an Individual is Imprisoned, the More Likely That Individual is a Drug or Alcohol Addict or Abuser

Substance use is tightly associated with recidivism. The more prior convictions an individual has, the more likely that individual is a drug abuser: in state prisons 41 percent of first offenders have used drugs regularly, compared to 63 percent of inmates with two prior convictions and 81 percent of those with five or more convictions. Only 4 percent of first-time offenders have used heroin regularly, compared to 12 percent of those with two prior convictions and 27 percent of those with five or more. Sixteen percent of first offenders have used cocaine regularly, compared to 26 percent of those with two prior convictions and 40 percent of those with five or more convictions. State prison inmates with five or more prior convictions are three times likelier than first-time offenders to be regular crack users.

Only 25 percent of federal inmates with no prior convictions have histories of regular drug use, but 52 percent of those with two prior convictions and 71 percent of those with five or more have histories of regular drug use. Among jail inmates, 39 percent with no prior convictions have histories of regular drug use, but 61 percent with two prior convictions and 76 percent with five or more convictions regularly used drugs.

The Growing Chasm in Substance-Abuse Treatment: Increasing Inmate Need and Decreasing Access

In state and federal prisons, the gap between available substance abuse treatment, inmate participation and the need for such treatment and participation is enormous and widening.

State officials estimate that 70 to 85 percent of inmates need some level of substance-abuse treatment. But in 1996, only 13 percent of state inmates were in any such treatment. The Federal Bureau of Prisons estimates that 31 percent of their inmates are hooked on drugs, but only 10 percent were in treatment in 1996. The proportion of jail inmates who need treatment has not been estimated, but given the similar alcohol and drug-abuse profiles of state prison and local jail inmates, it is likely to mirror the state estimate of 70 to 85 percent. Only eight percent of jail inmates were in treatment in 1992. As the number of inmates in need of treatment has risen in tandem with the prison population, the proportion receiving treatment has declined. Indeed, from 1995 to 1996, the number of inmates in treatment decreased by 18,360 as inmates in need of treatment rose by 39,578.

Not surprisingly given this lack of treatment, government spending on inmate drug and alcohol treatment is relatively small compared to the costs of imprisoning drug and alcohol addicts and abusers. CASA estimates that on average, states spend 5 percent of their prison budget on drug and alcohol treatment. In 1997, the Federal Bureau of Prisons spent $25 million on drug treatment—only 0.9 percent of the federal prison budget.

Treatment Effectiveness

Research in recent years indicates that well-designed prison-based treatment can reduce post-release criminality and drug and alcohol relapse, especially when combined with pre-release training and planning and community-based after care services, including assistance with housing, education, employment and health care.

Evaluations of prison-based treatment have focused on residential treatment programs and suggest that length of stay in treatment and the availability of aftercare following treatment are important predictors of success. Amity Rightum, a therapeutic community-based program at the R.J. Donovan medium-security prison in San Diego, for example, reduced reincarceration rates within one year of parole to 26 percent for Amity graduates who completed aftercare, compared with 43 percent for Amity graduates who did not participate in aftercare, 50 percent for Amity program dropouts and 63 percent for a matched comparison group.

Forever Free, a similar program operated by the California Department of Corrections for female inmates approaching their parole dates, reduced the rate of return to custody to 38 percent for all program graduates, compared with 62 percent for program dropouts. Participation in community-based treatment further increased the likelihood of successful outcomes—reducing the rate of return to custody to 28 percent for program graduates with some community treatment and 10 percent for graduates with at least five months of community treatment.

Beyond Treatment

Substance-abuse treatment alone is not enough. Most inmates who are drug and alcohol addicts and abusers also need medical care, psychiatric help, and literacy and job training. Drug and alcohol-involved inmates tend to have ailments—cirrhosis, diabetes, high blood pressure, malnutrition, sexually transmitted diseases, HIV and AIDS—that require medical care. Some have never worked or worked so sporadically in such low-level jobs that they need not only to improve their reading, writing and math skills, but also to acquire levels of socialization that most Americans take for granted. Without help in prison acquiring these skills, once released these inmates have little chance of resisting a return to lives of drug and alcohol abuse and crime.

To appreciate the heavy baggage substance abusing inmates carry, consider the histories of inmates who were regular drug users:

- Fifteen percent in state prison, 9 percent in federal prison and 20 percent in jail have been physically and/or sexually abused.
- Sixty-one percent in state prison, 44 percent in federal prison and 48 percent in jail did not complete four years of high school.
- Thirty-six percent in state prison, 33 percent in federal prison and 39 percent in jail were unemployed in the month prior to their offense.

Substance-Abuse Related Crime: It Runs in the Family

Like substance abuse itself, substance-abuse related crime runs in the family. Children of substance-involved inmates are at high risk of addiction and incarceration. Inmates whose parents abused drugs and alcohol are much more likely to abuse drugs and alcohol themselves. In state and federal prison, regular drug users are twice as likely to have parents who abused drugs and alcohol than inmates who are not regular drug users.

Regular drug users in prison and jail are likelier than the general inmate population to have a family member who served prison time: 42 percent of regular drug users in both state prisons and local jails and 34 percent in federal prison have at least one family member who served time in prison or jail, compared to 37 percent of the general state prison population, 35 percent of the local jail population and 26 percent of the general federal prison population.

Tobacco, Alcohol and Drugs in Prison

Prison policies regarding tobacco, alcohol and drugs set expectations and send important messages to inmates about official attitudes toward substance use. Unfortunately, not all prisons take advantage of this opportunity. While an estimated 29 percent of state and federal prisons are smoke-free, some state prisons provide free cigarettes to indigent inmates; a few provide free cigarettes to all inmates.

Although systematic evidence is lacking, anecdotal information suggests that drugs and alcohol are available in many prisons and jails. Current surveillance methods which occasionally test for drugs, at times with advance notice, are inadequate to eliminate drug dealing and use in prisons and to support treatment programs. Wider and more frequent random testing can help keep prisons drug-free, identify inmates in need of treatment and monitor those undergoing treatment.

The Cost of Drug- and Alcohol-Involved Inmates

Of the $38 billion spent on prisons in 1996, more than $30 billion dollars paid for the incarceration of individuals who had a history of drug and alcohol abuse, were convicted of drug and alcohol violations, were high on drugs and alcohol at the time of their crime, or committed their crime to get money to buy drugs. If current trends continue, by the year 2000, the nation will break the $100 million-dollar-a-day barrier in spending to incarcerate individuals with serious drug and alcohol problems.

Inmates who have abused alcohol or drugs often have special health needs that add expense to their incarceration. These include detoxification programs, mental and physical health care and AIDS treatment. State and federal inmates who regularly used drugs or abused alcohol are, on average, twice as likely as those who didn't to have histories of mental illness.

In addition to incarceration, there are other criminal justice system costs for arresting and prosecuting substance abusers. For example, the bill for arresting and prosecuting the 1,436,000 DUI arrests in 1995 was more than $5.2 billion, exclusive of the costs of pretrial detention and incarceration.

Prevention

Prevention is the first line of defense against drug- and alcohol-related crime. The tremendous costs of incarcerating so many drug- and alcohol-abusing inmates underscores the vital importance of developing, implementing and evaluating large-scale prevention efforts that are designed for the populations at risk for substance abuse and criminal activity. Since most addicts begin using drugs while they are teens, efforts to give youngsters the will and skill to say no are critical to keeping them out of the criminal justice system. The difficulties of recovering from drug or alcohol addiction are enormous even for middle- or upper-class addicts. For those with family histories of substance abuse, living in poverty, with limited educational and vocational skills and health problems, the treatment process can be extraordinarily difficult. Developing effective drug-prevention programs for children and teens and making our schools drug-free are key elements in any effort to reduce drug- and alcohol-related crime.

Missed Opportunity: Reducing Crime and Costs to Taxpayers

Preventing drug and alcohol abuse and providing effective treatment for drug- and alcohol-abusing inmates hold the promise of significant savings to taxpayers and reductions in crime. CASA estimates that it would take approximately $6,500 per year, in addition to usual incarceration costs, to provide an inmate with a year of residential treatment in prison and ancillary services, such as vocational and educational training, psychological counseling, and aftercare case management.

If current trends continue, by the year 2000, the nation will break the $100-million-dollar-a-day barrier in spending to incarcerate individuals with serious drug and alcohol problems.

However, if an addicted offender successfully completes the treatment program and returns to the community as a sober parolee with a job, then the following economic benefits will accrue in the first year after release:

- $5,000 in reduced crime savings (assuming that drug-using ex-inmates would have committed 100 crimes per year with $50 in property and victimization costs per crime);
- $7,300 in reduced arrest and prosecution costs (assuming that they would have been arrested twice during the year);
- $19,600 in reduced incarceration costs (assuming that one of those rearrests would have resulted in a one-year prison sentence);
- $4,800 in health care and substance abuse treatment cost savings, the difference in annual health care costs between substance users and nonusers;
- $32,100 in economic benefits ($21,400— the average income for an employed high school graduate— multiplied by the standard economic multiplier of 1.5 for estimating the local economic effects of a wage).

Under these conservative assumptions, the total benefits that would accrue during the first year after release would total $68,800 for each successful inmate. These estimated benefits do not include reductions in welfare, other state or federal entitlement costs, or foster care for the children of these inmates.

Given these substantial economic benefits, the success rate needed to break even on the $6,500 per inmate investment in prison treatment is modest. If only 10 percent of the inmates who are given one year of residential treatment stay sober and work during the first year after release, there will be a positive economic return on the treatment investment.

There are 1.2 million inmates who are drug and alcohol abusers and addicts (the other 200,000 of the 1.4 million substance-involved inmates are dealers who do not use drugs). If we successfully treat and train only 10 percent of those inmates—120,000—the economic benefit in the first year of work after release would be $8.256 billion. That's $456 million more than the $7.8 billion cost of providing treatment and training (at a cost of $6,500 each) for the entire 1.2 million inmates with drug and alcohol problems. Thereafter, the nation would receive an economic benefit of more than $8 billion for each year they remain employed and drug- and crime-free. That's the kind of return on investment to capture the imagination of any businessman.

The potential for reduction in crime is also significant. Estimates of property and violent crimes committed by active drug addicts range from 89 to 191 per year. On a conservative assumption of 100 crimes per year, for each 10,000 drug-addicted inmates who after release stay off drugs and crime, the nation will experience a reduction of one million crimes a year.

For a copy of the full report, contact CASA (212) 841–5200.

Inside the New Alcatraz

The ADX 'Supermax' prison redefines hard time

BY PETER ANNIN

DRIVING UP THE MAIN ROAD YOU pass a work camp, a medium-security facility and a maximum-security facility, all part of the big federal corrections complex outside Florence, Colo. Then you come to the place that is, literally and figuratively, the end of the line—the new Alcatraz, the toughest federal penitentiary in America. This is the Administrative Maximum Facility, also known as ADX. Inmates call it "the Big One" or the "Hellhole of the Rockies."

Since it opened in 1994, ADX has held the unique mission of confining "the worst of the worst"—400-plus inmates from all across the federal prison system, men so dangerous no other pen can hold them. Some, like terrorist Ramzi Yousef, mastermind of the World Trade Center bombing, were sent to ADX because authorities feared their supporters might try to rescue them: among other security features, the prison is specifically designed to thwart an attack from outside. Other cons were transferred there because they killed or assaulted guards or inmates. The cells look like they were designed for Hannibal Lecter. All furniture is concrete, to prevent occupants from making weapons out of bed frames or other metal parts, and each cell has a special vestibule where the inmate is shackled, hands behind his back, when he is being taken elsewhere in the prison. Solitary confinement is the norm: 40 percent of the cons stay in their cells 22 hours a day, and another 33 percent, the hardest of the hard core, are locked down 23 hours a day. They get out only for an hour of exercise—which they take all alone, in a room that looks like an undersize racquetball court. "It's not a prison where you have to worry about getting raped," one visitor says.

The triangular main building is like something out of M. C. Escher—full of angles and obstructions that aren't quite what they seem. The entry is underground, through a heavily guarded tunnel. Cells have slit windows that show only a sliver of sky. That makes it hard for inmates or visitors to tell precisely where they are within the prison building, which complicates planning rescues or escapes. But it also makes ADX one of the most psychologically debilitating places on earth. "Lock yourself in your bathroom for the next four years and tell me how it affects your mind," says Raymond Luc Levasseur, a veteran of the '70s radical underground who is serving 45 years for a series of bombings. "It begins to erode the five senses. It's dehumanizing."

Who's who at ADX is usually secret—another security precaution. But the names of high-profile inmates sometimes leak out. NEWSWEEK has learned that Oklahoma City bomber Timothy McVeigh and Ted Kaczynski, the Unabomber, share the same cellblock (and round-the-clock video surveillance) with Ramzi Yousef. Terry Nichols, McVeigh's accomplice, may be transferred to the prison soon. Gang leader Luis Felipe, head of New York's Latin Kings, is already there. Felipe, who was convicted of ordering at least six murders while serving time in a New York state prison, is prohibited from having any visitors other than his lawyer, Lawrence Feitell. According to Feitell, Felipe has broken down from the stress of his isolation. He has difficulty sleeping and eating and suffers from shakes or tremors, Feitell said; Prozac hasn't helped. "He falls into fits of weeping. He's written letters to the judge begging for some form of human contact," Feitell says. "The kind of mind it would take to create a place like that is beyond me."

The credit belongs to Norman Carlson. Director of the U.S. Bureau of Prisons until 1987, Carlson says ADX is a direct response to the sharp increase in "violent and predatory" inmates during the 1970s and '80s, particularly at the federal pen in Marion, Ill. Twenty inmates were murdered in 18 years at Marion—and on Oct. 22, 1983, two guards were stabbed to death by "two members of the Aryan Brotherhood who were just trying to outdo each other," Carlson says. The whole prison went on permanent, 23-hour lockdown and the "supermax" concept was born. Following the Feds' example, more than 30 states now have supermax pens.

This trend disturbs prison-rights activists, who argue that supermax prisons are a form of "cruel and unusual" punishment prohibited by the Constitution. "There has always been solitary confinement in this country," says Jamie Fellner of Human Rights Watch. "The difference is the length of time. We're not talking about putting someone in the hole for 15 days. We're talking about 15 years or life." But the federal courts have upheld the practice of 23-hour lockdowns, and that means ADX and the supermax concept are here to stay. Says architect John Quest, who designed the brick-and-concrete structure: "This building shows that prisons don't have to be ugly to be secure." The view from inside isn't nearly so pretty.

Room Without a View

Inmates at the ADX prison include Timothy McVeigh, Ted Kaczynski and Ramzi Yousef. They are locked up 23 hours a day and permitted few visitors. A look at the accommodations:

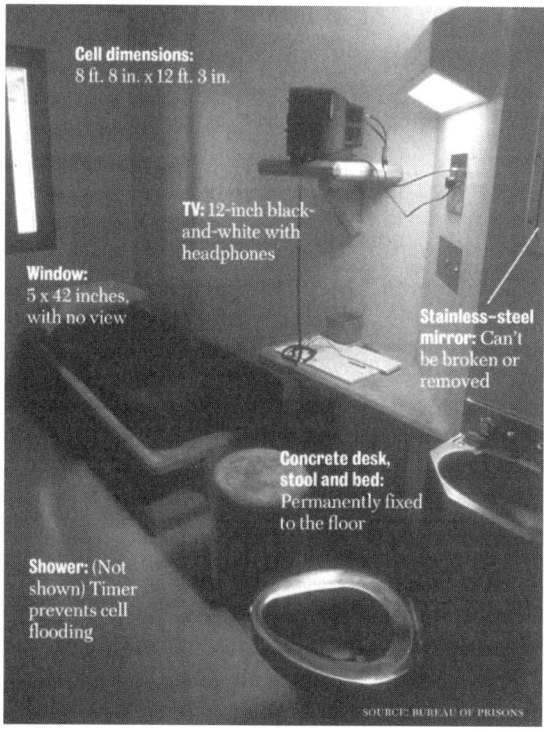

Cell dimensions: 8 ft. 8 in. x 12 ft. 3 in.

TV: 12-inch black-and-white with headphones

Window: 5 x 42 inches, with no view

Stainless-steel mirror: Can't be broken or removed

Concrete desk, stool and bed: Permanently fixed to the floor

Shower: (Not shown) Timer prevents cell flooding

SOURCE: BUREAU OF PRISONS
BOB DAEMMRICH—SYGMA

Article 11

Life on the Inside: The Jailers

In a wary world, battling tension, fear—and stereotypes

By Andrew Metz
STAFF WRITER

This is the job: One unarmed correction officer and 60 inmates, the jailer and the jailed, warily taking each other's measure, sparring for control. Right now, the officer is Cpl. William Roulis, and though it's only 6:30 in the morning, he's already on edge. Purple crescents hammock his eyes as he moves about a locked, windowed room in a second-floor cellblock at the Nassau County jail.

The inmates, men in orange jail jumpsuits, in on mostly drug and alcohol offenses, sluggishly walk through breakfast lines, picking up plastic trays of scrambled eggs, boxes of Fruit Loops, half-pints of milk, slices of white bread.

"Although we are charged with watching them, they watch us," Roulis says, studying through the glass one of the men who is using an empty peanut-butter jar as an oversized coffee cup. "They know what cologne you wear, the click of your heels."

Of all the things Roulis has learned over 10 years at the jail in East Meadow, the most important may be this: "You don't know what is going to happen, or when it is going to happen."

When two inmates will abruptly start brawling in front of the shower stalls, and he will have to order over the loud speaker, "lock in; everybody lock in *now*." Or when an inmate will barricade himself in his cell, and three officers will have to drag him out by the arms and

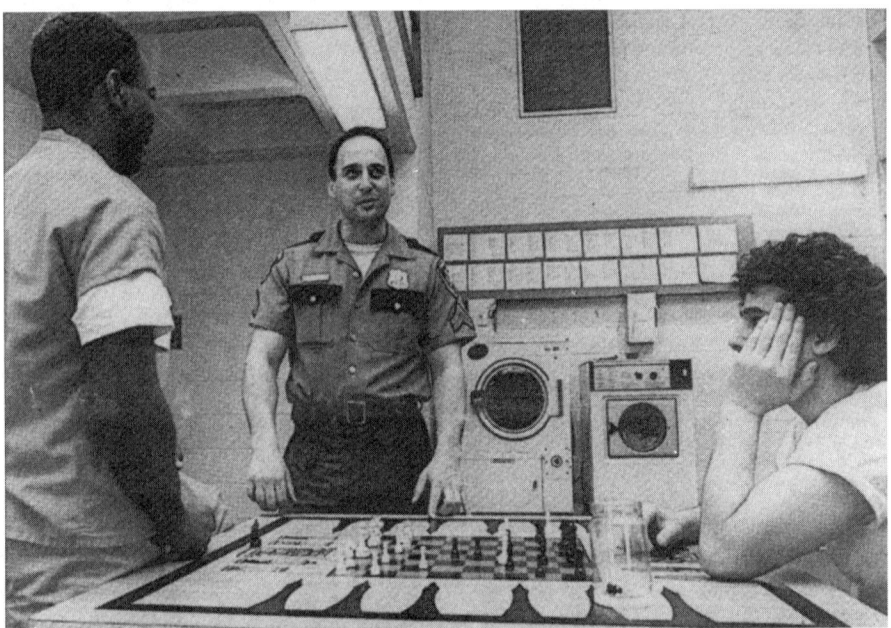

Newsday Photos/Dick Yarwood

Cpl. William Roulis talks with inmates in the housing unit at the Nassau County jail. Ten years on the job has taught him to expect the unexpected. "You don't know what is going to happen, or when it is going to happen," he says.

From *Newsday*, March 21, 1999, pp. A5, A50, A52. © 1999 by the Los Angeles Times. Reprinted by permission.

11. Life on the Inside

legs. Or when an inmate will taunt him from behind the bars, "I'm going to ____ me a Greek boy."

So, the 44-year-old officer is cynical, always expecting to be had. And this constant tension, this nerve-wracking wait-and-see imprisons him, too.

"You do 25 years, but a day at a time, a week at a time," he says, parting his lips in a faint smile. "When you come through the gates, you're in a different world."

There are about 1.8 million people in jails and prisons around the country, roughly 3,600 in Nassau and Suffolk awaiting trial or serving sentences of up to a year. But even as the public cheers the get-tough policing that fills correctional institutions, correction officers believe they are seen as brutes, only a shade better than the people behind bars.

This stigma is a sort of occupational hazard that is usually sloughed off. But for officers at the Nassau County Correctional Center, the past three months have brought the stereotype painfully close to home.

After an inmate was allegedly beaten to death by officers inside the jail in January, federal authorities stepped in to investigate the homicide and whether there is a pattern of brutality. And the whole situation has revealed a bevy of complaints and lawsuits brought by inmates with wide-ranging claims of mistreatment.

Inside lunch rooms and control rooms, in the trailers that function as the training academy and in dozens of posts throughout the facility, morale is dark. Officers say they have been wounded by recent headlines and newscasts.

They tell of being looked at askance by neighbors. Of wives being insulted in supermarkets. Of children confused by what they hear.

Few deny that abuses have occurred. But they insist any misbehavior is limited to rogues, to officers unable to rise above the depravity of jail culture.

"We spend our day with the kind of people you don't want next door," says Officer Bob Shanlin, 41, who in his 15 years at the jail has twice saved inmates who were trying to hang themselves with bedsheets. "We're like offensive linemen. You only hear our name when something goes wrong.... The vast majority of people here are not beating people. I wouldn't work with people that were."

One thousand and ten correction officers and commanders work at the jail, one of the largest county lockups in the country. In three shifts of around 120 officers each, they supervise and provide for about 1,800 inmates.

While keeping some of the jail off limits, including the building where the inmate allegedly was beaten in January, correction officials permitted closely monitored visits inside the jail in recent weeks. Days of observation and interviews—14 hours on one day—show just how complicated life on the inside can be. Locked in, officer and inmate move in a suspicious waltz, staking out positions, enduring the monotony, the indignities, the dependance.

One minute an officer is handing out toilet paper, the next he is explaining court papers. An officer is joking with two inmates playing checkers, and in an instant, he is ordering everyone to their cells.

This is the job: Put on a blue-and-gray uniform, pin a silver sheriff's badge to your shirt pocket and lace up black work shoes. Drive to a sprawling complex of concrete and metal, through 18-foot-high fences topped with thick coils of razor wire.

In a two-story building called the 832, bars open and seal shut behind you, and as you walk to the Muster Room to get your assignment, the odor of floor cleaner, the industrial kitchen and too many bodies carries you forward.

Soon you are locked inside a cellblock. You are outnumbered. Your only weapons are the wits you walked in with and the alarm on your waist. And when you set that off, officers come running, and more often than not it means inmates are swinging fists or throwing feces or food. For sure, they're yelling and swearing and refusing to lock down. Your life could be in danger.

You're enraged, and if you're honest, you're scared.

Newsday Photos/Dick Yarwood

Sgt. Daniel Dooley, left, with a new class of corrections officers in training. His instruction to the recruits: Your presence alone should be enough to control a situation—physical force should be used only as a last resort.

PRISON LIFE

"Anytime a body alarm goes off, your adrenaline starts pumping because you are running into a situation and you don't know what it is going to be like and it could be a war," says Shanlin, who can't recall being assaulted in his career, but has had a jar of urine thrown at him and has been insulted and threatened countless times. "You're an idiot if you... are not scared."

But all-out violence is rare, and you know it as you settle down behind a desk at the center of the cellblock. You supervise the "feedings," keeping track of each meal tray because almost anything can be made into a weapon.

Usually, the closest you come to using force is an unequivocal command or a firm grip on an elbow. No one wants to be locked down. No one wants weightlifting canceled.

At least every half-hour, you get up and pace the dimensions of the dorm, peering into each cell and inserting a key in a slot to record your passage. You sock away the paychecks that don't ever seem fat enough, rack up the overtime when you can and push your union to get a 20-year retirement clause in your contract. Police have one, after all.

You bristle when you're called a guard because guards work at Macy's and banks and don't stop dead in their tracks when they hear, "Yo, C.O.!" as they leave a mall and see five former inmates behind them. At the end of a day, you decompress however you can, if you can, and tell yourself you're an integral part of the criminal justice system.

"The public doesn't want to know about them," Officer Robert Koplar, 35, who has worked at the jail for 14 years, says of the inmates. "After they are caught, they forget about the other part. Where are you supposed to store them? Not the Marriott.

"... Someone has to watch them 24-7. Someone has to do it."

Few people actually plan on a career in corrections.

"I don't think you'll talk to anyone that says, 'Since I was 12 years old I wanted to be a correction officer,'" says Lt. Richard Plantamura, who is in charge of the jail's training academy.

Newsday Photo/Dick Yarwood

"I love what I do," says Officer Ronald Lanier, who is monitoring the visitors center. Lanier says he is a mentor for African-American inmates, who make up about half the jail population.

Of the dozens of new officers who each year routinely join the Nassau County Sheriff's Department, Division of Correction, most say they were looking for a position as a police officer.

They had taken a slew of civil service exams, perhaps not scoring high enough to land a police job at first. Then the jail made an offer.

Some eventually move to the Suffolk or Nassau police departments, where salaries are significantly higher. The first year of employment at the jail, base pay is about $28,000. A rookie Suffolk police officer makes about $45,000. And after two years, so does a new officer in Nassau.

Still, jail officials say attrition is low, and for men and women shopping for a civil service job, a job that doesn't require any college and eventually promises salaries more than $50,000, thousands in overtime, security and benefits, corrections is a coveted career.

"I love what I do," says Officer Ronald Lanier, a former Army enlisted man, who was driving a Drake's delivery route in Brooklyn, when he was offered a post at the jail eight years ago.

Standing tall, his black oxfords reflecting like mirrors, Lanier is monitoring visiting hours. As inmates hug mothers and girlfriends and wives, the 35-year-old says he sees his work as a calling.

"A lot of these guys I went to school with," he says, nodding his chin to the inmates. "I am here to do a job, but I care."

One of roughly 150 black officers, Lanier says he is a mentor for African-American inmates, who make up about half the jail population.

Lanier says he has been in only one physical tussle in his eight years and that was while breaking up a fight. Holding ground in a cellblock rarely comes down to force, he says. He lets the inmates know they're in his "house" now, and "this is how it's done."

"I don't go straight to C," he says. "I start at A and nine times out of 10 we end up at A."

And that, in the simplest sense, is the philosophy officers say they carry with them day to day: Force is supposed to be the last resort, and when it's doled out, it is meant to be measured.

11. Life on the Inside

As a rule, officers are unarmed. Supervisors have a can of pepper spray. The greatest tools, officers say, are composure and communication.

"The way you present yourself to people, how you communicate with people is going to get you through 90 percent of the time," says Sgt. Daniel Dooley, who teaches recruits. "Your communication skills will get you through. It's the easiest way to go."

In a cavernous jail gymnasium, Officer Kenny Sellers says he puts this to the test everyday. During a mid-morning recreation period, 77 inmates are pumping iron and dribbling basketballs and jogging. Sellers mingles with them all, smiles a lot. In small groups, he tries to quell brewing discontent this day, because both basketball hoops are being repaired.

The inmates are disappointed, but "they don't want to fight because they know if they do, they will lose out," says Sellers, 41, who at 6-foot-2, 240 pounds is as rippled as they come.

During 12 years as an officer, he says, he has forged a respectful discourse with inmates, giving them space—and sometimes advice on how to bulk up.

"They respect me," he says. "They know me."

This is the job: A 40-year-old officer makes a patrol along a guardwalk one Christmas. He sees the lights and snow outside and thinks of his family. He passes cell after cell and is pinched by a sorrow that takes years for him to understand.

"I thought, just on the other side of the bars are people thinking the same things I am," Lt. Richard Levering recalls.

Now, more than two decades later, Levering describes what hit him as the "incarceration feeling." He wrote poetry to make some sense of it:

Lonely, I stare through barred windows,
Watching the seasons go past.
In "lock-step," they march in a circle
And I can't tell the first from the last.
I listen with cautious compassion,
Keep my lamp of suspicion trimmed low
Enough to reveal hidden dangers
But not make me distrust those I know.
My day is a structured chaos
And the ominous slam of each gate
Reminds me that I am a captive
And the pleasures of freedom must wait.
I'm not serving time for some victim
To whom I brought pain, loss or fear.

Officer Ibrahim Zahran watching prisoners in the jail's law library, is one of the 1,010 correction officers who, in three shifts of about 120 officers each, supervise and provide for about 1,800 inmates. The Nassau jail is one of the largest county lockups in the country.

Newsday Photo/Dick Yarwood

PRISON LIFE

*I serve time in these dungeons of justice
For choosing a Correctional career.*

"We are all locked in here," says Levering, 66.

And that's a universal feeling for correction officers. Mel Grieshaber, of Michigan, who is the immediate past president of the International Association of Correctional Officers, likens corrections to combat.

"You are there coaching Little League one moment, then you get up the next day, brush your teeth and go to this . . . 100-percent hostile environment," says Grieshaber. "A lot of jobs are stressful, however this is the type of job where everything can be calm for periods of time, but you are always dealing with this little voice way deep down that says something could happen. So there is a certain edge all the time."

Up-to-date figures on the effects of corrections work are scarce and are more anecdotal than scientific. However, most correction experts agree that officers have excessively high rates of suicide, burn-out, divorce and alcohol abuse. Studies have shown they have heart attacks, hypertension and ulcers more than almost any other employment group. And a 1980s report by the American Federation of State and County Municipal Employees put their life expectancy at 59.

Nationally, officials estimate that seven died in the line of duty last year and more than 14,000 were seriously assaulted. At the Nassau jail, there were 38 assaults against officers last year, and two so far in 1999. Inmates assaulted one another 39 times last year, and already 35 times this year.

"It's a hard life to grow up in," Levering says. "I have often thought that no one should come on this job before 28 or 30."

He has had to tell inmates that relatives were killed, separate a baby from a mother, cut down a prisoner trying to hang himself.

Mostly, officers hope for a humdrum day. "A good day for me is when none of my officers get hurt," says Cpl. Bob Zizza, 37, who in 12 years has been assaulted five times.

In 1971, two professors in California embarked on a study of the psychology of imprisonment. In what became known as the Stanford Prison Experiment, they cast a group of college students in the roles of correction officers and inmates for six days. The results, the authors, Craig Haney and Philip Zimbardo declared, were shocking and forced them to halt the experiment.

Correction Officer Kenny Sellers with inmates in the jail's gym. Life inside the jail can be complicated, with officers one minute joking with inmates, the next ordering them to return to their cells.

Newsday Photo/Dick Yarwood

In under a week, they witnessed mock inmates and officers suffer trauma and stress. They watched many of the "officers," particularly those on the night shifts, harass and degrade and mistreat inmates. Others stood by and failed to report the abuses.

"You are talking about an environment that is constantly pushing against people" says Haney, a professor of psychology at the University of California at Santa Cruz. "This is really antithetical to what people are, and so prisoners are not at their best and not surprisingly correction officers aren't either."

And while the national corps of correction officers is more diverse, better educated and instructed than at any other time, according to experts, abuses persist.

Bob Gangi, head of the Correctional Association of New York, a nonprofit watchdog group, says that while the job breeds brutality, "correction officers have legitimate beefs that we as a society throw them down into the pits and ask them to do the dirty work and often don't really care about what goes on."

And so, correction officials and critics agree, in this field that constantly challenges moral bearings, rules and regulations are crucial compasses.

"You have to have structure for both the inmates and the officers," says Lt. Jerry Magnus, a supervisor who has worked in the Nassau jail for 27 years. He says the officers' rulebook is voluminous and "tells you how to do everything here except go to the bathroom."

Since the jailhouse death in January of Thomas Pizzuto and the federal probe, he says inmates are "thriving on the media," concocting accusations, even inflicting injuries on themselves and threatening to blame officers.

These are trying times, he says. "People have to put themselves in our place."

This is the job: Twelve hours after he first walked into his cellblock, Cpl. Roulis is in the same small bubble, monitoring the men in his charge.

It is 6:30 p.m. and the last feeding has finished. Inmates are talking on phones, talking to one another. Two TVs broadcast hazy images. A wiry, gray-haired inmate is sitting at a table, staring blankly at the floor.

"Look at that guy over there," says Roulis, a father of three. "He's done. He's left it all here."

A few minutes later, a mountainous man with thick hair bursting from his shirttop and a beard waits to be let inside the dorm. He is glowering and doesn't even turn his eyes as Roulis pushes a button to open the gate.

Roulis shakes his head. He says he "shudders to think if . . . [his children] ever got trapped in this world and couldn't get out."

In four hours, his double shift will be done. Then he'll drive home around 10:30 p.m. At 4 a.m., he'll pull himself out of bed again.

"Tomorrow's my last," before the weekend, he says, "and when I walk out of here, I'm running out of here. When I hit that parking lot, it's like I left the burden of the world behind me."

Article 12

PRISON CRIME IN NEW YORK STATE

DAVID R. EICHENTHAL
LAUREL BLATCHFORD
Office of the Public Advocate for the City of New York

The lack of attention devoted to crimes committed in prisons is striking given the important implications of the problem both for prison management and for public safety. This study examines reporting of crimes, referrals for prosecution and actual prosecution of crimes committed in New York State prisons. The authors find that there is no accurate means of tracking either prison crimes or prosecutions. But based on interviews, a review of state correctional department data, and a survey of prosecutors in more than one dozen counties where state prisons are located, they conclude that as many as 6,000 crimes may be committed annually in the New York State prison system. Yet few of these crimes are referred for prosecution or actually prosecuted.

PROBLEMS WITH UNDERENFORCEMENT OF PRISON CRIME

Some of the most violent criminals in New York State commit crimes without being punished under the criminal law. They reside in a jurisdiction with a population that would make it the state's seventh-largest city. In many cases, they assault individuals charged with the responsibility of policing their jurisdiction, yet they never get arrested. Even when criminals in this jurisdiction are arrested for their crimes, prosecutors often fail to prosecute criminal cases against them. In parts of the jurisdiction, prosecutors decline to prosecute as much as 75% of all cases referred to them. Prosecutors have also "decriminalized" virtually all misdemeanors. These crimes are committed by and among the population of New York's 63rd county—the 69,000-plus residents of the New York State corrections system.

The lack of attention devoted to crimes committed in prisons is striking given the important implicatons of the problem both for prison management and for public safety. Although research has yet to document a clear link between institutional offending and recidivism after release, it is intuitively plausible that inmates who commit crimes in prison may be more likely to continue their criminal activity once they return to their communities. Earlier this year, New York City Police Commissioner Howard Safir released a study showing that as many as 6% of all serious felonies are committed by individuals out of prison on parole. He, along with many others, has suggested that the state needs to abolish parole (Parole and Absconder Status of New York City Arrestees, 1996). But, perhaps it makes more sense to focus on those inmates who continue to commit crime in prison, as the present study does, without necessarily extending the confinement of those who show some signs of rehabilitation or aging out of their criminal career.

Regardless of its possible connection to subsequent street crime, continued criminal activity by inmates suggests a level of disrespect and increased risk for the corrections officers charged with maintaining order in correctional facilities. It is unclear whether administrative—as opposed to criminal—sanctions for offenses against corrections officers (or even other inmates) are adequate to deter further criminal conduct inside prisons.

To explore the extent of this problem in New York's prisons, this study was initiated by New York City Public Advocate, Mark Green. The findings and discussion that follow are based on interviews with corrections officials, review of state corrections department data, and surveys of prosecutors in more than one dozen counties where state prisons are located.

This research was conducted by the authors for the office of New York City Public Advocate Mark Green, and its findings were made available to the public in April 1997.

PROBLEMS IN MEASURING CRIME INCIDENCE AND PROSECUTION RATES IN NEW YORK STATE PRISONS

Although more than 69,000 New Yorkers currently reside in one of the 69 correctional facilities operated by the New York State Department of Correctional Services (DOCS), little information is kept regarding crimes committed in prison. If the current inmate population were concentrated in a single city, that city would be the seventh largest in New York State—more New Yorkers live in state prisons than in Binghamton, Mount Vernon, Schenectady, Elmira, or Plattsburgh (New York State Statistical Yearbook, 1995, p. 11). In each of those cities, crime is undoubtedly an important issue. But, except for inmates and correctional staff who may have been victimized, very few people seem to have been concerned about the amount of crime committed in state prisons.

There are three significant ways in which the amount of crime committed in the general population—outside of prisons—is counted: complaints (e.g., calls to the police department and other law enforcement agencies), victimization surveys (where individuals are surveyed to determine if they have been a crime victim in a given period), and arrest data. None of these data are precise because (a) not every crime victim files a complaint with law enforcement, (b) victimization results extrapolated from limited samples may contain flaws due to sampling error, and (c) arrest data may be a reflection of police productivity as much as actual criminal activity.

Strikingly, none of these data are available for crimes committed in state prison facilities. DOCS does not maintain a central database of criminal complaints or even of cases of criminal complaints resulting in referrals for criminal prosecution. To the extent that data exist, they are piecemeal and located at individual correctional facilities, prosecutors' offices, and with state police troops. In addition, DOCS maintains a record of all unusual incidents at state prisons. But, unusual incidents include both criminal conduct—assaults and possession of contraband—and noncriminal conduct—employee misconduct and disruptive behavior.

Data are even less available about what happens to prison crimes that are actually referred for criminal prosecution. Although a number of jurisdictions compiled such data at our request, even the most sophisticated prosecutorial offices in the state do not routinely maintain information on crimes committed in prisons.

- In New York County (Manhattan), where more than 2,500 inmates are housed in state correctional facilities, the Manhattan district attorney's office indicated that it "does not maintain a record of the number of referrals or declinations to prosecute in this type of case."[1]
- In Erie County, where more than 2,000 state inmates are in state correctional facilities, the district attorney's office indicated that "It is impossible in our computer system to distinguish inmate cases from the civilian population."[2]
- In Richmond County, where almost 1,000 state inmates are housed in Arthur Kill, District Attorney William Murphy responded that "Inasmuch as the current funding for my office precludes me from procuring the technology, and corresponding personnel, to maintain statistics such as those requested by you, I am unable to provide you with an analysis of this office's prosecution of internal prison crime."[3]

ROUGH ESTIMATES

Although data are limited, what we know about prisons in general and the limited information about prison crime in New York suggests that there may be an extraordinary amount of crime committed in state prisons annually. Years of criminal justice research document the intuitive—that prisons are violent environments. Thus, although many advocate incarceration as a means of incapacitating criminals, it is likely that incarceration in many cases merely shifts the locus of criminal activity away from neighborhoods to correctional facilities (Eichenthal & Jacobs, 1991, p. 303).

In 1995, DOCS reports that there were 8,304 unusual incidents in state prison facilities. There were 1,738 reported cases of inmate-on-inmate assaults, 962 cases of inmate assaults on staff, and 3,550 incidents involving possession of prison contraband (Unusual Incident Report, 1996, p. 4). If all of these had been reported crimes, there would have been more than 6,000 crimes committed in state prisons in that 1 year. One type of crime where fairly good data exist—both for crimes committed inside prisons and in the general population—is murder. In 1995, there were 1,551 murders reported in New York State: a murder rate of 8.6 per 100,000 New Yorkers.[4] In that same year, according to DOCS, there were 6 homicides at DOCS facilities: a murder rate of 8.7 per 100,000 state prisoners.

Criminal activity in New York's prisons may also take the form of multi-inmate incidents—riots or near riots. "Since 1994, DOCS has experienced 23 disturbances involving large numbers of inmates.... Six times in the past three years, DOCS has employed its Correction Emergency Response Teams to quell incidents" (Capacity Options Plan, 1997, p. 5). Yet, another serious form of inmate criminal activity is the use of illegal substances. Within the last 4 years, seizures of illegal drugs in New York State prison facilities have more than doubled (Purdy, 1995, p. 54).

Not every crime that is committed in prison—or in any setting—is automatically referred to a prosecutor for prosecution. If there may have been as many as 6,000 prison crimes committed in 1995, how many were referred for criminal prosecution? It is possible to develop an estimate of the number of referrals of crimes to local prosecutors based on referral data from those few jurisdictions that were able to report it.

One estimate—merely apportioning referrals on the basis of inmate population—suggests there were an estimated 1,000 internal prison crime referrals for prosecution in 1995. Another estimate can be derived from a comparison between referrals and unusual incidents. District attorneys in four counties—Chautauqua, Franklin, Oneida, and Washington—provided information on prison case referrals for prosecution. In 1995, the four district attorneys considered a total of 167 prison crime cases. In the same year, according to DOCS, there were 528 inmate assaults on staff or other inmates in the state prison facilities in those four counties. In other words, even assuming there were no other types of cases, fewer than 1 in 3 cases were referred for prosecution. If there were approximately 6,000 cases, that suggests that there may have been as many as 2,000 referrals for prosecution. This higher estimate has a historical basis; in 1985, when the state's prison population was approximately half the 1995 population, there were an estimated 1,018 referrals.[5] Anecdotal evidence suggests the number of referrals may be much higher still. In Cayuga County, where close to 3,000 inmates are housed in two state prisons, the local district attorney reported that he receives "approximately 600 referrals each year from the two facilities."[6]

Crimes committed in prisons are prosecuted by the district attorney of the county in which the prison facility is located. Because many of the state's prisons are located in small, rural counties, many of these local prosecutors lack the resources to prosecute a high volume of cases coming from state prisons. For example, the present public advocate survey elicited detailed responses from district attorneys in Cayuga, Chatauqua, Chemung, Clinton, Franklin, Oneida, St. Lawrence, Saratoga, Washington, and Wayne counties. State correctional facilities in these 10 counties hold more than 22,000 state inmates, or approximately one third the total state prison population. In those 8 counties, the average number of full-time assistant district attorneys was less than 4. Excluding Oneida County, on average, the remaining counties have just two full-time assistant district attorneys.[7] The result is that when prison crime cases are referred for prosecution, prosecutors frequently decline to handle the matter criminally. Prosecutors in 4 reporting counties declined 56.9% of felony prosecutions. By contrast, for all felony arrests, prosecutors statewide declined only 5.2%, with another 27.7% of felony arrests ultimately resulting in dismissals.

In Cayuga County, the local district attorney reported that he prosecutes only 5% of the hundreds of referrals he receives each year.[8] In Franklin County, where there are more than 1,800 inmates housed in two state prisons, the local district attorney declined to prosecute 75 out of 94 criminal cases referred by prison officials in 1995. In Clinton County, where approximately 4,000 inmates are housed in three prison facilities, the district attorney has adopted a policy to decline prosecutions involving assaults by inmates against other inmates unless there is a corrections officer witness. In addition, the district attorney will not prosecute most weapon possession cases unless there is evidence that the weapon was used or attempted to be used.[9]

Prosecutors in four counties—Cayuga, Chemung, Ulster, and St. Lawrence—where one dozen prisons house more than 10,000 inmates, report that they do not prosecute misdemeanors. Again, by contrast, prosecutors declined to prosecute only 3% of misdemeanor arrests and 29.1% were dismissed when the offenses took place in the general population. Prosecutors may be reluctant to prosecute inmates for misdemeanors because, if convicted to a consecutive sentence, the inmate would ultimately have to be housed in a local jail for punishment.

SPECIAL PROBLEMS IN PROSECUTING PRISON CRIME

Although a lack of resources may be one issue prompting prosecutors to decline high numbers of prison crime cases, prosecutors also identified a series of other problems. In inmate-on-inmate assault cases, prosecutors believe it is difficult to go forward without a noninmate witness. The lack of a credible witness was raised as a problem by six prosecutors, from Oneida, Wayne, Chautauqua, Chemung, Washington, and Franklin counties.

> We find it almost impossible to prosecute these crimes unless there are correction officers or prison employees as witnesses. (Washington County district attorney)

> The burden of proof cannot be sustained without forensic evidence corroborating the charges or correction officer's eyewitness testimony. (Franklin County district attorney)

In many cases, the problem is not even the credibility of a witness's testimony, it is the unwillingness to testify at all. District attorneys in three counties—Chemung, Oneida, and Ulster—indicated that this was a major problem in prosecuting inmate-against-inmate assaults.

Prosecutors in three counties—Chautauqua, St. Lawrence, and Oneida—also indicated that inmates involved in inmate-on-inmate assaults are frequently relocated to other state prisons, again creating an obstacle to successful investigation and prosecution. Two prosecutors—in Oneida and Franklin counties—indicated that prison crime prosecutions were limited by problems with the investigations conducted by DOCS personnel.

> Inadequate investigations clear defendants prior to our prosecution. (Oneida County district attorney)

> Inadequate criminal investigative training of DOCS personnel; failure by DOCS personnel to Mirandize inmates prior to questioning; failure to question inmates properly. (Franklin County district attorney)

Finally, two prosecutors—from Clinton and Ulster counties—expressed frustration with the existing Penal Law definition of physical injury for the purpose of prosecuting felony assault cases. Under Penal Law section 120.05(7), a person is guilty of Assault 2nd Degree when

> Having been charged with or convicted of a crime and while confined in a correctional facility, as defined in subdivision three of section forty of the correction law, pursuant to such charge or conviction, with intent to cause physical injury to another person, he causes such injury to such person or to a third person.

Under Penal Law 10.00(9), physical injury means "impairment of physical condition or substantial pain." The Clinton County district attorney has advised DOCS officials that "petty slaps, shoves, kicks and the like are not enough to meet this standard."[10] As a result, many simple inmate assaults are only prosecutable as a misdemeanor and, given the reluctance of county prosecutors to prosecute misdemeanors by inmates, are therefore not prosecuted.

INMATE CONSEQUENCES FOR CRIME IN PRISON

If inmates who continue to commit crimes while incarcerated are not punished under the criminal law, what happens to them? Many inmates who violate the criminal law are sanctioned internally through an administrative disciplinary process. These sanctions can include a loss of privileges, a change in conditions of confinement (e.g., solitary), and a loss of good time credit resulting in a longer period of incarceration. But, as the New York State Court of Appeals recently ruled, there is nothing that precludes imposing both administrative sanctions and criminal punishment on inmates who violate the law while in prison. In *Codero v. Lalor* (89 NY 2d 521) and *People v. Vasquez* (655 NYS 2d 870, 1997), the court held that under double jeopardy, a prior prison sanction does not create a bar to a criminal prosecution.

> Prison disciplinary action is not designed to "vindicate public justice," but rather to further the separate and important public interest in maintaining prison order and safety.... Prisoners, by virtue of their status (resulting from a prior violation of the Penal Law) are subject not only to criminal laws, aimed at vindicating societal interests, but also to a whole array of internal prison rules and regulations, which serve the separate, legitimate and important institutional purposes of preserving prison order and safety. A prisoner who commits a crime in prison breaks both sets of rules, and may thus be sanctioned both internally to carry out the goals of the penal institution, and through criminal prosecution to vindicate public justice. (New York Law Journal, 1997, pp. 27–28)

The reality, however, is that the vast majority of inmates who commit a criminal offense are never tried through a criminal prosecution "to vindicate public justice."

LEARNING LESSONS FROM SUCCESS: THE TEXAS MODEL

In a prior study of prison crime prosecutions, the authors concluded that "the special prosecutor model is well suited to the prosecution of prison crimes.... Their mandate is to prosecute all prison crimes where sufficient evidence exists. Furthermore, a special prosecutor could develop long-term relations with the department of corrections and a close familiarity with prison operations and the prisoner subculture" (Eichenthal & Jacobs, 1991, p. 300).

For the past 12 years, prison crimes in the state of Texas have been prosecuted by the statewide Special Prison Prosecutions Unit (SPPU). In that time, SPPU has developed an effective partnership with the Texas Department of Corrections (TDC) and local law enforcement officials in counties containing state prisons. SPPU investigators claim that they have developed experience and expertise in obtaining the cooperation of witnesses and victims and developing special techniques for the investigation of prison crime (Eichenthal & Jacobs, 1991, p. 301).

More than 6 years ago, in testimony before the New York State Assembly Correction Committee, the then chief prosecutor of SPPU, David Weeks, described how his office had succeeded in reducing the number of murders, aggravated assaults on inmates, and—working with TDC—had helped to control gang violence in prisons. According to Weeks,

> The biggest problem ... dealing with crimes inside the penitentiary is the code of silence that always exists.... But as we built our credibility, as inmates learned that they could talk to us and trust us ... we've been able to gain more and more information.... Unless you understand the dynamics of the prison system, you can't prosecute crimes there.

Weeks also addressed the investigative problems specific to prison crime.

> We've taught them about taking photographs, keeping the crime scene as complete a picture as possible, maintaining what inmates were there, writing down if they talked to the inmate, what did the inmate say. (Transcript of Public Hearing on Managing Rikers Island in the 1990s, Assembly Committee on Correction, 1990, November 8)

RECOMMENDATIONS

The findings of the public advocate's study mirror those of a 10-year-old study of prison crime nationally (Eichenthal & Jacobs, 1991). That study found a pattern of underreporting of prison crime, underenforcement of the criminal law, and many of the same obstacles identified by prosecutors in 1996. DOCS has recognized the problem and, in September of 1995, initiated a task force on prison crime. DOCS now regularly reaches out to prosecutors in prison counties to encourage prosecution and encourage prosecutors to seek reimbursement for the costs of prosecution under section 606 of the Correction Law.

But, more needs to be done to address this serious problem. The public advocate for the city of New York urges DOCS and the legislature to endorse a 5-point program to curb prison crime.

Create an Office of Special Prosecutor for Prison Crime. The state legislature should create an Office of Special Prosecutor for Prison Crime. The special prosecutor would have jurisdiction over all crimes committed in state correctional facilities.[11] For more than a decade, all crimes in Texas's state corrections system have been prosecuted by a special prosecutor, making it a national model.

Establish a joint state police or department of correctional services investigative team to centralize all prison crime investigations. Prisons are a unique and difficult setting in which to conduct criminal investigations. Prison crime investigators require special training in criminal investigations, which correction officers often lack, and a familiarity with the prison setting, which state police troopers often lack. To more effectively investigate and prosecute prison crime, the state police and DOCS should set up joint investigative teams specializing in prison crime investigations.

Create a single, centralized database to track all referrals of prison crimes for prosecution. DOCS should move immediately to establish a centralized reporting and tracking system for all crimes committed in state correctional facilities. All facilities should report on all referrals for prosecution and outcomes.

Amend the Correction Law to allow inmates convicted of misdemeanors committed in state prisons to be detained and serve out the misdemeanor sentence in state prison. It is unacceptable to decriminalize misdemeanors committed in state prisons. But local district attorneys are reasonably exercising their prosecutorial discretion because they are concerned that the burden of inmates serving consecutive sentences would shift to local jail facilities where misdemeanants are punished. The legislature should change the Correction Law to require state correctional facilities to hold misdemeanants who are convicted of offenses committed while serving in that facility.

Require DOCS to provide an annual report on prison crime to the state legislature. If measures such as these are taken, significant progress will have been made in addressing many of the problems identified above.

NOTES

1. Letter from Steven M. Fishner, executive assistant district attorney to Laurel Blatchford, Office of the Public Advocate, March 21, 1997.
2. Letter from Yvonne Vertlieb, executive assistant district attorney to Mark Green, February 25, 1997.
3. Letter from District Attorney William Murphy to Mark Green, February 26, 1997.
4. Data provided by New York State Division of Criminal Justice Services.
5. Eichenthal and Jacobs (1991, p. 286). Both 1985 and 1995 data are affected by the underprosecution of prison crime. In 1985, two thirds of all referrals came from two counties where there were an inordinately high number of referrals, but virtually no prosecution. Presumably, in other counties, underprosecution deterred prison and police officials from making criminal referrals—resulting in an undercount of the number of crimes that would have been referred for prosecution had they been committed in a nonprison environment. The 1995 data are based on extrapolation from statistics in four counties where district attorneys were actually able to provide data on referrals. Out of 167 referrals, 94 were from one county—Franklin County. There, prosecutors decline to prosecute cases more than 75% of the time.
6. Letter to Mark Green, public advocate for the city of New York, from James B. Vargason, district attorney of Cayuga County, April 9, 1997.
7. Given limited resources, prosecutors may be naturally reluctant to divert any resources to the prosecution of prison crime. Particularly where both offender and victim are inmates, there is no local political interest in the prosecution of prison crime. See Eichenthal and Jacobs (1991, p. 294): (As one prosecutor noted, "[Prison crime cases are] not politically attractive.... Most people in society think if it's one inmate assaulting another, well who cares?").
8. Letter to Mark Green from James B. Vargason, district attorney of Cayuga County, April 9, 1997.
9. Letter from Penelope D. Clute, Clinton County district attorney to Daniel Senkowski, superintendent of Clinton Correctional Facility, February 17, 1989: "ASSAULT ON ANOTHER INMATE... unless there is an employee witness, or the attacker admits the assault, a successful prosecution will be very difficult." Letter from Penelope Clute to Steve Pendergast, New York state police, January 3, 1991; "Until further notice, we will not prosecute charges of weapon possession for general population inmates where there is no evidence that the weapon was used or attempted to be used."
10. Letter from Penelope Clute to Steven Pendergrast, New York state police, January 3, 1991.
11. Legislation to create a special prosecutor has been proposed in both houses of the state legislature. A.6693 was introduced in the Assembly by Assembly member Daniel Feldman, Chair of the Correction Committee. S. 4784 was introduced in the Senate by Senator James Lack.

REFERENCES

Capacity Options Plan (1997, January). Office of the Director of Criminal Justice, State of New York.

Eichenthal, D., and Jacobs, J. (1991). Enforcing the criminal law in state prisons. *Justice Quarterly, 8*(3), 283–303.

New York State Statistical Yearbook (1995). Nelson A. Rockefeller Institute of Government, State University of New York.

Parole and Absconder Status of New York City Arrestees. (1996, November). New York Police Department.

Purdy, M. (1995, December 17). Officials ponder expansion of drug searches in prison. *The New York Times*, p. 54.

Unusual Incident Report: January–December 1995. (1996, April). State of New York, Department of Correctional Services.

STOPPING Abuse in Prison

Lawyers for women behind bars and human rights groups are making a difference

BY NINA SIEGAL

Widespread abuses of women behind bars barely received notice until seven or eight years ago. Across the country, there were incidents of prison or jail staff sexually molesting inmates with impunity. Slowly but surely, the nation's correctional facilities are responding to this abuse.

"Ten years ago, I think we knew it was going on, but we hadn't named it," says Brenda Smith, a Practitioner-in-Residence at Washington College of Law at American University. "Until you raise it as a problem, and until people start coming forward and talking about it, it is not perceived as a problem."

The changes are the result of several landmark legal cases, a shift in government policy, and the attention of human-rights groups. Still, problems remain. Guards continue to rape women inmates. But now there's a process to bring them to justice.

The stories were too consistent to be ignored. Numerous female inmates in three Washington, D.C.,

---

Nina Siegal is a reporter for "The City" section of The New York Times and a frequent contributor to The Progressive.

prison and jail facilities said they had been awakened at two or three in the morning for a "medical visit" or a "legal visit" only to be led into the kitchen, the clinic, the visiting hall, or a closet to have sex. Many inmates were becoming pregnant in a system that allowed no conjugal visits.

"There were a lot of places where people could have sex," says Smith. "A lot of it was in exchange for cigarettes." Prison employees offered other deals: " 'I will give you phone calls, I will make sure you get a better job assignment, I'll give you drugs if you have sex with me.' The sex involved not just correctional officers. It involved chaplains, administration, deputy wardens, contractors, and food-service workers. It involved not just male staff but female staff as well," Smith says.

In 1993, the National Women's Law Center and a District of Columbia law firm filed a class-action suit, *Women Prisoners vs. District of Columbia Department of Corrections*, in U.S. District Court. The suit alleged a pattern of discrimination against women in the jail, the Correctional Treatment Facility, and the Lorton Minimum Security Annex, a D.C. facility in Lorton, Virginia. A large portion of the case focused on issues of sexual misconduct, based on evidence that the law firm had collected during an investigation.

The following year, a judge found that there was a pattern and practice of misconduct so severe that it violated the Eighth Amendment protection against cruel and unusual punishment. The decision was appealed and is still in court.

As extreme as the D.C. situation was, it was not unique.

Lawyers in Georgia had been preparing a class-action suit on behalf of men and women in the state's prisons for almost ten years when they began to come across striking charges of sexual misconduct in the Georgia Women's Correctional Facility in Milledgeville and the nearby camp, Colony Farm. The alleged activities included rape, criminal sexual contact, leering, and abusive catcalling of inmates. One lieutenant had sex with at least seven prisoners from 1987 to 1991, directing women to meet him in various locations in the prisons for sex.

In 1992, the lawyers for the suit, *Cason v. Seckinger*, amended their complaint to add allegations of sexual abuse that had taken place over a period of fourteen years. Seventeen staff members were indicted. None were convicted, though several were dismissed from their jobs as a result of the lawsuit. The suit resulted in a number of federal court orders requiring the department to rectify many of its practices. It also influenced the department to close Milledgeville and move all the female inmates to a different facility.

These two suits—and the criminal prosecutions that ensued—were the first major legal attempts to address a problem that had been plaguing the criminal justice system for decades.

One of the biggest cases for the rights of women prisoners was settled last year. The case (*Lucas vs. White*) involved three inmates of a federal facility in Pleasanton, California, called FCI Dublin, who were sold as sex slaves to male inmates in an adjoining facility. Inmates paid guards to allow them into the cells of female inmates who were being held in the men's detention center, which is across the street from Dublin.

The plaintiffs settled their civil suit against the Federal Bureau of Prisons for $500,000 and forced the agency to make dramatic changes in the way it handles allegations of misconduct. According to the settlement, the Bureau of Prisons was to set up a confidential hotline, or some other reporting mechanism, so that inmates and staff can inform the authorities of problems inside. It was also supposed to provide medical and psychological treatment for inmates who have been victimized and establish new training programs for staff and inmates.

Geri Lynn Green, one of the two attorneys for the *Lucas* case, has been monitoring the changes at the prison since the case settled. After the lawsuit and the subsequent training, she says, "it appears there was a tremendous impact."

Brett Dignam, clinical professor of law at Yale University, agrees that the *Lucas* case made a big difference: "More prison staff members are resigning over issues of sexual misconduct."

Human rights advocates, too, have taken up the cause. In 1996, the Women's Rights Project at Human Rights Watch issued "All Too Familiar: Sexual Abuse of Women in U.S. Prisons."

The 347-page report detailed problems in California, Washington, D.C., Michigan, Georgia, and New York. "We have found that male correctional employees have vaginally, anally, and orally raped female prisoners and sexually assaulted and abused them," says the report. "We found that in the course of committing such gross misconduct, male officers have not only used actual or threatened physical force, but have also used their near total authority to provide or deny goods and privileges to female prisoners to compel them to have sex or, in other cases, to reward them for having done so."

Last June, the United Nations sent a special rapporteur, Radhika Coomaraswamy, to the United States to investigate sexual misconduct in the nation's women's facilities. She argued that stronger monitoring was needed to control widespread abuses.

"We concluded that there has been widespread sexual misconduct in U.S. prisons, but there is a diversity—some are dealing with it better than others," Reuters reported her saying in December. "Georgia has sexual misconduct but has set up a very strong scheme to deal with it. In California and Michigan, nothing has been done and the issue is very prevalent." In April, Coomaraswamy will give a final report to the U.N. Commission on Human Rights.

This March, Amnesty International released its own report, " 'Not Part of My Sentence': Violations of the Human Rights of Women in Custody," which includes a section on sexual abuse. "Many women inmates are subjected to sexual abuse by prison officials, including: sexually offensive language, observation by male officers while showering and dressing, groping during daily pat-down searches, and rape." In addition to the problems detailed in the Human Rights Watch report, Amnesty investigators found problems in Illinois, Massachusetts, New Hampshire, Texas, West Virginia, and Wyoming.

Lawyers and human rights groups have won some important reforms. In 1990, only seventeen states had a law on the books defining sexual misconduct in prisons as either a misdemeanor or a felony offense. Today, there are only twelve states left that do not criminalize sexual relations between staff and inmates—Alabama, Kentucky, Massachusetts, Minnesota, Missouri, Montana, Nebraska, Oregon, Utah, Vermont, West Virginia, and Wisconsin—according to Amnesty International, which is campaigning to get all these states to pass their own laws.

The U.S. Justice Department is also taking a more active role. It has filed two suits charging that the correctional systems in Michigan and Arizona were responsible for violations of prisoners' constitutional rights. The suits cite numerous allegations of abuse, including rape, lack of privacy, prurient viewing, and invasive pat searches. Both cases are still pending.

Meanwhile, state prison systems are training personnel. Andie Moss was a project director with the Georgia Department of Corrections in 1992 when the department was asked to help interview inmates for the class-action lawsuit. She ended up culling information from women who said they had been subjected to misconduct over a fourteen-year period. Today, Moss works with the National Institute of Corrections, part of the Bureau of Prisons. Her primary responsibility is to develop training programs to educate both staff and inmates about sexual misconduct, the new laws, and their rights.

Since her program, "Addressing Staff Sexual Misconduct," was initiated in early 1997, Moss and her team have provided training for more than thirty state correctional systems, and she expects to complete training for all fifty states by the end of 1999.

The training involves four basic elements: clarifying the departments' sexual misconduct policy, informing inmates and staff of the law in their state, telling inmates and staff how to report abuse that they witness, and giving examples of how people have intervened in the past.

"We know it's still an issue. We know corrections departments still need to work diligently on this," says Moss. "It's a constant effort because it is a cultural change. But if you could follow the change in the law, the change in policy and practice, there's been an amazing effort in the last three years."

Despite all the positive steps, however, women are still being abused in America's prisons and jails. Investigators from a number of California-based law firms who recently visited the Valley State Prison for Women in Chowchilla, California, heard stories of at least a dozen assaults by specific guards. They also found "a climate of sexual terror that women are subjected to on a daily basis," says Ellen Barry, founding director of Legal Services for Prisoners with Children, based in San Francisco.

"The instances of both physical and sexual abuse are much higher than any other institution where I've interviewed women," she says. "The guards are really brutalizing women in a way that we really haven't seen before."

Valley State Prison inmate Denise Dalton told investigators that a doctor at the facility groped her and conducts inappropriate pelvic exams. "If I need Tylenol, all I need to do is ask him for a pelvic and he will give me whatever I want," she said.

But most of the abusive conduct was of the type that, Barry says, made

13. Stopping Abuse in Prison

for "a climate of sexual terror" in the prison. Coreen Sanchez, another inmate, said that in December, she entered the dayroom at the facility and asked a correctional officer if the sergeant had come in, and he responded by saying, "Yeah, he came in your mouth." She also reported seeing correctional officers flaunt their erections in front of inmates.

Advocates for prisoners say there still needs to be a dramatic cultural shift within the system before women are safe from the people who guard them behind bars.

"I think we have to keep in perspective the limitations of litigation and advocacy work for truly making a change in this arena," says Barry.

One problem that advocates cite is the recalcitrance of the unions that represent prison guards. "The people we really have to win over are not legislators, but the unions," says Christine Doyle, research coordinator for Amnesty International U.S.A. "Guards look at this as a workplace violation, as something fun to do on the job. They don't look at these women as human beings. The message that these are human beings they are exploiting isn't getting through."

For them to get that message, says Doyle, corrections officers will have to hear it from within the unions, and not from any set of codes, procedures, or laws. "We have states that have legislation, and some of them are just as bad, if not worse, than states without legislation," Doyle says. "So, obviously, that doesn't work. If it comes from within, and the unions themselves say, 'We can do this internally,' workers will respond better."

Human rights groups, for now, are focusing on legislative solutions. In 1996, Human Rights Watch recommended that Congress require all states, as a precondition of receiving federal funding for prisons, criminalize all sexual conduct between staff and inmates. It also urged the Department of Justice to establish secure toll-free telephone hotlines for reporting complaints.

Amnesty International's new report takes an additional step, arguing that the role of male staff be restricted in accordance with the United Nations' Standard Minimum Rules for the Treatment of Prisoners, which state that "women prisoners shall be attended and supervised only by women officers."

Debra LaBelle, a civil rights attorney who filed a class-action suit on behalf of abused women inmates in Michigan, says she would like to see men taken out of women's institutions altogether.

"I resisted going there for a long time, but I don't know another solution," she says. "When we started out, they didn't do any training, much supervision, investigation. In the last three years, they've changed countless policies and yet it is still happening. Get them out of there. It's not like they're losing employment opportunities. There are, unfortunately, many more facilities that men can work in."

Sheila Dauer, director of the Women's Human Rights Program for Amnesty International, says the group's report aims to persuade the final thirteen states without laws against sexual misconduct to initiate legislation, starting with eight state campaigns this year. She says the campaign will also lend support to a federal bill that would do the same thing,

Amnesty's report, she says, is designed to "wake up the American public to the horrible abuses that women inmates are suffering in prison and stop the suffering."

Article 14

A Day in the Life

Four Women Share Their Stories of Life Behind Bars

By Gabrielle deGroot

Author's Note. When I first issued my request to talk to women incarcerated at the Maryland Correctional Institution for Women (MCI-W), I expected to hear stories of innocence and bitterness, and of the horrors of living behind bars. What I experienced instead was an unusually refreshing and candid glimpse into the lives of four women—women who had, perhaps, made the wrong choices in life, but who had taken full responsibility for those choices and who were trying desperately to make the best of a bad situation. These, then, are their stories, and this is what it's really like to be a woman in prison.

"It's hard to call SOMEONE A FRIEND"

We can only explain to you how we live. We can't make you understand, because we don't. We can never understand the politics or the system, ever."

That statement came from Laura, 39, a mother of three who is serving 20 years in prison without the possibility of parole for a drug conviction. But it could apply to any of the other three women who have agreed to share their stories of life behind bars: Cindy, 33, a slender, blond woman and former veterinary technician who killed her abusive husband; Donna, 34, a quiet woman who speaks of her former life as an intravenous drug user with equal parts candor and regret; and Shawnte, a petite, 18-year-old woman-child who says more with her silences than she does with her words.

They are four of some 850-plus female inmates at the Maryland Correctional Institution for Women (MCI-W), and part of a national trend that has seen the women's prison population climb from 3 percent in 1970 to more than 6 percent today. In 1997, more than 80,000 women were incarcerated in the United States, many of them for drug-related crimes.

For those who believe that female offenders are super-violent, or uneducated, or indifferent to their circumstances, these women beg to differ. While they have seen more in their short lives than most of us ever will, they also have learned more about themselves, their fellow inmates and the world than most people do in a lifetime.

From *Corrections Today,* December 1998, pp. 82-86, 96. Reprinted with permission of the American Correctional Association, Lanham, MD. © 1998.

"*Personally, it terrifies me—*
THE THOUGHT OF GOING **OUT THERE.**"

They have learned that the system is not always fair, but that rules and regulations are written for a reason, and those who break the rules cause trouble for all. They have learned that they can survive prison, mostly by relying on themselves and their own inner resources. And most important, they have learned that freedom is a gift that they squandered once through ignorance or greed or simply bad choices. All have vowed never to return once released. Whether they become successful outside the gates is entirely up to them.

"I want to be respected, you know?" says Donna, with a wistful smile. "I just want to be somebody that my mother can say, 'That's my daughter. I'm so proud of her.' I want my nieces and nephews to be glad to be in my company. That's how successful I want to be."

NEWS MEDIA REPORTS to the contrary, life behind bars is no picnic. Many of the women arise between 5:30 and 6 a.m. to shower and grab breakfast before they're locked in for the first count of the day at 7 a.m. After count clears at 8:30 a.m., they're free to report for work or school. Lunch is anywhere from 10:30 a.m. to 1 p.m., after which those women who are not working are free to go outside and enjoy the weather until the next count at 3 p.m. Then it's more work, or more school, or parenting classes, and then dinner, an hour or two of free time in the evening, and another count at 10 p.m.

Many of the women work for State Use Industries (SUI), a prison industries program that keeps them busy and allows them to earn some money. Of course, they're not earning much. The maximum amount a woman can earn is $2.50 a day, which she can use to purchase items from the commissary or to order clothing from a mail-order company.

While the women used to be able to receive packages from home, the practice was ended at all Maryland prisons when the male inmates in the prison next door abused the privilege. Likewise, the women are punished as a group when one woman acts out or disobeys the rules.

And therein lies the most difficult part of being incarcerated, these women say—maintaining one's individuality in the face of so much togetherness.

"Everyone views inmates as a group, as a class of people, and of course, we're the lowest class," says Cindy. "It's not that this individual inmate committed this individual crime, and has done A, B, C and D while incarcerated. When something happens, everybody gets punished. There is no individuality."

THAT STRIPPING OF ONE'S individuality, intentional or not, begins as soon as a woman enters the system. She is given a pink jumpsuit and a red jacket with MCI-W written in big, block letters on the back, which identifies her as being on "quarantine"—"newly arrived," in prison parlance. She wears pink for two weeks until properly classified, at which point she moves into a housing unit and is allowed to wear her own clothes.

Cindy remembers that period well. "I was petrified when I first came in," she says. "They took me off quarantine and put me on A-wing [the maximum security wing], and I cried. I actually cried in the hallway."

Shawnte still sleeps on A-wing, and insists that it isn't as bad as everyone says. "It's not a bad place to sleep," she says. She adds that "everyone sticks together," but later admits that there are only two people among the hundreds of women at MCI-W she can actually call friends. "I have two people that I can talk to about anything and not have to worry about hearing it again a hundred more times."

Laura doesn't allow herself to get close to anyone. "It's hard to call someone a friend," she says. "It's hard to get close to somebody because you never know whether they're going to stab you in the back," figuratively speaking, that is.

So how does one survive in a small place, with few friends and even fewer privileges? Most of these women set their sights on a goal—their freedom, their children, their families, the possibility of parole.

"I have one aim, one goal, and that's my freedom," says Donna, who is seven years into a mandatory 10-year stay for felony murder. "Every time that something is taken away from me, I just think, 'I don't want to retaliate, I just want to press forward, be positive.' I won't take any bitterness out there with me. I just want to take the lessons that I've learned and, you know, grow from this experience."

CINDY AND LAURA HAVE children waiting for them "on the outside." Laura's three children—two girls and a boy—live with their father, her ex-husband. Her son, who just turned 16, recently bought his first car. "I've missed a lot, and the guilt that I carry around for that . . ." Her voice trails off for a moment before she adds, almost defiantly, "If I can't fly the right way for myself, then I've got to for them."

Cindy's son, Kyle, was eight months old when she entered prison. He's eight years old now, and starting to ask questions. "He's always known that I killed his dad," Cindy says. "When they're very young, you have to say things to a child in very gentle terms. You can still be honest with them; they can handle the truth. But you have to come to their level. So, basically, we explained to him that his dad was going to hurt me. And he was able to understand that, but as he's grown, his questions have gotten more and more advanced. And recently, he asked about my husband's career. 'My dad did this, and did he do this well? And were people proud of him?' And, in fact, one time he asked me, 'How did my dad wear his hair when he

"I have one aim...
AND THAT'S MY FREEDOM"

was my age?' And I said to him, 'Just like you're wearing it. Just like you're wearing it.'"

Cindy sees her son and her mother, who is raising him, every other weekend, when they make the trip from Virginia to visit her. Other women are not so lucky. Laura sees her children sporadically, and Shawnte admits that her visitors are few and far between. "I don't get many visits," she says. "You know, when you first come down here, you get a whole lot. Then once you're here for a while, they get farther and farther apart. I have a little brother—he's four now, you know—and I sometimes sit around and wonder if he remembers who I am."

Cindy and Laura know their children will remember them, but they're nervous about the reactions their children might have when they get out of prison. "I wonder, 'Is he going to respect me?'" Cindy says. "Is my son ever going to look at me and say, 'You were in prison. Why am I going to believe you?' But then, I try to negotiate with my conscience and say, well, I've always been completely honest with him. I'm not in the hospital. I'm not at college. I'm in prison."

"The only thing I fear [about getting out of prison] is that my kids will be so different, and it bothers me a lot how they're changing and what I've missed," Laura says. "I called the other day, and my daughter, who's 13, said, 'We were getting ready to go to the mall.' And I said, 'Does that mean you'd rather not talk to me?' and she said, 'Dad's out in the car now, taking us.' So I said, 'OK, you go ahead.' I've missed parts that I can't get back."

BECAUSE THE WOMEN WITH whom we spoke had been incarcerated for at least three years, most were used to the routine and the rules, even if they didn't necessarily agree with them. "I don't have many fears about being here," Cindy says. "I'm used to it. I know what my place is. I know what I need to do."

But that doesn't mean that the routine itself doesn't pose its own challenges. After all, each day during the thrice-daily head counts, these women hear the doors clank shut behind them, and are reminded once again that they're in prison. "That's the worst; I hate it," says Laura. "I guess it's the idea of knowing that I'm stuck in here. This is part of the punishment. This is why I'm here, to be in this cell."

Partly because of the length of their stays at MCI-W, these women also have had plenty of time to think, to reflect on their lives, and to come to some realizations about what it means to live the good life.

"My first and second year here, I continuously thought, 'When I get out of here, I'm going to go get high,'" says Laura, who was convicted of possession with intent to distribute PCP. "I was going to have an ex-inmate pick me up, joint ready, at the gate. No doubt. The third year, I started saying, 'Hey, I don't like this life anymore.' You get sick of this. I don't want to be here the rest of my life. I want a man back in my life. I don't get to see my children—they're getting big. My parents are getting older. Somebody might die. What's going on here?"

Many of the women who arrive in pink jumpsuits each week are familiar faces—women who get out of prison for a few weeks or a few months, only to commit another crime, often drug-related. "Me, personally, I get frustrated when I see people coming back and forth, back and forth, because I don't have even one chance right now to step foot over the gate. If I did, you wouldn't see me again," says Shawnte, who is serving a natural life sentence for murder.

"I really believe that some people have found a place here," Cindy adds. "They might not like it here, but they know exactly where they fit in and they know exactly what's expected of them. In here, the only responsibility you have is the responsibility you choose to accept. Other than that, nothing is expected."

To succeed in prison, to become a better person, each of these women has had to call upon her own willpower, her own inner strength. "I pretty much deal with all positive people," Donna says. "That's a lesson that I've learned here. I could be with this crew that gets into trouble, but you know, I shun them now."

Hard lessons, learned the hard way.

CINDY, DONNA, LAURA AND SHAWNTE are all looking forward to the day they can leave the gates of MCI-W behind. But their fears for the future are as real and oppressive as the ones they brought to prison. "Personally, it terrifies me, the thought of going out there, where I have to get a job, get a car, be a mother and a daughter and a sister," Cindy says. "I have to get a driver's license, I have to pay taxes, I have to get car insurance. That responsibility—it's a huge load."

A printer with 18 years of experience, Laura isn't worried about landing a job when she's released. She does wonder about whether she'll lie on the form, when asked whether she's ever been convicted of a felony. "I'm a little fearful of will I tell the truth or will I lie on the application when it asks me, and I don't know what I'll do in any situation," she says.

"I fear that I'm going to go to a job interview and somebody's going to say, 'Have you ever been convicted of a felony?' And I'm going to be in that situation where I'm going to say yes or no," Cindy says. "My gut tells me that I want to say absolutely yes, I have, and be given the opportunity to explain. But the fear of maybe not getting the job wants me to say no."

"*I have two people* I CAN TELL **ANYTHING...**"

Each of the women realizes that she must re-earn the trust of her family and friends—a feat that will likely take years. And each realizes also, with some humor, that she must re-learn how to live.

Donna: "I can imagine going to a mall, and everybody will know I just came from prison..."

Cindy: "They put a fluorescent stamp on your forehead that only other people can see..."

Donna: "You go to a restaurant and you finish eating your food in, like, eight minutes..."

Cindy: "You know you've been a prisoner when you press your clothes under your mattress..."

Laura: "And then when they say, 'And here's your dessert,' you wrap it in a napkin..."

Cindy: "And tuck it in your bra..."

Laura: "Three o'clock, we're not going to know what to do with ourselves. We're going to be like, 'Do we shower? Can we get up? Can we move?'"

They laugh. It is shared laughter of an experience that no one, not even those who live it, can truly understand.

Gabrielle deGroot is managing editor of Corrections Today.

The Gangs Behind Bars

Prison gangs are flourishing across the country. Organized, stealthy and deadly, they are reaching out from their cells to organize and control crime in America's streets.

By Tiffany Danitz

A 40-year-old gang leader uses his cellular phone to organize an elaborate drug ring and order hits. He commands respect. He wears gang-banger clothing and drapes himself with gold chains. This man is responsible for an entire network of gang members across the state of Illinois. He is Gino Colon, the mastermind behind the Latin Kings. When prosecutors finally caught up with him last August, Colon was indicted for running the Latin Kings' drug-dealing operation from behind prison walls—the state penitentiary in Menard.

"People in society and correctional officers need to understand that immediate control over the prison system is often an illusion at any time," says Cory Godwin, president of the gang-investigators association for the Florida Department of Corrections or DC. "Contraband equals power."

Prison gangs are flourishing from California to Massachusetts. In 1996, the Federal Bureau of Prisons found that prison disturbances soared by about 400 percent in the early nineties, which authorities say indicated that gangs were becoming more active. In states such as Illinois, as much as 60 percent of the prison population belong to gangs, Godwin says. The Florida DC has identified 240 street gangs operating in their prisons. Street gangs, as opposed to gangs originating in prisons, are emerging as a larger problem on the East Coast.

Of the 143,000 inmates Texas houses in state pens, 5,000 have been identified as gang members and another 10,000 are under suspicion. Texas prison-gang expert Sammy Buentello says the state's prisons are not infested with gangs, but those that have set up shop are highly organized. "They have a paramilitary type structure," he says. "A majority of the people that come in have had experience with street-gang membership and have been brought up in that environment accepting it as the norm. But some join for survival."

After James Byrd Jr. was dragged to death in Jasper last June, rumors spread throughout Texas linking two of the suspected assailants to racially charged prison gangs. While authorities and inmates dismiss these rumors, the Jasper murder occurred only weeks after a San Antonio grand jury indicted 16 members of the Mexican Mafia, one of the state's largest and most lethal prison gangs, for ordering the deaths of five people in San Antonio from within prison walls.

"As they are being released into the community on parole, these people are becoming involved in actions related to prison-gang business. Consequently, it is no longer just a corrections problem—it is also a community problem," Buentello tells **Insight**.

According to gang investigators, the gang leaders communicate orders through letters. Where mail is monitored they may use a code—for instance, making every 12th word of a seemingly benign letter significant. They use visits, they put messages into their artwork and in some states they use the telephone. "It is a misnomer that when you lock a gang member up they fall off to Calcutta. They continue their activity," Godwin emphasizes. "It has only been in the last five years that law enforcement has realized that what happens on the inside can affect what happens on the outside and vice versa."

Of the two kinds of gangs, prison gangs and street gangs, the prison gangs are better organized, according to gang investigators. They developed within the prison system in California, Texas and Illinois in the 1940s and are low-key, discreet—even stealthy. They monitor members and dictate how they behave and treat each other. A serious violation means death, say investigators.

The street gangs are more flagrant. "Their members are going into the prisons and realizing that one of the reasons they are in prison is that they kept such a high profile," making it easier for the police to catch them, says Buentello. "So, they are coming out more sophisticated and more dangerous because they aren't as easily detected. They also network and keep track of who is out and so forth."

According to gang investigators and prisoners, the prison gangs were formed for protection against predatory inmates, but racketeering, black markets and racism became factors.

Godwin says Texas should never have outlawed smoking in the prisons, adding cigarettes as trade-goods contraband to the prohibited list. "If you go back to the Civil War era, to Andersonville prison," Godwin says of the prisoner-of-war facility for Union soldiers, "you will see that the first thing that developed was a gang because someone had to control the contraband—that is power. I'm convinced that if you put three people on an island somewhere, two would clique up and become predatory against the other at some point."

But protection remains an important factor. When a new inmate enters the prison system he is challenged to a fight, according to a Texas state-pen prisoner. The outcome determines who can fight, who will be extorted for protection money and who will become a servant to other prisoners. Those who can't join a gang or afford to spend $5 a week in commissary items for protection are destined to be servants. Godwin explains: "The environment is set up so that when you put that many people with antisocial behavior and criminal history together, someone is going to be the predator and someone the prey, and that is reality."

The Texas inmate describes a system in which gangs often recruit like fraternities, targeting short-term inmates because they can help the gang—pay them back, so to speak—when they leave prison for the free world. Most of the groups thrive on lifelong membership, according to the Florida DC, with "blood in, blood out" oaths extending leadership and membership beyond the prison into the lucrative drug trade, extortion and pressure rackets.

Prison gangs operating in Texas and Florida include Neta, the Texas Syndicate, the Aztecs, the Mexican Mafia, the New Black Panthers, the Black Guerrilla Family, Mandingo Warriors, Aryan Brotherhood, La Nuestra Familia, the Aryan Circle and the White Knights. Some of these gangs have alliances, and some are mortal enemies. Many on this list originated in California over the decades, some of them (such as the Texas Syndicate) to protect members from the other gangs. In addition, street gangs such as the Crips and Bloods and traditional racial-hate groups such as the Ku Klux Klan also operate in the prisons.

It is a misnomer that when you lock a gang member up they fall off to Calcutta. What happens on the inside can affect what happens on the outside and vice versa.

What prisoners may not realize is that because the gangs are monitored by prison authorities the law-enforcement community is becoming very sophisticated about the gangs. "Sixty percent of what we learn about what is going on in the city streets of Florida" is garnered in prison and not from observing the streets, says Godwin.

Prison officials say they concentrate on inmate behavior to identify gang members. They do not single out gang leaders to strike any deals because acknowledging the gang as anything other than a "security-threat group" gives them too much credibility. This has been a particular problem in Puerto Rico with the native and political Neta gang. Recognizing groups during the 1970s, in a system in which prisoners have the right to vote, has led to a tendency among politicians to award clemency to some inmates.

Officials in Texas have reacted most stringently to gang members. They isolate and place them in lockdown status to discourage membership. Buentello says this approach has produced a dramatic decrease in violence. In 1984, 53 inmates were killed due to gang violence. After the new policy was implemented in 1985, homicides dropped to five and then continued to decline.

Godwin says Florida uses a closed-management system that only locks up prisoners for 23 hours, with further enforcement based on inmate behavior.

"The reality is they are going to be able to get away with doing things when we have only a handful of prison staff," Godwin cautions, adding that the system needs to increase the professionalism of the staff with pay raises and training. Many employees are recruited out of the same neighborhoods as the prisoners, he explains.

Linda Washburn of the Massachusetts Department of Corrections, a much smaller system than Texas or Florida, says her state handles prisoner gangs just like Florida. According to her, size doesn't matter when it comes to prison-gang problems because no one is immune to it. "This issue crosses so many lines in society and in the prisons that it requires us in law enforcement and criminal justice to unite and confront the issue together ... as a team with one voice."

It isn't about bad guys killing bad guys. It's about drug dealers and racketeers profiting off the system. And Godwin warns that the direct effect on American neighborhoods is realized when the 16-year-old sent up for 25 years gets paroled and moves in next door.

The effects of the Duran Consent Decree

(negotiated agreement between the inmate population and the New Mexico Department of Corrections regarding prison operations)

Curtis R. Blakely

Although violence within corrections is fairly common, it only captures society's attention when it erupts on a large scale, such as a prison riot. On Feb. 2, 1980, perhaps the bloodiest prison riot in American history occurred at the New Mexico State Penitentiary at Santa Fe. In a macabre display of savagery, 33 inmates were brutally murdered. After 36 hours, the National Guard was ordered to enter and retake the facility. The cost of repairing and rebuilding was estimated at approximately $70 million.

While prison riots like New Mexico are rare, they nonetheless have served as catalysts for change and conduits for the upgrade and improvement of conditions. The Santa Fe riot provides a textbook example of extreme prison violence, and it has heightened awareness concerning security procedures throughout the country. This article will focus on the current agreement existing between inmates and the New Mexico Department of Corrections (DOC): the Duran Consent Decree, which is the negotiated agreement between the inmate population and the DOC regarding prison operations. It also will describe how the department has prepared itself to comply with this decree. Particular attention will be paid to the training academy, which has the unique distinction of being the first academy to be accredited by the American Correctional Association (ACA).

The Duran Consent Decree

The decree is credited as being the most enduring legacy of the 1980 riot. Although it took effect in 1979, it had little impact on the department until after the riot took place. According to this class-action suit, the plaintiffs (all present or future inmates) claimed that the totality of the conditions of confinement and practices of the department violated their rights under the Constitution and laws of the United States and the state of New Mexico.

On July 14, 1980, the decree was modified to resemble its present form. It specifies fourteen areas that needed to be improved and monitored. These include: correspondence, attorney visitation, food service, legal access, visitation, classification, living conditions, inmate activity, medical care, mental health care, staffing and training, administrative segregation, inmate discipline and pre-hearing detention/disciplinary segregation. In accordance with the decree, a special master monitors the operations of the DOC to ensure that progress toward substantial compliance is made. The special master must, at a minimum, file a report with the U.S. district court every six months regarding the department's compliance. When substantial compliance is achieved, the special master then recommends to the court that a period of self-monitoring and self-reporting be initiated for a period not to exceed two years. If, during this time, the special master determines that the facility has remained in substantial compliance, the decree will be vacated. All maximum and medium security facilities have vacated the decree except for the penitentiary. Central, Southern, Western and the New Mexico Women's Correctional Facility all have achieved ACA accreditation. Likewise, facilities at the penitentiary complex recently have undergone ACA audits.

The Training Academy

Section 11 of the Duran Consent Decree, which briefly addresses staffing and training, states that adequate staff and staff training must be provided to ensure the safety and protection of inmates and to allow the DOC to comply with all other orders and policy statements.

In order to accomplish this goal, DOC officials decided in 1991 that they would strive to be the first correctional academy to gain ACA accreditation. In January 1993, this goal was realized, making the New Mexico Corrections Academy the first to be awarded such distinction. Prior to this accomplishment, most training consisted of 40 hours of staff orientation. Today, the $11 million complex trains more than 1,200 staff annually in nine-week residential courses.

When new staff are brought into the academy, the department introduces them to the decree. New staff begin service equipped to maintain the safety of society and inmates, while being fully aware of the decree's mandates. The department's philosophy states that progress is possible only through the education and training of high-quality employees. By educating new staff and employees through orientation and yearly conferences, the department ensures that progress toward substantial compliance will continue. Likewise, all newly arriving inmates receive copies of the Consent Decree and are urged to become familiar with its mandates.

Conclusion

While correctional departments nationwide undoubtedly have undergone drastic changes during the past decade, the New Mexico DOC serves as an example of what can be accomplished when change is viewed positively. The training academy is arguably the finest in the country. Likewise, the department has constructed three additional facilities near the main unit to ensure the safety and security of both inmates and staff, and to maintain compliance with the decree. In September 1985, the North Unit was opened in order to house administrative segregation and close and medium security inmates. In April 1988, the South Unit began operation. It houses medium custody inmates. In September 1990, the Minimum Restrict Unit began operation. The addition of these three facilities ensures that inmates of similar classification are grouped accordingly. Likewise, these facilities ensure that crowded conditions similar to those that precipitated the 1980 riot will not reoccur; all four operate as one correctional complex.

In short, the New Mexico DOC is making substantial progress toward becoming a recognized authority on correctional issues. The department retains many of the most knowledgeable individuals within the fields of inmate classification, staff training and prison operations. It is through a combined effort of all the units comprising the DOC and the penitentiary complex that such rapid progress has been possible.

Curtis R. Blakely is a classification specialist at the Roswell Correctional Center, Roswell, N.M. Special thanks to Richard D. Sluder, Ph.D., Central Missouri State University.

The Constitution and the Federal District Judge

Frank M. Johnson

Modern American society depends upon our judicial system to play a critical role in maintaining the balance between governmental powers and individual rights. The increasing concern paid by our courts toward the functioning of government and its agencies has received much comment[1] and some criticism[2] recently. As governmental institutions at all levels have assumed a greater role in providing public services, courts increasingly have been confronted with the unavoidable duty of determining whether those services meet basic constitutional requirements. Time and again citizens have brought to the federal courts, and those courts reluctantly have decided, such basic questions as how and when to make available equal quality public education to all our children; how to guarantee all citizens an opportunity to serve on juries, to vote, and to have their votes counted equally; under what minimal living conditions criminal offenders may be incarcerated; and what minimum standards of care and treatment state institutions must provide the mentally ill and mentally retarded who have been involuntarily committed to the custody of the state.

The reluctance with which courts and judges have undertaken the complex task of deciding such questions has at least three important sources. First, one of the founding principles of our Government,[3] a principle derived from the French philosophers of the eighteenth century, is that the powers of government should be separate and distinct, lest all the awesome power of government unite as one force unchecked in its exercise. The drafters of our Constitution formulated the doctrine of separation of powers to promote the independence of each branch of government in its sphere of operation. To the extent that courts respond to requests to look to the future and to change existing conditions by making new rules, however, they become subject to the charge of usurping authority from the legislative or executive branch.

Second, our Constitution and laws have strictly limited the power of the federal judiciary to participate in what are essentially political affairs. The tenth amendment[4] reserves any power not delegated to the United States to the individual states or to the people. Reflecting the distrust of centralized government expressed by this amendment, courts and citizens alike since the Nation's beginning have regarded certain governmental functions as primarily, if not exclusively, state responsibilities. Among these are public education;[5] maintenance of state and local penal institutions;[6] domestic relations;[7] and provision for the poor, homeless, aged, and infirm.[8] A further limitation on the role of federal courts with respect to other governmental bodies lies in the creation and maintenance of these courts as courts of limited jurisdiction.

Last, federal judges properly hesitate to make decisions either that require the exercise of political judgment[9] or that necessitate expertise they lack.[10] Judges are professionally trained in the law—not in sociology, education, medicine, penology, or public administration. In an ideal society, elected officials would make all decisions relating to the allocation of resources; experts trained in corrections would make all penological decisions; physicians would make all medical decisions; scientists would make all technological decisions; and educators would make all educational decisions. Too often, however, we have failed to achieve this ideal system. Many times, those persons to whom we have entrusted these responsibilities have acted or failed to act in ways that do not fall within the bounds of discretion permitted by the Constitution and the laws. When such transgressions are properly and formally brought before a court—and increasingly before federal courts—it becomes the responsibility of the judiciary to ensure that the Constitution and laws of the United States remain, in fact as well as in theory, the supreme law of the land.

Published originally in 54 Texas L. Rev. 903, (1976).

17. Constitution and the Federal District Judge

On far too many occasions the intransigent and unremitting opposition of state officials who have neglected or refused to correct unconstitutional or unlawful state policies and practices has necessitated federal intervention to enforce the law. Courts in all sections of the Nation have expended and continue to expend untold resources in repeated litigation brought to compel local school officials to follow a rule of law first announced by the Supreme Court almost twenty-two years ago.[11] In addition to deciding scores of school cases, federal courts in Alabama alone have ordered the desegregation of mental institutions,[12] penal facilities,[13] public parks,[14] city buses,[15] interstate and intrastate buses and bus terminals,[16] airport terminals,[17] and public libraries and museums.[18] Although I refer to Alabama, I do not intend to suggest that similar problems do not exist in many of our other states.

The history of public school desegregation has been a story of repeated intervention by the courts to overcome not only the threats and violence of extremists attempting to block school desegregation[19] but also the numerous attempts by local and state officials to thwart the orderly, efficient, and lawful resolution of this complicated social problem.[20] Desegregation is not the only area of state responsibility in which Alabama officials have forfeited their decisionmaking powers by such a dereliction of duty as to require judicial intervention. Having found Alabama's legislative apportionment plan unconstitutional,[21] the District Court for the Middle District of Alabama waited ten years for State officials to carry out the duty properly imposed upon them by the Constitution and expressly set out in the court's order. The continued refusal of those officials to comply left the court no choice but to assume that duty itself and to impose its own reapportionment plan.[22] State officers by their inaction have also handed over to the courts property tax assessment plans,[23] standards for the care and treatment of mentally ill and mentally retarded persons committed to the State's custody;[24] and the procedures by which such persons are committed.[25]

Some of these cases are extremely troublesome and time consuming for all concerned. I speak in particular of those lawsuits challenging the operation of state institutions for the custody and control of citizens who cannot or will not function at a safe and self-sustaining capacity in a free society. Ordinarily these cases proceed as class actions seeking to determine the rights of large numbers of people. As a result, the courts' decisions necessarily have wide-ranging effect and momentous importance, whether they grant or deny the relief sought.

A shocking example of a failure of state officials to discharge their duty was forcefully presented in a lawsuit tried before me in 1972, *Newman v. Alabama*,[26] which challenged the constitutional sufficiency of medical care available to prisoners in the Alabama penal system. The evidence in that case convincingly demonstrated that correctional officers on occasion intentionally denied inmates the right to examination by a physician or to treatment by trained medical personnel, and that they routinely withheld medicine and other treatments prescribed by physicians. Further evidence showed that untrained inmates served as ward attendants and X-ray, laboratory, and dental technicians; rags were used as bandages; ambulance oxygen tanks remained empty for long periods of time; and unsupervised inmates without formal training pulled teeth, gave injections, sutured, and performed minor surgery. In fact, death resulting from gross neglect and totally inadequate treatment was not unusual.

A nineteen-year-old with an extremely high fever who was diagnosed as having acute pneumonia was left unsupervised and allowed to take cold showers at will for two days before his death. An inmate who could not eat received no nourishment for the three days prior to his death even though intravenous feeding had been ordered by a doctor. A geriatric inmate who had suffered a stroke was made to sit each day on a wooden bench so that he would not soil his bed; he frequently fell onto the floor; his legs became swollen from a lack of circulation, necessitating the amputation of a leg the day before his death.[27]

Based on the virtually uncontradicted evidence presented at trial, the district court entered a comprehensive order designed to remedy each specific abuse proved at trial and to establish additional safeguards so that the medical program in Alabama prisons would never again regress to its past level of inadequacy.[28] The State was ordered to bring the general hospital at the Medical and Diagnostic Center (now Kilby Corrections Facility) up to the minimum standards required of hospitals by the United States Department of Health, Education, and Welfare for participation in the medicare program.[29] The court also directed the Alabama State Board of Health to inspect regularly for general sanitation all the medical and food processing facilities in the prison system.[30] Finally, the court decreed that all inmates receive physical examinations by physicians at regular intervals of not more than two years.[31]

One of the most comprehensive orders that I have entered concerning the operating and management of state institutions relates to the facilities maintained by the Alabama Department of Mental Health for the mentally ill and mentally retarded. Plaintiffs in *Wyatt v. Stickney*[32] brought a class action on behalf of all patients involuntarily confined at Bryce Hospital, the State's largest mental hospital, to establish the minimum standards of care and treatment to which the civilly committed are entitled under the Constitution. Patients at Searcy Hospital in southern Alabama and residents at the Partlow State School and Hospital in Tuscaloosa joined the action as plaintiffs, thereby compelling a comprehensive inquiry into the entire Alabama mental health and retardation treatment and habilitation program.

At trial plaintiffs produced evidence showing that Bryce Hospital, built in the 1850's, was grossly overcrowded, housing more than 5000 patients.[33] Of these 5000 people ostensibly committed to Bryce for treatment of mental illness, about 1600—almost one-third—were geriatrics neither needing nor receiving any treatment for mental illness. Another 1000 or more of the patients at Bryce were mentally retarded rather than mentally ill. A totally inadequate staff, only a small percentage professionally trained, served these 5000 patients. The hospital employed only six staff members qualified to deal with mental patients—three medical doctors with psychiatric training, one Ph.D. psychologist, and two social workers with master's degrees in social work. The evidence indicated that the general living conditions and lack of individualized treatment programs were as intolerable and deplorable as Alabama's rank of fiftieth among the states in per patient expenditures[34] would suggest. For example, the hospital spent less than fifty cents per patient each day for food.[35]

The evidence concerning Partlow State School and Hospital for the retarded proved even more shocking than the evidence relating to the mental hospitals. The extremely dangerous conditions compelled the court to issue an interim emergency order[36] requiring Partlow officials to take immediate steps to protect the lives and safety of the residents. The Associate Commissioner for Mental Retardation for the Alabama Department of Mental Health testified that Partlow was sixty percent overcrowded; that the school, although it had not, could immediately discharge at least 300 residents; *and that seventy percent of the residents should never have been committed at all.*[37] The conclusion that there was no opportunity for habilitation for its residents was inescapable. Indeed, the evidence reflected that one resident was scalded to death when a fellow resident hosed water from one of the bath facilities on him; another died as a result of the insertion of a running water hose into his rectum by a working resident who was cleaning him; one died when soapy water was forced into his mouth; another died of a self-administered overdose of inadequately stored drugs; and authorities restrained another resident in a straitjacket for *nine years* to prevent him from sucking his hands and fingers. Witnesses described the Partlow facilities as barbaric and primitive;[38] some residents had no place to sit to eat meals, and coffee cans served as toilets in some areas of the institution.

With the exception of the interim emergency order designed to eliminate hazardous conditions at Partlow, the court at first declined to devise specific steps to improve existing conditions in Alabama's mental health and retardation facilities. Instead, it directed the Department of Mental Health to design its own plan for upgrading the system to meet constitutional standards.[39] Only after two deadlines had passed without any signs of acceptable progress did the court itself, relying upon the proposals of counsel for all parties and amici curiae, define the minimal constitutional standards of care, treatment, and habilitation[40] for which the case of *Wyatt v. Stickney* has become generally known.

During the past several years conditions at the Partlow State School for the retarded have improved markedly. It was pleasing to read in a Montgomery newspaper that members of the State Mental Health Board (the *Wyatt* defendants) recently met at Partlow and agreed that "what they saw was a different world" compared to four years ago; that "things are now unbelievably better," with most students "out in the sunshine on playground swings or tossing softballs[,] . . . responding to a kind word or touch with smiles and squeals of delight"; and that "enrollment has been nearly cut in half, down from 2,300 to just under 1,300 while the staff has tripled from 600 to 1,800."[41]

Persons incarcerated in state and local prison and jail facilities around the Nation increasingly have attacked the conditions of their confinement as unconstitutional. In recent years, federal courts in Alabama,[42] Arkansas,[43] Florida,[44] Maryland,[45] Massachusetts,[46] and Mississippi,[47] among others, have been forced to declare that the constitutional rights of inmates are denied by the mere fact of their confinement in institutions that inflict intolerable and inhuman living conditions. In Texas a federal judge has held unconstitutional the detention of juveniles in certain facilities maintained by the Texas Youth Council because of the extreme brutality and indifference experienced in these institutions.[48] In fashioning appropriate remedies in these cases, the courts have exhibited sensitivity to the real but not the imagined limitations imposed on correctional officials forced to operate penal facilities with the meager sums appropriated by legislators who see few or no political rewards in supporting constitutional treatment of prisoners. Some courts have ordered that entire institutions be closed and abandoned;[49] others have required substantial improvements in facilities and services as a precondition to their continued operation.[50]

Knowing firsthand the considerable time, energy, and thought that must precede any decision affecting mental hospital or prison conditions, I seriously doubt that any judge relishes his involvement in such a controversy or enters a decree unless the law clearly makes it his duty to do so. The Fifth Circuit adheres to the well-settled rule that federal courts do not sit to supervise state prisons or to interfere with their internal operation and administration.[51] The American system of justice, however, equally acknowledges that inmates do not lose all constitutional rights and privileges when they are confined following conviction of criminal offenses.[52]

James v. Wallace,[53] a recent class action tried before me objecting to conditions in Alabama's state penal facilities, presents another graphic example of how a state's irresponsibility in carrying out an essential governmental function necessitated federal judicial intervention to restore constitutional rights to citizens whose rights were systematically disregarded and denied. Preserving prisoners' rights is no less vital than safeguarding the liberties of school children, black citizens, women, and others who have found it necessary to resort to the courts to secure their constitutional rights.[54] The *James* trial began last August following extensive pretrial discovery, which included more than 1000 facts stipulated to by all parties and filed with the court. At the close of the defendants' case, the lead counsel for the Governor and the State Board of Corrections acknowledged in open court that "the overwhelming majority of the evidence... shows that an Eighth Amendment violation has and is now occurring to inmates in the Alabama prison system."[55]

Plaintiffs in *James* demonstrated the intolerability of life in Alabama's prisons by proof of both general living conditions and commonplace incidents. Fighting, assault, extortion, theft, and homosexual rape are everyday occurrences in all four main institutions. A mentally retarded twenty-year-old inmate, after testifying that doctors had told him he had the mind of a five-year-old, told in open court how four inmates raped him on his first night in an Alabama prison.[56]

The evidence showed that most prisoners found it necessary to carry some form of homemade or contraband weapon merely for self-protection. One prisoner testified that he would rather be caught with a weapon by a prison guard than be caught without one by another prisoner.[57] Seriously dilapidated physical facilities have created generally unsanitary and hazardous living conditions in Alabama's prison. Roaches, flies, mosquitoes, and other vermin overrun the institutions. One living area in Draper prison housing over 200 men contained one functioning toilet.

A United States public health officer, testifying as an expert witness after having inspected the four major prisons, pronounced the facilities wholly unfit for human habitation according to virtually every criterion used for evaluation by public health inspectors. He testified that as a public health officer, he would recommend the closing of any similar facilities under his jurisdiction because they presented an imminent danger to the health of the exposed individuals.[58] Moreover, all the parties to the lawsuit agreed that severe overcrowding and understaffing aggravated all these other difficulties. At the time of trial over 3500 prisoners resided in facilities designed for no more than 2300. The Commissioner of the Alabama Board of Corrections testified that although the prison system required a minimum staff of 692 correctional officers, it then employed 383.[59] Correctional experts testified that such an overflow of prisoners, coupled with the shortage of supervisory personnel, precludes any meaningful control over the institutions by the responsible officials. The facts bore out that conclusion. Prison guards simply refused to enter some dormitories at night,[60] and one warden testified that he would not enter a certain dormitory at his institution without at least four guards by his side.

Understaffing and lack of funds have deprived nearly all the inmates who are confined twenty-four hours a day of meaningful activity; usually they lie around idle. Most live in dormitories or barracks that afford them neither privacy nor security for their personal possessions. The defendants stipulated that over half of the prison population possessed no skills, and that in the first quarter of 1975 the average entering inmate could not read at the sixth-grade level. The few vocational training and basic education programs offered can accommodate only a tiny fraction of the inmates, and the entry requirements for the programs are highly restrictive. Alabama prisons do not have a working classification system, an essential ingredient of any properly operated penal system. A functioning classification system enables officials to segregate for treatment and for the protection of other prisoners not able or willing to function in any social setting. Currently, mentally disturbed inmates receive no special care or therapy, and are housed and treated like the general prison population. Consequently, violent and aggressive prisoners live together with those who are weak, passive, or otherwise easily victimized. For example, when the twenty-year-old inmate I spoke of earlier reported the rape to prison officials, the warden of the institution told him that he, the warden, could do nothing about it.

Since the final order in *James*, new reports have revealed other instances of what at best constitute questionable management practices. A committee of the Alabama Legislature investigating prison operations disclosed that financial records reflect the use of prison funds to purchase cases of caviar, evidently consumed in the course of entertaining legislators.[61] The committee also questioned a recent transaction in which the Alabama Board of Corrections approved the bartering of fifty-two head of beef cattle owned by the Board in exchange for three Tennessee walking horses. The Commissioner of Corrections publicly explained that the horses were acquired for breeding purposes.[62] It later developed that the horses obtained for breeding purposes were geldings.[63]

Based on the overwhelming and generally undisputed evidence presented at trial, the court granted immediate partial relief to plaintiffs in the form of two interim orders,[64] which remain in effect. One order enjoined the State from accepting additional prisoners, except escapees and parole violators, until each State prison facility decreases its population to its design capacity. The second ruling banned the use of isolation and segregation cells that fail to meet minimum standards. Before this order, as many as six inmates were confined in four-by-eight foot cells with no beds, no lighting, no running water, and a hole in the floor for a toilet that only a guard outside could flush.

The final opinion and order entered in *James* in January 1976 established a broad range of minimum standards[65] designed to remedy the broad range of constitutional deprivations proven at trial and conceded to exist by the State's lawyers. The standards govern staffing; classification of prisoners; mental and physical health care; physical facilities; protection of inmates; and educational, vocational, recreational, and work programs.

The fourteenth amendment,[66] which generates much of the litigation discussed above, forbids a state to "deprive any person of life, liberty or property, without due process of law" or to "deny to any person within its jurisdiction the equal protection of the laws."[67] The Supreme Court has interpreted the due process clause to require that the states fulfill most of the obligation toward citizens that the Bill of Rights imposes on the federal government.[68] Each state in all its dealing with its people must recognize and preserve their guaranteed freedoms. Nevertheless, state officials have frequently raised the tenth amendments's reservation of powers to the states as a defense to the exercise of federal jurisdiction over actions alleging state violations of constitutional rights. While the tenth amendment clearly preserves for the states a wide and important sphere of power, it does not permit any state to frustrate or to ignore the mandates of the Constitution. *The tenth amendment does not relieve the states of a single obligation imposed upon them by the Constitution of the United States.* Surely the concept of states' rights has never purported to allow states to abdicate their responsibility to protect their citizens from criminal acts and inhumane conditions. I find it sad and ironic that citizens of Alabama held in "protective custody" by Alabama had to obtain federal court orders to protect themselves from violent crimes and barbaric conditions.

The cornerstone of our American legal system rests on recognition of the Constitution as the supreme law of the land,[69] and the paramount duty of the federal judiciary is to uphold that law.[70] Thus, when a state fails to meet constitutionally mandated requirements, it is the solemn duty of the courts to assure compliance with the Constitution. One writer has termed the habit adopted by some states of neglecting their responsibilities until faced with a federal court order "the Alabama Federal Intervention Syndrome," characterizing it as

> the tendency of many state officials to punt their problems with constituencies to the federal courts. Many federal judges have grown accustomed to allowing state officials to make political speeches as a prelude to receiving the order of the district court. This role requires the federal courts to serve as a buffer between the state officials and their constituencies, raising the familiar criticism that state officials rely upon the federal courts to impose needed reforms rather than accomplishing them themselves.[71]

As long as those state officials entrusted with the responsibility for fair and equitable governance completely disregard that responsibility, the judiciary must and will stand ready to intervene on behalf of the deprived. Judge Richard T. Rives of the Court of Appeals for the Fifth Circuit, in joining a three-judge panel that struck down attempts by state officials to frustrate the registration of black voters, eloquently expressed the reluctance with which the vast majority of federal judges approach intervention in state affairs:

> I look forward to the day when the State and its political subdivisions will again take up their mantle of responsibility, treating all of their citizens equally, and thereby relieve the federal Government of the necessity of intervening in their affairs. Until that day arrives, the responsibility for this intervention must rest with those who through their ineptitude and public disservice have forced it.[72]

We in the judiciary await the day when the Alabama Federal Intervention Syndrome, in that State and elsewhere, will become a relic of the past. To reclaim responsibilities passed by default to the judiciary—most often the federal judiciary—and to find solutions for ever-changing challenges, the states must preserve their ability to respond flexibly, creatively, and with due regard for the rights of all. State officials must confront their governmental responsibilities with the diligence and honesty that their constituencies deserve. When lawful rights are being denied, only the exercise of conscientious, responsible leadership, which is usually long on work and short on complimentary news headlines, can avoid judicial intervention. The most fitting Bicentennial observance I can conceive would be for all government officials to take up the constitutional mantle and diligently strive to protect the basic human rights recognized by the founders of our Republic two hundred years ago.

Notes

1. See, e.g., L. Levy, Judgments 35–57 (1972); Mason, *Judicial Activism: Old and New,* 55 Va. L. Rev. 385, 394–426 (1969).
2. See, e.g., Griswold, *The Judicial Process,* 31 Fed. B. J. 309, 321–25 (1972).
3. See *The Federalist* Nos. 47, 48 (J. Madison).
4. *U.S. Const.* amend. X.
5. Cumming v. Richmond County Bd. of Educ., 175 U.S. 528, 545 (1899); Crews v. Cloncs, 432 F.2d 1259 (7th Cir. 1970).
6. Hoag v. New Jersey, 356 U.S. 464 (1958); Threatt v. North Carolina, 221 F. Supp. 858, 860 (W.D.N.C. 1963).
7. Ohio *ex. rel.* Popovici v. Agler, 280 U.S. 379, 383 (1930); Morris v. Morris, 273 F.2d 678, 682 (7th Cir. 1960); Ainscow v. Alexander, 28 Del. Ch. 545, 550, 39 A.2d 54, 56 (Super, Ct. 1944).
8. Adkins v. Curtis, 259 Ala. 311, 315, 66 So. 2d 455, 458 (1953); Beck v. Buena Park Hotel Corp., 30 Ill. 2d 343, 346, 196 N.E.2d 686, 688 (1964); Collins v. State Bd. of Social Welfare, 248 Iowa 369, 375, 81 N.W.2d 4, 7 (1957).
9. See, e.g., Marbury v. Madison, 5 U.S. (1 Cranch) 137, 170 (1803).
10. See, e.g., Brotherhood of Locomotive Firemen v. Chicago, R.I. & P.R.R., 393 U.S. 129, 136–37 (1968).
11. Brown v. Board of Educ., 347 U.S. 484 (1954).
12. Marable v. Mental Health Bd., 297 F. Supp. 291 (M.D. Ala. 1969).
13. Washington v. Lee, 263 F. Supp. 327 (M.D. Ala. 1966), aff'd, 390 U.S. 333 (1968).
14. Gilmore v. City of Montgomery, 176 F. Supp. 776 (M.D. Ala. 1959), *modified,* 277 F.2d 364 (5th Cir. 1960), *rev'd in part,* 417 U.S. 556 (1974).
15. Browder v. Gayle, 142 F. Supp. 707 (M.D. Ala.), aff'd, 352 U.S. 903 (1956).
16. Lewis v. Greyhound Corp., 199 F. Supp. 210 (M.D. Ala. 1961).
17. United States v. City of Montgomery, 201 F. Supp. 590 (M.D. Ala. 1962).
18. Cobb v. Library Bd., 207 F. Supp. 88Q (M.D. Ala. 1962).
19. United States v. United Klans of America, 290 F. Supp. 181 (M.D. Ala. 1968).
20. Harris v. Board of Educ., 259 F. Supp. 167 (M.D. Ala. 1966); Lee v. Board of Educ., 213 F. Supp. 743 (M.D. Ala. 1964).
21. Sims v. Frink, 208 F. Supp. 431 (M.D. Ala. 1962), aff'd sub nom. Reynolds v. Sims, 377 U.S. 533 (1964).
22. Sims v. Amos, 336 F. Supp. 924 (M.D. Ala), aff'd, 409 U.S. 942 (1972).
23. Weissinger v. Boswell, 330 F. Supp. 615 (M.D. Ala. 1971) (per curiam).
24. Wyatt v. Stickney, 324 F. Supp. 781 (M.D. Ala. 1971), *enforced,* 344 F. Supp. 373 (M.D. Ala. 1972) (mentally ill) *and* 344 F. Supp. 387 (M.D. Ala. 1972), *modified sub nom.* Wyatt v. Aderholt, 503 F.2d 1305 (5th Cir. 1974) (mentally retarded).
25. Lynch v. Baxley, 386 F. Supp. 378 (M.D. Ala. 1974).

26. 349 F. Supp. 278 (M.D. Ala. 1972), *aff'd in part*, 503 F.2d 1320 (5th Cir. 1974), *cert. denied*, 421 U.S. 948 (1975).
27. *Id.* at 285.
28. *Id.* at 286–288.
29. *Id.* at 286.
30. *Id.* at 287.
31. *Id.*
32. 325 F. Supp. 781 (M.D. Ala. 1971), *enforced*, 344 F. Supp. 373 (M.D. Ala. 1972) *and* 344 F. Supp. 387 (M.D. Ala. 1972), *modified sub nom.* Wyatt v. Aderholt, 503 F.2d 1305 (5th Cir. 1974) (affirming constitutional "right to treatment").
33. *Id.* at 782.
34. *Id.* at 784.
35. Wyatt v. Aderholt, 503 F.2d 1305, 1310 (5th Cir. 1974).
36. Wyatt v. Stickney, Civil No. 3195-N (M.D. Ala., Mar. 2, 1972) (emergency order). This order preceded the final order.
37. Wyatt v. Aderholt, 503 F.2d 1305, 1310 (5th Cir. 1974).
38. *See* Wyatt v. Stickney, 344 F. Supp. 387, 391 n.7 (M.D. Ala. 1972).
39. Wyatt v. Stickney, 325 F. Supp. 781, 785–86 (M.D. Ala. 1971).
40. 344 F. Supp. at 395–409 (Partlow State School); 344 F. Supp. at 379–86 (Bryce Hospital).
41. Reese, *Things Unbelievably Better at Partlow, Directory Says,* Alabama Journal, Feb. 20, 1976, at 13, cols. 3–4.
42. McCray v. Sullivan, Civil. No. 5620-69-H (S.D. Ala., Feb. 10, 1976); James v. Wallace, 406 F. Supp. 318 (M.D. Ala. 1976).
43. Holt v. Sarver, 309 F. Supp. 362 (E.D. Ark. 1970), *aff'd*, 442 F.2d 304 (8th Cir. 1971).
44. Costello v. Wainwright, 397 F. Supp. 20 (M.D. Fla. 1975), *aff'd*, 525 F.2d 1239, *rehearing in banc granted*, 528 F.2d 1381 (Mar. 3, 1976) (No. 75-2392).
45. Collins v. Schoonfield, 344 F. Supp. 257 (D.Md. 1972).
46. Inmates of Suffolk County Jail v. Eisenstadt, 360 F. Supp. 676 (D. Mass. 1973), *aff'd*, 494 F.2d 1196 (1st Cir.) *cert. denied*, 419 U.S. 977 (1974).
47. Gates v. Collier, 349 F. Supp. 881 (N.D. Miss. 1972), *aff'd*, 501 F.2d 1291 (5th Cir. 1974).
48. Morales v. Turman, 383 F. Supp. 53 (E.D. Tex. 1974).
49. *Id.*
50. James v. Wallace, 406 F. Supp. 318 (M.D. Ala. 1976); Costello v. Wainwright, 397 F. Supp. 20 (M.D. Fla. 1975), *aff'd*, 525 F.2d 1239 (5th Cir. 1976).
51. Novak v. Beto, 453 F.2d 661,. 671 (5th Cir. 1971); Newman v. Alabama, 349 F. Supp. 278, 280 (M.D. Ala. 1972), *aff'd in part*, 503 F.2d 1320 (5th Cir. 1974), *cert. denied*, 421 U.S. 948 (1975).
52. Washington v. Lee, 263 F. Supp. 327, 331 (M.D. Ala. 1966), *aff'd per curiam*, 390 U.S. 333 (1968).
53. 406 F. Supp. 318 (M.D. Ala. 1976).
54. Recently courts have recognized that prisoners retain all their constitutional rights except those necessarily diminished as an incident of incarceration. See Pell v. Procunier, 417 U.S. 817, 822 (1973); Jackson v. Godwin, 400 F.2d 529, 532 (5th Cir. 1968); James v. Wallace, 406 F. Supp. 318, 328 (M.D. Ala. 1976).
55. Record, vol. II, at 357. The eighth amendment prohibits "cruel and unusual punishments." *U.S. Const.* amend. VIII.
56. 406 F. Supp. at 325.
57. *Id.*
58. *Id.* at 323–24.
59. *Id.* at 325.
60. *Id.*
61. Montgomery Advertiser, Feb. 6, 1976, at 1, cols. 5–8.
62. *Id.*
63. Alabama Journal, Feb. 6, 1976, at 13, cols. 5–6.
64. 406 F. Supp. at 322, 327.
65. *Id.* at 332–35.
66. *U.S. Const.* amend. XIV.
67. *Id.*
68. Duncan v. Louisiana, 391 U.S. 145 (1968).
69. See *U.S. Const.* art VI, § 2.
70. See Mitchum v. Foster, 407 U.S. 225, 238–39 (1972); Zwickler v. Koota, 389 U.S. 241, 248 (1967); England v. Louisiana State Bd. of Medical Examiners, 375 U.S. 411, 415 (1964).
71. McCormack, *The Expansion of Federal Question Jurisdiction and the Prisoner Complaint Caseload*, 1975 Wis. L. Rev. 523, 536 (footnotes omitted).
72. Dent v. Duncan, 360 F.2d 333, 337–38 (5th Cir. 1966).

Unit 3

Unit Selections

18. **Like Mother, Like Daughter: Why More Young Women Follow Their Moms into Lives of Crime,** Toni Locy
19. **Percentage of Women on Probation and Parole Rising,** *Jet*
20. **Addressing the Needs of Elderly Offenders,** Connie L. Neeley, Laura Addison, and Delores Craig-Moreland
21. **Elder Care: Louisiana Initiates Program to Meet Needs of Aging Inmate Population,** Jean Wall
22. **Chaser: A Medication Addict,** Victor Hassine
23. **Mental Health and Treatment of Inmates and Probationers,** Paula M. Ditton
24. **Juveniles in Federal Prison,** Jack Kresnak
25. **Re-Forming Juvenile Justice: The New Zealand Experiment,** Allison Morris and Gabrielle Maxwell

Key Points to Consider

- Which of the "less common offenders" were you most surprised to find in prison and why?
- What were some of the unique problems that these different populations caused for the prison?
- Does the prison administration have an obligation to make prison more humane for all the different populations in the prison? Why or why not? What policies would you change to make prisons more humane for these different populations?
- Do you believe that the prison administration has an obligation to be considerate to the families of these different populations in the prison? What policies might you change to make prisons more humane for the families of some of these different populations? Which populations would you consider most important?
- What are some of the explanations offered for the changes in imprisonment rates for these unusual populations?
- Why would some inmates choose to be medicated for problems that are not caused by mental illness but by the living conditions in the prison?
- Why are we seeing more federal-level crimes and consequently more federal-level criminals?
- How does the experience of New Zealand mirror the experiences of the juvenile justice system in the United States? How similar are these problems to your area?

DUSHKIN ONLINE Links — www.dushkin.com/online/

19. **Basics of Juvenile Justice**
    http://www.uaa.alaska.edu/just/just110/intro2.html
20. **Behind Bars: Aging Prison Population Challenges Correctional Health Systems**
    http://www.nurseweek.com/features/99-7/prison.html
21. **Center for Rational Correctional Policy**
    http://pierce.simplenet.com
22. **Institute for Intergovernmental Research (IIR)**
    http://www.iir.com
23. **Juvenile Justice Documents: Corrections**
    http://www.ncjrs.org/jjcorr.htm

These sites are annotated on pages 4 and 5.

Unusual Problems and Unusual Populations

In this section the less common offenders in prison are examined. We look at some of the unique problems that this population generates.

The first article in the unit discusses the relationship between incarcerated mothers and their daughters, who see mom as both an offender and a role model. The next article points out that this situation is increasing with regard to women on probation and parole as well.

The elderly inmate is a unique and expanding population. "Addressing the Needs of Elderly Offenders" examines the problems of survival in a hostile environment, and discusses the changes that need to be made in prison structure and operations. Then, "Elder Care: Louisiana Initiates Program to Meet Needs of Aging Inmate Population" suggests ways to make the correctional environment more humane for this growing element of our correctional population.

Next, we turn our attention to a population that has been serving time in prisons and jails as long as prisons and jails have existed: the mentally ill. In the following two articles note how some prisons "medicalize" inmate misbehavior in order to justify the use of "chemical confinement" to simplify prison operations. Also note how the differences among mental illness, substance abuse, and criminal behavior have become blurred in recent years.

Finally, in the last two articles, observe how the federal government's interest in local crime control has resulted in increased numbers of juveniles in federal prisons. The problem of juvenile crime is not unique to the United States, and the problems faced in the United States are strangely similar to the problems faced halfway around the world in New Zealand, as the last article in this unit demonstrates.

Like mother, like daughter

Why more young women follow their moms into lives of crime

By Toni Locy

Anita Wallace was boasting. About how much she loves getting high, how much she loves stealing. She can't remember how many times she has been busted, she says. There have been so many. But her bravado vanishes as fast as a hit of the heroin she loves so much. Holding her pencil-thin arms close to her sides, she listens, for maybe the first time, as her daughter, Starr, tells how her mother made so many promises—then broke every single one. "Everybody else had their mom," says Starr, 18. "I know what it's like not to have my mom for a significant part of my life. I didn't know who to turn to, so I turned to myself."

From age 11, after her mother disappeared on a drug binge or got thrown in jail, Starr got the job of caring for her sister and younger brothers. She rebelled. Before too long, the good girl, as she called herself, went bad. She started drinking, stopped going to school. She went out with gang members. She robbed a guy delivering pizzas. Much as she despised her mother's lifestyle, Starr was following headlong in her footsteps. And like her mom, in the end, she was locked up, too.

Women have been going to jail for just about as long as there have been jails, but their numbers have always been far smaller than those of male inmates. That's still the case. Today there are about 83,000 women behind bars—about 6 percent of the nation's 1.2 million prisoners. But something new is going on—something frightening. Women today are being jailed at a rate much faster than men. Between 1986 and 1991, the incarceration rate for drug offenses for black women increased nearly twice as fast as for black men—828 percent over 429 percent. For women, generally, the incarceration rate jumped 516 percent between 1980 and 1998. There are reasons for that. Women who work in low-level roles in drug organizations are more likely to get caught by police and less likely to be able to cut deals with prosecutors.

But there's more to it than that. It has long been known that sons of criminal fathers often follow them to jail. Now, police and prosecutors are seeing the trend increasingly replicated among women. Women like Anita and Starr Wallace. To explore this trend, *U.S. News* polled juvenile-justice agencies nationwide. Twenty-one states responded. Of the 10 that provided data on boys and girls, all but one reported that more girls proportionately than boys had mothers who had been previously arrested. One state, Iowa, reported that 64 percent of its female juvenile delinquents said their mothers had criminal records. While it is still a rarity, more mothers and daughters are being locked up at the same time, for the exact same crimes.

Ties that bind. The *U.S. News* survey, the first of its kind, startled some experts. "Initially, I was surprised," said Meda Chesney-Lind of the University of Hawaii, one of the country's leading researchers on girls and crime. "There's no data on this issue. What you have done is illustrate that the damage done to girls is arguably more traumatic than it is for their brothers in having their mother incarcerated."

Why this may be so isn't clear. Welfare dependency, for instance, is known to have jumped from one generation to the next. A similar phenomenon may now be occurring among women who commit crimes, but the available data are insufficient to say so with certainty. What is clear is that the emotional ties between mothers and daughters are so strong that they are less likely to be broken than those of the opposite sex by abuse, absenteeism, or criminality. "The mother-daughter bond is so strong, so visceral, it can't really be explained just intellectually," says Evelyn Bassoff, a Boulder, Colo., psychologist who has written extensively on the subject. The connection between mothers and daughters is stronger than with sons, Bassoff says, because boys must break away from their mothers to become men. "But

18. Like Mother, Like Daughter

for a girl, there's never that break," Bassoff adds. "Her mother is her identity."

Even if that identity is one of a criminal or a drug user. The profiles of a typical adult female offender and a female juvenile delinquent are strikingly similar. Both are poorly educated, live in poverty, and make dismal choices in men. Both have been physically and sexually abused. Both have problems with drugs and alcohol, which they often use to medicate the pain of what has been done to them. History is repeating itself—only faster. The girls seem to be trying drugs and having babies at younger ages, with generations separated by as few as 13 or 14 years.

Some factors can be cited with reasonable certainty. A major culprit is crack. It didn't just make addicts of women; it made them criminals. Many women landed behind bars for selling or possessing the drug. But others got locked up for forgery, shoplifting, and prostitution while trying to make money to buy it. Justice Department studies say most crack orphans went to live with their grandmothers, aunts, or other female relatives when their mothers got locked up. Some went to live with their fathers, while the rest were placed in foster care. No one knows how many girls saw their lives so disrupted.

What is clear is that by the time a mother goes off to jail, her children's lives have already been turned inside out. In interviews with 30 mothers who are or have recently been incarcerated, and with 20 daughters, the pattern emerged again and again. Karen Denise Faulkner is one of the mothers. The 39-year-old from Amarillo, Texas, had it all: the kids, the husband, the house with the two-car garage. But at night, as her children slept, she slipped away, got into her car, and went to score crack. She'd stay up all night, getting high. When morning came, she'd hop back into bed to make her kids believe she'd been there all along.

Even when aberrant behavior is far more obvious, the ties between mother and daughter somehow manage to endure. Beverly Hamilton and her daughter, Esther Shawn, were incarcerated together at Minnesota's prison for women in Shakopee after they robbed an Arby's in 1997. Shawn, as she prefers to be called, claims she concocted the scheme so she could get money to leave her mother, a crack addict who had begun stealing from her children to buy drugs. Because Shawn and her friends didn't know how to drive, Shawn, now 20, asked her mother to drive the getaway car. The girls had a .22 rifle and went in at closing time. Beverly, now 37, wasn't there when they came out. Shawn and her friends, moneybags and gun in hand, ran down the street, searching frantically for Beverly. When they spotted her driving around aimlessly, they screamed to get her attention. They were almost home when police pulled them over; a customer at the drive-through had gotten the car's tag number. "I try not to blame her," Shawn says. "She shouldn't have done it. We both should've thought before we did it." Beverly, who has been released to a halfway house, says, "I should've been stronger." Someday, Shawn knows she will have to apologize to her own daughter. The 4-year-old lives with her father now. She doesn't remember who Shawn is.

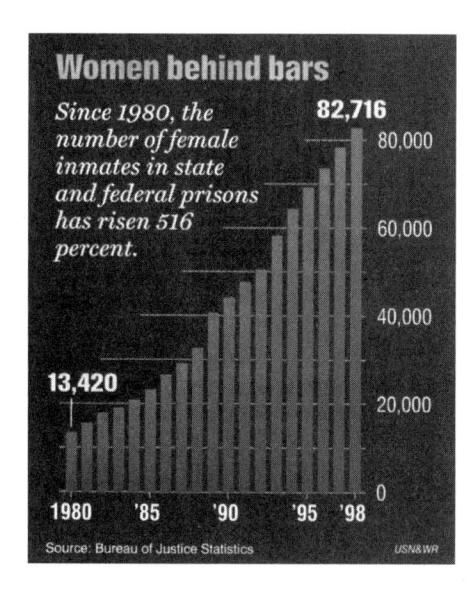

Women behind bars

Since 1980, the number of female inmates in state and federal prisons has risen 516 percent.

1980: 13,420 — 1998: 82,716

Source: Bureau of Justice Statistics — USN&WR

Drugs are an obvious lure into a life of crime for women, but so, surprisingly, are gangs. During her mother's first prison stint, Michelle Barnes was a member of a prison teen group that was set up to help mothers and children deal with the separation of incarceration. Now, she's an inmate, too. She and her mother, Mary Braxton, 50, are doing time together for a 1995 murder. "I've had the best my mom could give me," says Barnes, 27, formerly of Minneapolis. Barnes says she stabbed the victim because the woman was punching her mother. With them, history has repeated itself, double time. Braxton was locked up before at Shakopee for participating in a 1985 gang killing of a 16-year-old girl. Barnes says she grew up around violence because her mother was part of a gang. "I've seen murders. I've seen robberies. And this was all before the age of 14." Braxton says she knows how bad this looks. "I take the fault," she whispers. But Barnes defends her. She says she can separate the bad from the good in her mother. And she insists there is good. "I could've been a lot worse than I am," Barnes says. "It may not have been the ideal motherly type of thing, but I appreciate it."

Mommy dearest. *U.S. News* asked states as different as Iowa and Texas and Hawaii and Arizona to poll girls in custody, and they reached similar results. Iowa led, with 16 of 25 girls, or 64 percent, saying their mothers had been arrested. In Texas, 14 of 23 girls, or nearly 61 percent, said their mothers had been arrested. And in Hawaii, 5 of 10 girls said their mothers had criminal records, while 28 of 103 Arizona girls said their moms had been in trouble with the law. In California, according to a separate study by the National Council on Crime and Delinquency, more than half the nearly 200 girls locked up in four California counties said their mothers had been incarcerated during their childhoods.

"We thought, 'Wow!' " says Mary Nelson, Iowa's administrator of adult, children, and family services. "This certainly suggests that additional research is appropriate." Through the more scientific method of random sampling, Colorado, Florida, and Ohio found that 51 percent, 49 percent, and 44 percent of girls in their systems, respectively, had mothers who had been arrested or incarcerated. The entire survey is available at *www.usnews.com*

Social workers and probation officers at times urge troubled girls to cut ties to law-breaking mothers, but it's the rare teenage girl who can. From one sentence to the next, a letter from Arnessa Hardin to her mother, Cynthia, 37, in a prison in Gatesville, Texas, shows the roller coaster of feelings she has for her mother. "I wish you were here with me. Please hurry and come home," she writes. "I want a mother to let me know things." She also tries to be encouraging. "Mommy, please make your way through this time because now is all we have." But Arnessa is 15 and angry. "I know for a fact if you would have spent a little more time, I'd be a better person."

3 ❖ UNUSUAL PROBLEMS AND UNUSUAL POPULATIONS

Most people would tell Starr and Arnessa to get away from their mothers, that their moms deserve to be locked up and have their children taken from them. Angry as they are, many girls still want to be with their moms. Because of that loyalty, juvenile officials and child welfare workers say it is worth trying to help the mother to help the daughter. "We forget that when we take a child away from a mother, we put the child in an under-funded state program," says Warren Hurlbut, the Rhode Island Training School's superintendent. "These kids are not going to ideal situations . . . and they are not getting help."

Some probation officers and judges agree that foster care is often worse than leaving children with their drug-addicted mothers. James R. Milliken, presiding judge of San Diego County's juvenile court, says a child in foster care for more than three years will suffer psychological damage beyond repair. "We want them with Mom"—whenever possible, he says. That goal is at odds with recent state and federal laws that make it easier—and faster—to take children from their parents. Those laws may work for younger children, who are more easily adopted. But, says Rose Bruzzo, deputy director of social services for the District of Columbia's Superior Court, no one wants troubled teenage girls.

Grandma to the rescue. And the truth is that some mothers have had problems since they were teenagers. Dollie Richardson, 44, formerly of Ann Arbor, Mich., has spent most of the past 19 years in jail or prison, mainly for theft-type cases. She has a drug addiction that dates back to her early teens, and she doesn't feel comfortable outside prison walls. She has four children—all of whom were born behind bars. Cooking a Thanksgiving turkey terrifies her. "I don't want my life to be in vain," she says. "I love my kids. I really do. Maybe I just don't care enough about myself. But everything is, like, a struggle for me. I'm afraid."

Richardson's daughter, also named Dollie, is 16 and consumed with memories of her mother, like the time she watched her steal a fur coat. She also can't forget seeing her little sister, Marriah, a crack baby who is now 7, go through withdrawal. But Dollie doesn't feel completely abandoned, says Joyce Dixson, an ex-inmate and founder of Sons and Daughters of the Incarcerated in Ann Arbor, Mich. She has her grandmother. When the drug epidemic began in the 1980s, grandparents stepped in to help. At first, they thought that taking care of their grandchildren would be temporary, until their daughters kicked their drug habits and got their lives back together. But then the daughters started getting locked up.

Around the country, juvenile and child welfare authorities are realizing that girls are in trouble. "Until 1992, I didn't think much about girls either," says Judy Mayer of Maryland's juvenile-justice system. "But, holy cow, we started getting the data [on girls being locked up] and, my lord, we realized this is a terrible thing." So Maryland launched FIT (the Female Intervention Team) in Baltimore City, assigning all-female caseloads to probation officers trained to deal exclusively with girls. The program has kept many Baltimore girls from getting into trouble again and being pulled deeper into the system. Today, FIT's "gender-specific programming" is all the rage in juvenile-justice circles, where officials are finally accepting that girls are as different from boys as women are from men. "There isn't any magic to this," says Geno Natalucci-Persichetti, Ohio's juvenile services director, who believes social workers should get back to the basics and help families at the first signs of trouble. "What we need to do is get smart on crime."

Percentage of women on probation and parole rising
U.S. Justice Dept. Report

A report shows an increase in the percentage of women on parole and probation. The percentage of women on probation increased from 16% in 1985 to 21% in 1996, and female parolees increased from 7% in 1985 to 8% in 1990. Black women accounted for over ⅓ of probationers and ½ of parolees.

A growing number of people on probation and parole in the United States are women, according to the latest statistics from the U.S. Justice Department.

Last year, 515,600 women were on probation, which accounted for 21 percent of all adults on probation. The number increased from 18 percent in 1990 and from 16 percent in 1985.

The number of women on parole in 1996 was 79,300, which increased from 8 percent in 1990 and from 7 percent in 1985.

Men still account for four of every five arrests, but the number of women involved in crime is increasing, according to Allen Beck of the Bureau of Justice Statistics.

Beck told the Washington Post that the number of women arrested for driving while intoxicated increased sharply. In 1986, 5.5 percent of those charged were women, but 14 percent were women in 1995.

Beck said offenses such as fraud, larceny, theft and drug offenses are more prevalent among women parolees than men.

More than one-third of all probationers and about one-half of all parolees were Black. Nearly two-thirds of probationers and half of parolees were White. And Hispanics made up 15 percent of probationers and 20 percent of parolees.

Parole is supervised release after a prison term, while probation is a broad term covering supervision by a probation agency.

From *Jet*, September 8, 1997, p. 40. © 1997 by U.S. Dept. of Justice. Reprinted by permission.

Addressing the needs of elderly offenders

Medical Care, Physical Environment Are of Special Concern

Prison inmates who are aged 51 and beyond will make up 33% of total prison population by the year 2010. To accommodate the needs of the aging prisoners, corrections professionals are advised to adopt proactive prison management that takes into consideration humanitarian concerns, balance and safety, and money. Balance and safety refer to the accessibility of prison areas while humanitarian concerns involve keeping aged inmates in the prison workforce, helping them maintain family ties, and assuring them access to medical and mental health specialists.

Connie L. Neeley, Laura Addison, and Delores Craig-Moreland

The U.S. Census Bureau reports that the elderly are the fastest-growing segment of the population—a statistic which already is reflected in the increase in elderly inmates in America's prisons. Inmates over the age of 50 will comprise 33 percent of the total prison population by the year 2010, says Judy Hudson, chief of nursing services for the Missouri Department of Corrections. "Inmates are serving more mandatory sentences and longer terms, and release policies are becoming more restrictive."

How can corrections accommodate this aging prison population? According to geriatric criminal specialists, most prisons are built for young offenders who are locked up, taught a trade and sent back into society. But by the year 2000, an estimated 125,000 inmates will be 50 or older, and 35,000 of them will be over 65.

Corrections professionals must adopt proactive plans to provide for these elderly inmates, taking into consideration many elements of prison management, including balance and safety, humanitarian concerns and money. Balance and safety issues include the basics of designing spaces that are accessible to the elderly. They should be equipped with smoke alarms, fire alarms and sprinkler systems. The chief humanitarian concerns faced when managing elderly inmates involve keeping them in the work force of the prison, giving them responsibility for parts of their lives, and helping them maintain family ties to strengthen their hold on reality. Medical and mental health issues address both humanitarian concerns and—because of the cost of caring for elderly inmates financial considerations as well.

Correctional facilities will have to stretch their budgets to accommodate this mushrooming number of aging inmates. A growing elderly prison population will be more costly to accommodate than a younger one because elderly inmates require more medical and mental health services in special settings.

Demographics

Older inmates are not a homogeneous group. Many variables influence their classification and management, including each one's health and personal background, criminal lifestyle and life experiences, relationships with family members and peers, and religious beliefs.

Using a typology derived by geriatric criminal specialists Delores Craig-Moreland and William D. McLaurine Jr., elderly offender classifications can be broken down into four types: first offender, chronic offender, prison recidivist and one who has grown old as an inmate.

A first offender in his 50s or 60s probably already is maladjusted in society and is poor at adapting to change. Sixty-one percent have committed sexual crimes. The first offender has a volatile personality that poses a risk for suicide, violence against other inmates and poor mental health. Such an inmate would benefit from living in a segregated setting with other older inmates.

A chronic offender has a propensity for criminal activity but has not been confined before. He is able to socialize with others and does not feel stigmatized by his criminal label. Serving a long sentence, with the prospect of dying in prison, causes a great deal of stress for this inmate, who is likely to be violent.

A prison recidivist usually adjusts well upon re-entry because he already knows prison routine. He, too, has concerns about dying in prison and should be evaluated for potential health issues and supported in maintaining his self-respect. This inmate can be an asset in a separate living unit for older inmates. He can help first and chronic offenders adjust to prison life.

An inmate who has grown old as an inmate also is an asset to the first two types, and is the least volatile in daily interactions. He has had meaningful activities and a work history while in prison.

Housing

Older inmates can sometimes present correctional facilities with housing conflicts. While correctional administrators try to house elderly inmates near urban areas where medical specialists are available, these inmates often express a desire to be closer to their families and so may resist a move to an urban facility.

Older offenders do not like to be segregated or housed where their families cannot visit, agrees McLaurine. Yet, these inmates do better when they are away from the stress of interacting closely with younger offenders. Moving them out of traditional areas and into specially constructed sections can free up secure spaces needed for more violent inmates. Moving elderly inmates also makes it easier for correctional officers to monitor their medical and mental health needs.

Accessibility and safety are the two most important considerations in planning and designing housing for an aging prison population. Ramps and subtle grades, with handrails where necessary, enhance access. Doors should be three feet wide, with thresholds one-half inch or lower. Levers should be used in place of knobs, and the pulling force on door closers needs to be less than five pounds.

Rick Holbrook, a justice facilities specialist, says existing spaces can be remodeled to reflect changing needs. "You can retrofit existing facilities and improve their conditions to meet ADA requirements, making them as barrier-free as possible," he says.

A geriatric unit consists of sleeping quarters that can be made into a dormitory setting, with sleeping cubicles created by privacy screens. Holbrook recommends that each screened group not exceed four inmates.

Restroom facilities can be provided at the ratio of one toilet and sink per 12 male inmates, one per eight for females. Urinals can be substituted for up to half of the toilets in the men's quarters. Showers also should be supplied at a rate of one per eight, and at least one bathtub should be provided. Grab bars are required in showers and tub areas, as well as seats and flexible spray nozzles. The floor surfaces should be abrasive enough to minimize slipping when wet.

Activities

Designing a comfortable environment to meet the needs of older inmates is an important part of helping them adjust to prison life.

A day room in a prison geriatric unit should be a multipurpose space separate from the sleeping quarters. It can be a place for reading, playing games, watching television, talking and dining.

Crafts and other activities should be encouraged to keep the older population active creatively, although a crafts room will need supervision. An exam room for routine checkups may double as a dispensary for medication, a counseling room or an administrator's office.

Keeping physical therapy in its own room will be a key component in helping older inmates stay healthy. Inmates also should have access to an outside recreational area for exercise, with shaded areas and drinking fountains that can be winterized.

Of course, all areas of the geriatric unit must be fully visible to staff members in the security post set up within it. "Typically, the older inmate is not a security problem and does not require a high-security cell," Holbrook says. "A dorm-type facility is adequate for older inmates." Such a minimum security concept can bring costs down to approximately $100 per square foot, he adds, compared with $250 per square foot for a maximum security prison.

Impaired eyesight requires good lighting, but not just brighter, bigger lights. A sensitivity to glare, which can affect balance, orientation and memory span, also develops with age, so indirect lighting is more effective. Floor surfaces should not have high-gloss finishes or contrasting random patterns, and must be as non-slip as possible.

Sound control in day rooms can be accomplished with acoustical ceilings and low-pile carpet. The typical hard surfaces of detention facilities make it hard to distinguish one sound against a background of competing noises.

Medical Care

When older inmates take better care of themselves, they have fewer illnesses and make fewer trips to the infirmary. "It's essential to make the offender a partner in his or her health care through education on good health habits and compliance with treatment," says Missouri DOC's Hudson.

Keeping older inmates active is important. They should be offered activities that are practical for their ages and physical conditions, and should be allowed to keep reasonable assignments in the institutional work force as a way of maintaining dignity and positive self-images. Older inmates who have some sense of control over their daily lives adjust better. In addition, helping them maintain their family ties will reinforce their links to reality as they age.

Bobbie Huskey, former president of the American Correctional Association, suggests that a different classification system be used to identify the medical needs of older inmates. Instead of declaring inmates elderly by chronological age, each category of this system should address a level of physical impairment with its different medical care needs, programs and housing.

Acute-care inmates have infectious diseases and require skilled nursing care. Extended care offers 24-hour daily assisted living to those in the last stages of a terminal illness. Chronic care patients require daily access to health services, and to a medical unit if their mobility is severely restricted. Chronic, unstable patients also may require immediate access to health care for such services as dialysis. Chronic, stable patients are ambulatory and not in a special medical unit or separated from the general population.

According to Huskey, patients can move from category to category. For instance, after surgery or injury, an inmate may require daily nursing care or convalescent care in an infirmary, but only for a short period. After recovery, the inmate can be returned to a relatively self-sufficient life.

Some inmates' frailty and restricted mobility require protective housing, but not round-the-clock nursing care. Prisons have increased their use of hospice care for terminally ill inmates in recent years, she adds.

Conclusion

In a time of increasingly longer prison sentences and decreasing resources for dealing with special prison populations, corrections professionals should practice proactive planning to address the rapidly growing elderly inmate population.

Daily maintenance and attention are the best options in the long run. If the needs of the aging inmate population are neglected, it will create a more costly situation for the taxpayer down the road. According to Holbrook, everyone involved with housing prison populations needs to be involved in planning discussions with others in the field. "It's a proactive position on a major concern," he says. "We're all taxpayers."

Connie Neeley is a senior vice president for the architectural firm of Gossen Livingston Associates Inc. Laura Addison is a journalist in Wichita, Kan. Delores E. Craig-Moreland, Ph.D., is assistant professor at the Department of Administration of Justice at Wichita State University.

ELDER CARE

Louisiana Initiates Program to Meet Needs of Aging Inmate Population

By Jean Wall

In Louisiana, an inmate sentenced to life in prison is likely to die there, unless a court intervenes or the sentence is commuted by joint action of the board of pardons and the governor. There are 3,014 inmates with life sentences and approximately 1,850 more who have "practical life"—mandatory sentences so long as to effectively preclude release. These inmates represent the future of the already growing population of older inmates, a population that brings with it an increased potential for medical problems and emergencies, circumstances that often develop sooner in prison populations.

In 1980, 281 inmates (4.5 percent of the institutional population) were 50 years of age or older. In 1990, there were 857 (4.6 percent), and at the end of January 1998, there were 1,275 (7.4 percent). Truth-in-sentencing laws will push these numbers higher. More inmates will remain in prison for longer periods of time. And more inmates will grow old in prison.

Current Circumstances

In 1992, the Louisiana Legislature created a crime victims' "bill of rights," which, among other provisions, gave victims more say in probation and parole proceedings. Victim advocates argued that issues other than cost and risk must be considered when weighing the release of inmates from prison, regardless of age. In 1993, the state legislature passed a law excluding inmates sentenced for first- and second-degree murder from medical parole, even if they are terminally ill or permanently incapacitated.

After Congress enacted the Violent Crime Control and Law Enforcement Act of 1994, which offered construction grants and other incentives to states that ensure violent offenders remain incarcerated for substantial periods of time, the Louisiana Legislature passed a law requiring inmates who commit a crime of violence on or after Jan. 1, 1997, to serve 85 percent of the time imposed before qualifying for release. The state's first comprehensive felony sentencing guidelines, implemented in January 1992, were repealed, effective August 1995, amid insistent claims that they existed to shorten sentence lengths.

An Approach to the Challenge

Inmates in Louisiana state institutions live in dormitories in the general population—unless their behavior or assessed physical, mental or emotional needs indicate that cell block housing is required. This is true of geriatric inmates (the term used here to mean "aging" rather than "of advanced age"), just as it is of teen-age newcomers to the system, HIV-positive inmates, inmates with mental retardation and/or mental illness, and others. In that sense, older inmates are just one of various groups of special needs inmates within the state correctional system. Like the others, the elderly live in the general population as long as they can do so safely. For those who cannot live in the general population, the department has concentrated on upgrading medical and mental health services at the Louisiana State Penitentiary (LSP) at Angola in order to satisfy the needs of the department's most seriously medically and mentally ill offenders.

Intent on overcoming the constant shortage of doctors and nurses at LSP, the administration increased salaries for doctors and registered nurses, offered remodeled and modernized housing on the grounds to medical staff, and increased the hours of contract physicians.

Angola is in a rural area, and the prison is surrounded on three sides by the Mississippi River and bordered on the fourth side by the ravine-laced Tunica Hills. It is 59 miles from Baton Rouge and about 140 miles from New Orleans. The isolation that once made it the perfect place for a prison also made it a challenging location to maintain a full complement of necessary medical and mental health personnel. Once these limitations were acknowledged, other sites were examined for development of specialized units and services.

Special Needs Facilities

One special needs facility is being developed near Shreveport as a satellite of the David Wade Correctional Center (DWCC). Named the Dr. Martin L. Forcht Jr. Clinical Treatment Unit and referred to as Forcht-Wade, the unit will house male inmates who, by virtue of age and/or physical impairment, can best be handled in a special needs facility. The unit occupies the site of the old Caddo Parish Detention Center, which was donated by the parish to the state for development as a special needs facility. It is being renovated with assistance from federal crime bill funds. In September 1999, when renovations are complete, 330 of the unit's total 555 beds will be for special needs offenders.

Forcht-Wade is well-suited to serve as a special needs facility. It is close to the Louisiana State University Medical Center (LSUMC) in Shreveport, the premier teaching facility in the region. Plans are being developed to use medical center staff as consultants and to provide important medical components such as physical and occupational therapy through contracts with LSUMC's School of Allied Health Care.

A team of Forcht-Wade administrators, medical staff and the facility architect visited the Federal Medical Center in Fort Worth, Texas, and met with staff. Administrators are working with the Department of Gerontology of Northeast Louisiana University in Monroe to better prepare themselves to understand and serve the special needs of an aging population.

Currently, 166 beds at Forcht-Wade are occupied by minimum custody inmates who are housed there to help with renovations not provided by outside contractors. After renovations are complete, those beds will continue to be filled by inmates who are able to maintain the grounds and provide other service functions.

For four years, DWCC has shared a telemedicine linkage with LSUMC. Telemedicine technology utilizes interactive video and specialized diagnostic equipment to enable offsite physicians (usually in a hospital setting) to examine patients who are with medical personnel in a prison's infirmary. This arrangement has increased efficiency and decreased security risks. Where telemedicine is appropriate, a consultation that would require a 135-mile round-trip drive and two security officer escorts can be handled in about 45 minutes without taking inmates outside the secure perimeter of the institution. Telemedicine also has supported recruiting efforts by enabling physicians at DWCC's relatively isolated site to interact with medical colleagues. When Forcht-Wade is fully operational, the service will be expanded to that unit.

The Elayn Hunt Correctional Center (EHCC), located just outside the Baton Rouge metropolitan area and about 50 miles from New Orleans, was identified as the appropriate site at which to provide enhanced medical and psychiatric care in the system. Patients from LSP's Clinical Treatment Unit II were transferred to EHCC.

Planning and design monies have been authorized for a new 600-bed facility, which, when completed, will serve as a skilled nursing/mental health/HIV-AIDS facility and will deliver acute and chronic medical and mental health care. It will add new clinical areas and inpatient housing units, and supplement the state health care authority's efforts by providing services that have occupied but do not require a hospital's resources, in-

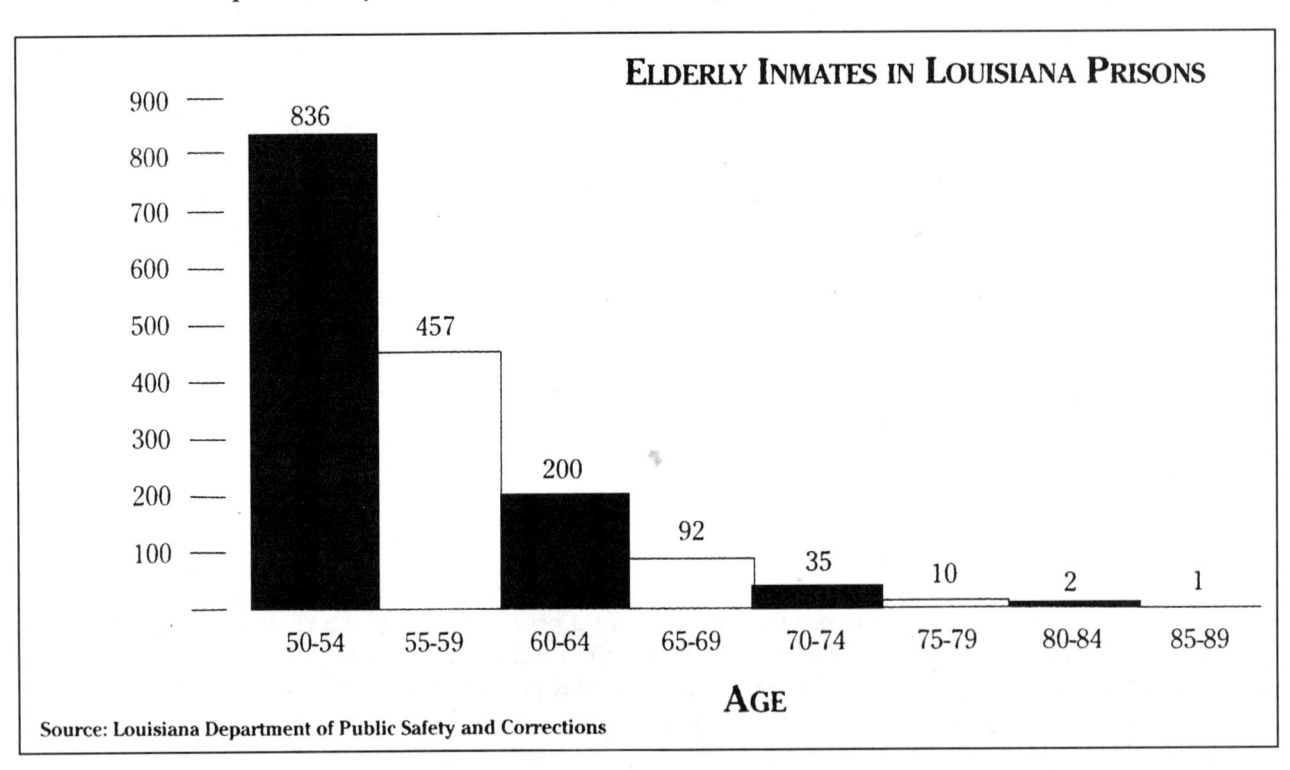

ELDERLY INMATES IN LOUISIANA PRISONS

Age	Number
50-54	836
55-59	457
60-64	200
65-69	92
70-74	35
75-79	10
80-84	2
85-89	1

Source: Louisiana Department of Public Safety and Corrections

cluding: infirmary care, frequent medical monitoring, long-term skilled nursing home care and hospice care. This facility also will be constructed with the help of federal crime bill monies. Funding for the required 10 percent state match has been included in this year's capital outlay budget request.

Meanwhile, pending completion of new special-needs beds at EHCC and DWCC, 70 existing beds have been set aside for the frail, elderly and infirm at EHCC, 120 at LSP and 30 at the Dixon Correctional Institute, where most male inmates requiring dialysis are housed. The Louisiana Correctional Institute for Women currently has 20 beds available for elderly or infirm inmates.

Special Programs

In 1991, an inmate suffered a heart attack while on his job; another, while watching television in his dorm. Before EMTs arrived, inmates recall, no one knew what to do. Major J. Lee Walker, director of Emergency Medical Services at LSP, was struggling with the same issue. Distances and standard security devices such as double interlock gates, where one door must slide shut before the other opens, complicate EMT access. One inmate, motivated by what he'd witnessed, submitted a detailed proposal to organize CPR classes for inmates.

Walker recalls that it took almost two years to put in place a program to train inmates in CPR. Two certified trainers from the prison's EMS department taught CPR to 20 inmate volunteers. Seventeen completed the first course and received certification as A-Level Basic Life Support practitioners, authorized by the American Heart Association to administer CPR. Some of the group wanted to learn more, but EMS personnel had other major responsibilities. CPR equipment is costly, and funds were an early obstacle. Inmates elected to use monies from the inmate-generated welfare fund to buy CPR mannequins, a television monitor, a videocassette recorder, training videos and other visual aids. The American Heart Association donated 30 instructor manuals.

Early newspaper reports quoted Walker as saying he would consider the program a success if 25 percent of the population learned CPR. By the summer of 1996, inmate CPR instructors had taught a six-hour CPR course to more than 2,000 inmates at LSP.

In February 1995, LSP's Emergency Medical Services Department earned certification as an advanced support service, the highest level for private or public ambulance operators in Louisiana. In 1997, LSP added telemedicine access, which allows immediate diagnostic assessment of inmates by physicians at the Medical Center of Louisiana (MCLA) in New Orleans, otherwise a round-trip of almost 250 miles.

Summary

Throughout the system, proactive health care measures for the aging population are coming into place. Annual TB testing of inmates and staff is mandatory. Regular age-appropriate health screenings are part of routine medical care. Inmate peer counseling addresses behaviors that increase the risk of HIV infection, heart attack and other diseases. Medical co-payments have been added as a means of curtailing abuse of prison medical services. Security officers certified as EMTs are widely used. Establishing additional telemedicine links between other prisons and large public hospitals is being pursued. Emergency medical furlough for inmates also remains an option.

The challenge of a growing and aging population, limited funds and public demand is great. We may, however, have access to more resources and choices in meeting it than we realize. We may need to centralize specialized programs but not necessarily all in one place; move specialized programs close to major population areas; tap crime bill monies; develop the ability to use emerging technologies; take advantage of training opportunities and grant monies; educate legislators, news media, victim advocates and the public about issues, choices and options; and innovate, innovate, innovate.

That's our job. In this, as in other tough situations, corrections professionals must find a way to balance public safety concerns and public demands for a government that operates with economy and efficiency and responds appropriately to legitimate correctional interests.

Jean Wall, an executive officer in the Louisiana Department of Public Safety and Corrections, is director of the department's Crime Victims Services Bureau. Contributors without whose help this article could not have been written are Warden Kelly Ward, David Wade Correctional Center, Assistant Warden Gary Frank, Executive Staff Officer Cathy Jett and Maj. Lee Walker of Louisiana State Penitentiary; and Executive Management Officer Dora Wheat.

ically at work preparing the answer to such problems as Chaser.

Chaser: A Medication Addict

Victor Hassine

Editor's Note

Prescription medications are ubiquitous in many prisons, and chlorpromazine tranquilizers are common in virtually all these institutions. Other medications, such as amphetamines, barbiturates, and diazopene tranquilizers, are routinely dispensed. Although these medications are given to inmates under the supervision of a physician, the actual distribution is often handled by guards and fellow prisoners. Since these prescription medications are readily available, their role in the underground economy is small. Any prisoner with a prescription can hoard pills, of course, and sell or give them to others.

The author's opinion of prescription medications and their use in American prisons is apparent in his interview with Chaser. Whether one agrees with him or not, medications have become part of the status quo in most prisons. Given the increasing use of penal institutions for housing the mentally ill, it is unlikely that the prevalence of prescription medications will abate in the near future.

I met Chaser in 1984, my fourth year at Graterford, when he first arrived to serve time on a robbery conviction. I can still remember the frightened look on his face that first day. As I was adapting to the rapidly changing rules and conditions of a prison in total meltdown, Chaser became the beneficiary of my hard-learned lessons on inmate survival. We managed to forge a mutual friendship.

Many outsiders who have met Chaser would comment, "He doesn't look like he belongs in here." I've heard this often when people encounter an inmate who doesn't have some grotesque feature that neatly fits their preconceived notion of the "criminal look." Experience has taught me that the less an inmate appears like a criminal, the more likely he is to be particularly vicious and unrepentant. Criminals who look like criminals keep people on guard; the honest-looking ones put them at ease, which allows them the greater advantage of misjudgment. But in Chaser's case they were right. He didn't belong in prison, let alone deserve to become a victim of the system.

I did my best to look after my friend until, about nine months later, he was transferred to the Rockview facility. This was a relief for me, since protecting a naive and scared young man from the predators at Graterford was no easy task.

Once he was transferred, I quickly forgot about Chaser. Frankly, it is nearly impossible for me to remember all the people that have come in and out of my life, especially nowadays with the influx of so many frightened young kids. Almost all my relations with fellow inmates today are superficial, as prison life becomes more and more a case of every man for himself.

What Chaser and I didn't know at the time was that prison administrators were fever-

From *Life Without Parole* by Victor Hassine, pp. 87–94. © 1999 by Roxbury Publishers, Los Angeles, CA. Reprinted by permission.

22. Chaser: A Medication Addict

ishly trying to figure out how to stop the imminent collapse of Graterford and other overcrowded prisons. With thousands of new, young Chasers coming in, it was becoming more impossible to feed, house, and clothe them all, let alone rehabilitate them. More importantly to officials, an increasing number of guards and staff were becoming victims of inmate attacks. As employee safety was their first priority, the administrators realized that something had to be done to shore up the cracks in Graterford's foundation—and it had to be quick, cheap, and effective. But Chaser and I never concerned ourselves with the administration's problems. After all, we had swag men to deal with and predators to avoid.

In 1990, as I made my way to chow at Rockview, I ran into Chaser again. He was walking out of the dining hall's special section reserved for the "nuts," whom the administration refer to euphemistically as "special-needs inmates." Chaser walked sluggishly with a disheveled, glassy-eyed appearance. In short, he *looked* like one of the nuts.

"Chaser, is that you?" I asked.

"Hey, Vic," he replied, "I've got to talk to you. It's real important. Meet me in the yard."

That evening in the yard, my old friend explained to me how he had returned to the streets two years earlier, only to lose his wife and son, develop a voracious drug habit, and end up committing burglaries to support his habit.

I was unmoved by Chaser's story, since almost every returning con I've ever met recounts a similar tale of woe. All I wanted to know was why he was on the nut block and why he was taking "brake fluid" [prescribed psychotropic medication]. It was obvious because of his very slow, disjointed movement and his shakes. Another alarming clue was the noticeable scars on his wrists from razor cuts.

Chaser described how his return to prison had exposed him to the "medicate-and-forget-them" system of modern prison management. This new system of mind-altering and mood-altering psychotropic drugs was rapidly becoming the prison administration's "quick, cheap, and effective" solution to warehousing masses of inmates into smaller spaces, while using fewer and fewer support services.

The reasoning seemed to be that every dose of medication taken by an inmate equaled one less fraction of a guard needed to watch that inmate, and one less inmate who may pose a threat to anyone other than himself. Hence, overcrowding had brought about a merging of the psychiatric and corrections communities. The resulting effect on inmates can be best described by Chaser during this 1994 interview.

"The first time [I came to prison] I was terrified because I didn't know what to expect and I knew no one. I was awkward and didn't know my way around. I had not acquired a prison or inmate mentality. The second time I was much more at ease because I knew a lot of people still in prison and I knew what to expect. I had also learned quite fast how to become as comfortable as possible. I had to take a lot of psychotropic drugs to achieve this comfortable state of mind....

"In November of 1989, after telling the shrink in the county prison that I wished I was dead, I was unknowingly given Sinequan which knocked me out for three days. But since I was in a special quiet section of the jail, I continued the medication, because to me it was better than being in population....

"I think the biggest difference between street drugs and psychotropic drugs is that street drugs give me some kind of feeling of well-being, high, confidence, euphoria, and contentment. But psychotropic drugs cause all feeling to cease. It stops self-awareness and sucks the soul out of a man. It slows or stops a man from striving to better himself and he stops caring about everything. It also creates total laziness. That laziness becomes his entire attitude and also is 100-percent habit-forming....

"After almost three months at the county prison in Philly, I was sent to Graterford to start my four-to-ten-year sentence. I had abruptly stopped taking the Sinequan and felt totally disoriented. I lasted three weeks in population. Looking for drugs, I ended up taking another inmate's Thorazine at times. I was out of control and all I could think of or look forward to was getting stoned.

"One day I got very drunk and went into a blackout and refused to lock up. Four guards carried me to a room and I was put into restraints. I was given nine months in the Hole. I did five at Graterford and was sent to Rockview to complete it....

"[Getting medication in Rockview] was quite easy. I said I wished I was dead, which was the same thing I said in the county. Every week the shrink would ask, 'How do you feel now?' All I had to do was say, 'Bad,' and ask for more or different meds. I always got what

I asked for, as long as I told them I thought of killing myself. . . . I took Sinequan, Melloril, Elavil, Klonopin, first separately, while always asking for Valium. Then in desperation, I mixed the medications and the dosages. The ultimate effect was total numbness. My body was numb. My feelings were numb, and then my mind was numb. I did not care what happened to me and just stopped thinking about anything. . . .

"While taking the meds, I was put on a special block and given a single cell. I got only a reprimand at misconduct hearings and did not have to go to work. I felt I was being placated and given special attention and I liked that. But when I stopped taking the meds, I was shook down [cell-searched] a lot and went to the Hole if I was ever given a misconduct. Once in the Hole, I would say I wish I was dead, and again they'd give me medication. . . .

"I admitted to staff many times that I had a severe drug addiction and that I had an abusive personality. I tried numerous times to get in the drug-therapy groups and on the D and A [Drug and Alcohol] Blocks. I was refused and ignored every time. . . .

"I lost all sense of dignity and self-worth. I had no pride. I lost all interest in the outside world and eventually did not care if I ever returned to it. All I knew or cared about was what times I went to get my fix. . . . [I] hurried to be first in line. I constantly had the shakes and inner tremors. My speech was slurred and slowed, and so was my thinking. I could not think ahead. I was like a small child only looking for instant gratification. My entire metabolism changed, and I gained a lot of weight fast. It damaged my memory, even to this day. . . .

"Since I was under constant supervision and being evaluated once or twice a month, pre-release and parole became much harder to obtain. So for the luxury of being comfortable and in a fantasy world, I had to abandon the idea of early release or furloughs. Since my number-one priority was no longer a goal, it became easy for me to forget or stop striving for what was once important to me. The side effects of the medication, such as tremors and shakes, made it impossible for me to get and keep a job. Education, reading, learning, and working to strengthen my mind became things of the past. Giving up became repetitious and habit-forming (not unlike street drugs) and eventually I lost and gave up my self-respect, dignity, and morals until my only interest in life was getting in line three times a day to receive my medication.

"I had given up on all these things, and I woke up one day and realized I was a very sad man. But I was willing to give up on life, because the medications I was taking made me think I was comfortable. . . . I had given up on Chaser. . . .

"I was seeking a shrink two times a week because I was depressed. I was not diagnosed as having any kind of mental illness or chemical imbalance, but despite that I was taking large dosages of Thorazine, Sinequan, Lithium, Elavil, and Melloril. I took them at 7 a.m., 11 a.m., 4 p.m., 8 p.m. . . .

"One night just before lockup, I got another misconduct. I didn't care if I went to the Hole or got cell restriction. What concerned me was that the administration might possibly take away my medication. So after weighing my options, it seemed only logical to kill myself, or at the least, give that appearance. I opened my window, pressed my wrists against the frozen bars, then took an old razor and opened my wrists. I figured that, if I died, that would be fine. But, if I lived, I would definitely get more medication, and that thought satisfied me. I lived this madness and insanity for well over a year, until I ran into you. You offered me your time and energy to explain to me what I was doing to myself and what I was becoming. Within six months, I was totally off the special-needs block and off 99 percent of the medication and my will to live and succeed returned . . . with a vengeance. I never needed the medications for my depressed condition. I just needed someone to say they cared. I needed a friend. I got both from you. I owe you my life, not the prison, and not the medication. . . .

"I have been medication-free for two years now and, although I'm usually uncomfortable with prison conditions, I can look in the mirror and see Chaser looking back with a smile. So to me, giving up the medication was a small price to pay to be myself again.

"[Psychotropic medication] is one of the easiest things to get in prison. It is easier to go to the shrink and ask for 500 mg of Thorazine than it is to get on the phone or get a pass to the Chapel. If a guy goes to the doc saying he feels depressed, violent, or suicidal, the doc will give him one of numerous medications. He is usually given a choice. All the medications are geared to slow a man down or fog his thinking so bad he can't think of why he's depressed, violent, or suicidal.

This will continue for years, as long as he says he needs the medications to a staff person once a month....

"I'd say 40 percent of the population here is taking some form of psychotropic medication. They are treated less harshly than those unmedicated. They are seen and talked to by staff much more often than those not on medications. They are given special consideration at misconduct hearings. They are permitted to come in from night yard earlier than the other inmates and, in a lot of cases, are given a single cell. When it comes to working, someone on psychotropic medication can usually pick whatever job he says he can handle. On the other hand, most of us were not required to work at all....

"I believe that, when a guard or any staff members puts on a uniform, they know it stands for authority. So they demand respect and control. When someone rebels or stands up to them, they feel their authority and control is threatened and they take steps to eliminate the rebellion. They put on the appearance of power, so they act cold, mean, negative, and harsh to display this power.

"Now when a guy is on medication, the threat is almost nonexistent. They [the staff] feel safe and secure with the men that are medicated. So the use of force and display of power is not necessary, and they act more leniently to the medicated inmate. They treat these men like children. To staff, a medicated inmate is a controlled inmate....

"[If all inmates were required to take psychotropic drugs], I would be shocked and scared. It would be like they were turning the prison into a brainwashing institution. I would think they had lost all control and were attempting to gain it back by stopping our wills and brains from functioning properly. I believe they are headed in that direction because of how easy the medications are to get and how many people are taking them....

"I think that, as the prison populations continue to grow and grow, and a younger and more violent crowd comes in, it will become harder and harder for the administration to control all the blocks. I think they are now learning that the best way to control inmates or pacify them is to totally medicate them. It may even become a reward system."

Psychotropic drugs are nothing new to the psychiatric community, which has been using them on the mentally ill for years. However, its use in corrections as a population-management tool and behavior modifier is relatively new. The effects of prolonged use of such medication on an ever growing number of inmates are unknown.

Just from the increasing size of medication lines and the growing number of inmates doing the brake-fluid shuffle, I have observed that psychotropic medications (also known as "chemical shackles") are defining the behavior of an increasing percentage of inmates in the general population.

As politicians and bureaucrats continue to debate the loftier issues facing the criminal justice system, the mother of invention has required front-line prison administrators to quickly implement any practice that might help them to keep their prisons intact and functioning. The practice of medicating inmates is becoming popular because it has proven to be a relatively inexpensive and efficient prison-control tool. The two governing estates of custody and treatment are being pushed aside by the rising third estate of psychiatric medication.

A bureaucratic system that subdues whole populations with drugs must certainly give us pause. The wisdom of turning means into ultimate ends in this way needs to be questioned. Today in prison, I find myself longing for any glimpse of an attempt to rehabilitate, not because I believe that treatment works, but because I worry about a society that no longer cares enough to try to help.

In my opinion, today's prison managers are only interested in their ability to confine an ever-increasing number of people for an ever-longer period of time. Since there is only so much that can be done in terms of cell and prison design, the research for solutions has focused not on changing the nature of prisons but on changing the nature of prisoners.

As of this interview, Chaser has been off medication for about two years. He has successfully gone through drug-rehabilitation therapy and is soon due for release. Once released, he will join a growing number of mind-altered men who are leaving prison and entering the mainstream of society. Only time will tell whether chemically treated inmates do in fact make law-abiding citizens. But, if you ask me, we should go back to trying to build a better mouse trap and, for God's sake, leave the mice alone.

Article 23

Mental Health and Treatment of Inmates and Probationers

By Paula M. Ditton
BJS Statistician

At midyear 1998, an estimated 283,800 mentally ill offenders were incarcerated in the Nation's prisons and jails. In recent surveys completed by the Bureau of Justice Statistics, 16% of State prison inmates, 7% of Federal inmates, and 16% of those in local jails reported either a mental condition or an overnight stay in a mental hospital. About 16%, or an estimated 547,800 probationers, said they had had a mental condition or stayed overnight in a mental hospital at some point in their lifetime.

Based on information from personal interviews, State prison inmates with a mental condition were more likely than other inmates to be incarcerated for a violent offense (53% compared to 46%); more likely than other inmates to be under the influence of alcohol or drugs at the time of the current offense (59% compared to 51%); and more than twice as likely as other inmates to have been homeless in the 12 months prior to their arrest (20% compared to 9%). Over three-quarters of mentally ill inmates had been sentenced to time in prison or jail or on probation at least once prior to the current sentence.

Over 30% of male mentally ill inmates and 78% of females reported prior physical or sexual abuse. Since admission 61% of mentally ill inmates in State prison and 41% in local jails reported they had received treatment for a mental condition in the form of counseling, medication, or other mental health services.

Prevalence of mental illness among correctional populations based on offender self reports

The findings in this report are based on the 1997 Survey of Inmates in State or Federal Correctional Facilities, the 1996 Survey of Inmates in Local Jails, and the 1995 Survey of Adults on Probation. In each survey, offenders selected through nationally representative samples were asked a series of mental

Highlights

Over a quarter million mentally ill incarcerated in prison or jail

Reported a...	State prison	Federal prison	Jail	Probation
Mental or emotional condition	10.1%	4.8%	10.5%	13.8%
Overnight stay in a mental hospital	10.7	4.7	10.2	8.2
Estimated to be mentally ill*	16.2%	7.4%	16.3%	16.0%

*Reported either a mental or emotional condition or an overnight stay in a mental hospital or program.

- About 10% of prison and jail inmates reported a mental or emotional condition; and 10% said they had stayed overnight in a mental hospital or program.
- Together, 16% or an estimated 283,800 inmates reported either a mental condition or an overnight stay in a mental hospital, and were identified as mentally ill.

Mentally ill inmates were more likely than others to be in prison for a violent offense

	State prisoners	
Offense	Mentally ill inmates	Other inmates
Violent	52.9%	46.1%
Property	24.4	21.5
Drug	12.8	22.2
Public-order	9.9	9.8
Criminal history		
None	18.8%	21.2%
Priors	81.2	78.8

- About 53% of mentally ill inmates were in prison for a violent offense, compared to 46% of other inmates.
- Mentally ill offenders were less likely than others to be incarcerated for a drug related offense (13% versus 22%).

Nearly 6 in 10 mentally ill offenders reported they were under the influence of alcohol or drugs at the time of their current offense

	State Prisoners	
Before entering prison	Mentally ill inmates	Other inmates
Homeless in 12 months prior to arrest	20.1%	8.8%
Physical/sexual abuse		
Male	32.8%	13.1%
Female	78.4	50.9
Alcohol/drug use		
At time of offense	58.7%	51.2%
Drug use		
In month before offense	58.8%	56.1%

Mental health treatment since admission	Mentally ill inmates	
	State prison	Jail
Any treatment	60.5%	40.9%
Medication	50.1	34.1
Counseling	44.1	16.2

- Mentally ill State prison inmates were more than twice as likely as other inmates to report living on the street or in a shelter in the 12 months prior to arrest (20% compared to 9%).
- Nearly 8 in 10 female mentally ill inmates reported physical or sexual abuse. Males with a mental condition were more than twice as likely as other males to report abuse.
- 6 in 10 mentally ill State inmates reported receiving mental treatment since admission to prison.

From *Bureau of Justice Statistics Special Report,* July 1999, pp. 1-11. © 1999 by the U.S. Department of Justice. Reprinted by permission.

Survey items used to measure mental illness

Do you have a mental or emotional condition? (prison and jail inmates only)
☐ Yes
☐ No

Have you ever been told by a mental health professional such as a psychiatrist, psychologist, social worker, or psychiatric nurse, that you had a mental or emotional disorder? (probationers only)
☐ Yes
☐ No

Because of an emotional or mental problem, have you ever—
Taken a medication prescribed by a psychiatrist or other doctor?
☐ Yes
☐ No

Been admitted to a mental hospital, unit or treatment program where you stayed overnight?
☐ Yes
☐ No

Received counseling or therapy from a trained professional?
☐ Yes
☐ No

Received any other mental health services?
☐ Yes
☐ No

Table 1. Measures of mental illness among State prison inmates, 1997

	State prison inmates Percent	Cumulative percent
Reported a mental or emotional condition	10.1%	10.1%
Because of a mental or emotional problem, inmate had—		
Been admitted to a hospital overnight	10.7%	16.2%
Taken a prescribed medication	18.9	23.9
Received professional counseling or therapy	21.8	29.7
Received other mental health services	3.3	30.2

health related questions. Respondents were asked if they have a mental or emotional condition and whether they had ever received treatment for a mental or emotional problem, other than treatment related to drug or alcohol abuse. (See survey questions in the box above.)

16% of State prisoners identified as mentally ill

For this report, offenders were identified as mentally ill if they met one of the following two criteria: they reported a current mental or emotional condition, or they reported an overnight stay in a mental hospital or treatment program. An estimated 1 in 10 State prison inmates reported a current mental or emotional condition (table 1). A slightly larger percentage (11%) of State inmates said they had been admitted overnight to a mental hospital or treatment program at some point in their life. Overall, nearly a third of all inmates reported they had a current mental condition or they had received mental health service at some time.

To take into account underreporting of current mental or emotional problems, past admission to a mental hospital was included as a measure of mental illness. Overall, 16% of State prisoners met these criteria, including 10% who reported a current mental condition and an additional 6% who said they did not have a mental condition but had stayed overnight in a mental hospital, unit, or treatment program.

Previously estimated rates of mental illness among incarcerated populations vary, depending on the methodology of the study, the institution, and the definition of mental illness. Estimates range from 8% to 16% among studies with more rigorous scientific methods, including random sampling and a standardized assessment or psychological testing. (See the box on this page.)

Past estimates of the rate of mental illness among incarcerated populations are higher than those for the U.S. general population. Among a sample of male jail detainees in Cook County (Chicago), Teplin found 9.5% had experienced a severe mental disorder (schizophrenia, mania, or major depression) at some point in their life, compared to 4.4% of males in the U.S. general population. The Epidemiologic Catchment Area program found that 6.7% of prisoners had suffered from schizophrenia at some point, compared to 1.4% of the U.S. household population (Robins and Regier).

283,800 mentally ill in prison or jail; 547,800 on probation

Using the same criteria described for State prison inmates, 16% of offenders in local jails or on probation and 7% of inmates in Federal prisons were identified as mentally ill in recently completed BJS surveys (table 2). Probationers were somewhat less likely than inmates in State prisons or local jails to report an overnight stay in a mental hospital or treatment program but more likely to report a mental or emotional problem. Fed-

Previous studies of the prevalence of severe mental illness in prison or jail

Study	Sample	Mentally ill*
Guy, Platt, Zwerling, and Bullock (1985)	Philadelphia jail pretrial admissions	16%
Teplin (1990)	Cook County jail admissions (males)	10%
Steadman, Fabisiak, Dvoskin, and Holohean (1987)	New York State prisoners	8%

*Generally includes schizophrenia, bipolar disorder, and major depression. See individual studies for variations in definition.

Table 2. Mental health status of inmates and probationers

	State prison inmates, 1997	Federal prison inmates, 1997	Jail inmates, 1996	Probationers, 1995
Identified as mentally ill*	16.2%	7.4%	16.3%	6.0%
Reported a mental or emotional condition	10.1	4.8	10.5	13.8
Admitted overnight to a mental hospital or treatment program	10.7	4.7	10.2	8.2

*Reported either a mental condition or an overnight stay in a mental hospital or treatment program.

Percent of females in State prison identified as mentally ill

Age	White	Black	Hispanic
Total	29%	20%	22%
24 or younger	37	17	23
25–34	23	20	21
35 or older	33	21	23

eral inmates had lower rates on both measures.

Assuming these rates have not changed since the surveys were conducted, an estimated 283,800 inmates in prison or jail were mentally ill as of June 30, 1998 (table 3). State prisons held an estimated 179,200 mentally ill offenders; Federal prisons held 7,900; and local jails, 96,700. Of those on probation at yearend 1998, an estimated 547,800 were mentally ill.

White inmates more likely than blacks or Hispanics to report a mental illness

Nearly a quarter of white State prison and local jail inmates and a fifth of white offenders on probation were identified as mentally ill (table 4). The rate of mental illness among black and Hispanic inmates and probationers was much lower. Among black offenders, 14% of those in State prison and local jails, and 10% of those on probation were identified as mentally ill. About 11% of Hispanic State prison and local jail inmates, and 9% of Hispanic offenders on probation had a mental illness.

Black and Hispanic inmates in Federal prison were half as likely as white inmates to report a mental illness. About 6% of black inmates and 4% of Hispanic inmates reported a mental condition or an overnight stay in a mental hospital, compared to 12% of white Federal prison inmates.

The prevalence of mental illness also varied by gender, with females reporting a higher rate of mental illness than males. Nearly 24% of female State prison and local jail inmates, and 22% of female probationers were identified as mentally ill, compared to 16% of male State prison and jail inmates and 15% of male probationers.

Offender mental illness highest among the middle-aged

Offenders between ages 45 and 54 were the most likely to be identified as mentally ill. About 20% of State prisoners, 10% of Federal prisoners, 23% of jail inmates, and 21% of probationers between ages 45 and 54 had a mental illness, compared to 14% of State inmates, 7% of Federal inmates, 13% of jail inmates, and 14% of probationers age 24 or younger.

The highest rates of mental illness were among white females in State prison. An estimated 29% of white females, 20% of black females, and 22% of Hispanic females in State prison were identified as mentally ill. Nearly 4 in 10 white female inmates age 24 or younger were mentally ill.

Table 3. Estimated number of mentally ill inmates and probationers, 1998

	Estimated number of offenders*			
	State prison	Federal prison	Local jail	Probation
Identified as mentally ill	179,200	7,900	96,700	547,800
Reported a mental or emotional condition	111,300	5,200	62,100	473,000
Admitted overnight to a mental hospital	118,300	5,000	60,500	281,200

*Based on midyear 1998 counts from the National Prisoner Statistics and Annual Survey of Jails and preliminary yearend 1998 counts from the Annual Probation Survey.

Table 4. Inmates and probationers identified as mentally ill, by gender, race/Hispanic origin, and age

	Percent identified as mentally ill			
Offender characteristic	State inmates	Federal inmates	Jail inmates	Probationers
Gender				
Male	15.8%	7.0%	15.6%	14.7%
Female	23.6	12.5	22.7	21.7
Race/Hispanic origin				
White*	22.6%	11.8%	21.7%	19.6%
Black*	13.5	5.6	13.7	10.4
Hispanic	11.0	4.1	11.1	9.0
Age				
24 or younger	14.4%	6.6%	13.3%	13.8%
25–34	14.8	5.9	15.7	13.8
35–44	18.4	7.5	19.3	19.8
45–54	19.7	10.3	22.7	21.1
55 or older	15.6	8.9	20.4	16.0

*Excludes Hispanics.

23. Mental Health and Treatment of Inmates and Probationers

Mentally ill more likely than other offenders to have committed a violent offense

Fifty-three percent of mentally ill State prisoners, compared to 46% of other State prisoners, were incarcerated for a violent crime (table 5). Approximately 13% of the mentally ill in State prison had committed murder; 12%, sexual assault; 13%, robbery; and 11%, assault. Among inmates in Federal prison, 33% of the mentally ill were incarcerated for a violent offense, compared to 13% of other Federal inmates. More than 1 in 5 mentally ill Federal prisoners had committed robbery (predominantly bank robbery). Among inmates in local jails, 30% of the mentally ill had committed a violent offense, compared to 26% of other jail inmates. An estimated 28% of mentally ill probationers and 18% of other probationers reported their current offense was a violent crime.

Nearly 1 in 5 violent offenders incarcerated or on probation were identified as mentally ill.

	Percent mentally ill among violent offenders
State prison inmates	18.2%
Federal prison inmates	16.6
Jail inmates	18.5
Probationers	22.8

Unlike those in State prisons, the majority of mentally ill offenders in jail or on probation had committed a property or public-order offense. Almost a third of mentally ill offenders in jail and on probation had committed a property offense, and a quarter had committed a public-order offense.

Mentally ill offenders were less likely than other inmates to be incarcerated for a drug offense. About 13% of mentally ill inmates and 22% of other inmates in State prison were incarcerated for a drug offense. In Federal prison, where the majority of inmates are incarcerated for a drug offense, 40% of those identified as mentally ill and 64% of other Federal inmates were in prison for a drug-related crime.

Half of mentally ill inmates reported 3 or more prior sentences

Mentally ill inmates reported longer criminal histories than other inmates. Among mentally ill inmates, 52% of State prisoners, 54% of jail inmates and 49% of Federal inmates reported three or more prior sentences to probation or incarceration (table 6). Among other inmates, 42% of State prisoners and jail inmates and 28% of Federal inmates had three or more prior sentences. About 10% of mentally ill prison inmates and 13% of jail inmates reported 11 or more prior sentences.

Mentally ill more likely than other inmates to be violent recidivists

Among repeat offenders, 53% of mentally ill State inmates had a current or past sentence for a violent offense, compared to 45% of other inmates. Forty-six percent of mentally ill jail inmates and 32% of other jail inmates with a criminal history had a current or past sentence or a current charge for a violent crime. Among Federal prisoners with a prior sentence, the mentally ill (44%) were twice as likely as other inmates (22%) to have a current or prior sentence for a violent offense.

Although offenders on probation had shorter criminal histories, nearly 3 in 10 of the mentally ill were recidivists with a current or past sentence for violence.

	Probationers	
Criminal history	Mentally ill	Other
None	43.4%	54.1%
Priors	56.6	45.9
Violent recidivists	29.1	17.1
Other recidivists	27.6	28.8

Table 5. Most serious current offense of inmates and probationers, by mental health status

Most serious offense	State prison Mentally ill inmates	State prison Other inmates	Federal prison Mentally ill inmates	Federal prison Other inmates	Local jail Mentally ill inmates	Local jail Other inmates	Probation Mentally ill probationers	Probation Other probationers
All offenses	100.0%	100.0%	100.0%	100.0%	100.0%	100.0%	100.0%	100.0%
Violent offenses	52.9%	46.1%	33.1%	13.3%	29.9%	25.6%	28.4%	18.4%
Murder*	13.2	11.4	1.9	1.4	3.5	2.7	0.5	0.9
Sexual assault	12.4	7.9	1.9	0.7	5.2	2.8	6.8	4.1
Robbery	13.0	14.4	20.8	9.1	4.7	6.9	2.0	1.4
Assault	10.9	9.0	3.8	1.1	14.4	11.0	14.0	10.5
Property offenses	24.4%	21.5%	8.7%	6.7%	31.3%	26.0%	30.4%	28.5%
Burglary	12.1	10.5	1.0	0.3	9.1	7.4	6.4	4.3
Larceny/theft	4.6	4.1	1.3	0.4	8.4	7.9	5.3	8.8
Fraud	3.1	2.6	5.0	4.9	5.2	4.4	11.7	9.2
Drug offenses	12.8%	22.2%	40.4%	64.4%	15.2%	23.3%	16.1%	20.7%
Possession	5.7	9.4	3.9	11.9	7.3	12.3	7.2	11.0
Trafficking	6.6	12.2	35.7	46.6	7.0	9.6	6.7	9.2
Public-order offenses	9.9%	9.8%	17.0%	14.6%	23.2%	24.6%	24.7%	31.6%

Note: Detail does not sum to total because of excluded offense categories.
*Includes nonnegligent manslaughter.

6 in 10 violent mentally ill State prisoners knew their victim

Mentally ill inmates who were incarcerated for a violent offense were more likely to report that the victim of the offense was a woman, someone they knew, and under age 18. Nearly 61% of mentally ill State prison inmates who had committed a violent offense knew their victim. An estimated 16% had victimized a relative and 12% an intimate, such as a spouse, ex-spouse, boyfriend, or girlfriend.

More than half of the mentally ill reported that they had victimized a female during the current offense. An estimated 15% reported that their youngest victim was a child, age 12 or under, and 12% reported the victim to be between ages 13 and 17. A weapon was used by 44% of the violent State prisoners who were mentally ill.

Victim characteristics and use of weapon, by mental health status of violent State prisoners

	Mentally ill inmates	Other inmates
Gender of victim(s)		
Male	44.3%	51.5%
Female	44.0	37.5
Both males and female	11.7	10.9
Age of youngest victim		
12 or younger	15.4%	10.2%
13–17	11.6	11.0
18–24	17.3	20.7
25–34	25.7	30.9
35–54	23.8	22.8
55 or older	6.2	4.3
Victim-offender relationship		
Knew victim[a]	60.8%	52.1%
Relative	15.6	10.3
Intimate[b]	11.6	8.6
Friend/acquaintance	29.8	27.7
Other[c]	6.5	6.9
Knew none of victims	39.1	47.9
Use of weapon		
Yes	44.0%	41.9%
No	56.0	58.1

[a] More than one victim may have been reported.
[b] Includes spouse, ex-spouse, boyfriend, girlfriend, ex-boyfriend, and ex-girlfriend.
[c] Includes those known by sight only.

These rates were at least double those for inmates who were not mentally ill.

About 4 in 10 inmates with a mental condition unemployed before arrest

Mentally ill offenders were less likely than others to report they were working in the month before arrest. About 38% of mentally ill State and Federal prison inmates and 47% of mentally ill jail inmates were not employed in the month before arrest, while 30% of other State inmates, 28% of other Federal inmates, and 33% of other jail inmates were unemployed.

An estimated 30% of mentally ill and 13% of other inmates in State prison received some type of financial support from government agencies prior to their arrest. More than 15% of the mentally ill received welfare, 17% supplemental security income or other pension, and 3% compensation payments, such as unemployment or workman's compensation.

Over half of mentally ill prison and jail inmates reported wages as their source of income prior to arrest, 23% of prison inmates and 20% of jail inmates reported income from illegal sources.

Offenders on probation were asked about their current employment and sources of income in the past year. Over half of mentally ill probationers and three-quarters of other probationers were currently employed. An estimated 52% of mentally ill probationers and 27% of other probationers said they received income from government agencies in the past year.

Homelessness more prevalent among mentally ill offenders

Mentally ill offenders reported high rates of homelessness, unemployment, alcohol and drug use, and physical and sexual abuse prior to their current incarceration. During the year preceding their arrest, 30% of mentally ill inmates in jail and 20% of those in State or Federal prison reported a period of homelessness, when they were living either on the street or in a shelter (table 7). About 9% of other State prison inmates, 3% of other Federal inmates and 17% of other jail inmates reported a period a homelessness in the year prior to their arrest.

Fewer inmates reported they were homeless at the time of arrest. About 4% of mentally ill State and Federal prison inmates and 7% of jail inmates reported they were living on the street or in a shelter when arrested for their current offense.

Table 6. Criminal history of inmates, by mental health status

	State prison		Federal prison		Local jail	
	Mentally ill inmates	Other inmates	Mentally ill inmates	Other inmates	Mentally ill inmates	Other inmates
Criminal history						
None	18.8%	21.2%	24.3%	38.8%	21.0%	28.4%
Priors	81.2	78.8	75.7	61.2	79.0	71.6
Violent recidivists	53.4	44.9	43.7	21.6	46.0	31.6
Other recidivists	27.8	33.8	32.0	39.6	33.0	40.0
Number of prior probation/ incarceration sentences						
0	18.8%	21.2%	24.3%	38.8%	21.0%	28.4%
1	15.5	19.4	14.0	18.2	14.7	17.9
2	13.8	17.0	12.9	14.7	10.1	11.5
3 to 5	26.3	25.5	23.6	18.9	23.5	19.7
6 to 10	15.6	11.6	15.4	7.3	17.6	14.6
11 or more	10.0	5.3	9.7	2.2	13.2	7.8

Family history of incarceration and alcohol or drug use prevalent among mentally ill

Overall, 55% of mentally ill State prison inmates, 42% of Federal prisoners, 52% of jail inmates, and 40% of probationers reported a family member had been incarcerated at some point (table 8). About 47% of other State prison inmates, 39% of other Federal inmates, 45% of other jail inmates, and 34% of other probationers reported a history of family incarceration. Nearly a quarter of mentally ill State inmates said their father or mother had served time in prison or jail; 42% said a brother or sister had been incarcerated.

When compared with other inmates and probationers, the mentally ill also reported higher rates of alcohol and drug abuse by a parent or guardian while they were growing up. Approximately 4 in 10 mentally ill State prisoners, jail inmates, and probationers, and 1 in 3 Federal inmates reported their parent or guardian had abused alcohol or drugs while they were growing up. About 42% reported alcohol abuse by a parent or guardian, and 13% reported drug abuse.

Table 7. Homelessness, employment, and sources of income of inmates, by mental health status

	State prison		Federal prison		Local jail	
	Mentally ill inmates	Other inmates	Mentally ill inmates	Other inmates	Mentally ill inmates	Other inmates
Homeless						
In year before arrest	20.1%	8.8%	18.6%	3.2%	30.3%	17.3%
At time of arrest	3.9	1.2	3.9	0.3	6.9	2.9
Employed in month before arrest						
Yes	61.2%	69.6%	62.3%	72.5%	52.9%	66.6%
No	38.8	30.4	37.7	27.5	47.1	33.4
Sources of income[a]						
Wages	56.7%	65.6%	54.0%	66.4%	62.9%	77.1%
Family/friends	22.0	17.7	20.1	12.3	19.7	15.4
Illegal sources	23.4	27.0	22.5	28.8	19.4	14.4
Welfare	15.4	7.8	13.7	3.9	21.9	12.3
Pension[b]	17.3	4.1	16.5	3.7	18.4	4.9
Compensation payments	3.1	1.9	4.7	1.8	3.0	2.1

[a]Detail sums to more than 100% because offenders may have reported more than one source of income. For prisoners detail includes any income received in the month prior to arrest. For jail inmates, detail includes any income received in the year prior to arrest.
[b]Includes Supplemental Security Income, Social Security, or other pension.

	Probationers	
	Mentally ill	Other
Currently employed		
Yes	55.9%	75.9%
No	44.1	24.1
Sources of income*		
Wages	69.3%	86.8%
Family/friends	17.9	16.3
Welfare	26.4	15.5
Pension	24.5	7.6
Compensation payments	10.2	7.7

*More than one source of income may have been reported.

At some point while growing up, a quarter of mentally ill State prisoners and local jail inmates lived in a foster home, agency, or institution. One in six mentally ill probationers reported living in a foster home or institution for a period of time during their childhood.

Mentally ill report high rates of past physical and sexual abuse

Mentally ill male State prisoners were more than twice as likely as other males to report physical abuse prior to admission to prison (27% versus 11%) and nearly four times as likely to report prior sexual abuse (15% versus 4%, table 9). Among male inmates 25% of the mentally ill in Federal prisons or in jails reported prior physical abuse, compared to 5% of other male Federal inmates and 8% of other male jail inmates. Mentally ill male probationers were 4 times as likely as other probationers to report prior physical abuse (21% and 5%, respectively).

The rate of physical abuse reported by mentally ill female inmates was over twice that reported by males. Nearly 70% of female State prisoners, 50% of female Federal prisoners, 60% of female

Table 8. Family background of inmates and probationers, by mental health status

	State prison		Federal prison		Local jail		Probation	
	Mentally ill inmates	Other inmates	Mentally ill inmates	Other inmates	Mentally ill inmates	Other inmates	Mentally ill probationers	Other probationers
Family member ever incarcerated	54.9%	46.5%	41.5%	38.5%	51.5%	45.1%	40.3%	34.0%
Parent	23.4	17.4	13.4	11.1	23.7	18.9	19.6	11.1
Brother/sister	41.8	36.5	29.5	29.9	36.2	32.8	25.7	25.6
While growing up—								
Ever lived in a foster home, agency, or institution	26.1%	12.2%	18.6%	5.8%	24.0%	11.5%	15.9%	6.5%
Parent or guardian abused alcohol or drugs								
Alcohol only	30.6%	22.2%	24.6%	16.0%	29.3%	21.9%	32.4%	19.2%
Drugs only	2.0	1.8	1.2	0.8	1.7	1.2	1.0	0.4
Both	10.9	5.7	8.5	2.8	11.01	6.1	9.0	2.4

3 ❖ UNUSUAL PROBLEMS AND UNUSUAL POPULATIONS

Table 9. Prior physical or sexual abuse of inmates and probationers, by mental health status

Reported by Offender	State prison Mentally ill inmates	State prison Other inmates	Federal prison Mentally ill inmates	Federal prison Other inmates	Local jail Mentally ill inmates	Local jail Other inmates	Probation Mentally ill probationers	Probation Other probationers
Ever abused before admission	36.9%	15.2%	34.1%	7.6%	36.5%	12.5%	38.8%	12.1%
Male	32.8	13.1	30.0	5.5	30.7	9.6	31.0	6.5
Female	78.4	50.9	64.1	36.1	72.9	40.3	59.4	35.7
Physically abused	31.0%	12.5%	27.5%	6.4%	30.0%	10.1%	28.1%	9.8%
Male	27.4	10.8	24.5	4.7	25.3	8.0	21.0	5.1
Female	67.6	40.2	50.0	29.4	59.8	30.8	46.7	29.7
Sexually abused	19.0%	5.8%	15.6%	2.7%	23.5%	5.9%	21.9%	5.8%
Male	15.0	4.1	11.6	1.5	17.2	3.4	14.2	2.4
Female	58.9	33.1	45.0	19.3	63.4	29.6	42.3	19.9

Table 10. Prior alcohol and drug use of inmates and probationers, by mental health status

Alcohol/drug use reported by offender	State prison Mentally ill inmates	State prison Other inmates	Federal prison Mentally ill inmates	Federal prison Other inmates	Local jail Mentally ill inmates	Local jail Other inmates	Probation Mentally ill probationers	Probation Other probationers
Alcohol/drug use								
At time of offense	58.7%	51.2%	46.5%	33.0%	64.6%	56.5%	49.0%	46.4%
Drug use								
In month before offense	58.8%	56.1%	48.1%	44.6%	57.6%	47.3%	39.5%	30.3%
At time of offense	36.9	31.7	29.3	21.9	38.8	30.4	18.1	12.6
Alcohol use								
At time of offense	42.7%	36.0%	27.9%	19.8%	44.3%	36.0%	41.4%	39.7%

Table 11. Alcohol dependence and experiences of inmates and probationers while under the influence of alcohol, by mental health history

	State prison Mentally ill inmates	State prison Other inmates	Federal prison Mentally ill inmates	Federal prison Other inmates	Local jail Mentally ill inmates	Local jail Other inmates	Probation Mentally ill probationers	Probation Other probationers
History of alcohol dependency*	34.4%	22.4%	23.9%	15.6%	37.9%	24.3%	34.8%	22.1%
Because of your drinking, have you ever —								
Lost a job?	16.7%	9.0%	8.7%	4.7%	18.0%	10.3%	19.4%	5.3%
Had job or school trouble (such as demotion at work or dropping out of school)?	24.0	13.8	15.4	7.1	..	..	25.2	10.5
Been arrested or held at a police station?	35.2	28.3	30.7	18.3	41.5	30.7	45.7	41.1
While drinking have you ever —								
Gotten into a physical fight?	45.7%	37.0%	36.4%	21.7%	49.8%	34.1%	43.9%	30.3%
Had as much as a fifth of liquor in 1 day, 20 drinks, 3 six-packs of beer, or 3 bottles of wine?	48.8	39.5	43.9	29.2	52.9	38.0	45.7	33.7

.. Not asked of jail inmates.
*Measured by 3 or more positive CAGE responses. For description of the CAGE diagnostic measure see text.

23. Mental Health and Treatment of Inmates and Probationers

jail inmates, and 47% of female probationers reported a history of physical abuse.

Nearly 60% of female mentally ill State prisoners, 45% of female Federal prisoners, 63% of female jail inmates and 42% of female probationers reported prior sexual abuse.

6 in 10 mentally ill State inmates under the influence of alcohol or drugs at time of offense

Mentally ill inmates were more likely than others to be under the influence of alcohol or drugs while committing their current offense. About 60% of mentally ill and 51% of other inmates in State prison were under the influence of alcohol or drugs at the time of their current offense (table 10). Rates of alcohol and drug use at the time of the offense were even higher among mentally ill jail inmates, where 65% of the mentally ill and 57% of other jail inmates were under the influence. Among probationers, 49% of the mentally ill and 46% of others reported alcohol or drug use at the time of the offense.

Like other inmates and probationers, the mentally ill were more often under the influence of alcohol than drugs at the time of the current offense. About 43% of mentally ill State prison inmates and 44% of jail inmates had been drinking when they committed their current offense. Thirty-six percent of other inmates in prison and jail reported they were drinking at the time of the offense.

Table 12. Maximum sentence length and time served by inmates, by offense and mental health status

	Mean maximum sentence length[a]		Mean time served			
			To date of interview		Total time to be served until release[b]	
Most serious offense	Mentally ill inmates	Other inmates	Mentally ill inmates	Other inmates	Mentally ill inmates	Other inmates
Local jail inmates						
All offenses	20 mo	26 mo	6.5 mo	6.7 mo	8.7 mo	10.7 mo
Violent	30 mo	37 mo	8.8 mo	9.3 mo	14.7 mo	16.0 mo
Property	26	26	5.3	8.0	7.4	11.6
Drug	18	25	8.9	8.4	8.6	13.5
Public-order	8	20	5.0	3.3	7.0	5.7
Other	10	8	8.4	1.6	10.0	5.3
State prison inmates						
All offenses	171 mo	159 mo	54.4 mo	49.3 mo	103.4 mo	88.2 mo
Violent	230 mo	225 mo	71.8 mo	69.7 mo	142.5 mo	130.7 mo
Property	128	118	38.8	36.6	75.0	62.2
Drug	103	111	30.3	28.5	49.8	49.5
Public-order	83	81	29.1	27.8	50.8	47.6
Other	120	104	32.5	47.8	60.1	80.6

Note: Because data on sentence length and time served are restricted to persons in prison and jail, they overstate the average sentence and time to be served by those entering prison or jail. Persons with shorter sentences leave prison and jail more quickly, resulting in a longer average sentence among persons in the inmate samples.
[a]Based on the total maximum sentence for all consecutive sentences.
[b]Based on time served when interviewed plus time to be served until the expected date of release.

A third of mentally ill offenders alcohol dependent

Based on the CAGE diagnostic instrument, 34% of mentally ill State prison inmates, 24% of Federal prisoners, 38% of jail inmates and 35% of mentally ill probationers exhibited a history alcohol dependence (table 11).

CAGE is an acronym for four questions used by the diagnostic instrument to assess alcohol dependence or abuse. Respondents are asked if they have ever attempted to (C)ut back on drinking; ever felt (A)nnoyance at others' criticism of their drinking; ever experienced feelings of (G)uilt about drinking; and ever needed a drink first thing in the morning as an (E)ye opener or to steady their nerves. A person's likelihood of alcohol abuse is assessed by the number of positive responses to these four questions. Clinical tests involving hospital admissions, found three or more positive CAGE responses carried a .99 predictive value for alcohol abuse or dependence. (See *Substance Abuse and Treatment, State and Federal Prisoners, 1997*, BJS Special Report, NCJ 172871, for additional information on the CAGE instrument.)

Mentally ill inmates and probationers were more commonly alcohol dependent, reporting three or more positive CAGE responses. About 38% of mentally ill jail inmates reported signs of alcohol dependence, while 24% of other jail inmates reported signs of dependence. Among State prison inmates, 34% of the mentally ill and 22% of other inmates reported three or more positive responses.

Mentally ill offenders report negative life experiences related to drinking

In response to questions concerning their life experiences with alcohol, about 17% of mentally ill and 9% of other inmates in State prison said they had lost a job due to drinking. Among jail inmates with a mental condition, 18% had lost a job due to drinking, while 10% of other

Table 13. Fights since admission and violation of prison or jail rules, by mental health status

	State prison		Federal prison		Local jail	
Discipline problem reported by inmate	Mentally ill inmates	Other inmates	Mentally ill inmates	Other inmates	Mentally ill inmates	Other inmates
Number of fights since admission						
None	64.3%	75.6%	79.4%	90.9%	80.9%	86.7%
1	11.4	9.6	11.6	5.2	9.4	7.0
2 to 3	12.8	7.8	5.2	2.5	7.0	4.1
4 or more	11.5	7.1	3.8	1.4	2.6	2.3
Charged with breaking prison or jail rules	62.2%	51.9%	41.2%	32.7%	24.5%	16.0%

3 ❖ UNUSUAL PROBLEMS AND UNUSUAL POPULATIONS

Table 14. Mental health treatment in prison or jail or on probation for those identified as mentally ill

	Percent of mentally ill offenders			
Since admission, the offender had—	State prison	Federal prison	Local jail	Probation
Been admitted overnight to a mental hospital or treatment program	23.6%	24.0%	9.3%	12.2%
Taken a prescribed medication	50.1	49.1	34.1	36.5
Received counseling or therapy	44.1	45.6	16.2	44.1
Received any mental health services	60.5	59.7	40.9	56.0

jail inmates reported losing a job. Nearly 20% of mentally ill probationers had lost a job; 5% of other probationers.

Amid other alcohol-related problems reported by the mentally ill, 35% of State prisoners had been arrested or held at a police station due to drinking, and 46% had gotten into a fight while drinking. Forty-nine percent of mentally ill State prison inmates, 44% of Federal inmates, 53% of jail inmates, and 46% of mentally ill probationers said they had consumed as much as a fifth of liquor (about 20 drinks) in 1 day.

Mentally ill jail inmates more often reported a prior stay in a detoxification unit for alcohol or drugs. An estimated 22% of the mentally ill in jail and 11% of other inmates reported they had been put in a detoxification unit.

Mentally ill expected to serve 15 months longer than other inmates in prison

Overall, mentally ill State prison inmates were sentenced to serve an average of 171 months in prison, or about 12 months longer than other offenders (table 12). On average, violent offenders with a mental illness were sentenced to 230 months (5 months longer than other violent inmates) and property offenders 128 months (10 months longer than other inmates).

Mentally ill jail inmates typically had sentences shorter than other jail inmates. On average, mentally ill inmates had a maximum sentence of 20 months, while other inmates an average of 26 months. Violent, drug, and property offenders identified as mentally ill had average sentences that were 6 to 12 months shorter than other offenders.

On average, mentally ill inmates in State prison are expected to serve more time in prison than other inmates. From the time of admission to prison to the time of the survey, mentally ill offenders had served on average 5 months longer than other offenders in State prison. Based on the time of admission to the time of expected release, mentally ill offenders expected to serve a total of 103 months in prison, 15 months longer than other offenders. The largest differences in time served were among violent and property offenders. The mentally ill expected to serve an average of at least 12 additional months for violent and property offenses.

Unlike State prisoners, mentally ill inmates in local jails expected to serve less time than inmates who are not mentally ill. Overall, both mentally ill jail inmates and other inmates had served about 6 1/2 months from the time of admission to the time of the survey. On average, mentally ill inmates expected to serve a total of 9 months in jail prior to release; other inmates expected to serve about 11 months.

Disciplinary problems common among mentally ill inmates

Mentally ill inmates in State or Federal prison, as well as those in jail, were more likely than others in those facilities to have been involved in a fight, or hit or punched since admission. Among State prisoners 36% of mentally ill inmates reported involvement in a fight, compared to 25% of other inmates (table 13). Mentally ill inmates in Federal prison were over twice as likely as others to report involvement in a fight (21% compared to 9%).

Twenty-four percent of mentally ill State prison inmates had been involved in two or more fights since admission, and 12% reported involvement in four or more fights. Among jail inmates 10% of the mentally ill had been involved in two or more fights, compared 6% of those not mentally ill.

Consistent with their more frequent involvement in fights, disciplinary problems were more common among mentally ill inmates than other inmates. More than 6 in 10 mentally ill State prison inmates had been formally charged with breaking prison rules since admission. About half of other inmates reported they had been charged with breaking the rules. Among Federal prison inmates 41% of the mentally ill had been charged with a rule violation, compared to 33% of inmates not identified as mentally ill.

6 in 10 mentally ill received treatment while incarcerated

An estimated 60% of the mentally ill in State and Federal prison received some form of mental health treatment during their current period of incarceration (table 14). Fifty percent said they had taken prescription medication; 44% had received counseling or therapy; and 24% had been admitted overnight to a mental hospital or treatment program.

Among jail inmates, 41% of those identified as mentally ill had received some form of mental health services since admission. The majority of those receiving treatment (34%) had been given medication. Fewer jail inmates (16%) than State prisoners (44%) said they had received counseling or therapy since admission.

Just over half of mentally ill probationers had received treatment since their sentence to community supervision. Counseling was the most common form of treatment (44%), followed by medication (37%), and an overnight stay in a mental hospital or treatment program (12%).

When sentenced to probation, an offender may be required by the court or probation agency to meet various conditions of the sentence, such as maintaining employment, submitting to drug testing, or participating in treatment. An estimated 13% of probationers were required to seek mental health treatment as a condition of their sentence. Forty-three percent of those required to participate in treatment had done so by the time of the survey.

Female mentally ill more likely than males to report treatment

Nearly 70% of mentally ill females in State prison, 77% of those in Federal prison, and 56% in local jails received mental health services while incarcerated, while 60% of males in State prison, 57% in Federal prison, and 38% in local jails reported treatment.

White mentally ill inmates reported higher rates of treatment than black or

23. Mental Health and Treatment of Inmates and Probationers

Hispanic offenders. About 64% of white State prison inmates identified as mentally ill had received treatment, compared to 56% of black offenders and 60% of Hispanic offenders.

Percent of mentally ill receiving mental health services

	State prison	Federal prison	Local jail
Gender			
Male	59.9%	57.4%	38.4%
Female	67.3	76.5	56.2
Race/Hispanic origin			
White	64.1%	65.4%	44.7%
Black	56.4	50.0	34.2
Hispanic	59.9	62.5	40.6

Overall, 17% of inmates in State prison, 10% in Federal prison, 11% in local jails, and 12% of those on probation had received some form of mental health services since their current admission to prison or jail or sentence to probation. The most common form of treatment in local jails was medication, reported by 9% of inmates. Probationers were more likely to have received counseling (10%) than to have taken medication (6%) while under supervision. Among State prison inmates 12% said they received medication while incarcerated, and 12% participated in counseling or therapy.

Percent of all offenders who received mental treatment

State prison inmates	17.4%
Federal prison inmates	10.0
Local jail inmates	11.4
Probationers	11.5

Methodology

Data in this report are based on personal interviews conducted through three BJS surveys, the 1997 Survey of Inmates in State and Federal Correctional Facilities, the 1996 Survey of Inmates in Local Jails, and the 1995 Survey of Adults on Probation. Detailed descriptions of the methodology and sample design of each survey can be found in the following: *Substance Abuse and Treatment of Adults on Probation, 1995* (NCJ 166611); *Profile of Jail Inmates, 1996* (NCJ 164629); and *Substance Abuse and Treatment of State and Federal Prisoners, 1997* (NCJ 172871).

Appendix table 1. Standard errors of mental health status for inmates and probationers

	Estimated standard errors			
	State prison inmates	Federal prison inmates	Jail inmates	Probationers
Identified as mentally ill	0.40%	0.55%	0.61%	0.89%
Reported a mental or emotional condition	0.33	0.45	0.54	0.84
Because of a mental or emotional problem, inmate had —				

Accuracy of the estimates

The accuracy of the estimates presented in this report depends on two types of error: sampling and nonsampling. Sampling error is the variation that may occur by chance because a sample rather than a complete numeration of the population was conducted. Nonsampling error can be attributed to many sources, such as nonresponses, differences in the interpretation of questions among inmates, recall difficulties, and processing errors. In any survey the full extent of the nonsampling error is never known. The sampling error, as measured by an estimated standard error, varies by the size of the estimate and the size of the base population. Estimates of the standard errors for selected characteristics have been calculated for each survey (see appendix tables). These standard errors may be used to construct confidence intervals around percentages. For example, the 95% confidence interval around the percentage of State prison inmates who were identified as mentally ill is approximately 16.2% plus or minus 1.96 times 0.40% (or 15.4% to 16.9%).

These standard errors may also be used to test the statistical significance of the difference between two sample statistics by pooling the standard errors of the two sample estimates. For example, the standard error of the difference between mentally ill State prisoners and other inmates who were incarcerated for a violent offense would be 1.49% (or the square root of the sum of the squared standard errors for each group). The difference would be 1.96 times 1.49 (or 2.91%). Since the difference of 6.8% (52.9% minus 46.1%) is greater than 2.91%, the difference would be considered statistically significant.

Estimating the number of mentally ill offenders under correctional supervision

Estimates of the total number of persons in prison, jail and on probation with a mental illness were obtained by multiplying the ratio of inmates or probationers identified as mentally ill from the personal interviews conducted in the three BJS surveys referenced above, by the total number of inmates in State prison, Federal prison, and local jails and the total number of offenders on probation.

For example, the total number of State prison inmates with a mental illness was estimated by multiplying the ratio of mentally ill offenders in State prison (16.2%) obtained from the 1997 Survey of Inmates in State Correctional Facilities, by the total State prison custody population at midyear 1998 (1,102,653) from the National Prisoner Statistics data collection.

References

Guy, Edward; Jerome Platt; Israel Zwerling; and Samuel Bullock. "Mental health status of prisoners in an urban jail." *Criminal Justice and Behavior.* 12(1), 29–53, March 1985.

Monahan, John. "Clinical and Actuarial Predictions of Violence" in Faigman, D and others, eds. *Modern Scientific Evidence: The Law and Science of Expert Testimony,* vol. 1. St. Paul, MN: West Publishing Company, 1997.

Mumola, Christopher. *Substance Abuse and Treatment, State and Federal Prisoners, 1997.* BJS Special Report, NCJ 172871, December 1998.

Powell, Thomas A.; John C. Holt; and Karen M. Fondacaro. "The Prevalence of Mental Illness among Inmates in a Rural State." *Law and Human Behavior.* 21(4), 427–438, August 1997.

Robins, Lee N., and Darrel A. Regier. *Psychiatric Disorders in America: The Epidemiologic Catchment Area Study.* New York: Free Press, 1991.

Steadman, Henry; Stanley Fabisiak, Joel Dvoskin, and Edward Holohean. "A Survey of Mental Disability among State Prison Inmates." *Hospital and Community Psychiatry.* 38(10), 1086–1090, 1989.

Teplin, Linda A. "The Prevalence of Severe Mental Disorder among Male Urban Jail Detainees: Comparison with the Epidemiologic Catchment Area Program." *American Journal of Public Health.* 80(6), 663–669, 1990.

Appendix table 2. Standard errors of selected characteristics of mentally ill inmates and probationers

Selected characteristic	State prison Mentally ill inmates	State prison Other inmates	Federal prison Mentally ill inmates	Federal prison Other inmates	Local jail Mentally ill inmates	Local jail Other inmates	Probation Mentally ill probationers	Probation Other probationers
Current offense								
Violent	1.36%	0.60%	3.65%	0.75%	1.71%	0.84%	2.74%	1.03%
Property	1.17	0.49	2.19	0.55	1.64	0.76	2.79	1.20
Drug	0.91	0.50	3.81	1.05	1.23	0.72	2.23	1.08
Public-order	0.81	0.36	2.92	0.78	1.55	0.83	2.62	1.24
Criminal history								
Any priors	1.06	0.49	3.33	1.07	1.47	0.89	3.03	1.35
Alcohol/drug use at time of offense	1.35	0.60	3.88	1.04	2.17	1.14	3.04	1.33
History of alcohol dependency	1.29	0.50	3.32	0.79	1.72	0.74	2.89	1.10
Ever abused								
Males	1.37	0.43	3.92	0.52	2.14	0.52	3.24	0.72
Females	1.93	1.30	5.63	4.03	2.38	1.46	5.92	3.03
Involved in fight or was hit or punched after admission	1.31	0.52	3.16	0.63	1.48	0.60	—	—
Homeless								
In year before arrest	1.09	0.34	3.01	0.38	0.91	0.26	—	—
At time of arrest	0.52	0.13	1.50	0.12	1.69	0.63	—	—

Acknowledgments

The Bureau of Justice Statistics is the statistical agency of the U.S. Department of Justice. Jan M. Chaiken, Ph.D., is director.

BJS Special Reports address a specific topic in depth from one or more data sets that cover many topics.

Paula M. Ditton wrote this report under the supervision of Allen J. Beck. Christopher Mumola provided statistical assistance. Tina Dorsey and Tom Hester produced and edited the report. Marilyn Marbrook, assisted by Yvonne Boston, prepared the report for publication.

July 1999, NCJ 174463

Appendix table 3. Standard errors of mental health treatment in prison or jail or on probation for those identified as mentally ill

Since admission, the offender had—	State prison	Federal prison	Local jail	Probation
Been admitted overnight to a mental hospital or treatment program	1.15%	3.32%	1.01%	2.00%
Taken a prescribed medication	1.36	3.91	2.22	2.90
Received counseling or therapy	1.35	3.88	1.26	3.03
Received any mental health service	1.33	3.84	2.16	3.03

Archive

This report and others from the Bureau of Justice Statistics are available through the Internet - http://www.ojp.usdoj.gov/bjs/

The data from the 1997 Surveys of Inmates in State and Federal Correction Facilities, the 1995 Survey of Adults on Probation, and the 1996 Survey of Inmates in Local Jails are available from the National Archive of Criminal Justice Data, maintained by the Inter-university Consortium for Political and Social Research at the University of Michigan, 1-800-999-0960. The archive may also be accessed through the BJS Internet site.

JUVENILES IN FEDERAL PRISON

By Jack Kresnak
From *Youth Today*

THE shackles linking the six youths clang as guards escort them outside for tonight's sweat. Hundreds, even thousands, of miles from home, they are among the "baddest" juveniles in the federal prison system. The guards unlock the chains and cuffs. The young Native Americans strip off their shirts and stoop to enter the dome-like tent of thick canvas stretched over bowed willow branches. They sit in a circle in the lodge, sprinkle sage and tobacco on rocks, meditate, beat a drum, chant, and sweat some more in communion with the Great Spirit.

Their lodge is at the Southwest Multi County Corrections Center, a two-story adult jail between a Perkins Family Restaurant and the Dakota Dinosaur Museum, in Dickinson, North Dakota, a struggling farming community 100 miles west of Bismark. The center is the largest maximum-security program for juveniles under federal authority—a tiny population that might grow significantly if Congress enacts juvenile crime legislation that would encourage more federal prosecution of youths.

Amid all the talk of charging more juveniles in federal courts, no one has answered some basic questions: How are juveniles treated in federal prisons now? And can federal prisons handle more juveniles?

"They're having trouble keeping up with their existing demand," says Michael Mahoney, president of Chicago's John Howard Association, and member of the youth-in-federal-custody task force, under the Coordinating Council on Juvenile Justice and Delinquency Prevention. "They are going to have an increased number of kids if some of these new laws pass."

The U.S. Bureau of Prisons (BOP) already struggles to handle 239 juveniles under its control. The federal prison system is built for adults; it has 116,000 of them. But the number of youths has risen from 111 in 1990. They are generally squeezed into small programs

---

Jack Kresnak is a reporter for Youth Today. *Condensed from* Youth Today, *7 (November 1998), 1, 48–50. Published by American Youth Work Center, from which subscriptions are available by contacting 1200 17th St. NW, 4th Floor, Washington, DC 20036-3006 (phone: 202-785-0764).*

carved out of adult facilities, like the one in Dickinson. Enactment of get-tough juvenile-crime legislation might well bring more youths here or to juvenile facilities that will have to be created.

"You can't imagine that they're incredibly well set up to handle an influx of juveniles," says Mark Mauer, assistant director of the Sentencing Project, based in Washington, D.C.

How big would that influx be? No one knows. BOP spokesman Todd Craig says that if the agency has done any projections about how the juvenile crime bills would impact the BOP's juvenile population, he can't reveal them. Indeed, even youth and criminal justice advocates who've been following every nuance of the legislation say they've heard no one discuss how BOP would handle more youths.

Regardless of the numbers, the idea of making more juvenile offenders eligible for federal prison raises the question of how the BOP handles the youths it has now. Some answers can be found in Dickinson.

It is not happenstance that many juveniles here are Native American—the ethnic background of two-thirds of all juveniles in the BOP system. While youths can land in federal prison for violations of federal law such as drug trafficking and bank robbery or for crimes on federal property, most are in for felonies committed on Indian reservations.

The BOP juvenile system consists of 30 institutions, both secure and nonsecure, under contract with the federal government. The youngest offenders the BOP takes are 13; there is currently one in New Mexico and one in South Dakota. Offenders can enter as youths up to age 18, but once in, can stay until 25, when they must be released. The average age of youths in the federal system is 17.

DAKOTA HORIZONS

The 40-bed juvenile facility here is run by the county, under a corrections center program called Dakota Horizons. The BOP pays Dakota Horizons $99.80 a day for each juvenile.

Is placing these kids hundreds or thousands of miles away from home really the answer?

Juveniles are here from as far away as Maine and Hawaii. About half of the juveniles in BOP facilities are over 250 miles from home. Distance is one of the main criticisms of putting juveniles in the BOP system. For rehabilitation to succeed, most experts agree, families of jailed youths should be involved in their therapy and their lives.

"Obviously, the government needs to cease using nonregional placement for kids," says Larry Brendtro, president of Reclaiming Youth International and, like Mahoney, a member of the juvenile justice coordinating council. "My concern for some time has been with this whole issue of the federal government placing kids hundreds or thousands of miles away from home," says Brendtro, who was part of a BOP team that audited Dakota Horizons.

"I send these kids up to the Dakotas, and that's a long way from Arizona for a 15-, 16-year-old kid," says U.S. District Court Judge Richard Bilby, of Tucson, who sentenced several juveniles to federal facilities.

It's an even longer way for an 18-year-old from Maine, such as Robert, one of several youths that Dakota Horizons made available for interviews. Being so far from home "is the toughest part of the whole thing," says Robert, here for crimes including car-jackings, home invasions, and robberies of drug dealers. He says his mother and siblings visited him here last year.

Dakota Horizons Director Norbert Sickler says the facility helps pay travel expenses for some families and offers free accommodations in the area. "From our experience, we have found that individuals who are from a greater distance, this has really not hampered the treatment program," says Sickler, former head of North Dakota's Bureau of Criminal Investigations. "We do encourage the kids to keep family connections both by writing and telephone."

The BOP plans to house all federal juveniles within 250 miles of their homes by fiscal year 2000, unless the sentencing judge rules otherwise, says Patricia Sledge, Deputy Assistant Director for the Bureau of Prisons' community corrections and detention division.

Even that might not be good enough, says James Bell, staff attorney for the Youth Law Center, in San Francisco. "By locking somebody up in Dickinson, North Dakota, I'm sure there's not a strong after-care component" for the youths when they are sent back home, especially to a reservation, he says. "There's no transition back to the community. The kids will pick up right where they left off. If we can keep them closer to home in a joint state/tribal venture of some kind and begin the transition back, I think that those dollars are better spent."

Indeed, John Echohawk, executive director of the National Indian Legal Defense Fund, says it would be better to treat Indian juveniles in their local communities. But that isn't always possible. "The tribes would like to handle these juveniles locally under tribal law with tribal facilities," Echohawk says. "But we've got such a tremendous problem related to a lack of funding for basic facilities, including juvenile facilities, that we don't really have any other choice but to use federal facilities off reservation."

Ironically, Dakota Horizons does not pass muster as a juvenile rehabilitation program under North Dakota law, says Terry Traynor, the North Dakota juvenile-justice specialist who administers federal Juvenile Justice Act funds in the state. "They're licensed under North Dakota law as a jail, and we can't, as state government, place juveniles there," Traynor says.

Sickler says his staff strives to maintain "sight and sound" separation of juveniles and adults, as required by federal guidelines, although occasionally adults and youths may see each other through a glass window. A construction project to expand the building will mean total separation for juveniles, Sickler says.

NOT REHABILITATING

The problem is that the BOP's facilities were built for adults, with modifications made for youths. James Cunningham, another juvenile-justice expert on the team that audited Dakota Horizons in August 1997, says that the BOP's "instruments were geared toward adult penal situations and not toward rehabilitating children.

"What they're doing is not meeting the needs of those children in terms of rehabilitating them," says Cunningham, who is director of the Detroit programs for Starr Commonwealth Schools, one of Michigan's leading agencies in rehabilitating delinquent youths. "They used standards that would apply to adults and not standards that would apply to children."

The BOP does plan to substantially upgrade programs for juveniles, says Sledge, of the agency's community corrections and detention division. Sledge was on the team that evaluated Dakota Horizons, and says she was "very much impressed with the staff they had there." She admitted that she is unfamiliar with the "therapeutic milieu" concept used in most juvenile-rehabilitation institutions, but says BOP psychologists and staff at Dakota Horizons are providing appropriate therapy.

Sickler says he is proud of the therapeutic services at his facility, and that they are expanding. While the audit team found that each youth got just 20 hours a week of programs including schooling, vocational training, counseling, and mental health services, Sickler says an audit last May put the figure at "approximately 45 hours. Our goal is to have 50." That will be the requirement under the BOP's new Statement of Work contracts.

Dakota Horizons provides psychological screening and counseling for juvenile inmates. A psychiatrist evaluates juveniles who may need behavior-modifying medications. The facility has three licensed addiction counselors; most of the juveniles have serious problems with alcohol, marijuana, and cocaine. Many of the youths come from facilities that couldn't handle them. "We're supposed to handle the toughest of the tough," says Loree Basaraba Thompson, head of mental health services at Dakota Horizons.

"It's a jail, but there are plenty of things we can do here," says Robert, the youth from Maine. He attends Alcoholics Anonymous meetings here.

The conditions at the BOP juvenile facilities are of particular interest to Native Americans. Fred LaMere, a Santee Sioux who works on homeschooling programs for Indian youth in Sioux City, Iowa, and also is a consultant on Indian affairs in Iowa's adult prisons, says prosecutors and judges are sending too many Indian youths to adult prison rather than juvenile facilities: "Basically, all the prisons are doing is allowing them [the youths] to have sweat lodges. As far as therapy and rehabilitation geared toward Native Americans, they're not doing that."

MORE IMPRESSED

Others are more impressed. Kevin Leckey, nondenominational minister at the Lower

Bruel Indian reservation south of Pierre, South Dakota, recently visited two former students who are serving time at Dakota Horizons. "I think it's one of the best [juvenile prisons] I've seen," he says. "That's because of the activities, the education, the process that they do with the kids. They give them something to look forward to each day rather than sitting in a cell with an empty mind."

Larry Foster, director and spiritual advisor for the Navajo Nation Corrections Project, in Arizona, knows several youths who have done time in Dickinson. He says the spiritual ceremonies, such as the sweat lodge, are significant for incarcerated Indians, and that getting such ceremonies into prisons has been a long struggle.

"The sweat lodge and pipe ceremonies are perhaps the most successful therapies for our youths who are incarcerated," Foster says. "The Native American youth are far removed from their homelands. They're isolated, and they need every opportunity to participate in their traditional beliefs. They benefit from this spiritual healing."

Could the BOP handle even more juveniles? Youth advocates, judges, and police have been critical of the movement to federalize crimes already handled by states. They see no advantage to sending kids to faraway prisons under federal jurisdiction, as opposed to state facilities that are set up for juveniles. In some states, however, the juvenile facilities might not offer as much programming as do BOP facilities such as Dakota Horizons.

"We're supposed to be a limited jurisdiction court," Judge Bilby says. "We're really supposed to only try those crimes that really affect the United States: treason, espionage, and dope. And they keep expanding jurisdiction and making it concurrent with the states. When you do that, you get into judge-shopping, with local police officials trying to find harsher penalties in one place or another, which can be very unseemly."

"I'm sure there would be somewhat of an increase" in the numbers of youths tried in federal court, Mauer says. The size of the increase, he says, would depend on several factors, including whether "the U.S. attorneys really want to take on additional cases."

RE-FORMING JUVENILE JUSTICE: THE NEW ZEALAND EXPERIMENT

ALLISON MORRIS
GABRIELLE MAXWELL
Victoria University of Wellington

This article describes the system of youth justice adopted in New Zealand in 1989, which introduced a number of radical and innovative features including the involvement of young people, families, and victims in deciding how best to deal with the offending. The principal mechanism for achieving this is the family group conference, which replaces or supplements the Youth Court as the principal decision-making forum in most of the more serious cases. Research data are presented that indicate that, to a large extent, this new process is working well and may be having an impact on reconviction figures.

INTRODUCTION

The Children, Young Persons and Their Families Act 1989 introduced into New Zealand a radical and innovative way of dealing with young offenders that is now being copied in parts of Canada, England, and Australia (Hudson, Morris, Maxwell, & Galaway, 1996) and examined by many diverse jurisdictions (for example, some states in the United States, South Africa, and Sweden). In essence, the New Zealand youth justice system moves some way toward a justice approach without abandoning the desire to achieve positive outcomes for young people who offend. Nothing experimental about that.

However, it also reflects certain innovative strategies: Families and the young people themselves are centrally involved in rather than excluded from decisions about how best the offending should be responded to; victims may also choose to be involved in determining these proposed sanctions; decisions are reached by the agreement of all the participants rather than externally imposed; and the process throughout should be culturally appropriate. These strategies are achieved partly through changes in police and court processes and practice but mainly through a new decision-making forum: the family group conference. This enables victims and offenders to meet together and to negotiate an appropriate penalty. This article primarily explores the potential of family group conferences in dealing with youth offending.[1] But first a brief description of the New Zealand system.

THE POLICE

The intention underlying the Children, Young Persons and their Families Act 1989 is to encourage the police to adopt low-key responses to juvenile offending wherever possible. Thus juvenile offenders cannot now be arrested unless certain tightly drawn conditions are met. The most important of these are that the arrest is necessary to ensure the juvenile's appearance in court, to prevent the commission of further offenses, or to prevent the loss or destruction of evidence or interference with witnesses. The most recent police statistics indicate that only about 8%–10% of juvenile offenders are arrested.[2] It is really only this arrested group who will subsequently appear in the Youth Court (we will discuss the Youth Court later).

Also, as in most jurisdictions now, it is expected that minor and first offenders will be diverted from prosecution by means of an immediate (street) warning. Where further action is thought necessary, the police can refer juveniles to the police Youth Aid Section (a specialist unit dealing only with juveniles) for follow-up—for example, a warning in the presence of the parents. The Youth Aid Section may also require an apology to the victim and give the child or young person an additional sanction (for example, some community work). During 1993, 25% of juvenile offenders were warned by the police, and a further 56% were dealt with by Youth Aid through police diversion: Thus the offenses of 81% of all known juvenile offenders in New Zealand are resolved by the police. The police clearly, then, stand as gatekeepers to the youth justice system.[3]

THE FAMILY GROUP CONFERENCE

Family group conferences lie at the heart of the new procedures and are held for those young people arrested and those not diverted or warned by the police: around 20% of all known juvenile offenders.[4] The family group conference has responsibility to formulate a plan about how best to deal with the offending. The range of possibilities here are limitless (as long as they are agreed on by the parties) but could include an apology, community work, reparation, or involvement in some program.

The family group conference is made up of the young person, his or her advocate if one has been arranged (usually in only arrest/court cases), members of the family and whoever they invite, the victim(s) or their representative, a support person for the victim if he or she so wishes, the police, the social worker if one has been involved with the family, and the youth justice coordinator (the employee of the Department of Social Welfare responsible for managing the youth justice process). The family and those it invites are entitled to deliberate in private during the family group conference or can ask for the meeting to be adjourned to enable discussions to continue elsewhere. Family group conferences can take place wherever the family wishes, provided (since 1995) the victim agrees. Common venues include facilities of the Department of Social Welfare, the family's home, community rooms, or marae (meeting houses).

The jurisdiction of the family group conference is limited to the disposition of cases where the young person has not denied the alleged offenses or has already been found guilty. The intended focus is the young person's offending and matters related directly to the circumstances of that offending. The Act clearly states that criminal proceedings should not be used to intervene in the life of the young person on welfare grounds, and this objective has been interpreted to imply that family group conferences themselves should primarily focus on issues of accountability rather than welfare. Welfare issues are usually only addressed as voluntary additions to offense-based sanctions or separately in care and protection proceedings.

The plans and decisions are binding when they have been agreed to by a family group conference and, for court-referred cases, accepted by the court. Where a young person fails to complete what the family group conference has decided, it may be reconvened to discuss that failure. At this stage, a new plan is formulated. At any stage, plans can include a recommendation for prosecution in court.

YOUTH COURT

A court process is reserved for a minority of young offenders. The Youth Court has been created as a branch of the District Court to deal with youth justice issues only, and its establishment underlines the importance of the principle that the offending of young persons should be premised on criminal justice not welfare principles; that is, on notions of accountability and responsibility for actions, due process, legal representation, requiring judges to give reasons for certain decisions, and imposing sanctions that are proportionate to the gravity of the offense.

The Youth Court is closed to the public to preserve the confidentiality of its proceedings. It operates an appointments' system in an attempt both to prevent young people associating with each other at court and to reduce the amount of time families are kept waiting. The Court routinely appoints a youth advocate (a barrister or solicitor) to represent the young person where the young person does not already have a legal representative. The Court may also appoint a lay advocate to support the young person in any proceedings in the Youth Court. Lay advocates are individuals of standing within the young person's culture, and it is their responsibility to ensure the court's awareness of cultural matters.

Where cases are referred to the Youth Court, the possible outcomes are as follows in order of severity: transfer to the District (adult) Court,[5] supervision with residence;[6] supervision with activity;[7] community work;[8] supervision;[9] fine, reparation, restitution, or forfeiture; to come up if called upon within 12 months (a type of conditional discharge); admonition; discharge from proceedings; and police withdrawal of the information. In addition, it is possible to order the disqualification of a driver involved in a traffic offense. The intention of the legislation is to allow families to influence outcomes. Thus the Youth Court cannot make a disposition unless a family group conference has been held, and it must take into account the plan and recommendations put forward by the family group conference.

DOES THE NEW ZEALAND SYSTEM "WORK"?

The success of the New Zealand youth justice system can be judged on the basis of conventional criteria derived from those objectives that are dominant trends in current juvenile justice policy in most jurisdictions—for example, diversion, de-institutionalization, and making young people accountable. In brief, here, our research shows that it has been relatively successful overall.[10] For example, few juvenile offenders now appear in courts, few of these receive any type of court order, and even fewer receive any kind of residential or custodial order. On the other hand, about 85% of the young people who took part in family group conferences agreed to carry out what we have called elsewhere "active penalties," that is to say, community work, reparation, and the like. If we add "apologies" to this, the figure comes closer to 95%.

But New Zealand's capacity to fundamentally re-form youth justice lies in its innovative features—participation by young persons, their families, and victims, and agreements reached by them about how best to deal with the offending. It is on these that we focus now.

FAMILY GROUP CONFERENCES, YOUNG PEOPLE, AND THEIR FAMILIES

An early concern was that young people and their families would simply not attend family group conferences. This turned out to be false, and the active involvement of parents in family group conferences is considerable. First, not only do they attend, but often the extended family does too. Second, in contrast to the exclusion that typifies conventional youth justice systems, more than two thirds of the parents we interviewed said they felt involved in the decision-making process and about two thirds also felt they had been a party to the decision. Thus holding parents responsible for their children's offending has been given a new and constructive meaning.

The young people we talked with were less engaged in the decision-making process. Only about a third felt involved, and less than a fifth (16%) felt that they had been a party to the decision. But what do these figures actually tell us? This lack of involvement may be because neither families nor professionals allow young people the opportunity to become involved, or it may be because young people themselves do not feel able to become involved. However, these figures for young people's involvement in the New Zealand system reflect real progress compared with the court-based decision-making processes in New Zealand in the past and compare favorably with young people's involvement in conventional criminal justice systems.

FAMILY GROUP CONFERENCES AND VICTIMS

Victims simply by their presence participate more in this system than traditionally, and for nearly half the family group conferences in our sample, at least one victim or victims' representative was present. When asked, victims gave a range of reasons for welcoming this opportunity. Some victims stressed the value of expressing their feelings to the offender and of making sure that the offender learned from the experience. Other victims wanted to contribute to the offender's rehabilitation or to show their support for the process or for offenders of their cultural group. Yet other victims emphasized their own interests: They wanted to make sure things were done properly and to get reparation.

Eighty-five percent of the victims who did not attend a family group conference gave reasons that related to poor practice: They were not invited, the time was unsuitable for them, or they were given inadequate notice of the family group conference. The Children, Young Persons and Their Families Act 1989 was amended (with effect from January 1995) to ensure that victims are consulted about the time and venue of family group conferences, and the proportion of victims attending group conferences has now certainly increased in some areas. There will always be a minority of victims who choose not to participate in a restorative process, but our research found that only 6% of victims, when asked, said that they did not wish to meet the offender.

Our research also showed that, when victims were involved, many found this a positive process. About 60% of the victims interviewed described the family group conference they attended as helpful, positive, and rewarding. Generally, they said that they were effectively involved in the process and felt better as a result of participating. Victims also commented on two other specific benefits for them. First, it provided them with a voice in determining appropriate outcomes. Second, they were able to meet the offender and the offender's family face to face so that they could assess their attitude, understand more why the offense had occurred, and assess the likelihood of it recurring. A smaller proportion of victims, about a quarter, said that they felt worse as a result of attending the family group conference. There were a variety of reasons for this. The most frequent and perhaps the most important was that the victim did not feel that the young person and/or his or her family were truly sorry.

About two thirds of the victims in our sample were satisfied with the outcomes, and this number was not related to the seriousness of the offense; around a third were dissatisfied. In part, this was because they saw the decision of the family group conference as too soft or too harsh. But, more frequently, victims were dissatisfied because the promised arrangements fell down afterward or they were simply never informed about the eventual outcome of the family group conference. The responsibility for this lay more often with professional staff than with the young person and his or her family. Overall, then, despite difficulties in developing effective practice, family group conferences seem more often and more effectively responsive to victims than conventional systems.

FAMILY GROUP CONFERENCES AND RECONVICTIONS

There is another sense in which we can ask whether family group conferences work: How successful are they at preventing reoffending? In some senses this is an unusual question in that family group conferences are a *process* of decision making rather than an outcome option. However, we analyzed data on the reconviction up to December 1994 of the original 1990–1991 family group conference sample (Morris & Maxwell, 1996a, 1996b). A matching sample against which to compare these data is not available. However, our general conclusion, after reviewing other local and overseas reconviction studies, is that the proportion reconvicted in the first year following a family group conference (26%) is certainly no worse and its possibly better than samples dealt with in the criminal justice system. Furthermore, there is some evidence from this study that the probability of reconviction was *reduced* when certain of the potentially restorative aspects of family group conferences were achieved. Victim's satisfaction was least often reported for persistent recidivists, and this group was also least likely to have completed the tasks agreed to at the family group conference. Regression analysis also suggested that those offenders who failed to apologize to victims were 3 times more likely to be reconvicted than those who had apologized.

CONCERNS ABOUT FAMILY GROUP CONFERENCES

A number of specific questions have been raised about family group conferences. We have dealt with these in detail elsewhere (Maxwell & Morris, 1996) and refer to them only in brief here.

DO FAMILY GROUP CONFERENCES PROVIDE A RATIONAL AND FAIR SYSTEM?

This can be tested in two ways: by examining the outcomes of family group conferences and by examining the views of those affected by the offense. We carried out a multiple regression analysis of family group conference outcomes and identified as important offense-related factors—the seriousness of the offenses committed, the number of offenses committed, and prior offense history. This indicates that the same factors are influential in family group conferences as in more traditional systems.[11]

Moreover, in our research, 95% of the family group conferences studied reached agreed decisions, satisfaction with outcomes was generally high (with the exception of victims), and the recommendations of the family group conference were usually followed by the Youth Court in those cases referred to it.

ARE FAMILY GROUP CONFERENCES SOFT OPTIONS?

There is little support from research for the suggestion that family group conferences are soft options. As we noted earlier, most young people dealt with in family group conferences received "active" penalties. Before the 1989 Act, a similar proportion of young people appeared before the court then as appear now at family group conferences, but only 60% of them received an active penalty, and apologies to victims were rare. It is true that custodial or residential penalties are rarely recommended by family group conferences. But we need to ask here whether anything positive would be achieved by a greater use of the "tough" options of custody and residential placement. Research generally indicates that these more severe penalties do not deter (Roeger, 1994).

DO FAMILY GROUP CONFERENCES WIDEN THE NET OF SOCIAL CONTROL?

Over the period 1991–1993, the proportion of young people warned by the police, dealt with by Youth Aid, and referred to family group conferences has remained relatively stable. It is difficult to compare this pattern with patterns in the past when there were only two possibilities: warning by the police or referral to the court. But, since 1989, diversion through the police has increased and also family group conferences have replaced court hearings for about three quarters of those who might otherwise have appeared in court. This suggests that net-widening is not occurring. Nor is there any evidence that the use of family group conferences has encouraged the referral of less serious offenders into the system. Generally, as we have noted previously, fewer young people now appear in court; fewer young people appearing in court now receive court orders; fewer young people are receiving sentences of supervision with residence, and those sentences are generally shorter (maximum 3 months); and fewer young people are remanded in custody. Young people are now much more likely to be dealt with by informal means, within the community and without a record of a conviction.

DO FAMILY GROUP CONFERENCE COERCE FAMILIES AND INCREASE STATE CONTROL?

Family group conferences *are* part of the system of social control. The involvement of families in decision making can be seen, cynically, as an effective way of expanding the system of social control by making families instruments of the state in this task. Certainly a number of our findings give cause to doubt that families were always free to choose: It was almost invariably the professionals who provided the informational basis for decisions, families were not always allowed time to deliberate on their own, and, sometimes, professionals argued strongly against the family's preferences. The fact that the police were generally satisfied with outcomes suggests that outcomes were, at least on occasion, pitched relatively high compared with those that a court might have given.

On the other hand, the involvement of families can lead to solutions different from those that would have been imposed by a court and potentially more meaningful for the young people concerned. Families also reported feeling involved in the decisions and being satisfied with the outcomes; this cannot be lightly dismissed. The argument that involving families in decisions merely increases the power of state control is fundamentally untestable. A system that produces outcomes that satisfy young people and their families and, at the same time, reduces the numbers of young people in court and in custody does not seem to be one that has increased social control.

CONCLUSION

There is much that is positive and novel about the New Zealand system of youth justice. It has succeeded in diverting the majority of young offenders from criminal courts, and reliance on the use of institutions has been much reduced. Families participate in the processes of decision making and are taking responsibility for their young people in most instances. Many of the concerns raised by commentators are not well founded. However, it would be wrong to finish without acknowledging a real concern that we have: inadequate resourcing. Although additional funding has recently been allocated to the service responsible for managing family group conferences, we have to note that the total budget for youth justice dropped from $34.5 to $27.5 million between 1991 and 1994, and, of this, the amount allocated for operational expenditure has declined even more dramatically from $11.5 million to $4.5 million. Over this period, the number of family group conferences held increased. It would be a great pity if the full potential of family group conferences remained unmet because of a failure to invest in the future of those young people who commit offenses.

NOTES

1. A separate system of family group conferences can deal with the abuse and neglect of children and young persons. See Hardin (1996) for a discussion of the relevance of these family group conferences for the United States.
2. This arrest figure contrasts with police estimates from 10 years previously of around 30% (Maxwell & Morris, 1993).
3. This "police diverted or warned" figure contrasts with a figure of 55% for 10 years previously (Maxwell & Morris, 1993).
4. The only exception is those young people who have committed murder or manslaughter.
5. Transfer to the District Court can only take place where certain conditions are met: The juvenile must be at least 15 years of age; the offense must be purely indictable, or the offense must be punishable by imprisonment for a term exceeding 3 months and the young person elects trial by jury; the nature of circumstances of the offense must be such that if the young person were an adult, he or she would be sentenced to custody; and the Court must be satisfied that any order of a noncustodial nature would be inadequate.
6. A supervision with residence order may last for up to 9 months and is made up of 3 months in the custody of the Department of Social Welfare (this is reduced to 2 months for good behavior during the custodial placement) and 6 months under the supervision of a social worker.
7. Supervision with activity involves an order of up to 3 months' structured supervised activity followed by up to 3 months' supervision.
8. Community work is for a minimum of 20 and a maximum of 200 hours and has to be completed within 12 months.
9. Supervision is limited to a maximum of 6 months.
10. In 1990 and 1991, we collected data on 195 young offenders referred to a youth justice family group conference (70 were also dealt with in the youth court). We observed and recorded what happened during the family group conference, collected data from police and social welfare files, and interviewed family members, young people, police officers, social welfare staff who were involved in the family group conference, and victims. For more information, see Maxwell and Morris (1993).
11. The proportion of variance accounted for by these factors was 29%, which indicates that nonoffense factors also played an important role. But this is equally true of adult courts.

REFERENCES

Hardin, M. (1996). *Family group conferences in child abuse and neglect cases: Learning from the experience of New Zealand*. Washington, DC: ABA Center on Children and the Law.

Hudson, J., Morris, A., Maxwell, G., & Galaway, B. (Eds.). (1996). *Family group conferences: Perspectives on policy and practice*. Annandale, New South Wales: Federation Press.

Maxwell, G. M., & Morris, A. (1993). *Families, victims and culture: Youth justice in New Zealand*. Wellington, New Zealand: Department of Social Welfare and Institute of Criminology.

Maxwell, G. M., & Morris, A. (1996). Research on family group conferences with young offenders in New Zealand. In J. Hudson, A. Morris, G. Maxwell, & B. Galaway (Eds.), *Family group conferences: Perspectives on policy and practice*. Annandale, New South Wales: Federation Press.

Morris, A., & Maxwell, G. M. (1996a). Family group conferences and offending. *Criminology, Aotearoa/New Zealand, 3*, 12–13.

Morris, A., & Maxwell, G. M. (1996b). Recidivism revisited. *Criminology, Aotearoa/New Zealand, 5*, 11–12.

Roeger, L. (1994). The effectiveness of criminal justice sanctions for aboriginal offenders. *The Australian and New Zealand Journal of Criminology, 27*, 264–281.

Unit 4

Unit Selections

26. **A House without a Blueprint,** Ted Gest
27. **Facts and Figures: A Costly Matter of Life or Death,** Belolyn Williams-Harold
28. **Stolen Lives: Men and Women Wrongfully Sentenced to Death Row,** Jenny Allen and Lori Grinker
29. **Death Row Justice Derailed,** Ken Armstrong and Steve Mills
30. **Point/Counterpoint: The Death Penalty Brings Justice,** Gov. George E. Pataki, and **Death at Midnight . . . Hope at Sunrise,** Stephen Hawkins

Key Points to Consider

❖ What are some of the "extra" protections a person gets in a death penalty case? How does the legal system justify these additional protections? What did the states do to satisfy these requirements for extra protection?

❖ What factors outside the actual facts of the crime have an impact on the potential for a sentence of death?

❖ What are some of the reasons that conservatives support or oppose the use of the death penalty? What are some of the reasons that moderates and liberals support or oppose the use of the death penalty?

❖ What were some of the reasons why those later discovered to be innocent were sent to death row? How did their families react to the sentence? How did it affect their families over time?

❖ What were some of the reasons that Illinois used to justify its moratorium on executions? Since the governor of Illinois has decided to temporarily suspend executions, do you think other states will follow? If so, which ones do you think will follow next, and why?

DUSHKIN ONLINE Links   www.dushkin.com/online/

24. **ACLU Criminal Justice Home Page**
    http://aclu.org/issues/criminal/hmcj.html
25. **Critical Criminology Division of the ASC**
    http://sun.soci.niu.edu/~critcrim
26. **Prison Law Page**
    http://www.wco.com/~aerick/prison.htm

These sites are annotated on pages 4 and 5.

Dying on the Inside: The Death Penalty

Few issues in the criminal justice system arouse as much debate as the death penalty. It is possible to find conservatives who oppose it (usually for financial reasons) and moderates who support it (usually as an attempt to achieve deterrence). The division, however, is not simply political. In this unit we explore the problems inherent in the utilization of a punishment that is completely irrevocable and has substantial and, at times, cumbersome constitutional protections.

In the first article, "A House without a Blueprint," Ted Gest uses a specific criminal case to demonstrate the practical problems of sentencing someone to die. This leads into the following article, "Facts and Figures: A Costly Matter of Life or Death," by Belolyn Williams-Harold, in which the financial burdens of following the federal guidelines for death-qualified cases are examined.

The next two articles explore the experience of being an innocent on death row, and how one state, Illinois, has made changes to its death penalty policies to keep this situation from reoccurring.

This unit concludes with a point-counterpoint presentation that shows both sides of the death penalty debate, and how each side considers specific material to the exclusion of other material, which, while valid, disagrees with their fundamental stance on the issue.

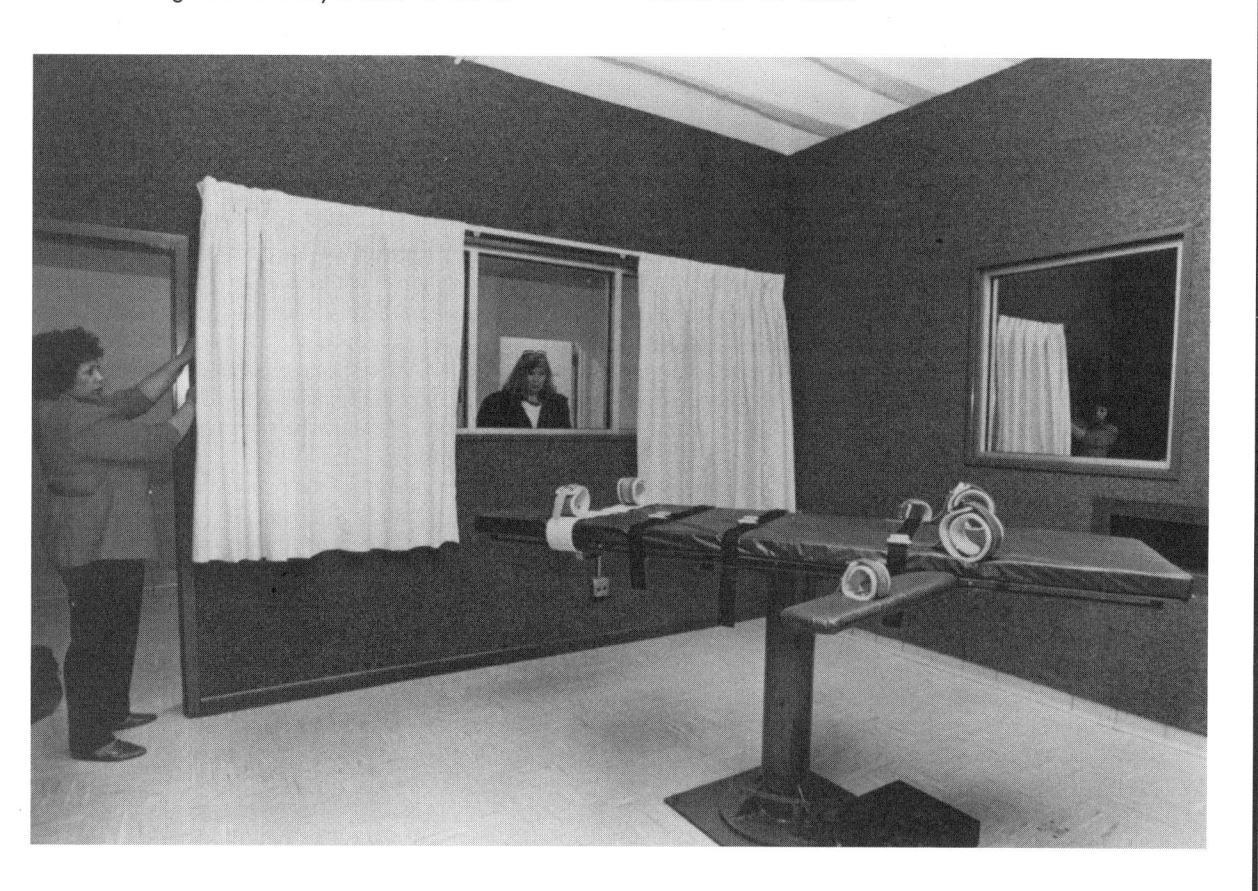

A house without a blueprint: after 20 years, the death penalty is still being meted out unevenly.

Ted Gest

There are currently 3,122 prisoners on death row, and critics of the system say that the death penalty is often administered unfairly. The location of the crime and the skill of defense attorneys often have more to do with who dies than the nature of the crime.

For years, most Americans have agreed that especially vicious murderers should be executed. Yet 20 years after the Supreme Court ended a four-year moratorium on death sentences, executions remain rare. The convoluted case of Gary Burris helps explain why.

On a freezing winter night in 1980, robbers took $40 from an Indianapolis taxi driver, forced him to disrobe and shot him in the head. His naked body was found the next morning, froze to the pavement. Burris admitted taking part in the murder, and he was convicted within a year. But his attorney failed to present evidence about Burris's early life—he grew up in a house of prostitution after being abandoned by his mother—that might have persuaded jurors to spare his life. That omission led to a series of appeals, a second sentencing and an execution initially set for last November. Two codefendants plea-bargained their way to lesser penalties, but 16 years after he was arrested, Burris is still on Indiana's death row, waiting for a test case he has brought over a new federal law to wend its way through the courts.

The flawed and seemingly endless Burris case reflects the huge gap between the rhetoric surrounding the death penalty and the reality of applying it. Despite wide public support for executions, only about 1 in 100 murderers ends up on death row, and in many ways the method of choosing who gets death and who gets life still resembles the lightning strike it was compared to in 1972, when the Supreme Court suspended executions and said states must devise more-rational sentencing methods.

The long wait. In the 20 years this week since the court allowed executions to resume, the justice system has been a model of inefficiency. Some 3,122 convicts occupy 36 death rows across the nation, and the annual execution total in the past two decades peaked last year at 56; there have been 18 in 1996. And the 31 men executed in 1994 had sat on death row for an average of 10 years.

Politicians and judges share the blame for the mess. While Congress and many state legislatures consistently have voted to make more crimes punishable by death, "the judicial system has tied itself in knots trying to carry out the popular will while also addressing the misgivings of those who have strong moral objections," says Alex Kozinski, a conservative California federal appellate judge who calls the death penalty "the ultimate run-on sentence."

The Supreme Court is a prime culprit. Two decades of decisions attempting to sort out the rules for executions have left prosecutors and defense lawyers more confused than enlightened. The complex doctrines, wrote legal scholars Carol and Jordan Steiker in the Harvard Law Review, have "grown like a house without a blueprint—with a new room here, a staircase there, but without the guidance of a master builder."

As the court tinkers with difficult but often peripheral issues, critics say that what should be the foundation of the process—the defense system—is increasingly shaky. Prominent suspects like O.J. Simpson and South Carolina mother Susan Smith get top-flight lawyering, and other defendants get good-quality help from public defenders. But many court-appointed attorneys lack competence, resources or both. Citing several states that allow private lawyers only $2,000 in public funds to prepare for trial, the Washington-based Death Penalty Information Center says that an attorney "diligent enough to put in the 500 to 1,000 hours" often needed in capital cases must work below minimum wage.

A crime's location and the quality of available lawyers nearby can have life-or-death consequences. A North Carolina man with an IQ of 70 was sentenced to death for killing a night watchman with his own clock, an unpremeditated act. "A more-zealous attorney could have avoided the death penalty," argues William Massengale, a Chapel Hill lawyer working on the man's appeal. "It's profoundly unfair that the selection of your lawyer may determine your fate."

Congress lowered the odds for many on death row this year when it halted funds for legal aid centers in 20 states

26. House without a Blueprint

ON DEATH ROW, RACE REALLY DOES MATTER

Of the 3,122 on death row, whites and minorities are represented almost equally:
White: 1,493 (48 percent)
Black: 1,272 (41 percent)
Latino: 236 (8 percent)

Although whites are victims in less than half of murders overall, most of those executed in the past two decades killed whites:
White defendant, white victim: 256 (57 percent)
Black defendant, white victim: 101 (23 percent)
White defendant, black victim: 5 (1 percent)
Black defendant, black victim: 51 (11 percent)

WRONG PLACE

Southern states have executed the most convicts since the Supreme Court allowed capital punishment to resume in 1976. Courts in these states are able to find only poorly paid lawyers for many defendants.
Texas: 106
Florida: 36
Virginia: 31
Louisiana: 23
Georgia: 20
Missouri: 19
Alabama: 13
Arkansas: 11

18 other states have executed 8 or fewer prisoners.
USN&WR–Basic Data: NAACP Legal Defense and Educational

---

their convictions and limited federal judges' powers of review.

Lawmakers and prosecutors were ecstatic about the legislation, but their enthusiasm may be short-lived. Even if the new law eventually helps streamline the process, it includes so many debatable provisions that, for now, it is likely to have the perverse effect of delaying executions rather than expediting them.

High-court concern. A key section, for example, instructs federal judges to limit reviews of state cases to a few significant categories, such as inmates who have fresh evidence of their innocence. But Congress barred appeals to the Supreme Court, a clause that prompted the high court to hold a rare special hearing a few weeks after the new law went on the books. The case was brought by Ellis Wayne Felker, who was convicted in the 1981 rape and murder of a Georgia college student. Felker, who claims he is innocent, lost one habeas appeal but argues that he has the right to file another.

Felker lost his own case, but last week the justices ruled that convicts may still ask them to review habeas petitions. The decision, however, is only the opening shot in a long battle over the new law. Opponents, who maintain that it wrongly tries to prevent the federal courts from enforcing a right enshrined in the Constitution, vow to file new challenges that could delay many executions for years.

Capital punishment's champions insist that the legal system is improving. The death chamber increasingly is reserved for "the baddest of the bad," says Carolyn Snurkowski, a Florida assistant attorney general who heads a national group of death-penalty prosecutors. "We bend over backward to find any aspect of a defendant's life that might mitigate the case for execution." Such intensified scrutiny helps explain why so few death-row inmates are executed. But given the varied ways capital cases snake through state and federal courts, the death penalty is likely to continue to be about as predictable as lightning strikes.

that help death-row inmates. Republicans complain that the units unnecessarily prolong appeals. The federal judiciary disagrees: Judges predict that the cut will delay rather than speed cases.

The ultimate risk is that innocent people will be executed. In the past two decades, 59 death-row inmates have been freed after establishing their innocence. Last year, Rolando Cruz escaped a death sentence for murdering a 10-year-old girl in Chicago after another man confessed. Also in Illinois, a death-row convict and two other men were released last month after Northwestern University journalism students discovered DNA and other evidence exonerating them in the murder of a couple.

Death penalty advocates say 1996 will be a year of one step forward, two steps back. The setback, ironically, stems from a new federal crackdown on sometimes repetitive appeals under a doctrine called habeas corpus that allows state prisoners to file federal lawsuits challenging their convictions. Conservatives long have complained that federal judges second-guess their state colleagues and overturn convictions long after trials are over. After a decade-long debate, Congress this spring required inmates to file habeas corpus cases within a year of

Facts & Figures:
A Costly Matter of Life or Death

By Bevolyn Williams-Harold

Taxpayers pay a high price for capital punishment

As weighty issues go, the death penalty certainly incites passionate debate. But emotional and moral arguments aside, an increasing number of states are looking at the financial toll capital punishment takes on taxpayers, and debating whether life imprisonment is a more cost-effective alternative.

Thirty-eight states have the death penalty. Currently, 3,387 men and women reside on death row—more than a third of them in California, Florida and Texas. A death penalty case in these three states costs taxpayers an average of $5.28, $3.2 and $2.3 million, respectively, according to the Death Penalty Information Center. In California, capital trials are six times more costly than non-capital cases.

While states pick up the final tab for death penalty cases, a heavy financial burden is placed on local governments. The county government is typically responsible for the costs of prosecution and the costs of the criminal trial, including attorney's fees, salaries for courtroom personnel and fees for expert witnesses. This money is spent at the expense of corrections departments and crime prevention programs, which are already strapped for cash.

As for those who argue that the death penalty is a powerful law-enforcement tool, a national poll found that police chiefs rate the death penalty as the least effective way to reduce violent crime.

Death Row USA
Total Number of Death Row Inmates: 3,387
(As of April 1, 1998)

Race of Defendant:		
White	1,611	(47.56%)
Black	1,420	(41.93)
Latino/Latina	265	(7.82)
Native American	45	(1.33)
Asian	25	(.74)
Unknown	21	(.62)

Average Cost Per Inmate Per Day	
1990	$48.07
1991	48.51
1992	50.22
1993	52.38
1994	53.24
1995	53.85
1996	54.25

Article 28

STOLEN LIVES

Men and Women Wrongfully Sentenced to Death Row

Jenny Allen and Lori Grinker

Fifty-three people have been released from death row since 1976 because of overturned convictions. Five men and women who gained release are profiled. Their stories point out flaws in the justice system that could allow the innocent to be executed.

The new comprehensive federal crime bill, among its many provisions, sharply increases the number of capital crimes and introduces the death penalty for crimes other than homicide.

Since 1976, when the Supreme Court reinstated the death penalty, 250 men and women have been legally executed in America. Fifty-three others have been released from death row because of probable innocence—a triumph for the accused, but an inescapable sign that the system has not been able to prevent the possibility of wrongful conviction.

The people in these pages have been to hell and back: Each was sentenced to die, then vindicated and allowed to go home—if a home awaited them. But will they ever be truly free?

A Shattered Family Picks Up the Pieces.

Andrew Golden's 26 months on Florida's death row were bitter ones, but today the former teacher is trying to leave all that behind: "I refuse to blame others. I don't hate. I don't seek revenge." Sadness is etched into his face, though, and slips into his conversation. "Once you've been convicted," he says, "it's almost impossible to regain your dignity." Golden will also never quite shake the heartache of his separation from Chip and Darin, the sons he dotes on. Despite his deep, sometimes nearly suicidal depressions in prison, he managed to assume a persistently cheerful attitude with his boys—knitting them slippers, writing them frequently, even helping by mail with college applications. Golden was desperate to maintain the normalcy his sons had known before their mother, his wife, Ardelle, drowned in September 1989, in a lake near what was then the family's home in Winter Haven, Fla. Andy and Ardelle had, as they often did, taken a drive to the lake; according to Golden, Ardelle went back later to fetch a forgotten cigarette case. She apparently died after accidentally driving down an unmarked, unlit boat ramp into the water. Police investigators and the medical examiner testified at the trial that the evidence did not

From *Life* magazine, October 1994, p. 64. © 1994 by Time Inc. Magazine Company. Reprinted by permission.

suggest foul play. Nonetheless, the jury opted for the prosecutor's version that Golden, heavily in debt, had killed Ardelle to collect on life insurance policies—and he was sentenced to die in the electric chair.

The Florida Supreme Court reversed his conviction on appeal 11 months ago, finding that the prosecution had failed to prove that Ardelle's death was anything but an accident—or Golden anything other than a loving husband. Now 50, he is reunited with his sons, basking in their attention. But what Darin, now 23 and a father himself, calls "the old Beaver Cleaver family" has vanished. The public scandal was hardest on Chip, who—although he graduated from high school with honors in June—felt battered by the local rumor mill. He had to find his solace in his father's indefatigable optimism: "It kept me from worrying about him." These days, their affection and solidarity are very much in evidence, buttressing Golden's determination during this post-prison time. "It's very important that I get this family back together," he says. "We want a home together... and it's up to me.

Sent to Death Row without a Trial

The day he won his freedom, Walter McMillian was asked if the success of his fifth appeal had restored his faith in the justice system. "No," said the Alabama pulpwood worker, "not at all."

The justice meted out to McMillian, 52, was pell-mell and perfunctory. In June of 1987 he was charged with the murder, eight months earlier, of an 18-year-old white woman, a clerk at a dry cleaner's, during a robbery at the store. Incredibly, McMillian was sent to death row within weeks after his arrest—over a year before his trial. He testified later that no one had ever heard of a capital defendant's being placed on death row prior to trial.

At the two-day trial, numerous witnesses testified that McMillian had been at home the morning of the murder, working on his pickup truck and helping his sister with a neighborhood fish fry. But the jury of 11 whites and one black chose to believe three other witnesses, all of whom benefited from trading incriminating testimony against McMillian for prosecutors' favors or reward money. The judge in southwestern Alabama's Monroe County Circuit Court, Robert E. Lee Key Jr., went the jury one better. He rejected the recommended sentence of life imprisonment without parole, citing the "vicious and brutal killing of a young lady in the first flower of adulthood," and ordered McMillian to die in the electric chair.

Seven times during his five years on death row in Alabama's Holman Prison, McMillian stayed up late to watch prison officials and witnesses file past his cell for midnight executions. "One day you're laughing and playing ball or going to church with a guy, and then you know he's going to die," says McMillian. "It was a rough feeling." After the electrocutions, he says, the sharp smell of burning flesh seemed to carry through the prison ventilation system. (Prison officials say this isn't possible, but other Alabama death row inmates have testified to the odor as well.) "Lord have mercy," says McMillian, "it scared me to death."

Prisoners in Alabama have no right to free legal assistance after their first appeal, but attorney Bryan Stevenson, then at the Southern Center for Human Rights in Atlanta, was outraged at what he considered a case tainted by "race, poverty and politics." His efforts, as well as a *Sixty Minutes* story and, finally, recantations from all three prosecution witnesses, brought an end to McMillian's ordeal. "Law enforcement... knew he was not guilty," says Stevenson. "When those three men admitted lying, the state had nothing left." McMillian's conviction was overturned by a state appeals court.

On March 2 of last year, he walked out of the Monroe County courtroom to ebullient cheers from family and friends. Welcome Home, read their handmade banner, God Never Fails. Four months later, wearing his oniy suit and a tie bought for the occasion, Walter McMillian appeared before a Congressional subcommittee on civil and constitutional rights. "I was wrenched from my family, from my children, from my grandchildren, from my friends, from my work that I loved, and was placed in an isolation cell the size of a shoebox, with no suniight, no companionship and no work, for nearly six years," he testified. "Every minute of every day, I knew I was innocent."

Building a Life behind Bars

At home in Los Angeles, Sonia "Sunny" Jacobs talks in a tumble of words, gesturing constantly, giggling, scooting to the edge of her seat. Sitting nearby, smiling at her childhood best friend's exuberance, is Micki Dickoff, a documentary filmmaker. It was Dickoffs herculean efforts that had set Jacobs free after 17 years in prison. "I don't even know what all she did," says Sunny. "I just know it worked."

This capacity for blind faith is what got Jacobs to death row in the first place. She doesn't deny it: "Love got me into this, and love got me out." Back in the '70s, when she was in her mid-twenties, the person she had turned her life over to was an ex-convict named Jesse Tafero.

In 1976, she and Tafero, with Tafero's prison friend Walter Rhodes, were parked at a rest stop on a Florida highway when two police officers approached. An argument ensued and gunfire erupted—killing both officers. Jacobs says she saw nothing because she, in the backseat, had flung herself protectively over her children, Eric, nine, from her first marriage, and Tina, her 10-month-old baby by Tafero. At trial, Rhodes, in a plea bargain that got him life imprisonment instead of the death penalty, testified that Jacobs and Tafero had fired the shots. Both were sentenced to the electric chair. (When Tafero was executed in 1990, an electrical malfunction sent flames shooting from his head.)

Jacobs was, in 1976, the only woman on death row in the country. (There are now 45.) The Florida penitentiary didn't even have a death row facility for women: Most of her five years there was lived in isolation; she saw only the silent guard who checked her cell. At first she paced all day; then she began to build a life, of sorts, and a self. She meditated, wrote letters, painted with a brush made from her own hair. "If you were outside looking in, I looked like a prisoner. Inside, looking out, I was a monk in a cave."

In 1981 the Florida Supreme Court commuted her sentence to a life term and released her into the general prison population. She brought her strengths with her, forging friendships, tutoring fellow prisoners and teaching meditation.

Micki Dickoff, who had seen Jacobs only once since their childhood years together in suburban Long Island, N.Y., wrote to her in 1990 after hearing about the case from family members. Months of letters and visits later, Dickoff was unshakably convinced of her friend's innocence. After probing the case deeply, she concluded that Walter Rhodes had fired the fatal shots. The evidence was strong enough to persuade an appeals court to order a new trial and to discourage prosecutors from attempting to reconvict Jacobs. In an unusual legal formality, Jacobs recognized that it was in her best interests to plead guilty, without actually admitting guilt. She was released in 1992.

At 45, a grown-up in the real world, she floundered: "I was angry and blaming." But gradually she learned to embrace her past. "I am the sum total of my experiences." That means, in part, teaching meditation and staying in close touch with former prison friends, "a little group from the lost planet." And spending time with Tina, now 18, and 27-year-old Eric, his wife and their little girl, Claudia Sonia. When Sunny first met Claudia, the five-year-old child asked, "Grandma, were you lost?" "Yes," replied Sunny, "I was."

Consumed by His Sense of Injustice

Except for a desk and chair, Muneer Deeb's Dallas-area apartment is bare of furniture. There's not even a bed. Deeb, 35, spends every spare moment at a word processor, writing a book about the ordeal that began when he was charged with the brutal 1982 murders of three teenagers in Waco, Tex. He also keeps tabs on his $100 million lawsuit against the officials who investigated and prosecuted him.

Deeb was accused of hiring a punk named David Spence to kill a young woman friend—a prospective employee in his Waco convenience store. The hit man and two companions mistakenly killed a different young woman and two of her friends. Spence was convicted and is himself on death row. One of his accomplices traded testimony against Deeb for a promise that he would not get the death penalty. Despite the lack of any physical evidence tying him to the deaths, Deeb was convicted and sentenced to death in March 1985.

In prison, Deeb, a Jordanian immigrant who came to the U.S. in 1979, began to learn law so he could, belatedly, defend himself. Batting his own inadequate English, the lack of a copying machine and the frequent ransacking of his documents by prison authorities, Deeb endlessly studied lawbooks from the prison library and copied out case law—including one 600-page text—on a manual typewriter. (He has discussed all these obstacles in speeches for Amnesty International's anti-death-penalty campaign.) "Very soon," he says, "I saw that my lawyers did not investigate properly, they did not discredit witnesses who lied against me. I became convinced that practically I had no lawyer at all."

Four years later—and in spite of a judge's warning that handling his own appeal would be akin to performing his own heart surgery—Deeb won a new hearing. For five hours he interrogated the same prosecutors and police officials whose investigations had led to his first trial—and earned himself the right to a new one. But it took two more years of filing motions to get a court date.

Deeb says he was offered various deals in exchange for a guilty plea—and turned them all down. "I would never plead something I did not do. That's my principle," he says. For the new trial, he had high-powered help from Houston defense attorney Dick DeGuerin, who called Deeb his "co-counsel" in court. On January 12, 1993, more than nine years after he was first arrested, Deeb was acquitted.

What's left is a residue of suspicion: Wary of hostility from area residents, Deeb moves often and doesn't reveal where he works. "I came here for the American dream," he says, laughing ruefully. "I got the American nightmare."

The Wrong Man, Twice Convicted

Everyone asks him what he appreciates most about being free, and now, just as he is about to dig into a breakfast of pancakes and thick scrapple, Kirk Bloodsworth has been asked again. It's gotten irksome—like being asked how being alive is better than being dead. Everything is better, he wants to say. Every single thing.

Kirk Bloodsworth, blocky and barrel-chested, is primarily a man of action, not of words. The outdoorsman has spent much of his 33 years hunting and fishing on Maryland's eastern shore. Still, he answers the question one more time. "I enjoy eating with a knife and fork instead of with a plastic spoon. I enjoy being able to get up and go to the door and open it myself," he says, choosing his words carefully, resolved to be patient. "You can't even go to the bathroom in prison without someone watching."

If Bloodsworth is edgy, even testy at times, it's understandable: He spent nine years in prison for a crime he didn't commit. In July 1984 the body of a nine-year-old girl was found in a wooded section of a Baltimore suburb. The child had been raped, her skull crushed by a rock. Bloodsworth, living nearby, was identified to police by an anonymous tip after a composite sketch of the suspect appeared in a local paper. In spite of the lack of physical evidence against Bloodsworth—and influenced, perhaps, by the public clamor to find a killer—a jury found the 24-year-old ex-Marine guilty. He was sentenced to die in the gas chamber. After 16 months on death row, Bloodsworth won a second trial. He was reconvicted and sentenced, this time, to two life terms.

Like others accused of crimes against children, Bloodsworth was reviled in prison—a pariah among exiles. "I got spat on, I got urine thrown at me, I got in fights," he says. "I was not well received." One friend, a man in the next cell, hanged himself "When he died," says Bloodsworth, looking no longer impatient but suddenly weary, "it hurt me through the heart." After his mother died, he considered suicide himself: "That nearly put me over the edge." But he persevered.

On June 28 of last year, a Baltimore County circuit judge ordered the case against him dismissed: DNA testing had shown that semen found in the child's underwear could not be Bloodsworth's. His lawyers had pressed for this sophisticated testing, unavailable at the time of his first and second trials, as soon as they realized its potential usefulness.

The day of his release, Bloodsworth strode through the prison gates, one hand raised in a clenched fist, and read a handwritten statement: "I was labeled a monster ... I've lost so much." He broke down twice before he finished. Later he added, "That's a system that needs an overhaul. If, say, they executed a thousand guilty people and one innocent man ... it isn't even close to being worth it."

A full pardon from the governor of Maryland and a $300,000 award for wrongful conviction have provided some compensation, but what's healing him most is living back on the pine-bordered property where he grew up, and returning to his old pleasures: trapping turtles, catching crabs. "I drink life up like a sponge," he says.

Death Row Justice Derailed

By Ken Armstrong and Steve Mills,
Tribune Staff Writers.

Capital punishment in Illinois is a system so riddled with faulty evidence, unscrupulous trial tactics and legal incompetence that justice has been forsaken, a *Tribune* investigation has found.

With their lives on the line, many defendants have been represented by the legal profession's worst, not its best.

They have been given the ultimate punishment based on evidence that too often is inconclusive, and sometimes nearly nonexistent.

They have seen their fates decided not by juries that reflect the community as a whole but by juries that include not a single member of their racial minority.

They have been condemned to die in trials so rife with error that nearly half of the state's death-penalty cases have been reversed on appeal.

Illinois has claimed the dubious distinction of having exonerated as many Death Row inmates as it has executed. But many of the circumstances that sent 12 innocent men to Death Row have been documented by the *Tribune* in numerous other capital cases.

In the first comprehensive examination of all 285 death-penalty cases since capital punishment was restored in Illinois 22 years ago, the *Tribune* has identified numerous fault lines running through the criminal justice system, subverting the notion that when the stakes are the highest, trials should be fail-safe.

The findings reveal a system so plagued by unprofessionalism, imprecision and bias that they have rendered the state's ultimate form of punishment its least credible.

The *Tribune* investigation, which included an exhaustive analysis of appellate opinions and briefs, trial transcripts and lawyer disciplinary records, as well as scores of interviews with witnesses, attorneys and defendants, has found that:

• At least 33 times, a defendant sentenced to die was represented at trial by an attorney who has been disbarred or suspended—sanctions reserved for conduct so incompetent, unethical or even criminal the lawyer's license is taken away.

In Kane County, an attorney was suspended for incompetence and dishonesty. Ten days after getting his law license back in 1997, he was appointed by the county's chief judge to defend a man's life.

• In at least 46 cases where a defendant was sentenced to die, the prosecution's evidence included a jailhouse informant—a form of evidence so historically unreliable that some states have begun warning jurors to treat it with special skepticism.

In one Cook County case, the word of a convicted con man, called a "pathological liar" by federal authorities, put a man on Death Row. In exchange for a sharply reduced sentence, the con artist testified that while in jail together the defendant confessed to him, even though a tape recording of their conversation contains no confession.

• In at least 20 cases where a defendant was sentenced to die, the prosecution's case included a crime lab employee's visual comparison of hairs—a type of forensic evidence that dates to the 19th Century and has proved so notoriously imprecise that its use is now restricted or even barred in some jurisdictions outside Illinois.

• At least 35 times, a defendant sent to Death Row was black and the jury that determined guilt or sentence all white—a racial composition that prosecutors consider such an advantage that they have removed as many as 20 African-Americans from a single trial's jury pool to achieve it. The U.S. Constitution forbids racial discrimination during jury selection, but courts have enforced that prohibition haltingly.

• Forty percent of Illinois' death-penalty cases are characterized by at least one of the above elements. Sometimes, all of the elements appear in a single case. Dennis Williams, who is black, was sentenced to die by an all-white Cook County jury; prosecuted with evidence that included a jailhouse informant and hair comparison; and defended, none too well, by an attorney who was later disbarred.

Williams and three other men—referred to as the Ford Heights Four—were wrongly convicted of the 1978 murders of a south suburban couple. Williams served 18 years, almost all on Death Row, before he was cleared by DNA evidence in 1996. He then filed a lawsuit accusing sheriff's officers of framing him.

"The feeling is emotionally choking," Williams said of being sentenced to die for a crime he did not commit. "It's inhuman. It's something that shouldn't be imaginable. Here are people who are supposed to uphold the law who are breaking it."

Illinois houses its condemned inmates at the Menard and Pontiac correctional centers and at the new prison in Downstate Tamms. They spend 23 hours a day in cells so narrow they can touch opposite walls at the same time.

To be sure, many of Illinois' Death Row inmates are guilty of horrendous crimes. But while lawfully condemning the guilty, the state's system of capital punishment has proved so vulnerable to mistakes that it threatens to execute the innocent as well.

The problems afflicting death-penalty trials in Illinois have generated great concern, even among some supporters of capital punishment, and have prompted the Illinois Supreme Court and the state legislature to examine possible reforms.

While it is impossible to calculate the exact financial costs imposed by the system's flaws, without question they are staggering. Taxpayers have not only had to finance multimillion-dollar settlements to wrongly convicted Death Row inmates—Williams alone received nearly $13 million from Cook County—but also have had to pay for new trials, sentencing hearings and appeals in more than 100 cases where a condemned inmate's original trial was undermined by some fundamental error.

Illinois Supreme Court Justice Moses Harrison II wrote last year in one Death Row inmate's appeal that he will no longer vote to uphold the death penalty, saying "so many mistakes" have been made in Illinois.

"The system is not working," Harrison wrote. "Innocent people are being sentenced to death. If these men dodged the executioner, it was only because of luck and the dedication of the attorneys, reporters, family members and volunteers who labored to win their release. They survived despite the criminal justice system, not because of it. . . . One must wonder how many others have not been so fortunate."

Flawed trial, flawed evidence

The case of Madison Hobley exemplifies how a man can be condemned to die in a flawed trial with questionable evidence of guilt.

In the predawn hours of Jan. 6, 1987, an arsonist's fire burned through a three-story apartment building on Chicago's South Side, forcing people to jump from windows and throw children to waiting arms below. Seven people died, including Hobley's wife and baby boy.

The crime was a so-called heater case, one that newspapers and television stations prominently recounted, applying additional pressure on police to solve the crime quickly.

Police arrested the 26-year-old Hobley within 24 hours. Three years later, a Cook County jury convicted Hobley and sentenced him to death. Prosecutors claimed Hobley was having an affair and set the fire to kill his family. Hobley admits the affair. He denies setting the fire.

His appeal alleges that prosecutors suppressed a report saying Hobley's fingerprints weren't found on the gas can he allegedly used, and that after Hobley's appellate lawyers learned of a second gas can possibly related to the investigation, police destroyed it. Last year, the Illinois Supreme Court found sufficient merit to those allegations to order a hearing on them. The court said it was "deeply troubled."

At trial, the lead prosecutor insisted there was no fingerprint report. Now, the state's attorney's office says there was a report and believes the defense was notified of that before the trial.

But the questions surrounding Hobley's conviction go further.

In a befuddling move, Hobley's trial attorneys allowed a suburban police officer to get on the jury. Most lawyers consider police officers the worst jurors imaginable for defendants because of their potential biases in favor of law enforcement. The officer became jury foreman. In an affidavit, another juror said the officer revealed his gun in the jury room and, citing his own experience, vouched for the police work in Hobley's case.

Hobley was interrogated by police officers under then-Cmdr. Jon Burge, whose name would become attached to one of the worst scandals in the modern history of the Chicago Police Department. At the center of the scandal were allegations that in the 1970s and 1980s, police tortured suspects to obtain confessions, using such means as electroshock and Russian roulette.

Fourteen men sentenced to death in Illinois were convicted with what they claimed to be false confessions obtained through torture by Burge's officers. Ten, including Hobley, remain on Death Row as their claims of abuse by a discredited police unit move through the appeals process.

29. Death Row Justice Derailed

Hobley, who worked for a medical-supplies company and had no prior criminal record, claimed officers wrapped a plastic bag over his head, struck his chest, kicked his shins and pushed their thumbs against his throat. The officers denied it.

Hobley's complaint went nowhere in an internal police investigation. But because so many suspects made similar claims, the department's Office of Professional Standards later conducted a far-reaching review of abuse allegations and, in 1990, found that Burge's officers engaged in systematic torture. Burge eventually was fired.

The police officers working for Burge said Hobley confessed; Hobley denies he did. Detective Robert Dwyer said he wrote down the confession, but testified that his notes got wet and torn, so he threw them away.

An arson detective's initial report indicated the fire started on the ground level. But Hobley allegedly confessed to starting the fire outside his third-floor apartment. At trial, the detective modified his analysis to say the fire could have started anywhere.

Other than the disputed confession, the prosecution's case hinged on a witness who said he saw Hobley filling a gas can shortly before the fire. But certain elements of that witness' testimony contradicted other evidence, and Hobley's attorneys have alleged the witness secretly received special consideration in a pending criminal case in exchange for his cooperation.

Prosecutors put into evidence a gas can found under a second-floor apartment's kitchen sink. They claimed Hobley used it to set the fire. But that can differed in size from the one Hobley reportedly had been seen filling, and Hobley allegedly confessed to throwing the can down a hallway, not into an apartment. In a deposition this year, one of the prosecutors said he doesn't believe Hobley used that can. Three months later, he wrote a letter taking that back and blaming a memory lapse.

Currently an inmate at Menard, Hobley has been on Death Row for nine years.

"I respected the law. I worked," he recently told the *Tribune*. "The only thing I did wrong was I was unfaithful."

Prosecutor misconduct

To win a death sentence, prosecutors in Illinois have repeatedly exaggerated the criminal backgrounds of defendants—turning misdemeanors into felonies, manslaughter into murder, innocence into guilt.

Prosecutors have lied to jurors, raising the possibility of parole when no such possibility existed.

They also have browbeaten jurors, saying they must return the death sentence, or they will have violated their oaths and lied to God.

Death-penalty cases in Illinois have included some of the most sympathetic victims, helping flare emotions at trial. Of the 285 cases since capital punishment's reinstatement, there were multiple murder victims in 104. In 44 cases, at least one victim was 12 years old or younger. In 15 cases, the victim was a police officer.

When the drive to avenge such crimes reaches the courtroom, a prosecutor's worst tendencies can come to a boil and spill over. More than 10 percent of Illinois' death-penalty cases have been reversed for a new trial or sentencing hearing because prosecutors took some unfair advantage that undermined a trial's integrity, according to the *Tribune's* review of appellate rulings. The misconduct by prosecutors has included misstating the law or evidence, using inflammatory arguments that appeal to jurors' prejudices, and even breaking a promise to a defendant not to seek the death penalty if he provided a written confession.

In securing a death sentence against Verneal Jimerson, another one of the Ford Heights Four who was exonerated by DNA evidence, prosecutors allowed their star witness to tell what they knew to be a lie, the Illinois Supreme Court ruled.

Jimerson, according to a previous *Tribune* investigation, is one of at least 381 defendants nationwide to have a homicide conviction thrown out because prosecutors concealed evidence suggesting innocence or knowingly used false evidence. That total underscores how questionable tactics marring Illinois death-penalty trials also course through other cases and states.

Although the great majority of misconduct by prosecutors occurs at trial, some prosecutors have run afoul while defending death sentences on appeal.

When Cornelius Lewis was convicted in 1979 of murdering a Decatur bank guard, the Macon County state's attorney obtained the death penalty by portraying Lewis as a career criminal with four felony convictions. On appeal, however, Assistant State's Atty. Jeff Justice and Assistant Illinois Atty. Gen. Neal Goodfriend discovered that was only half-true: One felony charge had been dismissed and another reduced to a misdemeanor.

But neither prosecutor notified Lewis' attorney or the courts that false evidence had been used to help secure Lewis' death sentence, according to court records. That information surfaced only because Lewis' attorney discovered it on his own. In 1987, a federal appeals court vacated Lewis' death sentence and called Goodfriend's and Justice's withholding of vital information "shocking" and "reprehensible." The court referred both to the state's lawyer disciplinary agency, but neither was sanctioned. At a new hearing, Lewis was sentenced to life.

"These prosecutors just sat on the information. They made a conscious decision not to tell me," said J. Steven Beckett, who represented Lewis on appeal. "What were those prosecutors thinking? That's advocacy taken to an extreme."

Another way that many prosecutors have bent or broken the rules in death-penalty cases has come at the trial's outset—when picking the jury.

Juries are supposed to represent a cross-section of the community, because people of different backgrounds, races and genders often have experiences and perspectives that can benefit a jury's deliberations. For example, an African-American from the Englewood neighborhood on Chicago's South Side might be more skeptical of a police officer's disputed testimony than a white resident of Schaumburg.

Having different races represented on juries would figure to be especially important in capital cases, where, in Illinois, nearly two-thirds of the defendants sentenced to death have been black or Hispanic.

Although the Constitution bars racial discrimination during jury selection, prosecutors often have flouted that prohibition. And reviewing courts, with rare exceptions, have let them, even after a 1986 U.S. Supreme Court ruling that was meant to crack down on the practice.

At least 35 black defendants condemned to death in Illinois since 1977 were convicted or sentenced by an all-white jury, the *Tribune* found. That accounts for 22 percent of all blacks sentenced to death.

Of 65 death-penalty cases in Illinois with a black defendant and white victim, the jury was all white in 21 of them, or nearly a third.

In the Death Row cases where blacks were convicted by an all-white jury, prosecutors frequently used their discretionary strikes to remove African-Americans from the jury pool. Such strikes allow attorneys on both sides to excuse an allotted number of jury pool members, usually without giving a reason.

In the 1983 trial of Andrew Wilson, who was convicted of murdering two Chicago police officers, Cook County prosecutors removed 20 African-Americans from the jury pool. In the 1979 trial of Farris Walker, who was convicted of the murder and attempted robbery of a retired lawyer, prosecutors struck 16 African-Americans. Such wholesale removal of black jury-pool members occurs less frequently these days, but even so, all-white juries are still selected, including one that earlier this year sentenced a black Cook County defendant to death.

Despite the long string of cases where prosecutors have removed an inordinate number of blacks from jury pools, only one conviction in an Illinois death-penalty case has been reversed because of a finding that prosecutors discriminated on the basis of race during jury selection.

Questions brushed aside

Reviewing courts have, at times, shown a willingness to uphold individual death sentences despite a host of troubling questions about a trial's integrity.

William Bracy was convicted and sentenced to death in Cook County in 1981 for the murders of three drug dealers in Chicago. The prosecution's chief witness was a man who had admitted taking part in the crimes and who, in exchange for his testimony, received a lenient sentence. Presiding at Bracy's trial was Thomas Maloney, who would become the only Illinois judge ever convicted of fixing murder cases. He was sentenced in 1994 to nearly 16 years in prison for fixing three murder cases in the 1980s.

To represent Bracy, Maloney appointed Robert McDonnell, a convicted felon who became the only Illinois lawyer ever disbarred twice. McDonnell was then between disbarments, reinstated despite concerns about his emotional stability and drinking, lawyer disciplinary records show. The prosecutors were Michael Goggin and Gregg Owen, a team that, according to court records, repeatedly committed misconduct during trials, racking up 35 instances of wrongdoing in one case alone.

The jury included the wife of a judge who had sentenced Bracy to prison in an unrelated case. In addition, prosecutors removed blacks from the jury pool, resulting in an all-white jury, according to an affidavit filed by one of the trial's lawyers.

Several aspects of Bracy's case gave reviewing courts pause, but none reversed. Misconduct by the prosecutors was deemed harmless. Issues concerning the jury's makeup and McDonnell's competence were raised and rejected. So was an argument that Maloney was motivated to make pro-prosecution rulings in order to protect his law-and-order reputation and to deflect suspicion that he was on the take in other cases.

When a federal appeals court denied Bracy's appeal in a 2-1 decision in 1996, dissenting Judge Ilana Diamond Rovner wrote: "I do not know which I find more shocking: the base quality of justice that Bracy and (co-defendant Roger) Collins received in the Illinois courts, or our holding today that the Constitution requires no more."

A fair trial requires an impartial judge, but "the State of Illinois placed the fate of William Bracy and Roger Collins in the hands of a racketeer," Rovner wrote.

The U.S. Supreme Court has since granted Bracy's attorneys the opportunity to find evidence showing Maloney penalized defendants who didn't bribe him. Maloney presided over nine cases in which a defendant received the death penalty.

Six of those defendants have received new trials on appeal: Two were acquitted, two were convicted again but sentenced to life and two await retrial, although prosecutors have told the Illinois Supreme Court that convicting them again will be difficult.

The other three defendants remain on Death Row.

String of errors, reversals

In Illinois, errors by judges, ineptitude by defense attorneys and prosecutorial misconduct have been so widespread in death-penalty

29. Death Row Justice Derailed

cases that a new trial or sentencing hearing has been ordered in 49 percent of those that have completed at least one round of appeals, the *Tribune* found.

That so many convictions and death sentences have been vacated shows that the Illinois Supreme Court, unlike the reviewing courts in some states, has not been a rubber stamp in capital cases. At the same time, the Illinois Supreme Court has upheld scores of death sentences while forgiving trial errors that benefited prosecutors, dismissing the errors as harmless.

In a chilling illustration of the death penalty's frailties, the very courts that have granted a new trial or sentencing hearing to nearly half of Illinois' Death Row population rejected the appeals of Anthony Porter, an innocent man who came within two days of execution.

Wrongly convicted in 1983 of shooting to death a couple as they sat in bleachers at a park on Chicago's South Side, Porter was saved not by the justice system, but by journalism students. Working with a private investigator, they proved Porter's innocence earlier this year by obtaining a videotaped confession from the real killer, who recently pleaded guilty.

Porter's appeals were denied even though his trial was seriously compromised. A juror was acquainted with one victim's mother and had even attended the victim's funeral, but she didn't disclose her potential bias during jury selection. In addition, Porter's attorneys tried the case on the cheap, failing to capitalize on available evidence that could have punched holes in the prosecution's case. They conducted a limited investigation, and in a sworn affidavit, one attorney even accused the other of having a judge sentence Porter instead of a jury to save time and money.

In words that now ring hollow, reviewing courts chose to excuse the shortcomings in Porter's trial, deeming such errors harmless because the evidence against Porter was so strong. "Overwhelming," the Illinois Supreme Court once called the evidence of Porter's guilt.

In Illinois, the majority of death-penalty cases reversed for a new trial or sentencing hearing have been attributable to errors by trial judges, such as inadequately screening jurors for bias or allowing prosecutors to present such dubious evidence as what a defendant supposedly muttered while sleeping, according to the *Tribune's* review of appellate records.

Judges have sweeping responsibilities. They are gatekeepers of trial evidence and instruct jurors on the law. At trial, there are numerous junctures where judges can commit errors affecting the outcome or leading to reversal.

Some judges have misstated the law to jurors, while others have demonstrated a profound ignorance of how capital trials are structured, sometimes depriving defendants of the right to have a jury impose the sentence instead of the judge.

Although many rules of death-penalty trials are unique, no specialized training is mandated in Illinois for the judges who preside over them.

Some of the most puzzling work by judges has been performed during Death Row appeals when cases have been returned to the circuit court for hearings on new evidence or various legal issues.

In Cook County, Judge John Morrissey mocked efforts by lawyers for Death Row inmate Ronald Jones to have DNA testing performed. "What issue could possibly be resolved by DNA testing?" Morrissey asked during a 1994 hearing.

Over the objection of Cook County prosecutors, the Illinois Supreme Court later allowed the tests, which exonerated Jones for the 1985 murder and sexual assault of a South Side woman and led to his being released from Death Row earlier this year.

The pervasiveness of reversible errors in Illinois capital cases has imposed substantial costs in court time and taxpayer money.

In Cook County, Dennis Emerson has been sentenced to die no fewer than three times for the 1979 murder of a woman during a tavern robbery on Chicago's South Side. A blend of errors by the trial judge, prosecutors and one of Emerson's attorneys has twice caused appeals courts to order a new trial or sentencing hearing. Now, 20 years after the murder, the appeals process for Emerson's third death sentence is just beginning.

And in a twist that adds police error to the mix, new evidence suggests Emerson may have committed a different murder that Chicago police pinned on an innocent man. James Newsome served 15 years of a life sentence for a South Side grocer's murder before being exonerated in 1995 by new technology that showed his fingerprints didn't match the gunman's. Instead, those prints belonged to Emerson, according to police.

Prosecutors had sought the death penalty against Newsome. Had they succeeded, Newsome would have pushed the state's number of exonerated Death Row inmates to 13—assuming he hadn't been executed first.

Calls for reform

The growing list of innocent men who have been sentenced to die in Illinois has attracted attention worldwide and become a rallying cry for opponents of capital punishment.

The Illinois Supreme Court and Illinois General Assembly have created committees to study the death penalty, and the reforms being considered include the dramatic step of creating minimum standards for prosecutors as well as defense attorneys in capital cases. But so far, the state's judicial and legislative officials have passed few rules or laws to shore up the capital-punishment system.

And in Cook County, where seven of the state's 12 exonerated

Death Row inmates were convicted, the string of wrongful convictions has barely stirred officials.

Compare the fallout from the cases of Dennis Williams and Guy Paul Morin.

Both were convicted of murder with jailhouse-informant testimony and hair-comparison evidence. And both were exonerated by DNA evidence—Morin in 1995, Williams in 1996. But while the crime pinned on Williams took place in Cook County, the one blamed on Morin occurred in the Canadian province of Ontario. Morin, convicted of murdering a 9-year-old girl, had received the country's maximum penalty: a life sentence.

Following Morin's release, top province officials appointed a special commission to investigate the case and recommend ways to prevent future miscarriages of justice. The inquiry lasted nearly two years. The commission called 120 witnesses, including criminal justice experts from around the world.

After reviewing thousands of documents, the commission issued a 1,200-page report, calling Morin's conviction a tragedy. "The system failed him—a system for which we, the community, must bear responsibility," the report said. The commission urged significant restrictions on hair and jailhouse-informant evidence, calling them generally useless or inherently unreliable. Ontario's government then turned the recommendations into policy.

Cook County, meanwhile, settled Williams' wrongful-arrest lawsuit for $12.8 million, thereby avoiding a trial and a public airing of the alleged misconduct by law-enforcement officers.

County officials have extended Williams an apology, but so far no reforms to go with it.

Point

The Death Penalty Brings Justice

by Gov. George E. Pataki

On March 7, 1995, I fulfilled a major campaign promise and signed legislation reinstating the death penalty in New York. For eighteen years, the Legislature—the people's voice—overwhelmingly supported capital punishment. For eighteen years, New Yorkers' demands were thwarted by gubernatorial veto.

Under this legislation, those who murder a police officer, a probation, parole, court or corrections officer, a judge, a witness or member of a witness' family are subject to the death penalty. Someone who murders while already serving life in prison or while escaping from prison, or who murders while committing other serious felonies also is eligible. Contract killers, serial murderers, those who torture their victims or those who have murdered before also can be sentenced to death.

In determining whether juries should impose the death penalty on anyone convicted of first degree murder, the bill expressly authorizes them to hear and consider additional evidence whenever the murder was committed as part of an act of terrorism or committed by someone with two or more prior serious felony convictions. This is an important step toward ensuring that the law is applied to criminals who commit crimes such as two-time convicted killer Thomas Grasso, the World Trade Center bombers, or Colin Ferguson of the Long Island Rail Road massacre. This law is balanced to safeguard defendants' rights while ensuring that the state of New York has a fully credible and enforceable death penalty statute.

The most important characteristic of government is the service and protection of its members from enemies, both foreign and domestic. In the United States, government is an instrument of the people. Therefore, legislation must reflect the will of those who entrust representatives to create the laws of society. In New York, the overwhelming majority of voters demanded the death penalty.

The relationship between a government and its people is referred to as a social contract. The notion of a social contract dates back to when our ancestors first started to live in groups, but became a formal political theory with Thomas Hobbes. The concept is simple. We relinquish a little bit of our autonomy in exchange for safety, security and a sense of community for the greater good. Hobbes proclaimed that, without this arrangement, life would be "poor, nasty, brutish and short."

As societies developed, governments were created, and the people in the United States created the government to enforce the rules they had established. These rules, or laws, protect us and give a sense of safety that allows us to be concerned with more than survival. Those who kill violate the most sacred of understandings that we as a society embrace. With this violation comes the legitimate demand on our government to provide justice for wrongs committed against us.

The death penalty is society's way of telling its members that when you commit a crime as horrendous as murder, you are not fit to live among us.

The death penalty will not bring back the victims of violent crime, but I am confident that it will act as a deterrent of crime and it will save lives. Those who disagree only need to look to the account of the August 1977 riot at Eastern Correctional Facil-

George E. Pataki is the governor of the state of New York.

ity, where correctional officers being held hostage overheard inmates deciding against executing the hostages because, at the time, it was a capital offense. The deterrent saved lives. Without the death penalty as a tool for jurists, a murderer can kill again without consequence.

Another flawed position held by death penalty opponents is that once a criminal is behind bars he or she no longer is a threat to society. Consider the case of Corey Jackson, an inmate who was serving a 25-years-to-life sentence for a 1994 homicide. On May 9, 1996, he was convicted of executing three teens, on a drug dealer's orders, and was sentenced to three more life sentences. While awaiting transfer to a state prison from the Brooklyn House of Detention, Jackson slashed a handyman at that facility, Robert Manning, in the face with a razor. The attack on Manning left him with 60 stitches and a permanent scar. Manning was lucky to escape with his life. What makes this case even more disturbing is the fact that Manning sat on the jury that found Jackson guilty of the teen murders, and after Jackson's savage attack on Robert Manning, he yelled "You thought I couldn't get you, but I got you." It is evident that Jackson has no regard for the rules of our society.

For too many years Americans have lived in fear of crime. This New York law alone won't stop crime, but it is an important step in the right direction. The citizens of New York have spoken loudly and clearly in their call for justice for those who commit the most serious of crimes by depriving other citizens of their lives. New Yorkers are convinced that the death penalty will deter these vicious crimes. I agree, and as their governor, I acted accordingly.

Counterpoint

Death at Midnight... Hope at Sunrise

by Steven Hawkins

If Connie Ray Evans was some awful monster deemed worthy of extermination, why did I feel so bad about it, I wondered. It has been said that men on death row are inhuman, cold-blooded killers. But as I stood and watched a grieving mother leave her son for the last time, I questioned how the sordid business of executions was supposed to be the great equalizer. I watched Connie's family slowly make their way to the parking lot, attempting to console each other over their private grief. "Is there ever an end to the pain?" I asked aloud, to no one in particular.

—Donald Cabana, Death at Midnight: The Confession of an Executioner

---

Steven Hawkins *is the executive director of the National Coalition to Abolish the Death Penalty.*

As warden, from 1984 to 1989, Donald Cabana gave the order to execute men at the Mississippi State Penitentiary in Parchman. Yet, with each execution, Cabana came to realize more and more the utter pain, the profound waste and the senseless duhumanization that the death penalty places upon our society. His recently released book, *Death at Midnight: The Confession of an Executioner*, is a powerful account of the failings and inconsistencies of the death penalty by someone in the best position to make such an observation—the person in charge of carrying it out. It has been more than 70 years since we have had the benefit of such a perspective—not since Lewis Lawes, the warden at Sing Sing, gave us *Man's Judgment of Death* in 1924. Through their first-hand experience with the death penalty, both Cabana and Lawes became firmly opposed to capital punishment.

The failure of the death penalty as a crime-fighting measure also has been noted by law enforcement officials. In January 1995, Peter D. Hart Research Associates conducted a survey of randomly-selected police chiefs from around the nation. The Hart survey found that police chiefs rank the death penalty as the least effective way of reducing violent crime, placing it behind such alternatives as curbing drug abuse, putting more police on the streets, lowering the legal barriers to prosecution and improving the economic condition. With respect to public safety, the police chiefs also ranked the death penalty last among cost-effective priorities, putting at the forefront community policing, police training and equipment, neighborhood

30. Death Penalty

watch patrols, drug and alcohol programs and anti-gang efforts.

Apart from the lack of any value in deterring crime, the death penalty continues to be tainted with all the problems of its troubled past. In 1972, the U.S. Supreme Court struck down capital punishment because it was arbitrary and completely unpredictable in its selected fury. The only discernable pattern suggested a punishment reserved for the poor and racial minorities. In 1976, the Supreme Court allowed the death penalty to return, but on the promise of fairness and justice in its administration. Twenty years later, that promise has not been fulfilled. The overwhelming majority of persons on death row still come from poverty-stricken backgrounds—more than 90 percent of them could not have hired a private attorney. And, more than half of the condemned still are members of racial and ethnic minorities. To make matters worse, nearly 60 people have been released from death row on grounds of their innocence.

While we have spent the last twenty years tinkering with the machinery of death—hopelessly trying to find a way to administer capital punishment in a consistent fashion, devoid of fatal error—the rest of the world has been moving away from the death penalty altogether. In fact, the majority of nations in the global community have abolished the death penalty either in law or in practice. Additionally, the execution of children (those under 18 years old at the time of the crime) has been eliminated in all but five countries—Iran, Pakistan, Yemen, Saudi Arabia . . . and the United States.

We may be at the midnight hour in our use of the death penalty, but there lies a dawn of hope as more people begin to question its legitimacy. The Academy Award-winning film, *Dead Man Walking*, shows us that sympathy for the pain and plight of victims does not have to be synonymous with support for capital punishment. It takes courage to stand up and recognize this basic fact, but stand we must. As Cabana writes at the end of his book: "This is not a particularly good time in which to find myself an opponent of capital punishment. Paradoxically, however, if this is the worst of times to be against the death penalty, it may also be the best of times. Never has there been a greater need for rationality and clear thinking. Absent the emotionalism and histrionics that always have been characteristic of the debate, the present offers greater opportunity than ever for pragmatism and calm deliberation. There is much need, and room, for both."

Unit 5

Unit Selections

31. **Correctional Treatment: Some Recommendations for Effective Intervention,** Paul Gendreau and Robert R. Ross
32. **Habilitation, Not Rehabilitation,** Dyan Machan
33. **A Decade of Experimenting with Intermediate Sanctions: What Have We Learned?** Joan Petersilia
34. **Eliminating Parole Boards Isn't a Cure-All, Experts Say,** Fox Butterfield
35. **Job Placement for Offenders: A Promising Approach to Reducing Recidivism and Correctional Costs,** Peter Finn
36. **Young Probation/Parole Officer Toughens with Experience,** Susan Clayton

Key Points to Consider

❖ Based on what you have read in this unit, should treatment of offenders be a priority of the criminal justice system? Can such treatment programs be effective? If so, what factors help to make these programs most effective?

❖ If treatment is not effective for certain offenders, should we create a system of justice that punishes some and treats others, even for the same offense?

❖ What differentiates parole from probation? Which one deals with more serious offenders?

❖ What defines a program as an "intermediate" sanction? What are some of the practical and political issues that ave affected the creation and support of intermediate sanction programs? Is there a relationship between political perspective and support for rehabilitation? Which political perspective tends to be most supportive of rehabilitation as a goal? Why?

❖ How have some states supported the ideal of abolishing parole and parole boards?

❖ How does the modern electronic monitoring/home confinement system operate? What are some of the problems inherent in its use?

DUSHKIN ONLINE Links   www.dushkin.com/online/

27. **American Probation and Parole Association (APPA)**
    http://www.appa-net.org
28. **VIP: Volunteers in Prevention**
    http://comnet.org/vip/

These sites are annotated on pages 4 and 5.

Living on the Outside: Intermediate Sanctions

As prison crowding increased in the 1980s, practitioners searched for a way to alleviate crowding while achieving the elusive goal of deterrence. A solution adopted by many states and localities was to allow low-level felons to serve part of their time in the county jail (rather than prison) and the remainder of their sentences on probation. From that time to the present, we have seen a burgeoning interest in the opportunity to intervene with offenders in that "intermediate" area between total incarceration and total release.

In this unit we explore the relationship between offender problems and the release process. In the first article, Paul Gendreau and Robert Ross point out the value of treatment programs and explore the difficulties that accompany the process of rehabilitation. Next, in "Habilitation, Not Rehabilitation," Dyan Machan shows that it is possible to be a "law and order" judge and still acknowledge both the causes of crime and the importance of treatment.

The final four articles explore the practice of intermediate sanctions and the policies and politics that surround their granting and governance. We begin with Joan Petersilia's examination of the "experiment" of intermediate sanctions, and her discussion of what has been learned since this experiment began. Next, Fox Butterfield offers some data on the recent restrictions placed on parole in some states and makes some predictions about the future of corrections if parole is eliminated. Then, Peter Finn, in "Job Placement for Offenders: A Promising Approach to Reducing Recidivism and Correctional Costs," describes successful approaches that allow large numbers of ex-offenders to remain employed and thus avoid reincarceration. Finally, Susan Clayton comments on the realities of being a parole/probation officer, and what a young officer finds the job to be at present as she works toward becoming a seasoned officer. The article also describes the promise and pitfalls of the process of electronic home detention.

Correctional Treatment
Some Recommendations for Effective Intervention

Paul Gendreau
Robert R. Ross

Martinson's well-publicized conclusion that in correctional rehabilitation "almost nothing works" (Martinson, 1974) touched off a debate that preoccupied the criminal justice system for more than a decade. Although there were a few dissenters who rejected the validity of Martinson's castigation of correctional treatment programs, there appeared to be a widespread endorsement of the view that treatment of the offender is an ineffective response to delinquent or criminal behavior. Proclamations about the apparent lack of evidence of the efficacy of correctional treatment undoubtedly have had major repercussions throughout the field of criminal justice (cf. Empey, 1979). Correctional managers, faced with dwindling budgets, have been loath to expend funds on treatment programs which, they were told, had little likelihood of success. Academicians and policy-makers disenchanted with correctional rehabilitation models of "medical" models which, they were told, had failed to live up to their extravagant promises, became enamoured with alternative models. Radical nonintervention (Schur, 1973), justice-as-fairness (Fogel, 1979), and deterrence (Tullock, 1974) along with a succession of others attracted loyal disciples eagerly seeking new panaceas. Perhaps the most significant effect of the "nothing works" proclamation was the promotion of a pervasive cynicism and feeling of hopelessness among correctional workers who were reminded again and again that their efforts at offender rehabilitation were of no value.

A further consequence of Martinson's "almost nothing works" assertion was that it motivated some researchers to reexamine the evidence for and against treatment effectiveness. Notable among these researchers was Ted Palmer (1975: 1978) who rejected Martinson's broad indictment of correctional programs by reference to evidence that Martinson himself had reported (and disregarded). Many of the programs that Martinson had reviewed actually were quite successful! Palmer's "revelation" was given short shrift in the debate on treatment effectiveness which unfortunately deteriorated into polemic and name-calling, becoming little concerned with more substantive matters, and less objective (Gendreau & Ross, 1979).

Recently, however, there appears to be a growing recognition that the "almost nothing works" credit is invalid. The evidence continues to mount that some programs do work and work well (Andrews, 1980: Gendreau & Ross, 1979, Peters, 1981). Even the most vociferous and persuasive proponent of the anti-treatment camp, Martinson recently acknowledged publicly that he could have been in error in his conclusion that correctional treatment was impotent (cf. Serrill, 1975; Martinson & Wilks, 1977). In our recent review of the published literature between 1973 and 1979 we found convincing evidence that some correctional programs significantly reduce recidivism (Gendreau & Ross, 1979). A number of these programs have been presented with additional follow-up data in a recent book (Ross & Gendreau, 1980).

In our view, the debate on correctional effectiveness should no longer focus on *whether* treatment programs are effective. That should now be viewed as an overly simplistic question. A more meaningful question which should now be addressed is *which* programs work. Equally important, questions should be asked about *why* some programs work and some do not.

The question of which programs work was addressed in previous publications which identified a substantial number of effective treatment programs (Gendreau & Ross, 1979; Ross & Gendreau, 1980). In this paper, we present a preliminary answer to the second question by discussing the characteristics of effective programs and suggesting some of the reasons why other programs fail.

It is not yet possible to speak with absolute assuredness about the essential ingredients of effective correctional programs but our examination of successful programs does suggest some guidelines which may help managers and policy-makers in the field of delinquency.

Effective Programs

Evaluation

The first characteristic of an effective program is not really a characteristic of the program *per se*, but of the evaluation of the program. Most of the recent successful programs we identified were conducted in methodologically impressive research. Of the studies, 33 percent employed true experimental designs with random assignment of subjects. Twenty-three percent employed a variety of baseline comparisons. Twenty-five percent used matched comparison groups. Clearly there has been a major improvement in the quality of research on the outcome of correction intervention. Hackler's (1972, p. 346) "well-known law" of delinquency program research asserts that "the more carefully you evaluate a program, the greater the probability that it will show little effect" is simply incorrect. The quality of program evaluation in the correctional treatment area is now in many cases far superior to the evaluation of other correctional approaches including deterrence (Gendreau & Ross, 1981).

Magnitude and Persistence of Effects

The effectiveness of programs has been demonstrated in a wide variety of correctional areas with both juvenile and adult offenders. Whereas the majority are community-based, remarkably successful programs have also been conducted in various institutional settings. The type of offenders involved range from pre-delinquents to sophisticated hard-core offenders and recidivistic adult criminal heroin addicts. Major reductions in recidivism have been demonstrated ranging in well-controlled studies from 30–60 percent (e.g., Alexander & Parsons, 1973; Chandler, 1973; Lee & Haynes, 1980; Phillips *et al.*, 1973; Ross & McKay, 1976; Walter & Mills, 1979). These are by no means short-term effects. Substantial beneficial results have been reported in follow-ups as much as three to 15 years after treatment! (e.g., Blakely, Davidson, & Saylor, 1980; Sarason, 1978; Shore & Massimo, 1979).

Program Conceptualization

The successful programs appear to share a number of characteristics that distinguish them from their less successful counterparts. We found no evidence of the effectiveness of programs which were derived from the medical (disease) or the clinical sociology model of criminology. Rather the majority of successful programs were based on a social learning model of criminal conduct (cf. Bandura, 1979; Nettler, 1978; Nietzel, 1979). In some instances, the intervention was in accord with specific assumptions of Differential Association Theory (Andrews, 1980; Burgess & Akers, 1966), developed not from assumptions about delinquents' psychopathology, but from assumptions about their clients' cognitive or social skills. Most attempted to broaden their social perceptions or their repertoire of adaptive behaviors rather than attempting to cure some underlying emotional disorder.

Program Types

Disappointing, of course, to panacea-seekers is the fact that no one therapeutic modality can be associated with success. The intervention techniques of successful programs vary greatly. They include family therapy, contingency contracting, behavioral counseling, role-playing and modeling, vocational and social skills training, interpersonal cognitive problem-solving training, and peer-oriented behavioral programs. All effective programs are, in fact, multi-facetted. The superiority of any one technique is yet to be demonstrated.

Program Components

Although the identification of the essential parameters of successful intervention is still in its infancy, much has been learned from some of the successful intervention research programs. In particular, the studies of Andrews & Kiessling (1980, p. 445, 446) are exemplary in this regard. They examined factors associated with effective supervision and counseling of probations and identified five sets of conditions which influence the outcome of intervention: (a) authority—where rules and or formal legal sanctions are clearly spelled out; (b) anti-criminal modeling and reinforcement—where the development of pro-social and anti-criminal attitudes, cognitions and behaviors are engendered and reinforced by appropriate modeling of pro-social behavior; (c) problem-solving—the client is assisted in coping with personal or social difficulties, particularly in the instances where they relate to fostering attitudes which have led him to experience pro-social behavior; (d) use of community resources; (e) quality of interpersonal relationship—an effective relationship consists of empathy, and the establishment of open communication and trust.

Our examination of successful programs suggests that each incorporates at least some of the factors identified by Andrews & Kiesling. As would be expected, there does exist considerable variation among successful programs in terms of the factors they emphasize. For example, Platt, Perry, & Metzger (1980) stressed the quality of interpersonal relationships and Ross & McKay (1976) emphasized an anti-criminal modeling and reinforcement approach.

Unsuccessful Programs

As we develop our knowledge about the types of programs that have a reasonable guarantee of success we also are acquiring insight as to the characteristics of programs and practices which are likely to fail.

Andrews (1979) has critically reviewed the studies of counseling programs in the correctional area. He found that counseling procedures which depend primarily on open communication "friendship" models, are non-directional, or involve self-help groups in which the offenders themselves are in charge of the program, typically have either had negligible effects or actually increase illegal behavior. A number of studies support this conclusion (e.g., Craft, Stephenson, & Granger, 1964; Fenton, 1960; Grant & Grant, 1959; Kassebaum, Ward, & Wilner, 1971). One implication of this observation is that with offender populations, trust, positive regard, warmth and empathy, though they may be necessary, are simply not sufficient in themselves to effect change. Anti-criminal program components (verbalizations, contracting or modeling, etc.) must be an integral part of the successful intervention, or else the "good relationship" will be less than effective. The Ross & McKay (1976) study illustrates this point. Their program clearly communicated respect and trust for their institutionalized chronic delinquents and utilized a peer therapist procedure. However, central to the intervention and a key to its success was a programmatic structure which was deliberately established to yield pressure towards pro-social behavior rather than anti-social behavior. The delinquents were directed towards responsible behavior which persuaded them that they were, in fact, pro-social individuals. Attempts to replicate this program by providing *only* the peer self-help aspects of the program were dramatically unsuccessful (Ross & McKay, 1979).

Behavior modification programs have enjoyed both impressive success and dramatic failure in corrections. The differences between those which have "worked" and those which have not are relatively clear. Reviews of this literature (Ross & McKay, 1978; Emery & Marholin, 1977) pointed out that many programs should never have been expected to succeed because they really never operationalized behavioral principles in their practices. They were operant conditioning programs in name only. Others completely distorted or bastardized the behavioral principles or attempted to change behaviors which had little relevance to the clients' anti-social or delinquent behavior. Ross & McKay's (1978) review revealed that unsuccessful programs had the following features: (a) they were imposed on the offenders who were never involved in the development of the program; (b) the target behavior; (c) they failed to neutralize or utilize in a positive way the offenders' peer group. The successful behavior modification programs (cf. Hoefler, 1975; Davidson & Robinson 1975) avoided or minimized these negative elements.

As we noted earlier, programs based on a "medical-model" disease conception of anti-social behavior (cf. Balch, 1975) have not been fruitful. Whether the disease is some form of psychopathology or biological deficit (e.g., extra chromosomes), we have not found one well-controlled positive report (Ross & Gendreau, 1980), although Hippchen (1976), among others, states that alleviating nutritional chemical deficiencies of delinquents reduces anti-social behavior. Unfortunately, studies purporting to support this view (e.g., Von Hilsheimer, Philpott, Buckely & Klotz, 1977) have been lacking in adequate controls.

Intervention programs based on a deterrence model were once proclaimed quite frequently (cf. Martinson, 1976) to be the "cure-all" for combating crime but the most recent evidence has provided a very sobering experience for deterrence proponents. Although there is the occasional study attesting to effective deterrence on a large societal scale for the short term (Gendreau & Surridge, 1978) or for a certain crime in a specific area (Schnelle, Kirchner, McRae, McNees, Eck, Snodgrass, Casey, & Uselton, 1978), there are many more studies showing mixed, if not negligible effects (cf. Blumstein, Cohen, & Nagin, 1978; Gendreau & Ross, 1981). Moreover, some studies indicate that deterrence programs were associated with increased offending (Critelli & Crawford, Jr., 1980; Erickson, 1977; Hart, 1978). The lack of evidence of effective deterrence may not entirely reflect the inadequacy of the deterrence model per se but shortcomings in its application. Attempts at applying the deterrence model have generally been so poorly conceptualized that no firm conclusions about the efficacy of deterrence could be reached (cf. Zimring, 1978). Moreover, there are profound and, perhaps, unresolvable methodological problems in deterrence research (cf. Gendreau & Ross, 1981) mitigating against finding easy, simplistic answers in the near future. Nevertheless, deterrence research should not be abandoned as there may be payoffs in considering how specific deterrence and treatment techniques can interact to produce effective intervention. The Hayes (1973) and Walter & Mills (1979) studies are two examples of this type of approach to intervention.

Confronting the Issues

Our review of the treatment research literature has confirmed that there are programs which can and have reduced recidivism and some which have not and probably cannot. However, we are not naive enough to assume that correctional agents and agencies will rush to replicate these successful programs nor will there be a marked modification of correctional policy in light of this recent positive evidence. There are any number of reasons for this despairing reality, one of these being that we are far from being an experimenting society (cf. Campbell, 1969; Tavris, 1975) at least in the criminal justice system. We seem neither to learn from our successes or failures, which is one characteristic we appear to share with the offenders we deal with—the failure to profit from experience. As we have documented previously (cf. Gendreau & Ross, 1981; Ross & McKay, 1978) panaceaphalia and negativism run rampant throughout the field. Fads are too enthusiastically embraced.

These characteristics are not, of course, indigenous to the criminal justice system; elements of this kind of thinking can be found in other applied fields where ready answers to complex problems have not been forthcoming. Likely, as the criminal justice system matures these characteristics will gradually extinguish. However, presently there are four issues that we feel are particularly crucial and must be urgently addressed. Failure to take a comprehensive view of the behavioral literature, the lack of therapeutic integrity, the neglect of differential treatment, and the failure to assess and examine the system itself can only lead to negative consequences.

Comprehensive View of the Literature

While the study of criminology purports to be a multi-disciplinary endeavor, in actual fact, the proponents of various positions have rarely taken the broad, well-informed view. The debate over rehabilitation centered on literature published before 1967 and various reviews (purportedly to settle the issue) have been highly selective and/or ignored large bodies of relevant material (Gendreau & Ross, 1979, p. 464-465). As Andrews (1980) incisively noted, the popularity of clinical sociology (Cressey, 1955) has never undergone any kind of thorough scrutiny whatsoever, as proponents of the model failed to test their assumptions and remained blind to the behavioral evolution that occurred outside their discipline. We have reported on a similar phenomenon occurring amongst deterrence proponents who have virtually ignored the fact that weaknesses in their model and theory building are in part due to a profound ignorance of basic experimental psychology (e.g., Carroll, 1978; Walters & Grusic, 1977) that directly touches upon their concerns.

In our opinion, the long-term consequences of failing to take an informed view has led to some of the barren theorizing that has characterized the criminal justice field. Only by ignoring the relevant literature, could one comfortably arrive at the policy positions characterized by the radical criminology, or radical non-intervention (Schur, 1973) or just desert models (Fogel, 1979). The former demands a wrenching radical change in Western society; the second (in some cases) suggests programs that have a good chance of increasing recidivism (Andrews, 1980, p. 449) and the latter theory besides demanding "justice-as-fairness" sounds the cheerful note that outside of killing people we cannot stop people from committing crimes (e.g., Fox, 1974).

Therapeutic Integrity

The major issue in service delivery has centered about the lack of quality and intensity of the service delivery systems developed to date. For example, "to what extent do treatment personnel actually adhere to the principles and employ the techniques of therapy they purport to provide? To what extent are the treatment staff competent? How hard do they work? How much is treatment diluted in the correctional environment so that it becomes treatment in name only?" (Gendreau & Ross, 1979, p. 467). As Quay (1977) and Sechrest *et al.* (1979) have reported, the above questions are rarely answered positively in delinquency intervention research.

This sort of problem, unfortunately, is not one of history. It still occurs. In the recent review of behavioral contracting programs with delinquents, Peters (1981) reported that "the single most important contributing factor to the success or failure of the programs is that quantity and quality to supervision provided to the therapists as they implement the programs...."

Differential Treatment

The potential of treatment programs has also been dismissed by those who naively require that in order for program effectiveness to be established, it must be demonstrated across-the-board with *all* offenders. It seems reasonable to think that in correctional programming, as in every other human enterprise, the effect of an action will depend upon the individual to whom the action is applied and the situation in which it occurs. A program which is effective with some offenders may not be so with other offenders. There are no cure-alls nor should we expect there ever will be. Thankfully, the failure to consider differential treatment effects is becoming less common in the delinquency literature (cf. Glaser, 1975; Warren, 1977). The majority of the effective programs examine individual differences and their interactions with treatment variables. They are crucial to assessing the value of employment programs (e.g., Andrews & Kiessling, 1980; Andrews, Wormith, Daigle-Zinn, Kennedy & Nelson, 1980: Jessness, 1975) and community-based and family therapy programs (e.g., Alexander, Barton, Schiavo & Parsons, 1976; O'Donnell & Fo, 1976).

Differential treatment is not a mere "will of the wisp" phenomenon as Martinson (1976) argued.

System Variables

Chaneles (1976) has noted that a very small percentage of correctional budgets are spent on offender programs. Berk & Rossi (1976) have pointed out that so many bureaucratic and political constraints have been placed on programs that their potential effectiveness is often neutralized. A great deal of the criticism of treatment programs should more properly be directed to criticizing the failure of program managers to attend to how system variables impinge on the program to influence its impact. There have been a few individual accounts (e.g., Rappaport, Seidman & Davidson, 1979; Reppuci, Sarata, Saunders, McArthur & Michlin, 1973) of how program policies in and of themselves can affect outcome.

But we need more concentrated efforts at systems analysis linking (a) setting factors—the physical and social structure of the program, (b) process and content of intervention, (c) intermediate targets, e.g., attitude change and (d) recidivism and cost-benefit (e.g., Andrews & Kiessling, 1980, p. 443). We need to examine how variables affecting the implementation of service systems affect outcome.

Finally, correctional administrators have sensed for a long time that political expediences often prevent the network of social service systems from functioning harmoniously so as to deliver services efficiently (e.g., McDougall, 1976). The extent to which this has happened has been ignored. Even in correctional and social service systems reported to be affluent and progressive, the system operates inefficiently in service delivery. Very often few offenders and their families receive services outside of the criminal justice system (Gendreau, Madden & Lepiciger, 1979). A few successful intervention programs have bridged this gap (See Gendreau & Ross, 1979, p. 488), but in most cases the services are simply not there or are not oriented towards offenders (Peters, 1981)—a reality that has escaped proponents of the advocacy-broker model and "leave the children alone" approach (Dell'Apa, Adams, Jorgenson & Sigurdson, 1976) of service delivery.

The systems and operations research must be drastically increased if any of our successful programs are to be entrenched and we are to even remotely approximate our claims as the experimenting society.

Conclusion

There are correctional programs that are effective. They can be distinguished from unsuccessful programs. There are perfectly good reasons why, in spite of our knowledge of what kinds of programs work, only limited success has been achieved to date, and it is within our means to be constructive in this regard. Admittedly, there are crime problems that go beyond the pale of what is possible given our current acceptance of what we construe to be moral and ethical correctional intervention (Gendreau & Ross, 1980, p. 25). Nevertheless, the majority of offender problems are well within bounds of our means to implement programs that work.

References

Alexander, J. F., Barton, C., Schiavo, R. S., and Parsons, B. V. Systems—Behavioral Intervention with Families' Behavior and Outcome. *Journal of Consulting—Clinical Psychology*, 1976, 44, 656–664.

Alexander, J. F. and Parsons, R. J. Short-term Behavioral Intervention with Delinquent Families: Impact on Family Process and Recidivism, *Journal of Abnormal Psychology*, 1973, 81, 219–225.

Andrews, D. A. The Friendship Model of Voluntary Action and Controlled Evaluations of Correctional Practices: Notes on Relationships with Behavior Theory and Criminology. Toronto: Ministry of Correctional Services, 1979.

Andrews, D. A. Some Experimental Investigations of the Principles of Differential Association Through Deliberate Manipulations of the Structure of Service Systems. *American Sociological Review*, 1980, 45, 448–462.

Andrews, D. A. and Kiessling, J. J. Program Structure and Effective Correctional Practices: A Summary of the CAVIC Research. In R. R. Ross and P. Gendreau (eds.) *Effective Correctional Treatment*. Toronto: Butterworths, 1980.

Andrews, D. A., Wormith, J. S., Daigle-Zinn, W. J., Kennedy, D. J., and Nelson, S. Low and High Functioning Volunteers in Group Counseling with Anxious and Non-Anxious Prisoners: The Effects of Interpersonal Skills on Group Process and Attitude Change. *Canadian Journal or Criminology*, 1980, 22, 443–456.

Balch, R. W. The Medical Model of Delinquency: Theoretical, Practical, and Ethical Implications. *Crime and Delinquency*, 1975, 21, 116–129.

Bandura, A. The Social Learning Perspective: Mechanisms of Aggression. In H. Toch (ed.) *Psychology of Crime and Justice* (Copyright (c) 1979), reissued 1986 Waveland Press, Inc., Prospect Heights, IL.

Berk, R. A. and Rossi, P. H. Doing Good or Worse: Evaluation Research Politically Re-examined. *Social Problems*, 1976, 23, 337–349.

Blakely, C. H., Davidson, W. S., Saylor, C. A., and Robinson, M. J. Kentfields, Rehabilitation Program: Ten Years Later. In R. R. Ross and P. Gendreau (eds.) *Effective Correctional Treatment*. Toronto: Butterworths, 1980.

Blumstein, A., Cohen, J., and Nagin, D. (eds.) *Deterrence and Incapacitation: Estimating the Effects of Criminal Sanctions on Crime Rates.* Washington, DC: National Academy of Sciences, 1978.

Burgess, R. L. and Akers, R. L. A Differential Association-Reinforcement Theory of Criminal Behavior. *Social Problems*, 1966, 14, 128–147.

Campbell, D. T. Reforms as Experiments. *American Psychologist*, 1969, 24, 409–428.

Carroll, J. S. A Psychological Approach to Deterrence: The Evaluation of Crime Opportunities. *Journal of Personality and Social Psychology*, 1978, 36, 1512–1520.

Chandler, M. J. Egocentrism and Antisocial Behavior: The Assessment and Training of Social Perspective-Taking Skills. *Developmental Psychology*, 1973, 9, 326–333.

Chaneles, S. Prisoners Can Be Rehabilitated Now. *Psychology Today*, 1976, 10, 129–133.

Cratt, M., Stephenson, G., and Granger, C. A. A Controlled Trial of Authoritarian and Self-governing Regimes with Adolescent Psychopaths. *American Journal of Orthopsychiatry*, 1964, 34, 543–554.

Cressey, D. R. Changing Criminals: The Application of the Theory of Differential Association. *American Journal of Sociology*, 1955, 61, 116–120.

Critelli, J. W. and Crawford, R. F. The Effectiveness of Court-Ordered Punishment: Fines Versus Punishment. *Criminal Justice and Behavior*, 1980, 7, 465–470.

Davidson, W. D. and Robinson, M. J. Community Psychology and Behavior Modification: A Community-Based Program for the Prevention of Delinquency. *Corrective and Social Psychiatry*, 1975, 21, 1–12.

Dell'Apa, F., Adams, W. T., Jorgenson, J. D. D. and Sigurdson, H. R. Advocacy, Brokerage, Community: The ABC's of Probation and Parole. *Federal Probation*, 1976, 40, 37–44.

Emery, R. E. and Marholin II, D. An Applied Behavior Analysis of Delinquency: The Irrelevancy of Relevant Behavior. *American Psychologist*, 1977, 32, 860–873.

Empey, I. T. From Optimism to Despair: New Doctrines in Juvenile Justice. In C. A. Murry and I. A. Cox, Jr. *Beyond Probation: Juvenile Corrections and the Chronic Delinquent*. Beverly Hills, CA: Sage, 1979.

Erickson, M. L., Gibbs J. P. and Jensen, G. F. The Deterrence Doctrine and the Perceived Certainty of Legal Punishments. *American Sociological Review*, 1977, 42, 305–317.

Fenton, N. Group Counselling in Correctional Practice. *Canadian Journal of Corrections*, 1960, 2, 229–239.

Fogel, D. *We Are the Living Proof: The Justice Model for Corrections.* Cincinnati: Anderson, 1979.

Fox, S. J. The Reform of Juvenile Justice: The Child's Right to Punishment. *Juvenile Justice*, 1974, 25, 2–9.

Gendreau, P. and Andrews, D. A. *Psychological Consultant*. New York: Grune & Stratton, 1979.

Gendreau, P., Madden, P., and Leipciger, M. *Norms and Recidivism* Rates for Social History and Institutional Experience of First Incarcerate: Implications for Programming. *Canadian Journal of Criminology*, 1979, 21, 416–441.

Gendreau, P., and Ross, R. R. Effective Correctional Treatment: Bibliotherapy for Cynics. *Crime and Delinquency*, 1979, 25, 463–489.

Gendreau, P., and Ross, R. R. Effective Corrections Treatment: Bibliotherapy for Cynics. In R. R. Ross and P. Gendreau (eds.) *Effective Correctional Treatment*. Toronto: Butterworths, 1980.

Gendreau, P., and Ross, R. R. Correctional Potency; Treatment and Deterrence on Trial. In R. Roesch and R. Corrado (eds.) *Evaluation Research and Policy in Criminal Justice*. Beverly Hills: Sage, 1981.

Gendreau, P., and Ross, R. R. Prescriptions for Successful Intervention. Manuscript under review, 1981.

Gendreau, P., and Ross, R. R. Getting Serious about the Deterrence of Offenders: Problems and prospects. Manuscript under review, 1981.

Gendreau, P., and Surridge, C. T. Controlling Gun Crimes: The Jamaican Experience. *International Journal of Criminology and Penology*, 1978, 6, 43–60.

Glaser, D. Achieving Better Questions: A Half-century's Progression in Correctional Research. *Federal Probation*, 1975, 39, 3–9.

Grant, J. D., and Grant, M. Q. A Group Dynamics Approach to the Treatment of Non-Conformists in the Navy. *Annals of the American Academy of Political and Social Science*, 1959, 322, 126–135.

Hackler, J. C. *The Prevention of Youthful Crime: The Great Stumble Forward*. Toronto: Methuen, 1978.

Hart, R. J. Crime and Punishment in the Army. *Journal of Personality and Social Psychology*, 1978, 36, 1456–1471.

Hayes, S. N. Contingency Management in a Municipally-Administered Antiabuse Program for Alcoholics. *Journal of Behavior Therapy and Experimental Psychiatry*, 1973, 4, 31–32.

Hippchen, L. J. Biomedical Approaches to Offender Rehabilitation. *Offender Rehabilitation*, 1976, 17, 115–123.

Hoetler, S. A., and Bornstein, Ph. H. Achievement Place: An Evaluative Review. *Criminal Justice and Behavior*, 1975, 2, 146–168.

Jeffrey, R., and Woolpert, S. Work Furlough as an Alternative to Incarceration; An assessment of its Effects on Recidivism and Social Cost. *Journal of Criminal Law and Criminology*, 1974, 65, 405–415.

Jessness, C. F. Comparative Effectiveness of Behavior Modification and Transactional Analysis Programs for Delinquents. *Journals of Consulting and Clinical Psychology*, 1975, 43, 758–779.

Kassebaum, G., Ward, D., and Wilner, D. *Prison Treatment and Parole Survival: An Empirical Assessment*. New York: Wiley, 1971.

Lee, R., and Haynes, N. M. Project CREST and the Dual-Treatment Approach to Delinquency: Methods and Research Summarized. In R. R. Ross and P. Gendreau (eds.) *Effective Correctional Treatment*. Toronto: Butterworths, 1980.

Martinson, R. "What Works? Questions and Answers About Prison Reform. *The Public Interest*, 1974, 35, 22–54.

Martinson, R. California Research at the Crossroads. *Crime Delinquency*, 1976, 22, 180–191.

Martinson, R., and Wilks, J. Save Parole Supervision. *Federal Probation*, 1977, 41, 23–27.

McDougall, E. C. Corrections Has Not Been Tried. *Criminal Justice Review*, 1976, 1, 63–76.

Nettler, G. *Explaining Crime*. New York: McGraw-Hill, 1978.

Nietzel, M. T. *Crime and Its Modification: A Social Learning Perspective*. New York: Pergamon, 1979.

O'Donnell, C. R., and Fo, W. S. O. The Buddy System: Mediator-Target Locus of Control and Behavioral Outcome. *American Journal of Community Psychology*, 1976, 4, 161–166.

Phillips, E. L., Phillips, R. A., Fixsen, D. L., and Wolf, M. W. Behavior Shaping Works for Delinquents. *Psychology Today*, 1973, 6, 75–79.

Palmer, T. Martinson Revisited. *Journal of Research in Crime and Delinquency*, 1975, 12, 133–152.

Palmer, T. *Correctional Intervention and Research*. Lexington, MA: Heath, 1978.

Peters, R. Deviant Behavioral Contracting with Conduct Problem Youth: A Review and Critical Analysis. Department of Psychology, Queen's University, Kingston, Ontario, 1981.

Platt, J. J., Perry, G. M., and Metzger, D. S. The Evaluation of a Heroin Addiction Treatment Program Within a Correctional Environment. In R. R. Ross and P. Gendreau (eds.) *Effective Correctional Treatment*. Toronto: Butterworths, 1980.

Quay, H. C. The Three Faces of Evaluation; What Can Be Expected to Work. *Criminal Justice and Behavior*, 1977, 4, 341–354.

Rappeport, J., Seidman, E., and Davidson II, W. S. Demonstration Research and Manifest Versus True Adoption: The Natural History of a Research Project. In R. F. Munoz, L. R. Snowden, and J. G. Kelly (eds.) *Social Psychological Research and Community Settings*. San Francisco: Jossey-Bass, 1979.

Repucci, N. D., Sarata, B. P., Saunders, J. T., McArthur, A. V., and Michlin, L. M. We Bombed in Mountville: Lessons Learned in Consultation to a Correctional Facility for Adolescent Offenders. In I. I. Goldenberg (ed.) *The Helping Professions in the World of Action*. Boston: D. C. Heath, 1973.

Ross, R. R. and Gendreau, P. *Effective Correctional Treatment*. Toronto: Butterworths, 1980.

Ross, R. R. and McKay, H. B. A Study of Institutional Treatment Programs. *International Journal of Offender Therapy and Comparative Criminology*, 1976, 20, 165–173.

Ross, R. R. and McKay, B. Treatment in Corrections: Requiem for a Panacea. *Canadian Journal of Criminology*, 1978, 120, 279–295.

Ross, R. R. and McKay, B. *Self-Mutilation*. Boston: Lexington, 1979.

Sarason, I. G. A Cognitive Social Learning Approach to Juvenile Delinquency. In R. D. Hare and D. Schalling (eds.) *Psychopathic Behaviour Approaches to Research*. New York: Wiley, 1978.

Schnelle, J. F., Kirchner, R. E., McRaie, J. E., McNees, M. P., Eck, R. H., Snotdgrass, S., Casey, J. D., and Uselton, P. H. Police Evaluation Research: An Experimental and Cost-Benefit Analysis of a Helicopter Patrol in a High Crime Area. *Journal of Applied Behavior Analysis*, 1978, 11, 11–21.

Schur, E. M. *Radical Nonintervention: Re-thinking the Delinquency Problem*. Englewood Cliffs: Prentice-Hall, 1973.

Sechrest, L., West, S. G., Phillips, M. A., Redner, R., and Yeaton, W. Some Neglected Problems in Evaluation Research: Strength Is Integrity of Treatments. In L. Sechrest, S. G. West, M. A. Phillips, R. Redner and W. Yeaton, *Evaluation Studies Annual Review* (Vol. 4). Beverly Hills: Sage, 1979.

Sechrest, L., White, S. O., and Brown, G. D. (eds.) *The Rehabilitation of Criminal Offenders*. Washington, DC: National Academy of Sciences, 1979.

Serrill, M. S. Is Rehabilitation Dead? *Corrections Magazine*, 1975, 11, 3–12, 21–26.

Shore, M. F. and Massimo, J. L. Fifteen Years After Treatment: A Follow-up Study of Comprehensive Vocationally-oriented Psychotherapy. *American Journal of Orthopsychiatry*, 1979, 49, 240–245.

Tayris, C. The Experimenting Society: To Find Programs That Work, Government Must Measure Its Failures. *Psychology Today*, 1975, 9, 47–56.

Tullock, G. Does Punishment Deter Crime?: *Public Interest*, 1974, 35, 103–111.

Von Hilsheimer, G., Philpott, W., Buckley, W., and Klotz, S. D. Correcting the Incorrigible: A Report on 229 Incorrigible Adolescents. *American Laboratory*, 1977, 101, 197–218.

Walter, T. L., and Mills, C. M. A Behavioral-Employment Intervention Program for Reducing Juvenile Delinquency. In J. S. Stumphauzer (ed.) *Progress in Behavior Therapy with Delinquents*. Springfield, IL: Thomas, 1979.

Walters, G. C., and Grusec, J. E. *Punishment*. San Francisco: Freeman & Co., 1977.

Warren, M. Q. Correctional Treatment and Coercion: The Differential Effectiveness Perspective. *Criminal Justice and Behavior*, 1977, 4, 355–376.

Zimring, F. G. Policy Experiments in General Deterrence: 1970–75. In A. Blumstein, J. Cohen, and D. Ngain (eds.) *Deterrence and Incapacitation: Estimating the Effects of Criminal Sanctions on Crime Rates*. Washington, DC: National Academy of Sciences, 1978.

Article 32

Does mandatory sentencing deter crime?
No, says this tough but compassionate judge.
To be effective, justice must be flexible.

Habilitation, not rehabilitation

By Dyan Machan

"JUDGE ROBERTS, DID YOU SPIT?" It might seem an impertinent question, but Burton Roberts, administrative judge for the 12th Judicial District of the Supreme Court of New York, knows exactly what I'm asking.

Roberts was immortalized as Judge Kovitsky in Tom Wolfe's bestselling book, *The Bonfire of the Vanities*. In one memorable scene, the judge comes upon a van of nasty, heckling prisoners. In Wolfe's words, "[Kovitsky's] pupils were like two death rays burning just beneath his upper eyelids." The judge peered into the van and spat at the prisoners.

From his Bronx courthouse chambers the judge insists, "I did not spit." Then he smiles. "It's something I could have done, but I did not," he says playfully.

After 25 years presiding over some of the nation's meanest streets, this 76-year-old jurist retires at year's end. Joining him in his roomy chambers, I wonder what's on his mind. As we sit down to Greek salads in tinfoil containers, I find out: mandatory sentencing. Nowadays, mandatory sentences are hugely popular with voters disgusted with coddled criminals and the politicians who cater to them. Some 46 states have established these laws, including New York.

How do these laws work? Instead of traditional minimum sentences of 6 to 12 years, a second-time armed robber receives 10 years flat. Instead of one-third of the time off for good behavior, there is only the possibility of one-seventh of the sentence being reduced.

Sounds like a good idea to me.

Roberts lifts his head from his salad. I think I see the death rays Tom Wolfe described.

"A terrible idea," he mutters. "Facing a surefire stiff penalty, the defendant, with nothing to lose, asks for a trial. The court can't lock people up indefinitely, so he's back on the streets on a pretrial release. What does a robber do when he's back on the street? He robs." Roberts hits the tin container with an olive pit by way of giving emphasis to his disapproval.

Why can't we keep these criminals locked up before their trial?

Tossing another olive pit, Roberts replies: "We don't have preventive detention in this state." Right. Innocent until proven guilty.

The judge takes a sip of his seltzer and sighs. "The guys who make these laws come from places with more trees than people." For non-New Yorkers, what he's referring to is that the state legislature sits in Albany, surrounded by rolling green hills, while he dispenses justice in a teeming urban setting. He thinks he knows criminals better than some legislator in the apple belt.

"It's not the severity of punishment that deters the crime," Roberts goes on, "Believe me, people who commit crimes don't sit around at dinner talking about whether a crime gets five years or ten."

I look into his death rays and dare: "Come on judge, you're telling me harsh punishment doesn't cut crime! In some countries thieves get their hands chopped off. There isn't much stealing."

Oh, he knows that. His fork hits the table like a gavel and he shoots back: "In old London, pickpockets got a public hanging. And when the people were gathered to watch the hanging, the other pickpockets had a field day. Hanging didn't seem to deter them!

"No, the only thing that works is speed and certain justice," he bellows. "Speed and certainty, not draconian sentences."

Wait a minute. Crime is down around the nation; in New York City

146   Reprinted by permission from *Forbes* magazine, November 2, 1998, pp. 90-94. © 1998 by Forbes, Inc.

alone, homicides are down 40% in the last five years. Certainly that's due to tougher sentences and better policing?

My naiveté has him fuming and he shoots back: "Crime is down as a result of demographics. Right now you have less people in the 15-to-25-year age group in which criminals are most active. But there is a rise in juvenile crime in ages 10 to 14. This group, just seedlings now—will grow to trees casting a terrible shadow over our urban centers."

Now he's back to those damned mandatory sentences. "The worst thing," he says, "is to take discretion away from a judge. It removes the judge's ability to evaluate the nuances of the crime and the nuances of the individual who committed it."

Roberts, a former district attorney and World War II hero, isn't a judge who worries a lot about what newspapers or politicians say about him. I suspect he enjoys it when he riles people. "A leader has to show by example and not cater to what the public wants. I can take it," he says with a shrug.

Just two years ago New York Mayor Rudolph Giuliani and New York Governor George Pataki attacked Roberts for setting bail too low for an accused cop killer. The judge held his ground and snapped: "I do not poll public officials in order to interpret the law." His explanation for the low bail: The death looked to be accidental.

My guess is that he can handle these verbal barrages because they are tame compared with the artillery barrages he endured in WWII. A 20-year-old U.S. Army infantryman, he repeatedly went into heavy fire in Italy and France in 1944 to rescue injured comrades. He was also wounded. Asked about his wartime experiences, Roberts says what a lot of heroes say: "The only ones who are brave are those who died."

After the war he attended Cornell University Law School on the GI bill, but was turned down in his first interview for a job in a law firm. Those were very different days. "In one conversation, the partner asked me what church I attended on Sunday," he says. That, of course, was a way of saying, "We want no Jews." Roberts, who is Jewish, chose to take a public sector job. After a stint as an assistant district attorney, he served as Bronx County's district attorney from September 1968 to January 1973, and was considered one of the most aggressive and effective D.A.s in New York City history.

Tense when talking about the law, Roberts relaxes when he tells an anecdote. "Let me tell you a story," he says, pushing aside his salad tin. "There was a kid whose specialty was robbing Chinese restaurants. He went to Brooklyn Tech and was a smart kid. I gave him youthful offender—the mildest treatment—and sentenced him to up to four years in state prison.

"When it came time for his release he wanted to stay in jail so he could complete the schoolwork he had started during prison at a community college. When he came out he went to Pace University. He became an actuary, with a good job at a big firm.

"Instead of throwing the key away, you treat these people with dignity. It's not popular to say, but the only chance we have is to habilitate these people. I won't say rehabilitate, because that assumes they were at one time okay."

Doesn't Roberts believe some people are lost causes? "Absolutely," he says, "Fifteen percent of criminals should be locked up forever.

"But let me tell you another story," says the judge. His subject is Nathan Giles Jr., who robbed, raped, sodomized and murdered a woman in 1978. "A death sentence would be too kind. I gave him 68½ years, 3 life terms and another plus 25 years. He was 34, which would make him eligible for release when he's 104. If the court has trouble finding me in 2044, I wrote into the decision that I want the court to show him as much sympathy as he showed his victim. He should die in jail."

At the Giles sentencing Roberts' final words were, "Good-bye, Nathan Giles—good-bye forever!" The jury rose and applauded.

Other visitors are awaiting. Judges who were queuing up outside are now settling into his office chairs. He says to one of the judges, "Hey, do you read FORBES?" The judges smirk. Roberts quips, "If you send me three subscriptions you will triple your circulation here." Everyone laughs.

That's his way of saying that there isn't much money in this forsaken part of New York City but that he loves it. He reads a bit of doggerel he wrote for the end of a recent speech. It ends in these lines: "I love thee, Bronx, I love thee well, anywhere else, a living hell."

Okay, he's not a poet. Nor is he a likely candidate for a rocking chair in the Florida sunshine. After retirement, he might join a law firm or become a TV legal commentator. "I want to work," he says. Then, breaking into an expansive smile, he adds, "Besides, my wife, Gerhild, married me for better or worse—but not for lunch."

Article 33

A Decade of Experimenting With Intermediate Sanctions: What Have We Learned?*

BY JOAN PETERSILIA, PH.D.
Professor of Criminology, Law, and Society, University of California, Irvine

THIS ARTICLE reviews what has been learned during the past 10 to 15 years about the restrictions and costs of intermediate sanctions, those mid-range punishments that lie somewhere between prison and routine probation. Various intermediate sanctions programs (ISPs) that incorporate intensive supervision, home confinement, community service, boot camps, and day fines have been developed in recent years.

For those of us whose research has focused primarily on community corrections, the end of the 1990s marks an important landmark. We have witnessed the natural progression of ISPs, beginning in the mid-1980s with the media's enthusiastic portrayal of them as the panacea of corrections; through program design and implementation; to evaluation and testing; and finally to institutionalization, redesign, or abandonment. It is critical for scholars, policymakers, and practitioners to look back and reflect upon what has been learned during these years.

When looking at ISPs, there are three important questions to consider: First, what did the ISP experiment consist of—who did what, with whom, and for what purpose? Secondly, how did ISPs affect program costs, recidivism, and prison crowding? And, perhaps most important, how is the knowledge gained from this experience influencing current practice?

Several conclusions can be drawn from the evaluations of ISPs:

- In terms of sheer numbers and investments, the overall ISP experiment was more symbolic in its achievements than substantive.
- Specific components must be in place for these programs to work.
- Research findings currently influence the design of corrections programs and, more important, contribute to an emerging community justice model that promises to create a major paradigm shift in community corrections.

The ISP Experiment Begins

In the mid-1980s, a broad-based consensus emerged as to the desirability of developing mid-range punishments for offenders for whom incarceration was unnecessarily severe and ordinary probation was inappropriately light. Three converging conditions and events drove the development of this consensus.

1. Crowded Southern prisons and a poor economy. First, prison crowding in the Southern United States, coupled with a poor regional economy, created early pressures for tough community-based options. Federal

---

*This article was originally prepared for the National Institute of Justice (NIJ) for use in its Crime and Justice Perspectives series.

33. Decade of Experimenting with Intermediate Sanctions

courts found several overcrowded prisons in the South to be in violation of the eighth amendment prohibition against cruel and unusual punishment and mandated that these states either build new facilities or find some other way to punish offenders. Because these states did not have the funds to build new prisons (as other states experiencing prison population growth initially did), judicial pressure created an incentive for them to develop tough but inexpensive sentences, specifically those that did not require a prison cell. Because the voters were not about to endorse "soft" social programs, the new programs were presented to the public as punitive rather than rehabilitative. In fact, some of the older, first-generation intensive supervision programs (which provided intensive rehabilitation services) changed their names to "intensive surveillance" programs while programs originally called "alternatives to incarceration" were renamed "intermediate punishments."

The State of Georgia developed the first well-publicized intensive supervision program, the hallmark of which was the assignment of 25 offenders to a supervision team of two probation officers. The team consisted of a surveillance officer, whose main responsibility was to monitor the offender closely, and a probation officer, who provided counseling and had legal authority over the case. While on intermediate sanction, each probationer was seen five times a week, performed community service, paid a supervision fee, and had to be employed or in an educational program.

Georgia's self-evaluation showed that ISP participants had extremely low recidivism rates (less than 5 percent), and most offenders maintained employment and paid restitution to victims. In addition, the monthly supervision fee made the program self-supporting. In 1985, Georgia Corrections Commissioner David Evans claimed the ISP had saved the state the cost of building two new prisons.

A great deal of national publicity followed. The *Washington Post* and the *New York Times* ran major stories touting the program's success and called Georgia's program "the future of American corrections." Proponents suggested that intermediate punishments could relieve prison crowding, enhance public safety, and rehabilitate offenders—all at a cost saving. Probation staffs also were enthusiastic, saying intermediate sanctions programs gave them an opportunity to "do probation work the way it ought to be done."

Illinois, Massachusetts, New Jersey, and Florida, among other states, quickly followed suit, and the intermediate sanctions movement was born. It is important to be clear about the initial motivation: modern ISPs were developed in direct response to prison crowding, and without that pressure, we would not be here today reviewing their performance.

2. First indepth study of U.S. felony probation. Research evidence produced at that time showed that the existing felony probation system was a failure in large urban areas. This evidence helped convince California and other large states that had not yet faced severe prison crowding that there were public safety risks in placing felons on routine probation. In 1983, the National Institute of Justice (NIJ) awarded a grant to the RAND Corporation to conduct the first indepth study of felony probation in the United States. The final report, *Granting Felons Probation: Public Risks and Alternatives,* documented the fact that serious felons were being granted probation. Furthermore, because of limited (and often declining) community corrections resources, these offenders were ineffectively supervised, and the public safety consequences were severe. Two-thirds of the nearly 2,000 felony probationers who were tracked during this study were rearrested within 3 years, and more than half were reconvicted of serious offenses.[1]

The study also generated a great deal of public attention because it clearly showed that overburdened probation staff often were unable to closely supervise felons or hold them accountable for their crimes. The researchers, however, did not call for the abandonment of probation for felons or their incarceration in the future but rather something in between:

> The justice system needs an alternative, intermediate form of punishment for those offenders who are too antisocial for the relative freedom that probation now offers but not so seriously criminal as to require imprisonment. A sanction is needed that would impose intensive surveillance, coupled with substantial community service and restitution.

The study concluded that mid-range punishments—such as those instituted in Georgia—were needed not only to relieve prison crowding but to relieve probation crowding as well. The dissemination of the NIJ-RAND study became the second event to increase the acceptance of ISPs.

3. Morris and Tonry's book on the polarization of sentencing. The third event that was critical in creating the impetus for the ISP movement was the publication of an influential book in 1990 by Norval Morris and Michael Tonry entitled *Between Prison and Probation: Intermediate Punishments in a Rational Sentencing System.*[2] Written by two of the nation's leading criminologists, this study acknowledged that U.S. judges faced a polarized choice between prison and probation, with a near vacuum of punishment options between these extremes. The study provided the needed conceptual framework for a more graduated sanctioning system that relied upon a range of sentences including fines, community service, house arrest, intensive probation, and electronic monitoring. Morris and Tonry argued that rigorously enforced intermediate punishments better serve victims and the justice system. A continuum that matches offenders to sanctions based on the seriousness of their crime is essential—regardless of any prison-crowding concerns—in creating a rational sentencing system, they wrote.

5 ❖ LIVING ON THE OUTSIDE: INTERMEDIATE SANCTIONS

The ISP Concept Gains Strong Support

What existed, then, were program models that appeared to work, research to show that without these programs the public was at serious risk, and a compelling theoretical justification for moving forward. A groundswell of support emerged for intermediate sanctions and, as one article noted about this period, "State legislators were virtually falling over each other" in an effort to sponsor legislation to implement these programs.[3]

The U.S. Department of Justice (DOJ) and several private organizations, particularly the Edna McConnell Clark Foundation, played a catalytic role in focusing this energy. In 1990, NIJ sponsored a national conference that brought together more than 300 federal, state, and local criminal justice administrators to explore the state of intermediate sanctions and their potential. In his keynote address, Attorney General Dick Thornburg emphasized the strong bipartisan support for developing intermediate sanctions. The Bureau of Justice Assistance (the "action" arm of DOJ) solicited agencies across the country to participate in a demonstration to test the costs and benefits of various types of ISPs. In addition, NIJ and the National Institute of Corrections (NIC) provided technical assistance, training, and research for a number of projects.

The 10 years between 1985 and 1995 could best be described as the period of ISP implementation and evaluation. Hundreds of programs were started, often with a great deal of ceremony. During this period, virtually every large probation or parole agency developed programs of intensive surveillance, electronic monitoring, house arrest, drug testing and, to a lesser extent, boot camps and day reporting centers.

A Closer Look Reveals Low ISP Participation and Shallow Funding

Most important, very few offenders, relatively speaking, participated in intermediate sanctions programs, and few dollars were spent on new ISP initiatives. Today, virtually every state and the federal government report having intensive supervision programs, but fewer than 6 percent of the 2.7 million adult probationers and parolees in the United States are estimated to be participating in them. (This number is, however, higher than anytime in the past.[4]) All 50 states report using electronic monitoring, and, despite what has often been characterized as explosive growth, the number of probationers and parolees monitored electronically is now at its highest level ever—about 1 percent.[5] Although 35 states report operating boot camps, the combined daily census has never exceeded 10,000 participants.[6] Finally, although nearly 125 day reporting centers operate in the United States, their combined daily population is less than 15,000.[7]

It appears that, at most, 10 percent of adult probationers and parolees participate in ISPs—a figure that is probably higher than at any time in the past. It is safe to say that the ISP experiment has not touched the bulk of those for whom it might be appropriate, such as felons with increasingly serious prior records and a history of substance abuse who are granted probation.

Moreover, when offenders were assigned to ISPs, the intensity of services and surveillance fell short of what the initial program models prescribed—most likely because sufficient dollars were not invested. As best as can be calculated, less than $10 million was invested by the federal government in ISP research and demonstration projects between 1985 and 1995. This can be compared to the $10 million the federal government invests in evaluations of community-oriented policing each year.

In no way is this intended to offend those responsible for making these funding decisions. The boom in ISPs took place in 1994—the same time that DOJ and NIJ budgets for research and demonstration programs were declining to a 20-year low. Competition for those scarce dollars was fierce, and corrections research—particularly community corrections research—has never attracted major financial support. Fortunately, Congress has increased funding to the Bureau of Justice Assistance (BJA), the Bureau of Justice Statistics (BJS), and NIJ, and corrections research has again found support.

What Did the ISP Experiment Really Consist Of?

It is beyond the scope of this presentation to fully describe the nature of ISPs or their evaluations. For anyone interested in such details, the recently published University of Maryland report entitled *Preventing Crime: What Works, What Doesn't, What's Promising* is recommended.[8] However, I will briefly summarize the specifics of the more popular programs.

As mentioned earlier, intensive supervision programs were the first—and still remain—the cornerstone of the intermediate sanctions movement. ISPs initially were developed as a means to divert low-risk prisoners to the community or place higher-risk probationers on smaller caseloads with more restrictions. Concurrent with the emergence of ISPs was a developing technology to permit greater surveillance of offenders. As the cold war wound down, the defense industry along with the developing computer and electronic industries saw the community corrections clientele as a natural place to put its energies—a growing market. Electronic monitoring, voice verification systems, cheap on-site drug testing, breathalyzers through the phone—all allowed community corrections the option of becoming more surveillance-oriented and using the offender's home as a place of incarceration.

Jurisdictions could choose from a menu of bells and whistles, which included surveillance and services, and the goal came to be toughness in appearance. Jurisdictions adopted what they wanted, what they could afford, and applied such programs to whomever they wanted—so that a wide variety of ISPs got implemented—and the name "ISP" really has no commonly agreed upon definition as a result. It simply means "more than" what offenders in that location would have gotten in the absence of the ISP.

As noted earlier, most of the programs implemented were much less intensive than the original Georgia model had called for. Recall that the Georgia ISP model called for caseloads of 25:2, and two face-to-face contacts, minimally per week, and I know of no large urban probation department that was able to sustain that level of caseload size and contact level for its felony probationers. Even programs that began with multi-week visits displayed a strong tendency to "regress to the mean" of only one or two visits per month to a client. Suffice to say that for offenders who did participate, their level of *both* service and surveillance fell below the desired intensity.

Moreover, failure to comply with ISP conditions did not mean that you would be violated from probation. Patrick Langan of BJS studied a nationally representative sample of all adult probationers and discovered that nearly half of them were discharged from probation *without* having fully complied with their court-ordered sanctions.[9] More than a third of all offenders were successfully discharged from probation without completing court-ordered drug treatment, drug testing, house arrest, or day reporting programs. And 40 percent of those discharged had not paid their victim restitution or supervision fees. He concluded that "intermediate sanctions are not rigorously enforced." Still, something different *did* happen in those communities that implemented ISPs and several good evaluations were conducted.

Program Costs, Recidivism, and Prison Crowding

Relative to the investment made, a tremendous amount was learned from these programs. Despite differences in the programs, the agencies that implemented them, and the characteristics of offenders who participated in them, three major findings are very consistent.

First, ISP participants, by and large, were not prison-bound but rather were high-risk probationers. In state after state, well-meaning program developers wrote guidelines for prison "diversions." Well-meaning judges and prosecutors ignored them and filled the programs with high-risk probationers. From the perspective of those who created these programs to save money and prison space, judges "misused" intermediate sanctions.

From the perspective of judges, they had endorsed the concept of a continuum of sanctions and preferred to use these options to increase supervision and accountability for felony probationers. The ISP experiment was definitely "net widening," but given the laxity of current supervision of serious felons on probation, it is more accurate to characterize it as "net repairing."

Second, ISP offenders were watched more closely, but ISP supervision did not decrease subsequent arrests or overall justice system costs. Technical violations, however, increased. Offenders on intermediate sanctions, electronic monitoring, boot camps, day fines, and drug testing programs were watched more closely—as evidenced by a greater number of contacts—but the programs did not reduce new arrests.

For example, the ISP national demonstration evaluated by Susan Turner and me, which involved 14 counties in 9 states, found no difference in arrests after 1 year (38 percent for ISP participants and 36 percent for routine probationers), more ISP than control offenders with technical violations (70 percent and 40 percent, respectively), and, as a result, more ISP than control offenders returning to prison or jail by the end of 1 year (17 percent and 19 percent, respectively).[10]

Because it is doubtful that ISP offenders committed more violations, close surveillance probably uncovered more technical violations. Whenever this happened, many ISP managers took punitive action—often revocation to prison—to maintain the program's credibility in the eyes of the judiciary and the community. Programs that were started primarily to save money and avoid the costs of prison often cost their counties more over the long term.

These results bring into question two basic premises of intermediate sanctions, i.e., that increased surveillance acts as a constraint on the offender and that the likelihood of detection acts as a deterrent to crime. The University of Maryland project, which summarized evaluations across the full range of intermediate sanctions, concluded: "Except in a few instances, there is no evidence that these programs are effective in reducing crime as measured by official record data."[11]

Third, an important and tantalizing finding—consistent across all the evaluations regardless of program design—points to the importance of combining surveillance and drug treatment program participation. In the RAND ISP demonstration, offenders who participated in treatment, community service, and employment programs—prosocial activities—had recidivism rates 10 to 20 percent below that of those who did not participate in such additional activities.

Researchers have found similar results in Massachusetts, Oregon, and Ohio, and a recent meta-analysis of 175 evaluations of intermediate sanctions programs concluded that the combination of surveillance and treatment is associated with reduced recidivism.[12] Paul Gendreau and Tracy Little conclude, "In essence, the supervision of high-risk probationers and parolees must be structured, [be] intensive, maintain firm accountability for program participation, and connect the offender with prosocial networks and activities."

The empirical evidence regarding intermediate sanctions is decisive: Without a rehabilitation component, reductions in recidivism are elusive. In sum, the ISP evaluations show that programs were seldom used for prison diversion but rather to increase accountability and supervision of serious offenders on probation. In addition, programs did not reduce new crimes, but instead increased the discovery of technical violations and ultimately increased incarceration rates and system costs. However, programs that provided treatment and additional services obtained some reductions in recidivism, particularly for high-risk offenders and for drug offenders more specifically.

Influencing Current Practice

How do ISP evaluations influence current practice? This is the most important of the three original questions because the ultimate goal of producing knowledge is to effect positive action. Still to be addressed are the same issues that motivated the intermediate sanctions movement—prison overcrowding, probation overload, insufficient resources, and public demand for accountability and punishment. How can this evidence be used to answer the central question, "If not prison, what?"

Researchers and policymakers cannot plead ignorance or abstain from the debate—because they know what is useful. Although they do not have all the answers, they have an obligation to engage in the debate and interject the known evidence because policy is made on these matters every day. It appears that this is happening in quiet but significant ways that may well result in a major paradigm shift for community corrections in the United States.

Program Redesign

First, the body of ISP evidence is being used to redesign programs that integrate surveillance with treatment opportunities. This is particularly true with juvenile justice programs but also with programs for adults, particularly drug offenders. The Office of Juvenile Justice and Delinquency Prevention Comprehensive Strategy for Youth endorses graduated sanctions and incorporates two principal components—increasingly strict supervision and a continuum of treatment alternatives.[13] Many states have adopted the Comprehensive Strategy. The California Legislature, for example, recently allocated $50 million to fund probation programs for delinquent youth and, drawing upon the evidence reviewed earlier, required that both surveillance and treatment be part of any funded program.

Other programs also have moved away from a singular focus on surveillance. Several boot camps, for example, are enhancing the therapeutic parts of their programs and shifting away from total reliance on physical, militaristic programming. UCLA's Mark Kleiman has proposed major funding for a national initiative labeled "coerced abstinence," which at its core will provide drug testing (a main ingredient in surveillance programs), plus treatment in and out of prison, followed by intensive aftercare upon release. A key component of his program is swift and certain response to drug-use violations.

One of the major recommendations of the recently published report by the Governor's Task Force on Sentencing and Corrections in Wisconsin, which draws heavily upon ISP experiences, calls for the elimination of probation for felons.[14] The task force recommends that felony probation be replaced with an arrangement named "community confinement and control" (CCC), which mandates electronic monitoring, urine testing, work or community service, and 18 to 20 contacts a month with a probation officer who has a caseload of no more than 17 offenders. CCC officers carry out "community-oriented probation" (similar to community-oriented policing), in which they provide active as opposed to passive supervision. They are required to engage the offender's family, employer, and neighborhood to create a support and supervision network. The Wisconsin Legislature has allocated the necessary resources to pilot the task force recommendation in two jurisdictions.

These are just a few of the ways in which ISP research results directly influence the design of future programs. It is safe to say that most corrections professionals are keenly aware of these findings. In terms of contributing to a cumulative body of knowledge about correctional programming, the ISP experiment can be considered a success.

Neighborhood Probation

The legacy of the intermediate sanctions experiment is likely to be far more important than simply the redesign of individual programs. ISPs have set the stage for an emerging model of community probation (also called community justice and neighborhood probation) in which probation officers partner with the police and community members to reduce public safety threats posed by offenders in their midst. Under this model, probation officers take an active role in community building and not just offender restraint. The probation and parole officers who are involved in ISP supervision programs are emerging as key players.

Interestingly, as community corrections officers move toward a tougher form of probation, which some liken to police work, police officers are embracing community-based policing, which some liken to probation or social work. Probation and police officers are getting out from behind their desks and out of their cars and into the community. "In your face" probation includes visiting the offender's home and work site and working with community agencies to develop and supervise community service obligations—a much more active type of probation.

Police, too, are getting out into communities, holding neighborhood meetings, and taking the pulse of neighborhoods they serve through comparatively well-funded community policing programs. One of the key goals of community policing is getting to know the people on the beat—offenders as well as law-abiding citizens. Police have heard repeatedly about residents' fear of offenders and the lack of justice and accountability for people who were arrested and placed on probation or released on parole. Victims felt crime was trivialized by a justice system that simply slapped the wrist of criminals and sent them home or imposed conditions that were not monitored. Repeat victimization was common, and the community wanted criminals who had committed serious offenses taken off its streets. Once that was done, community residents wanted programs to help the next generation become responsible citizens.

The police came to realize that to significantly reduce crime they had to get out in front of the problem and not merely react to reports of crime. They needed to be proactive rather than simply reactive. To be proactive, the police needed a variety of sources of information. Much of that information and—as it turns out—legal authority exist in the minds of the officers who operate intensive supervision programs in probation departments.

Historically, there has been animosity between police and probation officers—police believe they catch criminals, and probation lets them out. But this new "community justice" model creates a three-part collaborative between the police, probation, and members of the community.

Operation Night Light. Let me illustrate this for you by describing briefly what is happening in Boston, in a formal police-probation partnership program, one component of which is called "Operation Night Light." President Clinton praised this program in his State of the Union address and called for its expansion nationwide. No one can remember a President ever mentioning "probation" in a national address, and that alone is seen as important since probation supervises two-thirds of all correctional clients in the U.S. yet few in the public know much about it. The originators of the Boston project describe it in *Community Corrections: Probation, Parole and Intermediate Sanctions*.[15]

Community meetings organized by community policing officers in Boston revealed that, as a result of ISP experiments and other local corrections programs, probation officers knew a lot about high-risk offenders and locations in their neighborhoods as well as community resources and programs. Moreover, these neighborhood discussions revealed that many of these lawbreakers were already on probation or parole, but probation officers simply did not have the resources to monitor them, serve warrants, locate absconders, or secure treatment and other programs that these offenders needed. Because these offenders were on probation, their movements in the community could be limited by court order as a condition of probation. In fact, many of them were under court-ordered conditions—for example, nighttime curfews and weapons restrictions—that, if enforced, could be extremely useful in reducing the community's fear.

Admittedly, police and probation partnerships in the past usually began as a way to increase surveillance of high-risk offenders in the community. There was such a partnership in Long Beach, California, as early as 1987. The new community justice partnerships look and feel different from earlier efforts. For example, the Boston project has expanded to include clergy, youth workers, school personnel, and parents. In addition, interesting trends have developed. Judges are expressing greater confidence that such probation terms as curfews and geographical restrictions might be enforced. Police now have information on conditions of probation and feel that they can count on the probation system to hold offenders accountable when they violate those terms. Finally, because warrants are being served, police are reporting violations to probation officers.

By combining police and probation resources, probation supervision has become a 24-hour-a-day, highly accountable reality. What was impossible for probation to do alone (even in the most intensive ISPs) has become possible under the partnership between the police and the community.

This effort has required a lot of cooperation and coordination. Initially, probation officers were reluctant to partner with the police, and the police did not want to connect with "social workers." Over time, however, each group began to realize that everyone has something to gain from each other. Police are learning from community corrections officers and others about community resources such as employment and school truancy prevention programs. Boston police offenders attend joint training seminars, participate in strategic planning sessions with other organizations, and jointly participate in research projects. The police, probation, clergy, and lay people now attend monthly community meetings. Most recently, gang members and community mental health workers began to attend these meetings as well. The Boston program is expanding to incorporate new initiatives that employ the team approach. For example, police now help probation officers monitor high-risk, volatile domestic cases to reduce violence and school programs to reduce truancy. Probation absconders receive priority arrest status by police. The program has spread from Boston to a dozen other probation jurisdictions throughout Massachusetts.

Similar partnerships, now spreading across the nation, could not have been so easily forged without the ISP experiments of the past decade and the gradual acceptance by probation and parole staff of surveillance activities. Police and probation officers were moving in the same direction but did not realize it. Probation officers were getting out of their offices and monitoring offenders where they lived. Police officers were getting out of their cars and walking their beats, which allowed them to work with community members to identify problems and problem people. They stumbled onto one another; the collaborative prospects are exciting.

These programs are more than just surveillance, although admittedly surveillance plays a major role in some of them. Study after study has shown that probation and police officers, once they become familiar with individual communities and the people who live there, tend to develop less hardened attitudes. The following anecdote illustrates this.

Washington's SMART Partnership. The Washington State Supervision Management and Recidivist Tracking (SMART) Partnership for police and community corrections shares some of the characteristics of the Boston program.[16] One former director of corrections visited the community corrections field offices throughout the state annually to discuss priorities for the coming year. Each year, one particular field chief asked the director when probation officers would receive permission to carry weapons. This field chief complained at length about the personal risks he faced when making home visits to dangerous places and how drug use made offenders' behavior increasingly unpredictable and violent. However, the last time the former director saw this man, who had become an active participant in the SMART program, he said he did not need guns but needed more government funds to subsidize jobs for probationers. Clearly, a greater degree of community engagement occurs in these programs.

No Agency Is an Island

The ultimate legacy of a decade of experimenting with intermediate sanctions is the strong message that no one program—surveillance or rehabilitation alone—and no one agency—police, probation, mental health, or schools alone—nor any of these agencies without the community can reduce crime or fear of crime on its own. Crime is a complex, multifaceted problem that will not be overcome by simplistic, singularly focused solutions— whether they be boot camps, electronic monitoring, or intensive probation. Workable, long-term solutions must come from the community and be embraced and actively supported by the community.

This message of community support and involvement is a lesson we learn repeatedly. If the ISP evidence lends any scientific support or credibility to that message or to practitioners and researchers who are involved in this experiment, the money invested in intermediate sanctions will have been exceedingly well spent.

Notes

1. J. Petersilia et al., *Granting Felons Probation: Public Risks and Alternatives*. Santa Monica, CA: RAND Corporation, 1985.
2. N. Morris and M. Tonry, *Between Prison and Probation: Intermediate Punishments in a Rational Sentencing System*. New York: Oxford University Press, 1990.
3. T. Clear and P. Hardyman, "The New Intensive Supervision Movement," *Crime and Delinquency, 36*, pp. 42–61.
4. C. Camp and G. Camp, *The Corrections Yearbook*. South Salem, NY: Criminal Justice Institute, Inc., 1997.
5. Ibid, p. 143.
6. Ibid, p. 96.
7. D. Parent et al., *Day Reporting Centers*. Washington, DC: National Institute of Justice, 1995.
8. L. Sherman et al., *Preventing Crime: What Works, What Doesn't, What's Promising*. College Park, MD: University of Maryland, 1997. See, in particular, Chapter 9, "Criminal Justice and Crime Prevention," by Doris L. MacKenzie.
9. P. Langan, "Between Prison and Probation: Intermediate Sanctions," *Science, 264*, 1994, pp. 791–794.
10. J. Petersilia and S. Turner, "Intensive Probation and Parole," in M. Tonry, ed., *Crime and Justice: An Annual Review of Research*. Chicago, IL: University of Chicago Press, 1993.
11. L. Sherman et al., *Preventing Crime: What Works, What Doesn't, What's Promising*, p. 21.
12. P. Gendreau and T. Little, *A Meta-analysis of the Effectiveness of Sanctions on Offender Recidivism*. Unpublished manuscript, University of New Brunswick, Saint John, B.C., 1993.
13. J.C. Howell, *Guide for Implementing the Comprehensive Strategy for Serious, Violent, and Chronic Juvenile Offenders*. Washington, DC: Office of Juvenile Justice and Delinquency Prevention, 1995.
14. Wisconsin Governor's Task Force on Sentencing and Corrections, *Governor's Task Force on Sentencing and Corrections*. Madison, WI: Author, 1996.
15. R. Corbett, B. Fitzgerald, and J. Jordan, "Boston's Operation Night Light: An Emerging Model for Police-Probation Partnerships," in J. Petersilia, ed., *Community Corrections: Probation, Parole, and Intermediate Sanctions*. New York: Oxford University Press, 1998.
16. T. Morgan and S. Marrs, "Redmond, Washington's SMART Partnership for Police and Community Corrections," in J. Petersilia, ed., *Community Corrections: Probation, Parole, and Intermediate Sanctions*. New York: Oxford University Press, 1998, pp. 170–180.

Eliminating Parole Boards Isn't a Cure-All, Experts Say

By FOX BUTTERFIELD

Fifteen states so far have taken the politically popular step of abolishing parole boards, a vestige of what most Americans regard as a failed system of penal rehabilitation, and last week Gov. George E. Pataki of New York proposed to make his state the 16th.

But based on the experience of the other states, there is no proof that eliminating parole boards reduces crime, while it can lead to a further increase in the already swelling prison population, criminologists and other experts say.

For politicians promoting tough-on-crime platforms, it can have an unintended consequence: three states, including Connecticut, reinstituted parole boards after eliminating them because the resulting increase in inmates crowded prisons so much that the states were forced to release many of them early.

Yet a number of prison experts, including some who warn that eliminating parole boards could lead to shorter time served for less serious crimes, say the parole system is such a failure that abolishing it does not make much difference. Scrapping parole boards, they say, could save money that might be used on more effective anti-crime programs.

The parole system, like the modern prison, was an American invention in the 19th century. It consists of two parts, parole boards that have the authority to decide when to release prisoners, and parole officers who supervise convicts after their release.

Under Governor Pataki's proposal, New York would follow other states by eliminating the authority of the state parole board while keeping released prisoners subject to supervision by parole officers.

One argument against eliminating parole boards is that an inmate's release then becomes automatic, at the end of a set term.

"You decrease the ability to keep very dangerous offenders in prison," said Joan Petersilia, a leading authority on parole who is a professor of criminology at the University of California at Davis.

In California, Professor Petersilia pointed out, the convicted kidnapper Richard Allen Davis was rejected six times by the parole board, but after the state passed a law ending parole, he was released automatically because he had served a sufficient amount of time; a few months later he murdered 13-year-old Polly Klaas.

Some experts caution that the public's discontent with the parole system has also led to a change in the role of parole officers that has helped return more ex-convicts to prisons, swelling their populations.

As the penal system has moved away from rehabilitation, parole officers have been transformed from social workers who helped offenders find jobs or get drug treatment to law-enforcement agents who are more concerned with surveillance, from electronic monitoring and curfews to drug tests.

In California, 80 percent of parolees are failing to complete parole successfully. In 1997, 57 percent of the people entering the state's prisons were parole violators, not criminals convicted of new crimes, Professor Petersilia said.

Some experts say the parole system is so flawed that parole boards may as well be eliminated, but they caution that politicians should be honest with the public about the cost of lengthening prison sentences.

If all inmates serve longer terms, "you will break the bank," said Martin Horn, Pennsylvania's Secretary of Corrections and a former executive director of New York's Division of Parole. One way to avoid that, he said, is to sentence less serious criminals to shorter terms.

As for parole officers, Mr. Horn said, past efforts in New York have shown that when more money is spent on them, reducing their case loads, they tend to find more violations among their parolees, leading them to send more back to prison.

Mr. Horn suggested that New York could achieve a more cost effective crime policy by taking the $260 million it spent on its 60,000 parolees last year and spending some of it on vouchers that would enable parolees to get drug treatment and job training, and the rest on antipoverty programs that would help reduce crime.

New York's chief criminal justice official, Katie Lapp, said that Governor Pataki's proposal to end parole had been carefully studied to insure that the public knew how long criminals would actually spend in prison, and that she did not expect a jump in the number of inmates as California has experienced.

By contrast with California, Ms. Lapp said, only 20 to 25 percent of the offenders sent to prison in New York are parole violators, a sign that parole officers in New York are more thoughtful about their approach.

The movement to abolish parole began in the late 1970's after academic studies suggested that rehabilitative efforts in prison and early release on parole for good conduct had no measurable effect on reducing repeat offenses. Among the states that have eliminated parole boards are Arizona, California, Delaware, Illinois, Indiana, Kansas, Maine, Minnesota, Mississippi, Ohio, Oregon, New Mexico, North Carolina, Virginia, Washington. California counts itself among these states, although its parole board still considers a handful of cases of inmates who are serving life sentences. The Federal prison system has also got rid of the boards.

Only one state, Maine, has taken the additional step of dropping its system of parole agents to supervise inmates after their release.

As the nation has embraced harsher punishment for violent criminals, those states with parole boards have moved to restrict their authority to less serious criminals. And parole boards have become more hesitant to grant release. In Texas, the proportion of eligible inmates approved for parole in 1998 dropped to just 20 percent, from 57 percent in 1988.

But three states that eliminated parole, Connecticut, Colorado and Florida, have re-established the equivalent of parole boards after finding that abolition did not increase actual time served, because prisons became so crowded that some inmates had to be released early.

There is no statistical evidence that abolishing parole boards has lowered crime rates in any state, the experts say. But they acknowledge that keeping serious criminals in prison longer undoubtedly prevents some crimes.

Allen J. Beck, chief of corrections statistics at the Bureau of Justice Statistics, a branch of the Justice Department, said that ending parole by itself "has had no real impact on time served." Time served is going up everywhere, in states that still have discretionary parole boards and states that have abolished them, he said.

Job Placement for Offenders:

A Promising Approach to Reducing Recidivism and Correctional Costs

by Peter Finn

about the author

Peter Finn is an associate at Abt Associates Inc., a public policy and business research and consulting company headquartered in Cambridge, Massachusetts. His recent research has focused on life skills programs for inmates and job placement programs for ex-offenders. This article updates his previous article in the *Journal of Offender Rehabilitation*, 28(1/2), 1998, pp. 89–106.

Many newly released offenders have difficulty reintegrating into society. They may have a substance abuse problem or need a place to live and appropriate clothing; some may need to deal with the bureaucracy of a foster care system to regain custody of their children. Finding permanent employment is perhaps the most common obstacle for many ex-offenders, and one that researchers say may be associated with the chances that they will return to criminal behavior.[1] But offenders frequently face several barriers to finding permanent, unsubsidized employment after release: they often lack occupational skills, have little or no experience seeking employment, and confront employers who are uneasy about hiring individuals with criminal records.

A number of programs across the country are preparing inmates and parolees for employment and searching for a job by providing intensive educational and life skills services, social support, and postemployment followup,

A Snapshot of Offenders, Employment, and Recidivism

In informal polls, inmates often rank employment as one of their most serious problems. Below is a summary of some facts and figures about offenders, employment, and recidivism.

- **Number of inmates in jails and prisons, 1996:**[1]
  Jails: 510,000
  Prisons: 1,127,500

- **Number of releases from Federal and State facilities, 1996:**[2]
  1.1 million

- **Average recidivism rate after 4 years following release from prison, 1996:**[3]
  32.5 percent

- **Among adult probationers the percentage who had a disciplinary hearing, by employment status, 1995:**[4]
  Employed: 16 percent
  Unemployment: 23 percent

- **Percentage of jail inmates who were employed or unemployed before their most recent offense, 1996:**[5]
  Employed: 64 percent
  Unemployed: 36 percent

1. Bureau of Justice Statistics, *Correctional Populations in the United States, 1996: Executive Summary,* Washington, D.C.: U.S. Department of Justice, Bureau of Justice Statistics, March 1999 (NCJ 171684)
2. Camp, C. G. and G. M. Camp, *The 1997 Corrections Yearbook,* South Salem, NY: Criminal Justice Institute, 1997, pp. 46–47.
3. Camp, C. G. and G. M. Camp, *The 1997 Corrections Yearbook,* South Salem, NY: Criminal Justice Institute, 1997, pp. 46–47.
4. Bonczar, Thomas P., *Characteristics of Adults on Probation, 1995,* BJS Special Report, December 1997 (NCJ 164267).
5. Harlow, Caroline Wolf, *Profile of Jail Inmates 1996*, BJS Special Report, April 1998 (NCJ 164620).

5 ❖ LIVING ON THE OUTSIDE: INTERMEDIATE SANCTIONS

in addition to traditional job preparation and placement assistance.

These programs may have a much better chance of reducing recidivism than previous efforts of the 1960's and 1970's, which emphasized job placement more than job readiness and did not address underlying problems common to many offenders, such as substance abuse, mental illness, or lack of affordable housing.[2] (See "A Snapshot of Offenders, Employment, and Recidivism.")

Some of these programs are relatively new, while others have been in existence for more than 25 years. This article describes four such programs: the Safer Foundation in Chicago, the Center for Employment Opportunities (CEO) in New York City, Project RIO (Reintegration of Offenders) in Texas, and the Corrections Clearinghouse (CCH) in Washington. Although each program is unique, they all share programmatic features that can be replicated—basic services involving life skills training, job preparation skills, job placement, social support, and follow-up assistance. However, the diversity in the programs' context and administrative features offers a variety of alternatives for other jurisdictions to consider.

Chicago's Safer Foundation

Safer Foundation is a nonprofit organization (not a foundation, as the name implies) headquartered in Chicago, Illinois. Founded in 1972 by two former priests, the original program received a U.S. Department of Justice grant to provide vocational training to prison inmates and to help them get into unions and private industry after being released. By 1997, Safer had expanded to nearly 200 staff members in five additional locations in two States, including a State work release center and the Cook County Jail.

The Program. Most of Safer's clients are referred from probation and parole officers, and they receive basic educational and life skills classes and job placement assistance. According to Ron Tonn, Safer's Assistant Vice President for Programming, the program's mission "isn't to get ex-offenders a job but to provide avenues for them to let go of the criminal life and buy into the mainstream; getting and keeping a job is a means to that end."

Safer incorporates several unusual features. Under contract to the State, Safer runs the 200-bed Crossroads Community Correctional Center, the largest of four Illinois Department of Corrections (DOC) work release centers in the city. Although security is a paramount concern, the Center's major focus is on programs and service delivery, an approach that is difficult to pursue in a traditional DOC-run facility.

During orientation week, residents attend nine 90-minute minicourses on such topics as money management, job interviewing techniques, and stress management. Between these courses, Crossroads offers a basic reading and math skills course that uses a small-group peer learning approach in which groups of three to five students help each other with the aid of a professional instructor.

Safer also runs PACE Institute, or Program Activities for Correctional Education, a private school in Chicago's 10,000-bed Cook County Jail. Each semester, PACE provides 75–90 pretrial detainees and sentenced inmates with daytime basic education and life skills courses.

The basic skills course at the main Safer facility, open to 16- to 21-year-old ex-offenders, is designed primarily to prepare clients to continue their education after Safer. In addition to basic skills development, job developers teach students to complete job applications and prepare for job interviews. During and after the course, a job developer helps students find employment.

Safer makes extensive use of trained, closely supervised volunteers, enabling the program to provide services and secure expertise it could not otherwise afford. Under the supervision of a full-time paid coordinator, 200 volunteers provide one-on-one literacy tutoring during the evening as part of the PACE Institute, while 65 volunteers facilitate group discussions at Crossroads Community Correctional Center on topics ranging from parenting skills to goal setting.

Evidence of Safer's Effectiveness. Safer Foundation's data suggest the program has been effective in improving clients' basic skills. In-house data show that, for the program year 1995–96, all 72 students who completed Safer's youth basic skills program improved their scores on the

> "After I'd served 2 years in prison, I hooked up with Mike [an employment specialist] because my parole officer referred me specifically to him. 'Go talk to Mike, he'll help you find a job,' he said. In 2 weeks, Mike got me a job as a machine presser, and I was trained on the job. I couldn't land one on my own—I filled out applications, but no one would hire me. Mike also got me into an 8-month welding course, which will begin in 6 months, that I can do while I'm still working."
>
> —*Safer Foundation Client*

General Educational Development (GED) test by an average of 12.5 percent.[3] Safer clients' average GED score upon intake was 189, which is approximately equivalent to grade level 5 or 6. By the end of the program, 34 percent of participants scored above 225 and 64 percent scored above 200. Participants' overall average score increased to 213. Of 94 inmates who attended the basic reading and math skills course offered in the work release center that Safer runs, 91 percent improved their basic skills test scores. The improvement for all participants was an average of 16 percent, while 12 percent improved their scores by at least 25 percent.

Safer's figures for job placement are particularly significant because the program changed its definition of "placement" in 1996 to include—and to claim government reimbursement for—only participants who remain on the job for at least 30 days. The program helped 1,102 of the 2,759 participants enrolled in the program find work during the fiscal year ending June 30, 1996. Using the program's 30-day placement criterion, 650, or 59 percent of those clients who found jobs, officially qualify as placements.

Safer has begun to track clients' work histories for 10 months after they have found a job. Among a sample of clients who remained employed for 30 days, 81 percent were still employed (with the same or another employer) after 2 months, 75 percent after 3 months, and 57 percent after 9 months. Of 72 participants completing Safer's basic skills program for youth, 67 percent entered school, vocational training, or employment, with 58 percent of these participants maintaining their placements after 180 days. Ninety nine percent of participants who completed the program had not been convicted of a new crime after 180 days.

Cost Implications. Safer Foundation's 1996 budget was $8,506,142. More than 6 percent of the funds—just over $510,000—came from private contributions and grants, with the rest provided by State and local governments. After excluding the costs of running Crossroads Community Corrections Center and PACE Institute, and other expenses unrelated to the program's job placement services, Safer's cost per participant placed was $1,369 in 1996; its cost per participant placed who remained employed for at least 30 days was $1,956.

New York City's Center for Employment Opportunities

In the late 1970's, the Vera Institute of Justice, a nonprofit organization in New York City, established what became CEO because many newly released offenders were being rearrested, usually for petty property offenses. At the same time, it appeared that offenders who were able to stay straight were finding day-labor jobs in their own neighborhoods. In 1978, Vera decided to try to develop work crews that could offer day-labor employment in neighborhoods where offenders were living and that lacked these types of jobs. Within a year, Vera added vocational development services because work crew members wanted better jobs and because social problems, such as the lack of health insurance and housing, were making it difficult for many of them to continue crew work.

A Safer Foundation counselor presents options to a client attending a substance abuse prevention program. Photo: Powell Photography, Inc.

Over time, the program's paramount goal changed to providing ex-offenders with permanent, unsubsidized, higher paying employment, with the work crews seen as an indispensable means of achieving that objective. Vera launched CEO as an independent organization in 1996.

The Program. CEO assigns exoffenders—two-thirds of whom are mandated to join the program as a condition of release from the State's shock incarceration ("boot camp") program—to day-labor work crews. Assigning participants to crews soon after they have been released from prison provides an opportunity to capitalize on the discipline they have acquired in prison before it wears off. The crews provide participants with structure and activity, good work habits, daily income, and a test of their readiness for placement in a permanent job. In mid-1996, 40 crews with more than 200 participants were operating each day in more than 25 locations in all 5 city boroughs.

Crews operate from 9:00 a.m. to 5:00 p.m. and from 4:00 p.m. to midnight. Assignments, paid for by city and State agencies, include providing custodial services to court buildings, painting dormitories and classrooms in schools, providing roadside cleanup along piers and State highways, maintaining nature trails, and performing

> Then a CEO representative called me because one of my customers had hired a CEO participant and told the program about me. The CEO person told me that they screen these people, offer money for me to train them, and CEO and the parole board both monitor them. If there's a problem, they'll find it out and either solve it or get the person out. I don't have a human resources department to screen people, and with a newspaper ad you never know what kind of person you're getting. So I interviewed a few [participants], hired one, and it worked out fine."
>
> —Shop owner with 35 employees who has employed CEO clients

A CEO crew member providing custodial services. Photo: Harvey Wang.

general grounds-keeping. The program pays crew members at the end of each day in order to provide them with immediate spending money, reinforce dependability, and promote self-esteem. Field supervisors coordinate the required work with the customer's facility manager and train participants in the work requirements.

Participants spend their first 4 days at CEO—Monday through Thursday—attending all-day job readiness classes designed especially for difficult-to-employ populations. On Friday, participants receive a 90-minute orientation to the work crews and meet with their assigned employment counselor to develop an employment plan. Each participant's counselor then picks a day of the week when, instead of working on a crew, the participant comes to the office to pursue job leads the counselor has developed between meetings.

Although CEO has placed some participants with large corporations, according to Tani Mills, who runs CEO's vocational development activities, "We have found a niche with small and medium-sized companies: large companies have their own human resource departments, so they don't need CEO so much.... Besides, many participants can't handle the anonymity of a big company."

Evidence of CEO's Effectiveness. CEO annually placed an average of 766 participants in permanent jobs between 1992 and 1996, for an average placement rate of 70 percent. Approximately 75 percent of placed participants were still on the same job after 1 month, with 60 percent still on the job after 3 months. Half of those who remained on the job for 1 month were still on the same job after 6 months. In 1996, the average hourly wage of placed participants was nearly 50 percent higher than the minimum wage at the time ($4.25). Nearly two-thirds of the jobs provided full benefits.

Cost Implications. Program revenue in fiscal year 1996–97 at CEO totaled just over $7.4 million. The program's income in fiscal year 1996 included $1.9 million from government agencies for vocational development (life skills classes and job placement services) and $5.6 million from customers who hired work crews. In 1996, CEO covered all but $416,000 of its work crew expenses with revenue from work crew customers. As a result, in calculating CEO's cost to taxpayers, it is necessary to add only the unreimbursed cost of the work crews to the cost of vocational development activities, for a total of $2,316,800. With an average of 766 placements per year, the average cost per placement to the taxpayer is $3,025.

Texas's Project RIO

Texas's Project RIO, which started as a two-city pilot program in 1985, has become the most ambitious State government program in the Nation devoted to job placement for ex-offenders. Operating out of the Texas Workforce Commission, RIO's 106 staff members in 62 offices provide job placement services to nearly 16,000 parolees (representing 85 percent of all releases) each year in 92 Texas towns and cities.

As with Safer Foundation and CEO, RIO traces its origins to the need to reduce recidivism. In 1984, the head of the parole division and the chief of job service operations at the Texas Workforce Commission persuaded the Governor to use some of his discretionary money to provide specialized employment services to ex-offenders as a means of keeping them out of prison. As a result, the Governor used Federal funding to pilot test two collaborative experiments in Dallas and Houston. When an independent evaluation suggested that Project RIO was reducing recidivism, the Texas legislature agreed in 1987 to fund the program from general revenues and to expand the program to Texas's five other largest cities. In 1991, the legislature increased RIO funding still further to include parolees and inmates in the rest of the State.

The Program. Project RIO provides services to the entire State through full-service offices in each of Texas's seven largest cities. In smaller municipalities, one half-time to three full-time staff work out of local Texas Workforce Commission offices, while in rural communities "itinerant" services providers travel periodically from the local commission offices to spend a day or two a week in various locations.

Like Safer Foundation, Project RIO also serves offenders while they are in prison. By providing funds to the existing prison school district, RIO offers inmates life skills classes, individual job readiness counseling, and help assembling birth certificates, Social Security cards, school transcripts, and other needed documents so that they can begin looking for employment the moment they are released. Project RIO's prison activities also serve an important outreach function by publicizing RIO's availability to help every paroled inmate. On release day, RIO staff give every group of departing inmates a 30-minute orientation to the program, including a card with the RIO hotline, which generates approximately 150 calls per month. Project RIO staff also have arranged for a number of employers who have hired RIO participants to spend a day in prison talking to inmates about job opportunities for ex-offenders.

Project RIO's services to released offenders include the standard combination of assessment, placement, and followup. Full-service offices also provide clients with a resource room that includes computerized job listings, telephone books, and a telephone.

Evidence of Project RIO's Effectiveness. During fiscal year 1995, Project RIO served 15,366 parolees, representing about 40 percent of all ex-offenders and 47 percent of all parolees released from prison that year. Almost 74 percent of clients in 1995—11,371 parolees—found employment at an average wage that was 21 percent above the minimum wage.

Project RIO clients appear to be much more likely to get jobs than are ex-offenders who do not participate in the program. An evaluation of RIO found that, after a 1-year followup, 69 percent of program participants found employment, compared with 36 percent of non-RIO parolees, even though both groups of ex-offenders had similar demographic characteristics and risk of reoffending. The evaluators also found that minority ex-offenders did especially well in RIO: 66 percent found employment, compared with only 30 percent of African Americans and 36 percent of Hispanics who were not enrolled in the program.[4]

When it comes to recidivism, employed ex-offenders who found jobs through RIO had reduced recidivism rates, compared with unemployed ex-offenders who did not enroll in RIO. During the year after release—when most recidivism occurs[5]—48 percent of RIO high-risk clients were rearrested, compared with 57 percent of non-RIO parolees; 23 percent were reincarcerated, compared with 38 percent of non-RIO parolees. Project RIO has been of greatest benefit to ex-offenders who were considered the most likely to reoffend.[6] (See "Rearrests and Reincarcerations by Risk of Recidivism and RIO Participation.")

It is possible that parolees who were most likely to succeed on their own were the ones who took advantage of RIO's services. However, the evaluators found that there were few differences between RIO participants and nonparticipants and that the differences were unlikely to have influenced the findings.[7]

Cost Implications. In 1995, the Texas legislature provided Project RIO with $15 million for 2 years. Of this, $4.69 million was funneled through the Texas Workforce Commission to the Texas Department of Criminal Justice for its prison-and parole-related RIO contributions, and $2.9 million was paid to the State prison's school district. This left the Workforce Commission with approximately $4.1 million per year for running Project RIO. The program

Rearrests and Reincarcerations by Risk of Recidivism and RIO Participation (n=1,200)

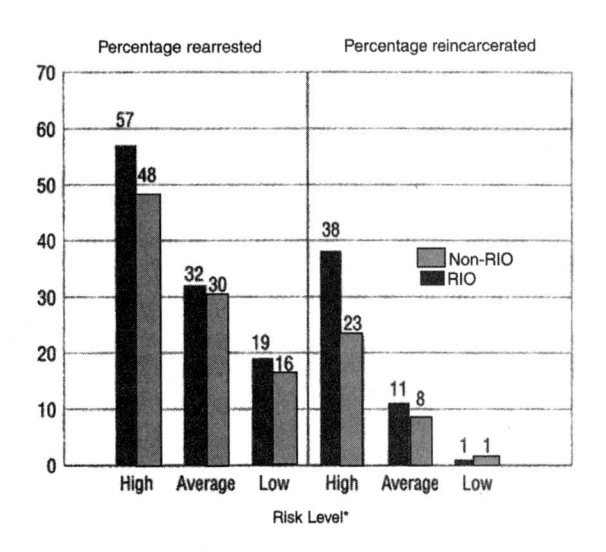

Risk Level	Percentage rearrested Non-RIO	Percentage rearrested RIO	Percentage reincarcerated Non-RIO	Percentage reincarcerated RIO
High	57	48	38	23
Average	32	30	11	8
Low	19	16	1	1

*Based on 23 factors, such as substance abuse history, living arrangements, correctional officers' impression of risk, academic level, vocational skills, and employment history.

spent $361 in 1995 for each of the 11,371 clients who were placed in jobs.

Washington State's Corrections Clearinghouse

The decline of the Seattle area airplane manufacturing industry in the early 1970's resulted in fewer job opportunities and a less optimistic outlook for newly released inmates seeking employment. The Washington State legislature responded by providing funding for the Employment Security Department to establish an Ex-Offender Work Orientation Program to help ex-offenders find jobs. Based on that effort's success, the Employment Security Department and the Department of Corrections formalized their relationship in 1976 by establishing the Corrections Clearinghouse (CCH). Over time, CCH's original mission—to coordinate job search activities for adult offenders being released from prison—expanded to include providing services within correctional facilities and serving juvenile offenders. In 1997, CCH employed 23 professional staff members.

The Program. The Corrections Clearinghouse provides direct services and acts as a central point for brokering and coordinating the services available through a network of State and local agencies.

In terms of direct services, CCH staff in adult prisons offer several prerelease employment-related courses, as well as vocational assessments in one facility and industrial safety courses in two facilities. At the Washington Corrections Center for Women, CCH offers two transition-to-trades initiatives tailored to women. One initiative, funded by three unions, guarantees union membership to women who successfully complete an in- prison trades-related apprenticeship coaching program, thereby improving their chances of being hired after release. Juvenile institution managers can choose from a menu of services CCH offers, ranging from vocational testing to employment preparation classes. However, CCH's most requested service is assessment of individual juveniles' employability and development of a portfolio outlining the offender's needs and a service strategy for meeting them.

Inmates work in Safer's peer learning group at Crossroads Community Center. Photo: Powell Photography, Inc.

At five prisons, CCH instructors register their students with the Employment Security Department, enabling them to access the department's JobNet computerized job data bank so that they can discover job leads while still in prison. CCH contracts with six community-based organizations and one employment security job service center to operate the "Ex-O" program, which provides job search assistance to adult and juvenile ex-offenders, including ongoing postplacement services. Service providers also are contracted to help clients gain promotions that provide higher wages.

The program brokers a number of services—that is, acts as the agent for other groups to pool their resources and collaborate to provide new services. Staff members arrange meetings among high-level administrators of two or more groups that are responsible for addressing similar problems. CCH may provide one-time travel expenses so the groups can begin working together. For example, CCH brokered the establishment of a college program for ex-offenders in recovery for chemical dependency. Called Vocational Opportunity Training and Education (VOTE), the program consists of a 7-week return-to-work workshop, along with counseling to address alcohol and other drug abuse recovery issues. Initially, CCH and the Employment Security Department matched contributions from a local college and the State Division of Alcohol and Substance Abuse to pilot test the program. When the program proved a success, the college and division made it permanent.

CCH has coordinated numerous activities, but one in particular stands out. The Case Management Resource Directory is a listing of 2,500 resources in Washington State, from places to obtain free clothing to substance abuse treatment, that employment specialists, welfare offices, and others can use to steer clients to sources of help. CCH staff arranged with a correctional center and the local college's inmate computer instructor to devise a prison industry program involving six inmates who designed and wrote the computer software for the disk version of the directory, update the entries quarterly, and staff toll-free telephone and fax lines for ordering copies, receiving updates, and adding resources.[8]

Evidence of CCH's Effectiveness. In fiscal years 1997–98, at least 3,082 inmates completed a CCH program. The seven Ex-O contractors enrolled 1,312 ex-offenders, 59 percent of whom found work. Of these, 99 percent were still employed after 15 days and 68 percent were employed after 45 days. A 1994 study conducted by CCH staff with the assistance of the DOC's Office of Research compared the recidivism rates of 500 Ex-O clients who found employment with the historical recidivism rate among all department releasees. (Recidivism excluded ex-offenders who might have been jailed.) The recidivism rate for the Ex-O clients after 1 year was 3 percent, compared with 10 percent for all releasees. After 5 years, the recidivism rate was 15 percent for the Ex-O clients, compared with 30 percent for all releasees. However, the study did not control for the possibility that the Ex-O clients might have been lower risk or more motivated than other releasees.

Cost Implications. The Corrections Clearinghouse's 1997–98 budget was $3,209,131. The program receives slightly more than half of its funding from the Employment Security Department's Penalty and Interest Fund. (Employers who are delinquent in paying their State unemployment insurance taxes pay penalties and interest into the fund.) The Department of Social and Health Services provides CCH with $644,992, $500,000 of which is earmarked by the State legislature for the Juvenile Rehabilitation Administration. The Division of Alcohol and Substance Abuse provides the department's remaining $144,992 for the VOTE program. In fiscal year 1996–97, CCH spent $361,500 on Ex-O contractors. In helping 766 ex-offenders to secure jobs through Ex-O contractors, CCH's cost per placement was $465; with an enrollment of 1,312 ex-offenders, its cost per enrollee was $276.

Replication Issues and Success Factors

The ultimate goal of the four programs is to change the mindset of ex-offenders so that they buy into the mainstream philosophy of holding an honest job and preferring the "straight life" to a life of crime. While job placements are one strategy for achieving this goal, program staff believe that, to be successful in preventing recidivism, they also must provide basic education classes, life skills training, support services, and where possible, begin to reach this population before inmates are released.

Unique circumstances helped each of these programs to get established and succeed. It was the efforts of two socially conscious former priests in Chicago—one of whom remained as president until 1995—that made Safer Foundation a reality. An unusual justice system reform organization in New York City made it possible to launch CEO. The program's work crews succeeded in part because the city's massive public transportation system enables members to commute easily from home to work. Several unusual factors helped Project RIO to flourish, including consistently high employer demand for workers and the need to reduce the enormous cost of housing the second highest number of State prison inmates in the Nation. In addition, because the Texas Workforce Commission has had offices around the State since 1935—most with good reputations in their local jurisdictions—Project RIO had a head start in getting cooperation from employers to hire ex-offenders. The decline of the Seattle area airplane manufacturing industry in the 1970's and some prison riots, coupled with the Employment Security Department Deputy Assistant Commissioner's experience as a former parole officer, generated the momentum to establish the Corrections Clearinghouse.

Although many jurisdictions should be able to replicate these types of programs, there appear to be two key prerequisites to success: collaboration with other agencies and the provision of support services and followup to clients.

Collaboration With Other Agencies. All four programs rely heavily on good working relationships with other agencies—especially their respective State departments of corrections—for allowing access to inmates in prison or securing referrals after their release. As one program director said, "We are a guest in the House of Corrections." The relationship between each of the four programs and its respective corrections department has evolved into a partnership because each organization shares the same two goals: reducing recidivism and corrections costs.

All four programs constantly face the challenge of balancing the needs of multiple clients—inmates and ex-offenders, State agencies, employers, and, in Safer's case, private funders. For example, although employers consider Safer's post-placement support services essential to keeping ex-offenders on the job, the program has had to shape its grant proposals—and therefore its services—to accommodate the public sector's primary interest in placing ex-offenders in jobs, not providing follow-up services.

Providing Support Services and Followup. Many ex-offenders have problems related to substance abuse, affordable housing, child care, emotional difficulties, and other barriers to securing and maintaining employment. As a result, all four programs devote resources to helping ex-offenders address these problems. Of course, individual job developers vary considerably in the amount of time and creativity they devote to helping clients with these problems. The best, however, are like the employment specialist in Austin, Texas, who arranged for a client whose jaw was broken and wired due to a volleyball collision just before he left prison to get free cans of a liquid diet supplement, clothing, medical care, and eyeglasses.

All four programs also follow up with clients after placement. Safer has specially designated case managers, called "lifeguards" who do nothing but remain in touch with placed clients for a year after they have found jobs, offering help with any problems that arise, from finding child care to meeting a parole mandate to entering substance abuse counseling. Job developers at CEO continue to monitor placed participants' performance for 6 months, including, as needed, telephoning the employer, visiting the work site, and counseling the employee. The program's computerized case tracking system produces monthly reports that indicate when follow-up contacts are due. The program continues to offer job development and support services indefinitely to former participants who run into problems through no fault of their own.

A Promising Approach to Reducing Recidivism

As of June 1998, State prison systems in the United States housed more than 1 million inmates, a more than two-fold increase over 1985's inmate population.[9] As the prison population grows, there is substantial pressure on public officials to reduce the number of prisoners or, as is increasingly the case, to build more prisons. One method of controlling prison populations is to reduce the high rate of recidivism among ex-offenders. The evidence suggests that programs like Safer Foundation, CEO, Project RIO, and the Corrections Clearinghouse can succeed in placing a large number of ex-offenders in jobs. The data are insufficient to state conclusively that these types of programs are succeeding in helping large numbers of ex-offenders to remain employed and to avoid reincarceration. Nevertheless, the programs hold sufficient promise of achieving these goals to warrant replication—as one piece of society's multipronged effort to reduce recidivism.

Notes

1. Berk, R.A., K.J. Lenihan, and P.H. Rossi, "Crime and Poverty: Some Experimental Evidence From Ex-Offenders' *American Sociological Review,* 45(1980):766–86; Harer, M.D., "Recidivism Among Federal Prison Releasees in 1987: A Preliminary Report," Washington, D.C.: U.S. Department of Justice, Federal Bureau of Prisons, Office of Research and Evaluation, Unpublished Paper, 1987; McGinnis, R.D., K.L. Klocksiem, and C. Wiedeman, "Probation and Employment: A Report on the Bergen County, New Jersey, Probation Department," *Offender Rehabilitation,* 1 (1977): 323–33; Piehl, A.M., "Learning While Doing Time," Cambridge, MA: Harvard University, John F. Kennedy School of Government, Unpublished Manuscript, 1994.
2. McDonald, D.C., "Offender Employment and Training Programs: A Review of the Research," Cambridge, MA: Abt Associates Inc., Unpublished Manuscript, 1994.
3. The GED is administered by the American Council on Education. It is designed to measure high school equivalency by comparing test-takers' knowledge and skills in five subject areas with those of recent high school graduates. The minimum passing standard set by the GED Testing Service is a minimum score of 40 on each test and an average of 45 overall—or 225 total standard score points. Most U.S. jurisdictions use this passing score requirement. According to Tonn, it is possible to score 160–165 points simply by guessing, so Safer considers scores in the range of 165–225 "functional."
4. Menon, R.C., D. Blakely, D. Carmichael, and L. Silver, *An Evaluation of Project RIO Outcomes: An Evaluative Report,* Austin, TX: Texas A&M University, Public Policy Resources Laboratory, 1992.
5. Beck, R. A., and B.E. Shipley, *Recidivism of Prisoners Released in 1983,* Washington, D.C.: U.S. Department of Justice, Bureau of Justice Statistics Special Report, 1989; Hoffman, P., and B. Meierhoefer, "Post-Release Experiences of Federal Prisoners: A Six-Year Follow-Up," *Journal of Criminal Justice,* 7(1979): 193–216.
6. Menon et al., *An Evaluation of Project RIO Outcomes: An Evaluative Report,* 1992.
7. Ibid:
8. In 1997, the National Institute of Corrections (NIC) provided funding to CCH to convert the Case Management Resource Directory into a computer program that States, counties, or any other geographic area could customize for their jurisdictions using inmate labor. Upon completion of the 18-month project, NIC's Office of Correctional Job Training and Placement expects to seek funding to provide technical assistance to State and local correctional systems that are interested in implementing the system.
9. Gilliard, Darrell K., *Prison and Jail Inmates at Midyear 1998,* Washington, D.C.: U.S. Department of Justice, Bureau of Justice Statistics, March 1999 (NCJ 173414).

For More Information

Publications

The following documents are available from the NIJ Web page at http://www.ojp.usdoj.gov/nij or by contacting the National Criminal Justice Reference Service, P.O. Box 6000, Rockville, MD 20849-6000, 1-800-851-3420. Use the NCJ number when ordering.

Chicago's Safer Foundation: A Road Back for Ex-Offenders by Peter Finn, NIJ Program Focus, June 1998 (NCJ 167575)

Successful Job Placement for Ex-Offenders: The Center for Employment Opportunities by Peter Finn, March 1998 (NCJ 168102]

Texas Project RIO (Reintegration of Offenders) by Peter Finn, NIJ Program Focus, June 1998 (NCJ 168637]

Washington State's Corrections Clearinghouse: A Comprehensive Approach to Offender Employment by Peter Finn, July 1999 (NCJ 174441).

World Wide Web Addresses

American Correctional Association: http://www.corrections.com/aca/

National Institute of Corrections' Office of Correctional Job Training and Placement: http://www.nicic.org/inst

Office of Correctional Education, U.S. Department of Education: http://www.ed.gov/offices/OVAE/OCE/index.html

Rachelle White

Young Probation/Parole Officer Toughens With Experience

by Susan Clayton

"Kal-e-FOR-nyuh. Kal-e-FOR-nyuh. BAS-ket-bol. BAS-ket-bol. TEM-per-chuer. TEM-per-chuer. Be-RAM-et-er. Be-RAM-et-er."

"Sam" repeats these words over and over again as a computerized box tries to make a template of his voice. The box is part of the electronic monitoring equipment that will allow Baltimore, Md., Home Detention Agent Rachelle White to keep track of him.

White runs to the back room to check the computer screen. She is making sure the box is taking Sam's voice print correctly. The computers in the back room, which are monitored 24 hours a day, will randomly call Sam's home to make sure he is there.

While she's in the back, White checks her messages and learns that one of her other clients was out of range when the unit's computer called to check on him. The usually soft-spoken agent grabs her client's file and quickly dials his number. White's manner changes as she throws her arm down on the desk. "This cannot happen again," she tells her client, adding, "You need to stay within range of your box at all times."

White says she used to be fairly quiet and shy before she started at the Home Detention Unit. "I'm not anymore. I learned to be tougher," she says. "There is no room for shyness in this job. You lose it pretty quickly." She claims she has to be strong so that clients don't take advantage of her. "You have to be stern and try to make them follow the rules," White says. "Sometimes they will try to get the best of you and will if you let them."

After hanging up the phone, White realizes that Sam's computerized box is not working properly and she must switch boxes. "BAS-ket-bol. BAS-ket-bol." Sam begins repeating the words over again. "Slow down and don't put any extra accents or stress on the words," White reminds him.

After about an hour, Sam has successfully recited all of the words and the computer has recorded and stored his voice in its memory. Now, White can attach a small monitor to his ankle, which he must wear at all times. She reminds her client that if he fails to comply, the ankle monitor will send an out-of-range signal to the computerized box, which will notify her office immediately.

On the way to Sam's house, White explains to him how home detention works. He is not permitted to leave the house unless he has an agent's permission and he must remain within range of the box. After they arrive, she hooks the box up to his phone line so the department's computers can dial into his box at any time to make sure he's home. If he isn't, the computer will detect that either there is no answer or the voice does not match.

White also meets her client's sponsor, who is required to support him during his time on home detention. The sponsor agrees in writing to keep the house free of alcohol and drugs and to encourage him along the way. Before she leaves, White explains how the ring of the phone will sound when the department's computers call in and how it differs from the ring of a regular phone call. Finally, she reminds her client of his urinalysis appointment the following week.

Although she works the 4 p.m. to midnight shift, White, whose typical caseload is 12 to 15 clients, is always busy. Things never slow down in the Home Detention Unit. Officers are on duty 24 hours a day and can surveil their clients at all times. If a parolee disappears, White and her fellow agents are dispatched immediately.

Home Detention Unit Manager Vernon Skuhr says that until 1992, his agents had no authority to make arrests. "In 1992 we finally convinced the legislature that we needed to be able to arrest and use electronic monitoring," says Skuhr. The law granting this authority took effect July 1, 1992. All Maryland home detention agents had to complete a 10-week training program through the Maryland State Police Department to qualify for a position within the unit.

A uniformed and armed agent, White can arrest and place new charges, such as a drug possession or parole violation, on parolees who are on home detention. "This gives us the ability to do our job more effectively," says White, adding, "It allows us to enforce the rules and conditions of the program."

White says becoming a parole officer was something that she never gave much thought to while she was a student. She only began thinking about it four years ago, after earning her undergraduate degree in psychology. Now a three-year veteran, White can't imagine doing anything else. "I enjoy doing what I do, especially when I see someone who has a lot of problems turn his or her life around."

> **White says that she encourages her clients to get jobs. "Some of them don't want to listen, but there are others who really do want to change their lives."**

White's unit is part of the Maryland Division of Parole and Probation's Correctional Options Program, which began in 1994 and is an alternative to incarceration to help ease crowding in the state's correctional facilities. "The Options program diverts money from incarceration to supervision and keeps the individual safely in the community," says Tom Williams, program director.

The program is voluntary. Inmates sign a contract while they are still incarcerated agreeing to comply to certain guidelines. The program targets five options: boot camp prison, regimented offender treatment center (ROTC), home detention, day reporting and intensive supervision. White says the program is successful because of the types of alternatives it offers. "Options allows for increases and decreases in supervision levels depending on how the offender is responding."

White's colleague Patrick McGee, a field supervisor, says nonviolent offenders can benefit from the program. "We are trying to connect treatment and corrections—respond rather than incarcerate."

Offenders on home detention are monitored by both structured and random visits to their homes. White says they also must report twice a month for urinalysis testing. If they test positive for drugs, they are reprimanded by White and her supervisor, Lieutenant Bill Cheney. "This is their second chance. If they test positive again they are put into drug therapy or can be sent to ROTC, the 40-day detoxification program," says White.

To qualify for home detention, an offender must have a release or trial date within the near future. All types of offenders are eligible, except child abusers. According to White, after 90 days on home detention, the offender is reevaluated. An offender could spend months on home detention depending on the parole board's order. Thirty days to six months is the typical length of stay on home detention; however, an agent can recommend an extension. If a parolee is having problems complying with the conditions of his or her parole, the individual's supervision can be upgraded to home detention in lieu of incarceration. White says her home detention clients come straight from the parole board or are referred to her from a unit within the Division of Parole and Probation.

Making a Difference

White says that she encourages her clients to get jobs. "Some of them don't want to listen, but there are others who really do want to change their lives," White says. She claims that sometimes her job can become frustrating. "For example, if someone has done well and I reward him by allowing him to work and then he slips up and has a positive urine test, it's very difficult," White says. "I feel like I have done so much for the person and he or she has taken advantage of my trust."

White notes that as she goes along she tends to react by how her clients interact with her. "Sometimes they don't want to talk and be truthful with you. Others will be open and honest, and then you can be more open with them."

Despite some disappointments, White says she is confident that the Options program makes a difference. "All of the units work well together." She notes communication between the units is essential. "Often it seems like a revolving door, with some clients moving in and out of the different supervision levels."

White claims the successes are what makes her job rewarding. "It's great when I get clients who decide they truly want to turn their lives around," says White. She adds, "It feels good to know I might have had some positive influence on them and their future."

Susan Clayton is the associate editor for Corrections Today.

Unit 6

Unit Selections

37. **New Bedlam: Jails—Not Psychiatric Hospitals—Now Care for the Indigent Mentally Ill,** Spencer P. Harrington
38. **A Get-Tough Policy That Failed,** John Cloud
39. **The Deterrent Effect of the Three Strikes Law,** John R. Schafer
40. **"Lock 'em Up and Throw Away the Key": A Policy That Won't Work,** William H. Rentschler
41. **Education As Crime Prevention: Providing Education to Prisoners,** Research Brief
42. **Probation Department in Michigan Finds Volunteers Make Fine Officers,** Brian M. Smith
43. **Correctional Privatization: Defining the Issues and Searching for Answers,** G. Larry Mays
44. **Chain Gangs Are Right for Florida,** Charlie Crist, and **Chain Gangs Are Cruel and Unusual Punishment,** Rhonda Brownstein
45. **Restorative Justice: The Concept,** Howard Zehr
46. **Rough Justice in the Youth Courts,** Kirsty Milne
47. **HIV/AIDS Education and Prevention Programs for Adults in Prisons and Jails and Juveniles in Confinement Facilities,** Journal of the American Medical Association
48. **It's Time to Open the Doors of Our Prisons,** Rufus King

Key Points to Consider

❖ What type of social situation might create behavior that would result in a mentally ill person being placed in jail? How might a shift to a more law-and-order philosophy place more mentally ill in both prison and jail?

❖ Based on the readings, do you believe the "three-strikes" laws have helped or harmed our society? Upon what evidence do you base your belief?

❖ Why could it be considered "political suicide" to oppose prison construction? How can privatization save a state money at the outset, but cost the state more over the long term? What are some of the more controversial methods a state might use to save money or generate money from the criminal justice system?

❖ What is restorative justice? What criminal justice factors caused it to be created, and with what types of crime would it be most attractive and useful?

❖ How do the debates in the English parliament regarding juvenile justice reflect the same problems that the United States is having?

❖ How has hysteria about crime and social safety helped to create our present criminal justice system? What can be done to undo some of these negative aspects?

Dushkin Online Links

www.dushkin.com/online/

29. **ACLU: Corrections: News**
    http://aclu.org/issues/criminal/hmcj.html
30. **Campaign for Equity–Restorative Justice (CERJ)**
    http://www.cerj.org
31. **National Center for Policy Analysis (NCPA)**
    http://www.public-policy.org/~ncpa/pd/law/index3.html
32. **National Institute of Corrections (NIC)**
    http://www.nicic.org/inst/
33. **National Institute of Justice (NIJ)**
    http://www.ojp.usdoj.gov/nij/lawedocs.htm

These sites are annotated on pages 4 and 5.

Future Issues in Corrections

In this unit we explore many current issues in the field of corrections. As you may have noted by now, the corrections system is at risk whenever change occurs in any part of the criminal justice system as well as when change occurs at the societal level. This unit includes materials that help to indicate the extent of the risk and clarify the type and degree of the impact.

The unit begins with an article that deals with a topic visited earlier in this edition: the mentally ill in our corrections system. In this article Spencer Harrington discusses how social change and prison crowding have caused more mentally ill to be handled by the criminal justice system, and how the jails are ill-equipped to handle this influx.

The following three articles discuss the causes and the impacts of the nation's renewed interest in deterrence, and how legal changes associated with this interest have affected the function of the criminal justice system. In the first of these three articles, John Cloud in "A Get-Tough Policy That Failed," discusses the goal of deterrence as it applies to mandatory sentences, and how some of the elements critical to deterrence are not present in the current sentencing structure.

While mandatory sentencing as a way to achieve deterrence is not an easy approach in actuality, the idea has merit at the philosophical level. In the next article, John Schafer discusses the goal of deterrence and how the "three strikes" laws are achieving their goal of hindering crime.

Then, William Rentschler offers his view of the imprisonment binge, and comments on how this "lock 'em up" philosophy is not a crime-controlling mechanism but rather a response to social pressures and political aspirations.

Following these articles, we turn our attention to some of the "new" ideas in criminal justice. This section begins with an article that explores the impact of education on crime and crime prevention, including the question of providing higher education to inmates. This article is followed by three articles that examine financially motivated changes in the criminal justice system. In the first of these three, Brian Smith examines a successful program in Michigan that matches members of the public with probationers to allow these nonpaid volunteers to assist in the supervision process. Next, G. Larry Mays discusses privatization in the corrections field. He shows that the savings, while potentially significant at the outset, can easily disappear as costs of operation increase and the potential risks to the state materialize. Lastly, a point-counterpoint discussion of the financial and social costs of utilizing inmate chain gangs to perform menial labor for the state pits Charlie Crist against Rhonda Brownstein.

The final four articles in this unit represent current issues within corrections. First among them is an examination of the concept of restorative justice. In this overview article, Howard Zehr explains the philosophy of restorative justice, and shows how this concept can both aid the victim and help an overburdened legal system to use its resources more wisely and effectively.

Then, Kirsty Milne discusses how the English justice system is facing many of the same challenges experienced in the United States and is responding in a similar manner, even though that response has not achieved the most promising results here. Next, this unit turns to a recent but continuing problem in corrections: HIV and AIDS in the inmate population. An article in the *Journal of the American Medical Association* discusses HIV/AIDS intervention programs in prisons. The effectiveness of such programs is examined, with the idea that, if effective, they should be copied in other institutions.

Finally, the unit and the text concludes with a brief article by Rufus King that makes the case that hysteria, not crime, has spurred the increases in sanctions that have resulted in the rapid and unending increases in prison population. King makes the argument that the criminal justice system needs more compassion and must look to solutions other than vengeance in order to control the problem of crime in our society.

The New Bedlam

Jails—Not Psychiatric Hospitals—Now Care for the Indigent Mentally Ill

by Spencer P. M. Harrington

When Timothy Williams arrived last year at the Alexandria Adult Detention Center (AADC) in Alexandria, VA, he'd just come off a spree of nine burglaries, mostly stealing VCRs and other home electronics to support his crack habit. Williams, 37, an Alexandria native, is dually cursed with a drug habit and paranoid schizophrenia, and during his last term in a Virginia penitentiary had tried to commit suicide by cutting his arms 200 times with a razor. He was off his anti-psychotic medication: "When I'm on medication," he says, "I'm a nice guy to be with. When I'm off it, I'm a damn devil." Fortunately, this time Williams was jailed at the AADC, which has a model mental health unit. He says counselors there patiently persuaded him to get back on his anti-psychotic medication. "If they hadn't come to me, I'd have been dead now by suicide."

Sadly, many U.S. jails are nowhere near as hospitable to the mentally ill as the AADC, and newspapers are full of suicides of inmates with a history of mental illness. A 1997 Justice Department investigation of the Men's Central Jail in Los Angeles included a report of an inmate who, despite a known history of mental illness and suicide attempts, was not being housed in a suicide observation cell. Repeated requests for anti-psychotic medication by the inmate and a social worker were ignored, and he was soon found hanging in his cell, "cold to the touch." The Justice Department report describing this incident reads like a series of truthful parables illustrating how detainees with mental illnesses slip through the cracks, wither, and die behind bars.

With incarceration rates rising yearly, more and more people with schizophrenia, severe depression, and manic-depressive disorder (the so-called severe mental illnesses) are serving time in jails, which have become de facto the largest providers of mental health services in many cities around the country. Between 600,000 and one million men and women jailed each year suffer from severe mental illness, and studies of men in large urban jails have shown rates of schizophrenia, major depression, and manic-depressive disorder to be two to three times higher than in the general population. The jailed mentally ill are usually poor people with no money, friends, or family to bail them out.

The Cycle Begins

People with mental illnesses end up in custody because public mental health centers have, for a variety of reasons, been unwilling or unable to help them. Without the medication they need to keep their illness in check, they sometimes lapse into psychosis and behave in bizarre ways that attract the attention of police. Because police often find the local mental health care system unresponsive, they resort to arresting people with mental disorders. Jailed on misdemeanor charges and released within a year, the indigent mentally ill forage for services as best they can until, unmedicated, they relapse into psychosis and commit a small offense that again lands them in jail. In some cases the mentally ill are incarcerated scores of times; George Wooten, a Denver man with schizophrenia, was jailed 100 times on misdemeanor charges in the 1980s.

In too many states, a ping-pong game has developed between jails and community mental health centers, in which the indigent mentally ill are swatted back and forth between institutions. This situation benefits no one, least of all the mentally ill. Most jails were not designed to be mental hospitals, and most jailers were not trained to care for psychotics. Budgetary constraints, antiquated facilities, and the short sentences imposed on misdemeanants compound the difficulties of mental health treatment in jails. Finally, the ping-pong game is expensive and not in the best interests of public safety. Better community treatment for the indigent mentally ill would result in fewer costly psychiatric hospitalizations, reduced jail expenses and more space for serious criminals, and more street time for police freed from responding to mental-health emergencies. California now spends between $1.2 and $1.8 billion annually on the mentally ill in its criminal justice system; comprehensive community treatment programs might reduce these expenses and turn some former inmates into productive members of society.

An unhappy truth revealed by a study of nineteenth-century mental health reform in America is that the central issue confronting activists of the 1840s is the same one confronting activists today: removing the mentally ill from jails. It was widespread practice in eighteenth-century America to house insane paupers, as they were then called, in jails and poorhouses. But the 1820s and 1830s brought an era of heightened social consciousness, spearheaded by Unitarian and Quaker reformers. In 1842, Dorothea Dix, a former Boston schoolteacher steeped in Unitarian theology, wrote *Memorial to the Legislature of Massachusetts,* a 32-page text vividly describing the plight of the impoverished mentally ill. Dix considered herself an instrument of divine will and imbued the Memorial with evangelical fervor. Confining the criminal and the insane in the same building, she wrote, was "subversive of the good order and discipline which should be observed in every well-regulated prison." While campaigning to build a mental institution in New Jersey, Dix wrote that while jails were built "to detain criminals, bad persons, who willingly and willfully [transgress] the civil and social laws," lunatics were innocents, guilty of nothing but "laboring under disease." Jailing the mentally ill, she wrote, made as much sense as jailing someone for contracting tuberculosis. In the remaining 45 years of her life, Dix would badger and shame state legislatures around the country into opening 30 psychiatric hospitals for the indigent. By 1880, only 397 of 91,959 insane persons (0.4%!) were housed in jails. Dix's humanitarian appeals were clearly effective.

Activism in the Twentieth Century

But by 1945, the mental hospitals Dix had lobbied for were in a shambles, the subject of newspaper and magazine exposes. A *Life* magazine article reported that many facilities had been allowed "to degenerate into little more than concentration camps on the Belsen pattern." Until 1961, though, activists had sought to reform conditions at mental hospitals. But in that year intellectuals published attacks on asylums that provided ammunition for those who would shut the hospitals permanently. In *Asylums*, the sociologist Erving Goffman contended that much of the unusual behavior he had observed during research at a Washington mental hospital was learned in reaction to the institutional setting. If psychiatric patients were freed from the hospitals, he suggested, their strange behavior would disappear. In *The Myth of Mental Illness,* the psychoanalyst Thomas Szasz argued that mental disorders did not exist, but were convenient labels used to describe behavior that society did not like. Four years later the French thinker Michel Foucault, in *Madness and Civilization*, would lambast the mental hospital as a coercive form of social control. As the decade progressed, this intellectual critique of the asylums soon became yoked to the broader social movements of the sixties; the mentally ill were viewed as an oppressed group in need of liberation.

In the next decade, a number of factors conspired to restrict the use of public mental hospitals. Breakthroughs in the treatment of people with mental illnesses also called into question the necessity of long-term confinement in hospitals. By the mid-1950s, the first anti-psychotic drugs were becoming widely available and appeared to control some of the symptoms of severe mental illness. Mental hospitals, moreover, were a drain on state budgets and carried the stigma of the abuse and neglect. Federal social welfare programs enacted in the 1960s also hastened deinstitutionalization. Needy people with mental illnesses became eligible for programs such as Medicare, Medicaid, Supplemental Security Income, Social Security Disability Insurance, and subsidized housing once released from state hospitals. This provided great incentive for states to shut their hospitals, sending ex-patients in need of intensive care to nursing homes and other facilities where the federal government would help pick up the tab. Between 1955 and 1994, the number of patients confined in state psychiatric hospitals dropped from 558,239 to 71,619.

The 1960s also witnessed the tightening of state laws regulating involuntary hospitalization. Whereas in the past, psychiatrists had considerable latitude in deciding whom to hospitalize and medicate against their will, now they could only do so if a patient was a danger to himself and others. By the late 1970s, every state had changed existing laws or enacted new ones to restrict psychiatric hospitalization to the dangerousness criterion. This ensured that there would be a vastly reduced constituency for mental hospitals in the future.

Indigents who had previously been confined in the hospitals were now meant to live in the community and receive medication and counseling at public clinics called Community Mental Health Centers, which were built and staffed with $3 billion in federal money. By the early 1970s researchers were noticing that some former patients were slipping through cracks in the community mental health care system, ending up homeless, psychotic, and arrested by police. In 1972, Marc Abramson, a California psychiatrist, published a prophetic article in which he coined the term "criminalization of the mentally ill" to describe the increasing numbers of people with mental disorders who were being arrested. He predicted that as more people with mental disorders were released into the community, "there will be an increase in pressure for use of the criminal justice system to re-institutionalize them." A 1984 study showed that suspects exhibiting signs of mental illness were 20 percent more likely to be arrested than those who appeared not to be mentally ill. A year later, another study of 65 patients released from a state mental hospital showed that 32 percent had been arrested and jailed within six months of release. Many researchers and mental health professionals were now seeing criminalization as one of deinstitutionalization's many malign and unintended consequences.

Treating the Worried Well

Of all the reasons why the community mental health centers have failed people with serious mental illness, the most damning is that they have given preferential treatment to people with minor coping problems, the so-called "worried well." Though the community centers were established to care for people with serious mental illnesses as the state psychiatric hospitals were being shut, the federal government failed to mandate any relationship between the hospitals and the new community centers. When the hospitals closed, the mentally ill were often not referred to the community centers, which in their absence began to treat people with life-adjustment problems. E. Fuller Torrey, a Washington, D.C.-based research psychiatrist who has written extensively on deinstitutionalization, characterizes the community centers' neglect of the indigent mentally ill as an abdication of their psychiatric responsibility. "If you have public psychiatric services," he says, "you have to decide what your priorities are and how those services are going to be allocated. If a woman whose teenage daughter is no longer speaking to her has the same right of access as people with brain diseases who are hearing voices... society is going to pay a certain price for that decision. People with voices in their head have to get priority."

Community mental health providers are also ill-equipped to deal with the constellation of problems often accompanying the indigent mentally ill. "The problem is that most of these people have long-term, serious substance-abuse problems," says Bonita M. Vesey, a mental health policy researcher. "Sometimes their crimes are violent—30 percent are convicted of violent crimes—and they're homeless, resistant to treatment. These are probably the most difficult people to engage and treat." Linda Teplin, director of the Psycho-Legal studies program at Northwestern University Medical School, says that few states have established agencies to treat both mental illness and drug and alcohol addiction, and that people with both disorders are often seen as too disruptive to be treated by either mental health or detox clinics. "We train counselors as if people were pure types," she says, "and we fund programs as if people were pure types. You're either this or that. There are fewer pure types than we would like. Pure types are easier to treat."

Funding issues may also play a part in the decision of clinics to get rid of the mentally ill as soon as possible. "If I'm running a public health center," says Fuller Torrey, "my job is not to spend any more money than I have for housing and board or placement for mentally ill people. So if there are a thousand mentally ill folks out there on any given day, and 150 of them are in jail, then they are not my responsibility. They are going to cost the department of corrections money, but they are not going to cost me money." The same attitude, he says, is prevalent in the jails: "If I'm running a jail system... and if 16 percent of my cells are loaded up with mentally ill people, that's coming out of my budget and I'm going to do whatever I can to get these folks back over to the public mental health services as quickly as I can."

Torrey blames the mental health community for favoring the budgetary shell games to treatment: "Mental health professionals in large number are contributing to this kind of sloughing off of responsibility back and forth," he says. "It's almost like it's part of our training. We have a greater ability to rationalize why [the mentally ill are] not our responsibility than the average man in the street."

Lacking treatment programs in the community, mentally ill ex-offenders are likely to drop off their medicine. Timothy Williams, the inmate at the AADC, says he stops taking his medication when he gets frustrated. This happens not in jail or prison, but on the street, where he is particularly vulnerable: his parents are dead, and he never learned to read or write. Friends in his neighborhood are bad influences, he says, because they tell him he doesn't need the medication. He adds that, in the past, he didn't want to associate himself with the mentally ill, a group often portrayed on TV as homicidal maniacs. Only after being medicated is he able to understand that he's committed crimes. "By then I'm in jail and it's too late."

Incarcerating the Mentally Ill

Police encounters with the mentally ill can be frustrating and time consuming. Police often must decide whether to arrest, to seek out a community mental health center during its hours of operation, or to find a hospital emergency room. The latter two options may be closed because of limited space for police referrals, restrictive admission criteria, and a general reluctance to take on problem cases. According to Bonita Vesey, police can be "tied up for six to eight hours trying to get somebody hospitalized. Most emergency rooms require officers to sit with a person until they're seen by a physician."

Lacking any options, police generally arrest the mentally ill, usually on misdemeanor charges. A 1991 telephone survey of 1,401 families of people with mental illnesses revealed that 40 percent of the disordered people in this group had been arrested at some point in their lives. The rate of arrest among the severely disordered who use public mental health facilities is probably higher. Two University of Pennsylvania researchers recently predicted that if current rates of incarceration continue, a majority of the public mental health clientele will have experienced criminal detention. Ironically, many mentally ill appear dangerous enough to be arrested, but not dangerous enough to be hospitalized.

While laws limiting involuntary hospitalization to the dangerousness criterion have been applauded by some as a victory for civil liberties, others have attacked them for denying treatment to all but the sickest. Police are arresting and courts jailing disordered people in jurisdictions where it's nearly impossible to get an involuntary commitment, says Torrey. "Being a danger to yourself or others means you either have to be trying to kill yourself in front of your psychiatrist, or trying to kill your psychiatrist," he says. "It's not at all infrequent for an official to tell a family, "Bring charges on your son. That's the only way we're going to get treatment for him.... Swear out a warrant, say that he's beaten up his sister. Then we can get him in jail, and then we can get treatment for him.'"

Bonita Vesey, who serves as a consultant to jails seeking to improve mental health services, says she sometimes worries she is inadvertently encouraging incarceration. "The problem," she says, "is that when the services provided in the jails are superior to those provided in the community, judges and police know that at least when they can get people in jail, they will receive treatment."

But how much treatment do the mentally ill get in jail? That depends on the jurisdiction. Cities like Alexandria run model programs, while others ignore legal mandates to provide psychiatric check-ups. Funding appears to be the issue. "It's expensive," says Teplin. "Not only do jails have to retain a psychiatrist... but once they find someone who has a serious disorder, they have to make arrangements to treat them. It's much easier not to do it and not to know whom you have."

With jails in the country's 25 largest jurisdictions at 96 percent capacity, they are overburdened, underfunded, and ill-equipped to become treatment facilities for large numbers of mentally ill. "The states have forgotten that it's their responsibility to ensure that there are adequate resources for local criminal justice and mental health agencies," says Stephen J. Ingley, executive director of the American Jail Association, a nonprofit training and support group. "They've abdicated that responsibility." Ingley says he hears complaints from jail directors "all the time" about how they are incarcerating increasing numbers of mentally ill. "It comes down to another unfunded mandate," he says. "Jails are forced to care for these individuals.... The frustration is that these people keep coming back and back and back, because jails don't have the resources to provide them with the treatment they need."

Once in jail, the mentally ill generally do not fare well. Mental disorders place the inmate at risk of being victimized or sexually abused, and at increased risk of suicide. At least half of all inmates who committed suicide either had a major mental disorder at the time or had been hospitalized for one in the past. Since many disordered inmates have no insight into their illnesses, they can deny treatment and medication and can become extremely disruptive without meeting the criteria for hospitalization. Jail administrators "hate these people," says Teplin. "They are a pain in the ass to deal with. They set fires. Other prisoners hate them, and they get picked on all the time. They cause fights." Timothy Williams says that while in prison he "didn't behave like other inmates did. I would throw feces and eat them."

Jail guards, who sometimes have no mandated mental-health training, can issue symptomatic inmates disciplinary tickets that lead to their incarceration for longer periods. Unlike many inmates, the mentally ill usually serve out their jail terms, largely because the courts do not consider them good candidates for work-release or other alternatives to incarceration programs. Periods of hospitalization are sometimes not counted toward time served on sentences; sick detainees with no insight can be hospitalized multiple times, extending their jail time by months.

When mentally ill inmates finally are released, jails often do not engage in discharge planning. A study Vesey conducted last year revealed that only 20 percent of jails do so nationwide, while a 1992 jail survey found that 46 percent of respondents were unaware of whether their disordered inmates received follow-up care in the community. The 1992 survey also estimated that only one-third of seriously mentally ill inmates received continuing psychiatric services once they left jail. "I think jails still really think that they stand alone," says Vesey. "That they have a criminal justice mission that picks up as soon as people walk through the door, and that they have no other responsibilities as soon as the person walks out the door."

Fearing life on the street without medication, Timothy Williams says he tried to lengthen his prison term by threatening to punch a guard. His behavior illustrates how psychiatric aftercare is the gravest problem an inmate with mental illness faces upon release. The mentally ill can wait between one and two months to be seen by a clinic after leaving jail. Another barrier to treatment is that if jail mental health service providers are different from those in the community, then confidentiality laws prevent psychiatric histories and other medical records from being shared. Jail and community mental health workers may diagnose inmates differently and prescribe different medications. "So it's as if everyone's starting with a clean slate," says Vesey. "And this has everything to do with jail staff not being able to communicate with community staff."

A Breakdown in Communication

The breakdown in communication between jails and community mental health groups can have serious ramifications for public safety. Jails have an embarrassing history of releasing mentally disordered inmates with a history of violence without arranging for any follow-up treatment. While medicated, people with mental disorders are no more prone to aggression than the general population. However, without medication, some mentally ill can become violent. A 1987 study of 85 mentally ill felons, more than half of whom had committed violent crimes and were found not competent to stand trial, revealed that 38 percent had been released without plans for follow-up two years after jailing. While violence is difficult to predict, there is evidence that a history of violent behavior among the mentally ill is a good indicator of future behavior. A 1989 study of released mental patients revealed that between 25 and 30 percent of men with at least one violent incident in their past were violent within a year of release from the hospital.

Counties recognizing that mentally ill offenders are a community issue, not just the responsibility of jails or public mental health agencies, stand the best chance of offering humane treatment. Some jurisdictions are experimenting with diversion programs, establishing 24-hour psychiatric crisis centers where police can bring people they would normally arrest. Other counties attempt to sustain continuity of care and get around confidentiality laws by maintaining the same mental health providers in the jails as in the community.

The AADC mental health program is used as a demonstration project by the National Institute of Corrections, a federal agency providing assistance to jails and prisons. The jail's program is administered by the City of Alexandria Community Services Board, which also oversees mental health care in the city. The sheriff's department, which administers the jail, splits the cost of care for mentally ill offenders with the Community Services Board. Seven mental health workers oversee a psychiatric housing area in the jail, which holds 410 people. Case managers within the Community Services Board's mental health and substance abuse offices know some AADC inmates before incarceration, explains William Gimblett, director of the jail's mental health services. "So when they learn that someone they know has come to the jail," he says, "they are in touch with the staff here to collaborate on their treatment plan." When inmates finish their time at the AADC, jail staff contact community providers to ensure they are alerted.

According to Richard Ruscak, the undersheriff overseeing the jail, the program is effective because it quickly links mental health services to offenders. "They used to get arrested and [the county department of] mental health wouldn't know they were in jail," he says. "Mental health just thought they were out on the street and not coming back for therapy. But now that it's known that they're in jail, service linkage is much quicker."

Unfortunately, there is only so much a jail program can do. Because of his rash of burglaries, Timothy Williams awaits transfer to a Virginia prison to serve a six-year sentence. "When I go to the penitentiary I'll try to find someone there who can hook me up with a community program, group home, or something," he says. "If I don't [manage to do that]," he says, "all I can do is a lot of praying that I don't end up walking the streets again."

Spencer P. M. Harrington is a freelance writer. He has attended John Jay College of Criminal Justice in New York and worked as a senior editor at *Archaeology* magazine for ten years. This article was written with the support of a grant from the Dick Goldensohn Fund, which supports investigative journalism.

A Get-Tough Policy That Failed

Mandatory sentencing was once America's law-and-order panacea. Here's why it's not working

By JOHN CLOUD

REMEMBER LITTLE POLLY KLAAS? SHE was the 12-year-old Petaluma, Calif., girl whisked from a slumber party in 1993 and found murdered two months later. Her father Marc, horrified to learn that her killer was on parole and had attacked children in the past, called for laws making parole less common. He joined with others backing a "three strikes and you're out" law for California—no parole, ever, for those convicted of three felonies. Klaas went on TV, got in the papers, met the President—all within weeks after his daughter's body was found.

Then he began studying how the three-strikes law would actually work. He noticed that a nonviolent crime—burglary, for instance—could count as a third strike. "That meant you could get life for breaking into someone's garage and stealing a stereo," he says. "I've had my stereo stolen, and I've had my daughter stolen. I believe I know the difference."

Klaas began speaking against three strikes. But his daughter had already become a symbol for the crackdown on crime, and California's legislature passed the three-strikes law. It now seems politically untouchable, despite horror stories like the one about a Los Angeles 27-year-old who got 25 years to life for stealing pizza. Last year two state senators tried to limit the measure to violent crimes, but the bill didn't make it out of committee. Governor Pete Wilson vetoed a bill simply to study the effects of the law.

Wilson probably knew what the study would conclude: while three-strikes laws sound great to the public, they aren't working. A growing number of states and private groups have scrutinized these and other "mandatory-minimum laws," the generic name for statutes forcing judges to impose designated terms. The studies are finding that the laws cost enormous amounts of money, largely to lock up such nonviolent folks as teenage drug couriers, dope-starved addicts and unfortunate offenders like the Iowa man who got 10 years for stealing $30 worth of steaks from a grocery store and then struggling with a store clerk who tackled him (the struggle made it a felony).

How much are we spending? Put it this way: mandatory minimums are the reason so many prisons are booming in otherwise impoverished rural counties across America. The U.S. inmate population has more than doubled (to nearly 2 million) since the mid-'80s, when mandatory sentencing became the hot new intoxicant for politicians. New York (the first state to enact mandatory minimums) has sloshed $600 million into prison construction since 1988; not coincidentally, in the same period it has sliced $700 million from higher education. Americans will have to spend even more in the future to house and treat all the aging inmates. California has already filled its 114,000 prison beds, and double-bunks 46,000 additional inmates.

More important, mandatory minimums for nonviolent (and arguably victimless) drug crimes insult justice. Most mandatory sentences were designed as weapons in the drug war, with an awful consequence: we now live in a country where it's common to get a longer sentence for selling a neighbor a joint than for, say, sexually abusing her. (According to a 1997 federal report, those convicted of drug trafficking have served an average of almost seven years, nearly a year longer than those convicted of sexual abuse.) Several new books, including Michael Massing's *The Fix*, point out that the tough-on-drugs policies of the past 15 years haven't had much impact on the heart of the drug problem, abuse by long-term urban addicts.

DERRICK SMITH

The 19-year-old was accused in New York City of selling crack. Distraught at how many years he could get, he leaped out a window to his death

Likely sentence 15 years to life

PORSCHA WASICK

"Oh my, that's a long time!" the Ohio judge exclaimed on learning of the tough sentence awaiting this college student convicted of selling LSD in 1996

Sentenced to up to 25 years

Even the usually hard-line drug czar Barry McCaffrey has written that "we can't incarcerate our way out of the drug problem." He has urged Congress to reduce mandatory minimums for crack, which are currently 100 times as heavy as those for powdered coke and impact most on minority youth.

This injustice is most palpable on city streets. In places like New York there are more black and Hispanic kids in prison than in college. That injustice may have played a role in the fate of Derrick Smith, a New York City youth who in October faced a sentence of 15 years to life for selling crack. At the sentence hearing a distraught Smith told the judge, "I'm only 19. This is terrible." He then hurled himself out of a courtroom window and fell 16 stories to his death. "He didn't kill anyone; he didn't rob anyone," says his mother. "This happened because we are black and poor."

Worst of all, mandatory minimums have done little to solve the problems for which they were crafted. Casual drug use has declined since the 1970s, but the size of the addict population has remained stable. And even conservative criminologists concede that demographics (i.e., fewer young men) and better policing are more responsible for the dropping crime rate than criminals' fear of mandatory minimums. John DiIulio Jr., the Princeton professor who wrote a 1994 defense of mandatory sentencing for the *Wall Street Journal* with the charming headline LET 'EM ROT, now opposes mandatory minimums for drug crimes. He points out that more and more young, nonviolent, first-time offenders are being incarcerated—"and they won't find suitable role models in prison."

But even some older, repeat offenders are getting punishments that seem ridiculously disproportionate to their crimes. Consider Douglas Gray, a husband, father, Vietnam veteran and owner of a roofing business who bought a pound of marijuana in an Alabama motel for $900 several years ago. The seller turned out to be a police informant, a felon fresh from prison whom cops paid $100 to do the deal. Because Gray had been arrested for several petty crimes 13 years earlier—crimes that didn't even carry a prison sentence—he fell under the state's "habitual offender" statutes. He got life without parole.

The good news is that a consensus is emerging among judges (including Reagan-appointee Chief Justice William Rehnquist), law enforcers and crime experts—among them many conservatives who once supported the laws—that mandatory minimums are foolish. The Supreme Court last week declined to hear a case challenging the California three-strikes law, but four Justices expressed concern about the law's effect and seemed to invite other challenges. A few brave politicians have gingerly suggested that the laws may be something we should rethink. Some states are starting to backtrack on tough sentencing laws:

■ **MICHIGAN** Last February former Republican Governor William Milliken called the "650 Lifer Law" his biggest mistake. The 1978 law mandated a life-without-parole term for possession with intent to deliver at least 650 g (about 1.4 lbs.) of heroin or cocaine. But though the law was intended to net big fish, few major dealers got hit. In fact, 86% of the "650 lifers" had never done time; 70% were poor. "A lot of them were young people who made very stupid mistakes but shouldn't have to pay for it for the rest of their lives," says state representative Barbara Dobb, the Republican who began a reform effort. In August, G.O.P. Governor John Engler signed a law allowing 650 lifers to be paroled after 15 years.

■ **UTAH** In March 1995, Republican senate president Lane Beattie, concerned about the excesses of mandatory minimums, introduced a bill to eliminate them in certain cases. Worried about the political fallout, he did so near midnight on the last day of the legislative session. The bill passed quietly, without debate, but victims' groups noticed. Though a public outcry followed, the G.O.P. Governor said he agreed with the bill and refused to veto it.

■ **GEORGIA** In the final minutes of the 1996 legislative session, state lawmakers nixed mandatory life sentences for second-time drug offenders. State statistics showed that four-fifths of those serving life had hawked less than $50 in narcotics. Even state prosecutors backed the change.

■ **NEW YORK** John Dunne, a former Republican legislator who helped devise the Rockefeller Drug Laws, the mandatory-sentencing legislation promulgated in the 1970s by Governor Nelson Rockefeller, is lobbying to end them. "This was a good idea 25 years ago, but the sad experience is that it has not had an effect," says Dunne, who also served in the Bush Administration. "Behind closed doors, virtually everyone will say these drug laws are not working, but they cannot say that publicly."

Certainly no one in Washington is saying it publicly. The House Judiciary Committee didn't even hold hearings on the bill that created the current minimums, which coasted to victory just in time for the 1986 midterm elections. Congress and the President last year added a new mandatory minimum to the books: five years for 5 g of crystal meth, the crack of the '90s. Mandatory minimums remain political beasts, and it would probably take Nixon-goes-to-China leadership from a Republican to turn public opinion against them. Either that or more Jean Valjeans serving 10-year sentences for stealing steaks.

—With reporting by Andrew Goldstein and Elaine Rivera/New York, Viveca Novak and Elaine Shannon/Washington, Kermit Pattison/St. Paul and James Wilwerth/Los Angeles

JEDONNA YOUNG
After 20 years in prison for heroin possession, she was ordered released on Friday under a new Michigan law allowing parole in drug cases

Sentenced to life, now freed

2 million Number of people behind bars in the U.S., including local jails—twice as many as a decade ago

60% Portion of federal prisoners jailed for drug crimes, up from 38% before mandatory-sentencing laws were passed in 1986

36% Portion of drug offenders who committed nonviolent, low-level crimes

DOUGLAS GRAY
Alabama police caught him buying a pound of pot. Earlier petty crimes made him a "habitual offender"

Sentenced to life, no parole

The deterrent effect of three strikes law

Results of a survey about the deterrent effect of California's three strikes law revealed that criminals are deterred from committing future crimes when they face specific, long-term sanctions for repeated offenses.

John R. Schafer

Since their inception, societies have attempted to control their members in one form or another. The particular behaviors that become the focus of that control can vary from one culture to another; however, the mechanisms that regulate the behavior remain constant. Essentially, punishment or the threat of punishment for social noncompliance represents the mechanism that deters individuals from engaging in deviant activity.[1] The penalty for unwanted behavior can take the form of legal prosecution, social sanctions, or a combination of both. Researchers have labeled this phenomenon perceptual deterrence.[2]

The concept of deterrence can be divided into two categories: general deterrence and specific deterrence.[3] General deterrence occurs when potential offenders see the consequences of other people's actions and decide not to engage in the same behavior. Specific deterrence is triggered when offenders realize the consequences of their own past behavior and decide not to commit the same acts.[4]

Building on the deterrence principle, three strikes laws often are seen as the answer to crime problems in America. Such laws attempt to reduce crime either by incarcerating habitual offenders or deterring potential offenders from committing future crimes. By 1997, 24 states, as well as the federal government, had enacted some form of mandatory sentencing.[5] Although all of these laws are referred to as three strikes laws, the provisions and enforcement of each vary greatly from state to state.

In California, for example, offenders accrue strikes when they get convicted of serious or violent felonies, and offenders with two strikes receive a third strike when they get convicted of any subsequent felony, violent or nonviolent.[6] As of December 1996, the state had prosecuted over 26,000 offenders for their second or third strikes.[7]

But questions remain: Will the advent of three strikes laws deter crime, and, more important, will offenders become more likely to kill victims, witnesses, and police officers to avoid a life sentence? These questions represent important concerns as the cost of implementing mandatory sentencing laws may well include human lives in addition to monetary resources.

California's Experience

The deterrent effect of three strikes laws can be measured best by examining the law's impact on crime in California, which aggressively prosecutes offenders under the provisions of the state's three strikes law. Moreover, because young adults remain responsible for the majority of the crimes, any deterrent effect of this group should significantly reduce the crime rate.

Since California enacted its three strikes law in 1994, crime has dropped 26.9 percent, which translates to 815,000 fewer crimes.[8] While the three strikes law cannot be given sole credit for the drop in crime, in many cases it proved an essential missing piece of the crime control puzzle. Furthermore, in the year prior to the law's passage, California's population of paroled felons increased by 226 as felons from other states moved to California. In the year after the law's enactment, the number of paroled felons plunged as 1,335 moved out of California.[9] Though not conclusive, this decrease may portend the deterrent effect of the state's three strikes law.

Critics of the three strikes law cite the fact that the overall crime rate in 1996 declined nationwide and, more germane, that crime fell in states with no mandatory sentencing laws. These critics attribute the drop to demographics and cite the unusually low number of males in their mid-teens, the crime-prone years. Researchers predict that the crime rate will increase dramatically in the near future because the number of juveniles currently in their preteens far exceeds the normal demographic expectation.[10]

The Juvenile Factor

In truth, crime remains an activity for the young, particularly young men. In 1996, males under age 25 made up 45 percent of the individuals arrested in the United States for index offenses.[11] This group also committed 46 percent of the violent crimes and 59 percent of property crimes.[12] Another well-replicated study found that approximately 6 percent of all juveniles commit more than half of the crimes in the United States.[13]

Not surprisingly, although the overall crime rate in the United States has declined, the juvenile arrest rate for the 5-year period from 1992 to 1996 increased by 21 percent, while adult arrests rose only 7 percent during the same time period.[14] A more frightening statistic reveals that each generation of juvenile offenders has been more violent then the generation that preceded it.[15] The data suggest that a small number of young offenders commit numerous unpunished crimes because the courts, especially the juvenile justice system, provide the offenders with countless "second chances." These offenders are not held accountable for their actions and thus are not motivated to change their criminal behavior.

In 1899, Illinois passed the first Juvenile Court Act in the United States. This act removed adolescents from the formal criminal justice system and created special programs for delinquent, dependent, and neglected children.[16] Over the ensuing century, juvenile justice has remained cyclical.[17] The cycle typically begins when a juvenile or group of juveniles commits an unusually heinous crime that evokes a public outcry. In turn, lawmakers pass stronger legislation for reform. After the tempest subsides, society once again retreats to a position of indifference, only to be aroused by yet another reprehensible act. This cycle is punctuated by attempts to rehabilitate juvenile offenders; however, these attempts largely have failed. No evidence exists to indicate that traditional one-on-one or group psychotherapy reduces the recidivism rate.[18] Other variables—such as education, vocational training, social worker intervention—or any other methods tried to date have not proven effective in deterring crime.[19]

In short, the current juvenile justice system does little to rehabilitate or deter young offenders from a life of crime. This lack of success has frustrated the public to the point where long-term incarceration appears to be the only solution. For this reason, under the provisions of some three strikes laws, an offender could enter prison as a juvenile and, after a long sentence, be paroled as a middle-aged adult. Long prison sentences incapacitate chronic offenders during their crime-prone years and allow them to reintegrate into society when they have grown less likely to commit additional crimes.

In an effort to measure the perceived deterrent effect of California's three strikes law, the author administered an 18-question survey to all of the 604 offenders housed at Challenger Memorial Youth Center (CMYC), an all-male, residential lock-down facility under the authority of the Los Angeles County Probation Department, in Lancaster, California. Five hundred and twenty-three juvenile offenders chose to complete the survey over a 3-day period in March 1997.

The Survey

The author designed the survey to measure the offenders' experiences with the consequences of their own crimes (specific deterrence), the offenders' vicarious experiences with the consequences of other people's crimes (general deterrence), and the likelihood that the offenders would kill to avoid a life sentence. Three questions measured specific deterrence, three measured general deterrence, and one measured the offenders' intent. The data was sorted according to the following variables: race, age, education, family upbringing, offspring, and gang membership.

Results

The survey found that 78 percent of the offenders surveyed understood the provisions of California's three strikes law. The questions that addressed the individual components of the law demonstrated both a specific and general deterrent effect. Specifically, 61 percent of the offenders said they would not or probably would not commit a serious or violent crime if they knew their prison sentence would be doubled; 70 percent said they would not or probably would not commit the crime if they knew they would receive life in prison, thus demonstrating a specific deterrent effect. By comparison, these percentages decreased to 32 percent and 42 percent, respectively, when offenders were asked if they thought someone else would commit a crime facing similar prison terms, illustrating a general deterrence effect.

However, when offenders viewed the law in general terms, no deterrent effect existed. That is, when the question asked if offenders thought the "three strikes law" would stop them or someone else from committing a serious or violent crime, most offenders said no. These findings suggest that when offenders are confronted with the severity of their punishment in specific, personal terms, the law has a deterrent effect, but if the law is defined in general terms, the deterrent effect wanes.

In addition, the survey found that 54 percent of the offenders indicated that they would kill or probably would kill witnesses or law enforcement officers to avoid a life sentence. This figure rose to 62 percent among offenders who claimed gang membership. These findings should serve as a warning to all law enforcement officers that when offenders, especially gang members, have two or more strikes, the likelihood of violence increases substantially.

The survey also determined that race, age,[20] and education did not significantly impact the specific or general deterrent effect of the law. Rather, family upbringing, gang affiliation, and offspring proved the most important variables related to deterrence. The family had a positive influence on offenders, while gang affiliation produced a negative effect. Offenders raised in a home with both parents said they would be less likely to kill witnesses to avoid life in prison and more likely to be deterred by the three strikes laws.

Interestingly, offenders with children were less likely to be deterred by the three strikes law than offenders without children. Conventional thinking would suggest that offenders with children of their own would lead more responsible lives in an effort to care for their children; however, this was not the case. One explanation for this finding is that individuals who do not foresee the consequences of their actions routinely engage in risky behavior and so become more likely to have children as juveniles.

An overwhelming majority of the offenders who responded to the survey believed that the three strikes law was not fair and that offenders should receive more than three chances. During the postsurvey discussions with the offenders, most believed that the number of chances afforded offenders should equal one more than the number of crimes for which they themselves had been convicted.

Recommendations

In view of the findings of this study, additional data should be gathered from offenders in California, as well as other states, to determine if the results of this study are part of a greater phenomenon or specific to the offenders surveyed. If these findings hold true, the consequences of three strikes law should be explained to offenders in specific terms, in order to maximize their deterrent effect.

In addition, as more states enact and enforce three strikes laws, the number of offenders willing to use violence to escape arrest likely will increase, as well. Accordingly, law enforcement officers should approach suspects with extra caution and, whenever possible, should run National Crime Information Center and criminal history checks prior to confronting suspects.

In many respects, the findings in this survey are not surprising. The family unit in America has deteriorated slowly over the past few decades. Many children grow up in broken homes with few, if any, role models to teach them right from wrong, much less instill them with the courage to make morally correct decisions. Indeed, gang rituals have replaced family traditions; gang violence has replaced family values. Thus, crime prevention strategies

Offender Demographic and Socioeconomic Data

Category	Number	Percent
Sex		
Male	523	100
Female	0	0
Age		
Under 10	2	.4
11 to 14	36	7
15 to 17	375	72
18 to 20	105	20
Over 20	5	1
Race		
White	49	9
African American	118	23
Hispanic	323	62
Asian	23	4
Other	10	2
Education		
Elementary school	9	2
Middle School	97	19
Some high school	348	67
High school diploma/general equivalency	62	12
Some college technical school	7	1
College degree	0	0
Children		
Yes	131	25
No	392	75
Gang Membership		
Yes	273	52
No	250	48
Family Upbringing		
Both parents	245	47
Single parent	227	43
Other	51	10

Note: Percentages may not equal 100 due to rounding.

that target entire families and intervene early, combined with swift and sure punishment for lawbreakers, including aggressively enforced three strikes laws, may produce the greatest deterrent effect.

Conclusion

Many offenders who have been through the criminal justice system repeatedly have learned through experience that the punishment for their actions is not severe enough to deter them from reaping the rewards of future criminal acts. Juvenile offenders learn the same lesson at an age that may make them destined for a life of crime. Yet, the results of a survey of a group of juvenile offenders in California suggest that when young criminals face specific, long-term sanctions for repeated offenses, they may be deterred from committing future acts. Thus, strictly enforced three strikes laws may break the cycle of crime that often begins early in a youth's life.

Scholars and practitioners alike continue to debate whether criminals are products of their genes or their environments. Those who believe criminals are born advocate incarceration as a means of incapacitation, while those who think criminals are made favor rehabilitation. The continuing controversy of whether the purpose of incarceration is for rehabilitation or incapacitation will continue for some time to come. Until this debate is resolved, offenders, at least in states with three strikes legislation, will have fewer opportunities to prey on innocent victims.

Notes

1. Robert F. Meier and Weldon T. Johnson, "Deterrence as Social Control: The Legal and Extra-legal Production of Conformity," American Sociological Review 42 (1977): 292–304.
2. Daniel S. Nagin and Raymond Paternoster, "The Preventive Effects of the Perceived Risk of Arrest: Testing an Expanded Conception of Deterrence," Criminology 29, no. 4 (1991): 561–587.
3. Raymond Paternoster and Alex Piquero, "Reconceptualizing Deterrence: An Empirical Test of Personal and Vicarious Experiences," Journal of Research in Crime and Delinquency 32 (August 1995): 252–286.
4. The concept of deterrence also includes certainty and swiftness of punishment. For a more in-depth review of the literature, see Raymond Paternoster, "Decisions to Participate in and Desist from Four Types of Common Delinquency: Deterrence and the Rational Choice Perspective," Law and Society Review 23, no. 1 (1989): 7.
5. U.S. Department of Justice, Office of Justice Programs, National Institute of Justice, "Three Strikes and You're Out: A Review of State Legislation," Research in Brief (Washington, DC, September 1997), 1.
6. California Penal Code, Section 1170.12.
7. Supra note 5.
8. Attorney General Dan Lungrin, press release no. 98-034, March 5, 1998.
9. Ibid.
10. John J. Dilulio, Jr., "Arresting Ideas: Tougher Law Enforcement Is Driving Down Urban Crime," Policy Review 74 (Fall 1995): 5.
11. The FBI classifies the following crimes as index offenses: murder and nonnegligent manslaughter, forcible rape, robbery, aggravated assault, burglary, larceny-theft, motor vehicle theft, and arson. Supra note 8, 214.
12. Supra note 8, 214.
13. M.E. Wolfgang, R.M. Figlio, and T. Sellin, Delinquency in a Birth Cohort (Chicago: University of Chicago Press, 1972), 67.
14. Supra note 5, 213.
15. James Wootton and Robert O. Heck, "How State and Local Officials Can Combat Violent Juvenile Crime," The Heritage Foundation, State Backgrounder, no. 1097/S, October 28, 1996, 2.
16. Anthony M. Platt, The Child Savers (Chicago: University of Chicago Press, 1978), 9.
17. William E. Thornton, Jr. and Lydia Voigt, Delinquency and Justice (New York: McGraw Hill Inc., 1992), xxv.
18. Charles E. Silberman, Criminal Violence; Criminal Justice (New York: Vintage Press, 1980), 247.
19. Ibid.
20. This survey did not examine differences by age, which may have a deterrent effect when offenders consider the likelihood they will be transferred to adult court for prosecution.

"LOCK 'EM UP AND THROW AWAY THE KEY": A Policy That Won't Work

"Prisons are an enormously costly failure for controlling and reducing crime, expensive beyond belief, . . . and efficient breeders of even more serious future offenses against society."

by William H. Rentschler

AMERICANS no longer build soaring cathedrals that stir people's souls. Instead, they build countless grim prisons that smother hope. It is a depressing trade-off.

A single mean, bleak prison cell, with its thin mattress, basic plumbing, 60-watt bulb, and concrete floor, costs beleaguered taxpayers—from Portland, Ore., to Pensacola, Fla.; Portland, Me., to Albuquerque, N.M.; and all points in between—a minimum of $45,000 and as much as $125,000 to build.

These are precious tax dollars that could be applied to hot breakfasts for poor kids, updated schoolrooms and textbooks, decent education, care of the infirm elderly and mentally ill, repair of crumbling roads and bridges, and countless other pressing needs. This is merely the beginning of the enormous cost of imprisoning wrongdoers who often do not fit the media profile of slavering brutes, but instead may be young first offenders whose minor, frequently victimless crimes pose no threat or danger to the public.

To cage a human being once the prison cell is built represents a cost of $12-30,000 per prisoner each year from tight state and Federal budgets. Because of its high labor costs, New York City spends $50,000 yearly to keep an inmate in jail. The average annual tab is almost $69,000 for the increasing numbers of older inmates over 55, whose health care and other special needs balloon the bill.

These numbers apply for every year an inmate serves for whatever crime he or she committed. Moreover, they continue forever as a taxpayer penalty, since every cell that exists anywhere in the U.S. is guaranteed to be occupied in a national criminal justice system where overcrowding is a grim, unchanging fact of life, no matter how many new facilities are added. This huge annual burden covers the ever-rising costs of punishing and segregating criminals. Taxpayers are stuck with the bill for warehousing, feeding, clothing, and guarding these convicted felons while they are incarcerated.

In the final decade of the 20th century, prisons in the U.S. have assumed a status of near sanctity, almost like a hallowed monument or cathedral in another era. One who dares oppose the construction of yet another new prison is adjudged "soft on crime," tolerant of severe wrongdoing, and likely, if facing election for public office, doomed to defeat.

Today in America, there is virtually no enlightened dialogue or consideration of

---

Mr. Rentschler, publisher of The Rentschler Report, *a national journal of independent opinion, is a three-time winner of the Peter Lisagor Award from the Chicago Headline Club and a five-time Pulitzer Prize nominee.*

what works and what doesn't in criminal justice, how much should be paid to satisfy the lust to punish, and whether there are better ways to attack such age-old ills. Howard Peters III, director of Illinois' Department of Corrections, has said. "The public needs to understand that prisons aren't free." Yet, he is in the forefront of the drive for a new "supermax" prison to house the deadliest felons convicted in Illinois, even though the state already has three of the toughest institutions in the nation. The reason Peters seeks more space is that the present prisons are about half filled with inmates who logically could be transferred to medium-security facilities or released early without risk to the community.

When a task force appointed by Illinois Gov. Jim Edgar proposed the new $60,000,000 state-of-the-art institution early in 1993, he was beset by fiscal woes and unable to meet the state's bills on time. Accordingly, Edgar took a cautionary approach and put the massive project on hold stating. "It's not enough to be tough on crime. We have to be smart on crime too." Weeks later, under severe pounding from the prison lobby—those who profit from building, supplying, and staffing jails—and the one-dimensional, lock-'em-up law enforcers, Edgar waffled, urging the General Assembly to go ahead with this gargantuan new house of incarceration. His turnabout has touched off a mad scramble by communities throughout Illinois, whose townspeople see the huge prison as a major source of jobs and local spending, and thus are angling furiously to be chosen as the site for its construction.

Something similar occurred in Florida. where Gov. Lawton Chiles caved in under intense pressure from National Rifle Association and car rental lobbyists, along with the State Legislature, and approved a massive prison-building measure, despite opposition from the state's most influential newspapers, civic groups, and tax-conscious residents. On the day of the vote, several small planes, paid for by lobbyists and trailing banners exhorting the legislators to approve the $165,000,000 bill, circled the state capitol as a far-from-subtle reminder of their clout.

The public generally hasn't the foggiest idea of the tremendous long-term tax burden of the nationwide prison binge they generally support. Meanwhile, no politician or prosecutor or prison-builder is about to tell voters anything resembling the truth—that prisons are "bought" by states with debt, typically long-term bonds. As with mortgages, financing charges greatly inflate upfront construction costs, which are fed gingerly to the public and represent only the tip of the vast iceberg of obligation over many years.

Far beyond the construction cost and debt service is the commitment by government to pay operating and maintenance costs for decades to come. The National Council on Crime & Delinquency (NCCD), the premier private research and advocacy agency in the U.S., provides this sobering statistic: Over a 30-year period, roughly the duration of a life sentence, the cost of building and operating a typical prison bed (or cell), including debt service, is approximately $1,300,000. At a time when tax dollars are scarce, precious, and fought over by legislators, lobbyists, and local officials, this nation squanders countless billions on ineffective, self-defeating state and Federal prisons and criminal justice policies that increase, rather than control, reduce, or suppress crime.

America long was accustomed to being first in most measures of economic and human progress. Recently, however, it has "achieved" the "honor" of having the highest rate of incarceration in the world, outdistancing by a comfortable margin every other nation in prison inmates per 100,000 residents. Even more damning, a study by The Sentencing Project, a private prison research organization, showed that four times as many black males per 100,000 are incarcerated in the U.S. as in South Africa. This nation quite literally has created its own version of apartheid. Over all, the U.S. cages three to five times as many of its people as Great Britain, France, and other industrialized nations, according to Barry Krisberg, president of the NCCD.

In the mid 19th century, author Fyodor Dostoyevsky wrote that "the degree of civilization in a society can be judged by entering its prisons." By that measure, and the extent to which it incarcerates people, America must be classified as backward, even barbaric, based on the condition and number of prisons, criminal sentencing and correctional practices, and public attitudes toward crime and punishment. This is especially so because a surprisingly high percentage of the more than 1,000,000 human beings incarcerated in this country on any given day are non-violent first offenders whose crimes are of a relatively minor, non-threatening nature.

A costly failure

Prisons are an enormously costly failure for controlling and reducing crime, expensive beyond belief, debilitating, demeaning, counterproductive, dangerous to prison staff and the non-violent majority who are imprisoned, and efficient breeders of even more serious future offenses against society. They simply don't work except to remove from the streets the relatively small percentage of persistently and irrationally violent, dangerous, and repeat offenders.

Despite the costliest prison-building binge in U.S. history over the past decade, which continues apace, there is no room in the system for more convicted criminals. This fetish with locking people up is a scandal that has deprived America of meeting some of its most urgent needs.

Many blame it on the magnitude of the drug problem. Most prison admissions today indeed are drug-related, but the vast majority have little or nothing to do with controlling the drug plague. A high percentage is jailed for low-level possession of drugs, the most minor felony class. Few have prior records of violence. Many are suburban teenagers. Most big fish in the drug trade manage to evade the reach of the law, despite costly, overblown "drug wars."

U.S. judges, contrary to popular myth and mass media overkill, impose harsher, longer sentences than those anywhere else in the world. Nevertheless, they are forced by determinate sentencing laws to impose still longer mandatory sentences, which often make no sense at all and strip judges of their discretionary powers.

Syndicated columnist Garry Wills observes pointedly that "a blind will to be tough rather than intelligent makes us keep overloading this ineffectual system. Put in another way, social vindictiveness is our costliest pleasure." The ranting and raving of those who would bury every wrongdoer behind prison walls bring America no closer to eliminating the terrible ravages of violent crime.

California criminologists James Austin and John Irwin, in a paper prepared for the NCCD, argue that "There is only one viable solution that would have an immediate and dramatic impact on prison crowding: shorter prison terms." This, of course, triggers howls of outrage.

Austin led a research study in Illinois which showed the state saved about $50,000,000 by releasing 21,000 carefully screened inmates 90 days early to relieve severe overcrowding. While the program was in effect, the state's crime rate actually declined. Austin, a recipient of the Peter Legins Award from the American Correctional Association, believes such initiatives, on a much wider scale, dramatically could relieve overcrowding and improve the attack on crime at a fraction of the cost. "Political and media harangues about street crime," maintain Austin and Irwin, "have resulted in irrational fear and an excessive, ineffective, punitive response to crime."

"The clamor for more and stronger prisons and stiffer sentences makes no sense," according to Michael J. Mahoney, executive director of Chicago's John Howard Association, a private prison and criminal justice watchdog agency. "We can't build our way out of the crime plague. It's counterproductive and economically impossible. High walls, barbed wire, and armed guards give people a certain sense of security, but it's largely illusory. Very few dangerous criminals, are locked up at any one time."

Such conclusions by credible professionals fly in the face of what most people have been led to believe. Prisons have failed to bring about the end of crime.

What long prison terms can accomplish, and usually do, is to turn a minor street miscreant into a hardened lifetime professional. It is time to seek an end to the misguided, self-defeating, enormously costly reliance on prisons and to reject their continued existence, *except* as the punishment of last resort, to be reserved for violent, dangerous, and chronic offenders.

U.S. prisons today are desperately, dangerously overcrowded because of the myopia of too many judges, prosecutors, legislators, community leaders, editors, demagogues, and well-meaning, but frightened, citizens who wrongly see prisons as the panacea for escalating crime.

The gauge of success for any undertaking is the achievement of its prime objectives at acceptable cost over a reasonable span of time. The measure of a prison system's success would be the ultimate reduction of crime and the restoration of much of the prison population to law-abiding citizenry. By that standard, prisons have failed dismally, and crime continues to escalate in those countries where such facilities are the cornerstone of the criminal justice process.

In the U.S., running counter to all logic, prisons comprise a "growth industry" that defies recession, functions without competition, creates a vast bureaucracy, draws its clients from a massive government-operated-and-supported judicial/prosecutorial/ criminal justice apparatus, and is ever stimulated by a shadowy, self-seeking "prison/industrial complex." On a smaller, but fast-expanding, scale, this is akin to the vast, powerful "military/industrial complex" a visionary Pres. Dwight D. Eisenhower warned against. Both these institutions maintain a vise-like grip on the White House, Congress, governors' mansions, and state legislatures.

In the U.S., a disproportionate percentage of inmates are young, black, poor, undereducated, and unemployed when they enter prison. When they finally are released—as 95% one day will be—they are likely to be embittered, unskilled, penniless, fearful of the future, bereft of all hope, and trained only to continue along the path of crime. Their aim is to get out and get even. Society bears the burden.

Education as Crime Prevention

Providing education to prisoners

This research brief presents the most recent data on the impact of education on crime and crime prevention, and examines the debate on providing higher education to inmates.

> "WE MUST ACCEPT THE REALITY THAT TO CONFINE OFFENDERS BEHIND WALLS WITHOUT TRYING TO CHANGE THEM IS AN EXPENSIVE FOLLY WITH SHORT-TERM BENEFITS— WINNING BATTLES WHILE LOSING THE WAR."—FORMER U.S. SUPREME COURT CHIEF JUSTICE WARREN BURGER[1]

In response to the American public's growing fear of crime and the call for more punitive measures to combat such fear, many legislators and policymakers have promoted building more prisons, enacting harsher sentencing legislation, and eliminating various programs inside prisons and jails.

With re-arrest rates averaging around 60%, it is clear that incarceration alone is not working. In fact, the drive to incarcerate, punish, and limit the activities of prisoners has often resulted in the elimination of strategies and programs that seek to prevent or reduce crime.

For instance, research shows that quality education[2] is one of the most effective forms of crime prevention. Educational skills can help deter young people from committing criminal acts and can greatly decrease the likelihood that people will return to crime after release from prison. Despite this evidence, educational programs in correctional facilities, where they have proven to be extraordinarily effective, have in many cases been completely eliminated.

Over 1.6 million individuals are housed in adult correctional facilities in the United States,[3] and at least 99,682 juveniles are in custody.[4] The majority of these individuals will be released into the community unskilled, undereducated, and highly likely to become re-invovled in criminal activity. With so many ex-offenders returning to prison, it is clear that the punitive, incarceration-based approach to crime prevention is not working. We need to promote policies and procedures that are successful. Education, particularly at the college level, can afford individuals with the opportunities to achieve and maintain productive and crime-free lives, and help to create safer communities for all.

THE EDUCATIONAL LEVEL OF OFFENDERS IS LOW

Most individuals involved in the criminal justice system come from low-income, urban communities, which are also the most likely to be under-served in terms of educational support programs. Not surprisingly, a disproportionate number of the incarcerated are undereducated. To a great extent, the inadequate education of juvenile and adult offenders reflects the failures and inadequacies of public inner-city education.

Juvenile Offenders

While illiteracy and poor academic performance are not direct causes of criminal behavior, young people who have received inadequate education or who exhibit poor literacy skills are disproportionately found within the criminal justice system.

- According to a study conducted by Project READ, a national program designed to improve reading skills, youth that are confined to correctional facilities at the median age of 15.5 years and in the ninth grade read, on average, at the fourth-grade level.[5] More than one-third of all juvenile offenders of this age group read below the fourth-grade level.[6]
- Ninety percent of teachers providing reading instruction in juvenile correctional facilities reported that they had "students who [could not] read material composed of words from their own oral vocabularies."[7]
- Approximately 40% of youth held in detention facilities may have some form of learning disability.[8]

With such high rates of learning disabilities and poor educational skills, juvenile offenders are desperately in need of quality education, yet are likely to be denied it. For example, juvenile offenders in adult prisons can be prevented from participating in GED programs because of their age, and those requiring special education services are, in some facilities, no longer eligible to receive such education upon incarceration.[9]

In most cases, once juveniles are incarcerated, even for a short time, their line to education is forever broken. Most juvenile offenders aged 16 and older do not return to school upon release or graduate from high school.[10]

There is a strong link between low levels of education and high rates of criminal activity, and one of the best predictors of adult criminal behavior is involvement with the criminal justice system as a juvenile. With so few resources devoted to the education of juvenile offenders, it is not surprising that so many remain invovled in the criminal justice system well into their adult lives.

Adult Offenders

Like their juvenile counterparts, adults involved in the criminal justice system are severely undereducated. Nineteen percent of adult inmates are completely illiterate, and 40% are "functionally il-

41. Education as Crime Prevention

THE HISTORY OF HIGHER EDUCATION IN PRISON

In 1965, Congress passed Title IV of the Higher Education Act, which explicitly permitted inmates to apply for financial aid in the form of Pell Grants to attend college. The passage of Title IV allowed for the expansion of what had been a smattering of higher education programs in correctional facilities. The number of programs peaked in 1982 at over 350 available in 90% of the states.[41]

In the 1970s, studies[42] were conducted to determine the achievements of correctional higher education. Success was measured by the rate of re-arrest and the offender's ability to obtain and maintain employment upon release. The results were overwhelmingly positive, indicating that higher education was responsible for reducing an individual's chances of returning to crime, which in turn resulted in savings by reducing the costs of incarceration and victimization, and by providing skilled workers to the economy.

In the early 1990s, elected officials began introducing legislation to prohibit federal tuition assistance to inmates. A counter-effort, started by educators, correctional officials, prison advocates, and prisoners themselves managed to stave off the legislation until 1994, when the Violent Crime Control and Law Enforcement Act effectively dismantled correctional higher education.

FIGURE I: Literacy Levels for U.S. Adults

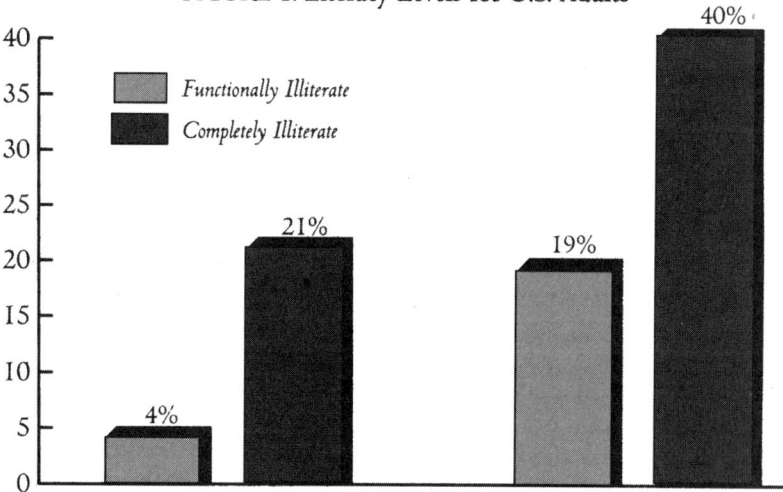

[Bar chart showing: General Population — Functionally Illiterate 4%, Completely Illiterate 21%; Incarcerated Adults — Functionally Illiterate 19%, Completely Illiterate 40%]

literate," which means, for example, that they would be unable to write a letter explaining a billing error.[11] Comparatively, the national illiteracy rate for adult Americans stands at 4% with 21% functionally illiterate (see figure I).[12]

The rate of learning disabilities in adult correctional facilities runs high, at 11%, compared to 3% in the general population.[13] Low literacy levels and high rates of learning disabilities within this population have contributed to high dropout rates. Nationwide, over 70% of all people entering state correctional facilities have not completed high school, with 46% having had some high school education and 16.4% having had no high school education at all.[14]

EDUCATION LOWERS RECIDIVISM MORE EFFECTIVELY THAN CURRENTLY SUPPORTED PROGRAMS

Nationally, reported rates of recidivism for adult offenders in the United States are extraordinarily high, ranging from 41%[15] to 60%.[16] The difficulty in pinpointing specific rates of recidivism is often due to a confusion of terms. The national re-arrest rate, around 63%, is different from the re-imprisonment rate, which averages around 41%.[17] Programmatic efforts to reduce recidivism have ranged from boot camps and shock incarceration facilities to prison-based education efforts. The effectiveness of these programs varies, but research shows that prison-based education and literacy programs are much more effective at lowering recidivism rates than either boot camps or shock incarceration. For example, in a recent report on crime prevention programs conducted at the request of the U.S. Justice Department,[18] researchers at the University of Maryland found that teaching reading skills to juveniles worked significantly better to reduce crime than boot camp programs.[19]

> "CORRECTIONAL EDUCATION APPEARS TO BE THE NUMBER ONE FACTOR IN REDUCING RECIDIVISM RATES NATIONWIDE."—ALABAMA STATE BOARD OF EDUCATION.[20]

According to the Federal Bureau of Prisons, there is an inverse relationship between recidivism rates and education. The more education received, the less likely an individual is to be re-arrested or re-imprisoned.[21]

• A report issued by the Congressional Subcommittee to Investigate Juvenile Delinquency estimates that the national recidivism rate for juvenile offenders is between 60% and 84%.[22] For juveniles involved in quality reading-instruction programs, the recidivism rate can be reduced by 20% or more.[23]

• A five-year follow-up study conducted by the Arizona Department of Adult Probation concluded that probationers who received literacy training had a significantly lower re-arrest rate (35%) than the control group (46%), and those who received GED education had a re-arrest rate of 24%, compared to the control group's rate of 46%.[24]

• Inmates with at least two years of college education have a 10% re-arrest rate, compared to a national re-arrest rate of approximately 60%.[25]

• Research studies conducted in Indiana, Maryland, Massachusetts, New York, and other states have all reported significantly low recidivism rates for inmate participants in correctional higher-education programs, ranging from 1% to 15.5%.[26,27]

As with all research on prisons and jails, data on correctional education tends to focus on specific localities or states. Texas is one jurisdiction which has done extensive research on the success of correctional higher education.

The overall recidivism rate for degree holders leaving the Texas Department of Criminal Justice between September 1990 and August 1991, was 15%, four times lower than the general recidivism rate of 60%. A two-year follow-up report found that the higher level of degree awarded was inversely related to the level of recidivism—individuals with associate's degrees had a recidivism rate of 13.7%, those with bachelor's degrees had a rate of 5.6%, and those with master's degrees had a rate of zero (see figure 2).[28]

CORRECTIONS OFFICIALS SUPPORT CORRECTIONAL EDUCATION

The vast majority of corrections officials believe that educational programs not only benefit inmates, but also the facility's administration and staff. Inmate students are better behaved, less likely to engage in violence, and more likely to have a positive effect on the general prison population.[29] Educated inmates can be a "stabilizing influence in an often chaotic environment, enhancing the safety and security of all who live and work in the correctional facility."[30] Indeed, 93% of prison wardens surveyed in a 1993 study conducted by the Senate Judiciary Committee of the United States Senate strongly supported educational and vocational programming in adult correctional facilities.[31]

CORRECTIONAL HIGHER EDUCATION IS A BARGAIN

The expense of providing higher education to inmates is minimal when considering the impact upon rates of recidivism and the future savings of preventing re-arrest and re-imprisonment.

New York State estimates that it costs $2,500 per year, per individual to provide higher education in a correctional facility. In contrast, the average cost of incarcerating an adult inmate per year is $25,000 (see figure 3).[32] Why are correctional education programs so inexpensive? For the most part, higher education in correctional facilities is provided by community col-

FIGURE 2: Recidivism Rates for Degree Holders Leaving the Texas Department of Criminal Justice, 1990–1991

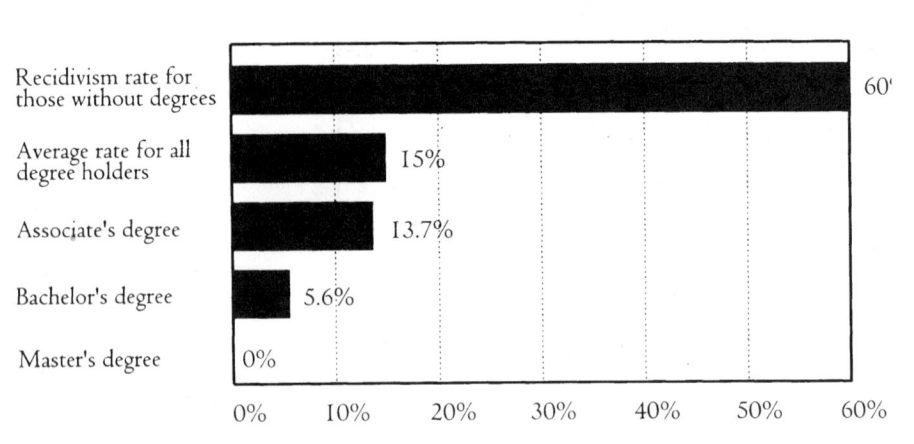

Recidivism rate for those without degrees	60%
Average rate for all degree holders	15%
Associate's degree	13.7%
Bachelor's degree	5.6%
Master's degree	0%

leges and universities that offer moderately priced tuition.

> "SOCIETY SHOULD RECOGNIZE THAT THE COST OF COLLEGE IS REALLY VERY INSIGNIFICANT WHEN YOU COMPARE THE COST OF THE DAMAGE DONE BY CRIME." —J. MICHAEL QUINLIN, FORMER DIRECTOR OF THE FEDERAL BUREAU OF PRISONS][33]

A combination of funding sources support an inmate's education, including in-kind donations from universities and colleges, outside support (foundations, community-based organizations, private donations), and individual contributions from inmates themselves, garnered while working at prison-based jobs. Until 1994, federal support in the form of Pell Grants did provide a substantial amount of tuition funding (see sidebar on next page).

THE SAVINGS OF PROVIDING CORRECTIONAL HIGHER EDUCATION ARE SIGNIFICANT

Even in a hypothetical situation with a comparatively expensive correctional higher-education program ($2,500 per year, per inmate in New York State) and one of the highest recorded rates of recidivism upon completion of such a program (15%), the savings of providing higher education are still substantial:

The cost of incarcerating 100 individuals over 4 years is approximately $10 million. For an additional 1/10 of that cost, or $1 million, those same individuals could be given a full, four-year college education while incarcerated. Assuming a recidivism rate of 15% (as opposed to the general rate of 40–60%), 85 of those initial 100 individuals will not return to prison, saving U.S. taxpayers millions of dollars each year.

In addition to the millions saved by preventing an individual's return to incarceration and dependence on the criminal justice system, providing higher education to prisoners can save money in other ways. The prevention of crime helps to eliminate costs to crime victims and the courts, lost wages of the inmate while incarcerated, or costs to the inmate's family.

WHY SHOULD PRISONERS RECEIVE HIGHER EDUCATION?

The available statistical evidence overwhelmingly demonstrates the positive impact of higher education opportuni-

FIGURE 3: Cost of Incarceration vs. Higher Education in Correctional Facilities, per Year, per Inmate

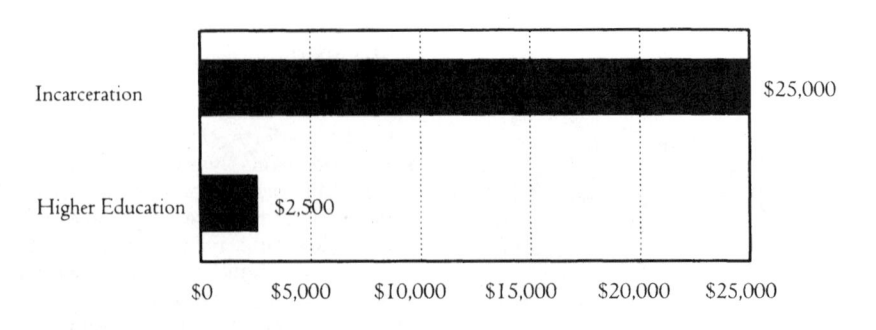

Incarceration	$25,000
Higher Education	$2,500

THE ELIMINATION OF FEDERAL SUPPORT FOR CORRECTIONAL HIGHER EDUCATION

Despite tremendous evidence supporting the connection between higher education and lowered levels of recidivism, the U.S. Congress included a provision in the Violent Crime Control and Law Enforcement Act of 1994 which denied all prisoners access to federal Pell Grants. The provision was initiated to appeal to the notion that prisons have become places of leisure, and that inmates were given access to higher education at the expense of law-abiding taxpayers.

Yet prisoners who were eligible for federal tuition assistance never received support for college tuition at the expense of those in the free world. Pell Grants are non-competitive, need-based federal funds available to any and all qualifying low-income individuals who wish to attend college degree programs. The pool of money available for Pell Grants is not limited, and is only dictated by the number of individuals who apply and qualify. Whether in or out of prison, an individual must meet the exact same criteria to be awarded a Pell Grant.

For qualifying individuals in correctional facilities, the average Pell Grant award was less than $1,300 per year.[43] The total percentage of the Pell Grants' annual budget that was spent on inmate higher education was 1/10 of 1%.[44]

ties on the prison population. Some of the resulting benefits are as follows:

• An estimated 97% of adult felony inmates are eventually discharged from confinement and released into the community.[34]

• Studies have shown that individuals who receive higher education while incarcerated have a significantly better rate of employment (60–75%) than those who do not participate in college programs (40%).[35]

• The financial and societal savings of providing an inmate higher education are enormous. Upon an inmate's release, the cost-benefit of reducing recidivism will begin to be realized immediately. If we consider the additional benefit of this individual obtaining work, paying taxes, and contributing to the general economy, and the prevention of costs to victims of crime and the criminal justice system, the benefits are significantly greater.

• The RAND Corporation, a public policy think tank based in California, recently released a study showing that crime prevention is more cost-effective than building prisons. Of all crime prevention methods, education is the most cost-effective.[36]

• Higher education has a stabilizing influence on the correctional environment and can help a facility to run more smoothly and less violently than correctional institutions without educational programs.

• The educational level of a parent is a clear predictor of both the educational achievements of a child and the level of parental involvement in a child's education.[37,38] As the majority of prisoners are parents,[39] the education of adults in prison can have a positive and long-lasting impact upon the lives of their children.

• Well-run, high-quality higher education programs in correctional facilities can inspire correctional officers to pursue additional education, and in some instances scholarship moneys can be made available to those who work inside the facilities. The positive impact of education in prisons should inspire better public education for all citizens, both in and out of our prisons and jails.

RECOMMENDATIONS

Ensure quality education for juveniles involved in the criminal justice system.

A child's involvement in the criminal justice system, can be a critical intervention point to prevent future criminal activity. Because we do know that education can be a catalyst for change, it is essential to provide appropriate programs, including special education, to juvenile offenders. Particular attention must be paid to juveniles housed in adult correctional facilities, and programs designed to assist juveniles in their transition from incarceration into the community must be supported and evaluated to ensure the best possible opportunities for successful reintegration upon release.

"MY INVOLVEMENT WITH COLLEGE...HAS OPENED MY EYES TO ALL OF THE THINGS THAT WERE WRONG IN MY LIFE. NOW I HAVE A SENSE OF PRIORITY, A SENSE OF ACCOUNTABILITY, AND HAVE MADE A LEGITIMATE PREMISE FOR MYSELF ON WHICH TO BUILD.... MY NEEDS ARE STILL IMPORTANT, BUT NOT AT SOMEONE ELSE'S EXPENSE."—STATEMENT BY AN INMATE STUDENT.[40]

Garner financial support for correctional education programs from various sources.

With all of the evidence available supporting the positive impact of correctional higher education, it is critical that programs be fully maintained to allow for the maximum number of qualified participants. The reinstatement of federal financial assistance in the form of Pell Grants to inmates is crucial. Alternative and varied sources of funding must also be considered. For example, in New York state, a variety of sources, including university assistance, private and in-kind donations, and the individual financial contributions of inmates and their families, have combined to provide the financial support for correctional higher-education programs.

Implement and fund post-release supportive services.

The benefit of higher education is clearly an incentive to maintain a crime-free life. However, because of the dearth of supportive services, many individuals may find themselves released without access to employment opportunities and/or additional training and education programs. As the first few months after release are critical, it is imperative that supportive services are in place and that ex-offenders are provided with access to them.

Fund evaluation of educational programs.

While it is clear that there is a strong link between quality education and

As a relatively small percentage of inmates attended higher education programs and actually received federal tuition assistance, Pell Grant support directly affected only a small part of the prison population.[45] Still, this support had a large and lasting impact on entire correctional systems.

- Educated prisoners often serve as teachers and tutors for other inmates, and often as examples and role models.

- Educational programs help to provide structure and lessen the need for supervision, and in the words of one federal prison warden, "help to keep the prison running smoothly."[46]

As the impact of federal higher-education tuition support was felt beyond the lives of individual recipients, the denial of financial assistance to inmates has also reverberated.

- At least 25 states have cut back on vocational and technical training programs since the Pell Grants were cut.[47] In 1990, there were 350 higher education programs for inmates. In 1997, there are 8.[48]

- 25,168 college students in correctional facilities were recipients of Pell Grants for the school year 1993–1994, the last year federal tuition support was available to them.[49] While no follow-up study has been done to track these individual students, it is highly likely that the majority of them were unable to continue their college education.

lowered levels of recidivism, there are difficulties in determining exactly which types of educational programs are most effective. Public and private funders should support evaluation of correctional education programs, which would include long-term follow-up to determine the impact of programs upon employment and the chance of re-involvement in the criminal justice system for both female and male ex-offenders and their children.

If we are serious about preventing and reducing crime, it is critical to adopt the most effective, humane, and cost-efficient means of doing so. As a reasonably priced, highly efficient, and continually beneficial method of crime prevention, education is clearly one of the most successful means we have.

REFERENCES

1. Taylor, J. M. (1993, January 25). Pell Grants for prisoners. *The Nation*. p. 90.

2. The use of the term 'quality education' is meant here to distinguish between programs implemented to fulfill federal and/or state guidelines requiring the education of both adult and juvenile offenders but which are rarely tested or evaluated for effectiveness, and educational programs that have a documented success rate at both providing education that meets community standards and reducing recidivism.

3. Gilliard, D. K. and Beck, A. J. (1997). *Prison and jail inmates at midyear 1996.* (NCJ Publication No. 162843). Washington, DC: U.S. Department of Justice, Bureau of Justice Statistics, p. 1.

4. Juvenile is defined as an individual under the age of 18. It is difficult to collect data on juvenile offenders. This total does not include the number of juveniles in police lock-ups, and only reflects the results of a 1-day census count at private and public juvenile facilities, adult jails, and state and federal correctional facilities. See: DeComo, R., Tunis, S., Krisberg, B., Herrera, N. C., Rudenstine, S., and Del Rosario, D. (1995). *Juveniles taken into custody: Fiscal year 1992 report.* (NCJ Publication No. 153851). Washington, DC: Office of Juvenile Justice and Delinquency Prevention, p. 28.

5. Project READ. (1978). *To make a difference.* Silver Spring, MD: READ, Inc. p. 27. In Brunner, M. S. (1993). *Reduced recidivism and increased employment opportunity through research-based reading instruction.* (NCJ Publication No. 141324). Washington, DC: Office of Juvenile Justice and Delinquency Prevention, p. 5.

6. Project READ. (1978). *To make a difference.* Silver Spring, MD: READ, Inc. p. 27. In Brunner, M. S. (1993). *Reduced recidivism and increased employment opportunity through research-based reading instruction.* (NCJ Publication No. 141324). Washington, DC: Office of Juvenile Justice and Delinquency Prevention, p. 5.

7. Brunner, M. S. (1993). *National survey of reading programs for incarcerated juvenile offenders.* (NCJ Publication No. 144017). Washington, DC: Office of Juvenile Justice and Delinquency Prevention. p. 29.

8. Gemignani, R. J. (1994). *Juvenile correctional education: A time for change.* (NCJ Publication No. 150309). Washington, DC: Office of Juvenile Justice and Delinquency Prevention, p. 2.

9. Juvenile Law Center. (1996, December). *1996 Annual Report.* Philadelphia, PA: Juvenile Law Center. pp. 8–9.

10. Gemignani, R. J. (1994). *Juvenile correctional education: A time for change.* (NCJ Publication No. 150309). Washington, DC: Office of Juvenile Justice and Delinquency Prevention, p. 3.

11. There is not a statistically significant difference between the literacy rates of male and female offenders. See: Haigler, K. O., Harlow, C., O'Conner, P., and Campbell, A. (1994). *Literacy behind prison walls: Profiles of the prison population from the national adult literacy survey.* (NCES Publication No. 94-102). Washington, DC: U.S. Department of Education, National Center for Education Statistics, p. 124.

12. U.S. Department of Education, National Center for Education Statistics. (1992). *1992 national adult literacy survey.* Washington, DC: National Center for Education Statistics. [On-line]. Available: http://www.ed.gov/NCES/nadlits/overview.html.

13. Haigler, K. O., Harlow, C., O'Conner, P., and Campbell, A. (1994). *Literacy behind prison walls: Profiles of the prison population from the national adult literacy survey.* (NCES Publication No. 94-102). Washington, DC: U.S. Department of Education, National Center for Education Statistics, p. xxiii.

14. Maguire, K. and Pastore, A. L. (1996). *Sourcebook of criminal justice statistics—1995* (NCJ Publication No. 158900). Washington, DC: U.S. Department of Justice, Bureau of Justice Statistics. p. 567.

15. Harer, M. D. (1994). *Recidivism among federal prison releases in 1987: A preliminary report.* Washington, DC: Federal Bureau of Prisons, Office of Research and Evaluation. p. 2.

16. News and views: A possible reprieve for prisoner higher education. (1995, December 31). *The Journal of Blacks in Higher Education.* paragraph 5.

17. Bureau of Justice Statistics. (1997). *Criminal offender statistics.* [On-line]. Available: http://www.ojp.usdoj.gov/bjs/crimoff.htm.

18. Sherman, L. W., Gottfredson, D., MacKenzie, D. L., Eck, J., Reuter, P. and Bushway, S. *Preventing crime: What works, what doesn't, what's promising.* (NCJ Publication No. 165366). Washington, DC: National Institute of Justice.

19. Sherman, L. W. (1997, August 6). Crime prevention's bottom line. *The Wall Street Journal.* p. A15.

20. Mosso, G. E. (1997, Winter). The truth about prison education. *Prison Connections.* Volume 1, Number 3. [On-line] Available: http://persephone.hampshire.edu/wmpig/VIN3/prisoned.html.paragraph 2.

21. Harer, M. D. (1994). *Recidivism among federal prison releases in 1987: A preliminary report.* Washington, DC: Federal Bureau of Prisons, Office of Research and Evaluation. p. 4.

22. Brunner, M. S. (1993). *Reduced recidivism and increased employment opportunity through research-based reading instruction.* (NCJ Publication No. 141324). Washington, DC: Office of Juvenile Justice and Delinquency Prevention. p. 1.

23. Brunner, M. S. (1993). *Reduced recidivism and increased employment opportunity through re-*

search-based reading instruction. (NCJ Publication No. 141324). Washington, DC: Office of Juvenile Justice and Delinquency Prevention. p. 6.

24. Siegel, G. R. (1997). *A research study to determine the effect of literacy and general educational development programs on adult offenders on probation.* Tucson, AZ: Adult Probation Department of the Superior Court in Pima County.

25. Marks, A. (1997, March 20). One inmate's push to restore education funds for prisoners. *The Christian Science Monitor,* paragraph 14.

26. Bettendorf, E. (1996, October 25). Prisoner poets. *The State-Journal Register.* paragraph 52.

27. Tracy, C. and Johnson, C. (1994). *Review of various outcome studies relating prison education to reduced recidivism.* Windham School System: Huntsville, TX. pp. 6–7.

28. Data is averaged and does not add up to 100 percent. Tracy, C. and Johnson, C. (1994). *Review of various outcome studies relating prison education to reduced recidivism.* Windham School System; Huntsville, TX. p. 7.

29. Taylor, J. M. (1993, January 25). Pell Grants for prisoners. *The Nation.* p. 88.

30. Consortium of the Niagara Frontier. (no date). *The benefits to New York state of higher education programs for inmates.* [pamphlet]. Amherst, NY: Consortium of the Niagara Frontier. paragraph 4.

31. Elikann, P. T. (1996). *The Tough-on-Crime Myth: Real Solutions to Cut Crime.* New York, NY: Insight Books. p. 151.

32. Taylor, J. M. (1993, January 25). Pell Grants for prisoners. *The Nation.* p. 88.

33. Marks, A. (1997, March 20). One inmate's push to restore education funds for prisoners. *The Christian Science Monitor.* paragraph 13.

34. Boyce, C. J. (1994, July 15). For those behind bars, education is rehabilitation. *Minneapolis Star Tribune.* paragraph 12.

35. Taylor, J. M. (1993, January 25). Pell Grants for prisoners. *The Nation.* p. 88.

36. Greenwood, P. W., Model, K. E., Rydell, C. P. and Chiesa, J. (1996). *Diverting children from a life of crime: Measuring costs and benefits.* Santa Monica, CA: Rand.

37. Brown, P. C. (1989). *Involving parents in the education of their children.* Urbana, IL: ERIC Clearinghouse on Elementary and Early Childhood Education. [On-line]. Available: http://www.ed.gov/databases/ERIC_Digests/ed308988.html.

38. U.S. Department of Education. (1996). *The digest of education statistics 1996.* Washington, DC: National Center for Education Statistics. [On-line]. Available: http://www.ed.gov/NCES/pubs/D96/d96t024.html.

39. Over 75% of female inmates and 64% of males have children. See: Snell, T. L. and Morton, D. C. (1994, March). *Women in prison.* (NCJ Publication No. 145321). Washington, DC: U.S. Department of Justice, Bureau of Justice Statistics, pp. 6–7.

40. Consortium of the Niagara Frontier. (no date). *Prison higher education programs: Statements by inmate students and graduates.* [pamphlet]. Amherst, NY: Consortium of the Niagara Frontier. paragraph 6.

41. Taylor, J. M. (1993, January 25). Pell Grants for prisoners. *The Nation.* p. 88.

42. Taylor, J. M. (1993, January 25). Pell Grants for prisoners. *The Nation.* p. 88.

43. U.S. Department of Education, Office of Correctional Education. (1995). *Pell Grants and the incarcerated.* [pamphlet]. Washington, DC: U.S. Department of Education.

44. U.S. Department of Education, Office of Correctional Education. (1995). *Pell Grants and the incarcerated.* [pamphlet]. Washington, DC: U.S. Department of Education.

45. Less than 1% of inmates received federal Pell Grants in their final year of availability. See: U.S. Department of Education, Office of Correctional Education. (1995). *Pell Grants and the incarcerated.* [pamphlet]. Washington, DC: U.S. Department of Education.

46. Worth, R. (1995, November). A model prison. *The Atlantic Monthly.* paragraph 7.

47. Worth, R. (1995, November). A model prison. *The Atlantic Monthly.* paragraph 12.

48. Bettendorf, E. (1996, October 25). Prisoners poets. *The State-Journal Register.* paragraph 50.

49. Office of Correctional Education. (1995). *Pell Grants and the incarcerated.* [pamphlet]. Washington, DC: U.S. Department of Education.

The Center wishes to thank Michelle Fine, Ph.D., Professor of Psychology at The Graduate Center, CUNY, and Paula H. Mayhew, Ph.D., Dean of the Faculty at Marymount Manhattan College, for their comments on a draft of this research brief.

Probation Department in Michigan finds volunteers make fine officers

Abstract: A volunteer probation officer program is useful in reducing caseloads as it utilizes volunteers from comprehensive training programs, as evident in Oakland Country, Michigan. The candidates are screened carefully for good communication skills, sincerity, possible criminal records and driving records. Psychologists, postal workers, store owners and law students are selected for assistance in supervising community service programs.

Brian M. Smith

How much responsibility should correctional volunteers be given? At the 46th District Court Probation Department in Michigan, we have found that with proper screening and training, community volunteers can capably supervise low-risk, non-violent first offenders. A volunteer probation officer program is an effective way to enhance a probation department and involve the community in the criminal justice system.

The probation department, located north of Detroit in Oakland County, Mich., serves a caseload of about 1,100 offenders. The caseload is covered by a probation supervisor, three probation officers and a staff of volunteers and student interns who assist the probation officers.

The VPO Program

Recruitment and training are the pillars of our volunteer probation officer program. We usually conduct recruitment by advertising in local newspapers. Anyone interested in becoming a volunteer probation officer, or VPO, must complete an application for volunteer service. The department screens applications carefully before scheduling interviews. In general, we look for people with good communication skills, enthusiasm, a desire to assist others and a commitment to the community.

Jana Olivarez, the probation supervisor, and Gertie Garber, our volunteer coordinator, then interview the most qualified volunteer candidates. The final step is a background investigation, which includes criminal history and driving record checks.

Our volunteers reflect a cross-section of the communities we serve. Current volunteers include a psychologist, a speech pathologist, a postal worker, a homemaker, a retired auto worker and a furniture store owner. The court also recruits volunteers from the private sector. Many local employers allow employees to work for community agencies during their normal work day as part of a corporate communty involvement program.

Our volunteer probation program normally has 20 to 25 VPOs at any given time. New volunteers are recruited when the number drops below 20. Turnover is not a major problem; many volunteers have been with the program more than five years. Garber, who is herself a volunteer, has served the court since 1978.

Before volunteers are assigned cases, they attend an orientation and training session. The session, conducted by Olivarez and Garber, lasts from four to six hours. It includes a review of the department's policies and procedures, descriptions of situations volunteers are likely to encounter and role playing scenarios. VPOs receive a training manual that is updated annually. We also have regular in-service and occasional off-site training for all VPOs and staff.

VPOs handle about 15 percent of the probation department's total caseload. Each volunteer generally supervises seven to 10 low-risk, non-violent first offenders. (Our full-time officers handle about 250 offenders.) Garber attempts to match VPOs to probationers based on volunteers' educational level, occupation and career training. For a volunteer program to be successful, it should not create more work for the paid staff or place additional demands on an already heavy workload. This is one reason VPOs are given lower risk, non-violent offenders.

Volunteers who have been in the program for several years and who have received advanced training are assigned more complex or difficult cases. By developing expertise on particular types of cases, VPOs learn how to handle their caseload and provide the best possible service. We have found that offenders generally do not differentiate between volunteer and paid probation officers. VPOs say they enjoy volunteering because it puts them in touch with what is going on in the community and gives them a sense of pride in their work.

Student Intern Program

We also have a student intern program that complements the VPO program. Students are recruited from colleges and universities throughout Southeast Michigan, including the University of Michigan, Michigan State University, Oakland University and Wayne State University. Most are criminal justice or pre-law students.

Interns, who are asked to commit to a minimum of nine months of service, work up to 20 hours a week. We usually have one or two interns at a time. They

From *Corrections Today,* August 1993, pp. 80-83. Reprinted with permission of the American Correctional Association, Lanham, MD. © 1993.

are not paid for their work but do receive college credits toward their degrees and valuable hands-on experience working with offenders.

Interns conduct pre-sentence investigations, handle caseloads averaging 30 offenders and help the probation officers. They also assist with record keeping and other special projects.

Offender Community Service Program

In addition to VPOs and college students, the department uses volunteers to supervise its community service program. The sentencing option of ordering offenders to perform community service has grown in popularity in recent years, placing an additional personnel burden on the probation department and the court.

The program has grown steadily since its inception in 1982. Community service is now ordered in about 80 percent of the cases the probation department supervises.

The program is directed by Al Cliette, a retired U.S. Army colonel who volunteers 16 to 20 hours a week in the probation department. Among other duties, he is responsible for establishing contacts with the non-profit, community agencies the program works with.

During Cliette's five years with the court, the list of court-approved nonprofit community agencies has grown from 20 to 180. He contacts each agency every six months to ensure that the agency listing, particularly the name of the contact person, is accurate.

Examples of the court's community service agencies are churches, synagogues, hospitals, the Michigan Humane Society, the Michigan Cancer Foundation and the American Red Cross. Typical community service work includes office or clerical duties, general maintenance and work with youth groups such as the YMCA or YWCA.

In Michigan, courts are not required to provide liability insurance for offenders sentenced to community service. Agencies that agree to accept offenders for community service are responsible for handling injury claims.

In 1992, offenders performed about 58,000 hours of community service work, more than three times as many hours as in 1988. Cliette logs and forwards all correspondence and completion information from the community service agencies to the probation officers. He also helps probation officers document the number of community service hours offenders work.

Cliette thoroughly explains the responsibilities and procedures of the community service program to the offenders and is available to help them with their paperwork. We have found that this assistance increases the level of offender compliance.

Volunteers and student interns are an integral part of the 46th District Court Probation Department. Their overall level of service to the court has been excellent. Although much time and effort has been devoted to establishing and operating our volunteer programs, we have found that they benefit the department and increase the community's understanding of the correctional system.

VPOs with Juveniles

by Raymond Lescher

The Ramsey County Community Corrections Department in St. Paul, Minn., has a strong volunteer program called Volunteers in Corrections (VIC) that emphasizes working with juveniles.

Most of the program's 200 volunteers are matched with youths at three juvenile probation branch offices and in two juvenile institutions—the Juvenile Detention Center and Boys Totem Town, a residential treatment facility for 65 youths ages 13 through 18. In addition, some VIC participants work with adults on probation or parole, at a local minimum security work facility, and with families in family court.

Most of the work with juveniles is in a traditional one-on-one role. Volunteers build trusting relationships with adolescents and help them follow court conditions such as school attendance, financial restitution and community service. Other important duties include providing substance abuse and family counseling, helping them find jobs, tutoring, and offering advice. Volunteers also have set up no-smoking programs, arts and crafts classes and an African American mentor program. The immense power of adult role models giving freely of their time is a powerful influence in the lives of juvenile offenders. Frank Hosch, superintendent at Boys Totem Town, has 50 volunteers in his facility. "They are invaluable," he says. "Their contributions of experience, expertise and time have allowed for expanded programming and services to be made available to residents here."

Ramsay County first began using correctional volunteers in October 1970, when six men and women attended a three-hour orientation. Since then the program has grown immensely. The 99th group of volunteers recently underwent orientation, which now lasts 12 hours. In nearly 23 years, more than 2,000 citizens have made the one-year commitment, which includes a minimum of two hours of weekly participation.

In 1987, VIC's advisory board began fund-raising to provide scholarships for tuition and book costs to current and former residents who wanted to continue their education past high school. So far, 44 scholarships totaling more than $17,000 have been granted to students at area colleges, junior colleges and trade and vocational schools.

The remarkable service provided by volunteers hasn't gone unnoticed. In 1992, the Minnesota Corrections Association honored the volunteers with its prestigious President's Award and President George Bush named the program as his 939th Point of Light. And this past April, VIC was awarded the International Association of Justice Volunteers' Creative Criminal Justice Award.

Raymond Lescher is the manager of Volunteers in Corrections Inc., a non-profit agency that works with the Ramsey Country Community Corrections Department in St. Paul, Minn.

Correctional Privatization: Defining the Issues and Searching for Answers

G. Larry Mays
New Mexico State University

INTRODUCTION

The move toward privatization of governmental services was a major topic of discussion during the decade of the 1980s (President's Commission on Privatization, 1988). In particular, a wide range of criminal justice services were offered by the private sector either for-profit or on a non-profit basis. Today there are examples of private delivery of police, court, and correctional services. For example, the private sector employs roughly twice as many police personnel as the public sector (see, e.g., Abadinsky & Winfree, 1992:213). In the area of the courts, some jurisdictions permit parties in civil actions to "rent-a-judge" (a lawyer or retired judge) to expedite the hearings of certain types of disputes. And, in the realm of corrections, private service providers conduct presentence investigations, operate community-based programs, and finance, build, and operate prisons.

The issue of correctional privatization is both very old and very new. The private provision of "correctional" services goes back at least as far as the first juvenile institutions—the houses of refuge created in cities like New York in the 1820s (Durham, 1989, 1991; Rogers & Mays, 1987). Additionally, probation began with John Augustus in 1841 essentially as a private, voluntary alternative to prison or jail (Champion, 1990).

Privatization is new as well. In fact, it seems that privatization was rediscovered or reborn, largely as a result of the prison "crowding crisis" of the 1980s (Durham, 1989; Sullivan, 1989; Turner, 1988). Since then, privatization has been depicted on the one hand as a policy capable of saving American corrections from total collapse, or on the other hand as a complete abrogation of governmental responsibility for public safety (Mahoney, 1988). As with most policy changes, especially those that seem to depart significantly from past practice, there is both truth and error in either of these extreme interpretations.

What follows in this introduction is neither a call for more expansive application of privatization, nor an utter condemnation of the use of the private sector to provide correctional services. Instead, it is an attempt to *clearly* define the issues, to frame the appropriate policy questions in the most objective, least polemical way, and to suggest options that policymakers and taxpayers alike might consider.

However, before defining the parameters of the field of play, it is important to issue an implied, but essential, caveat: very few people are truly objective or impartial about privatization; we all have biases of one kind or another. Nevertheless, perhaps the clash of biases presented will provide all of us with a more complete picture of the things correctional privatization can and cannot do.

PHILOSOPHICAL ISSUES

Incarcerating or otherwise supervising convicted offenders typically is viewed as a necessary, but unpleasant, task. Often university students will say "I want to work in criminal justice, but not in prisons." The general public typically lacks knowledge about corrections generally and prisons in particular; thus, the world of corrections, for the most part, is out of sight and out of mind. This holds true unless a major event like a prison riot reminds the public once again that there are prisons and "bad people" are incarcerated in them.

In all of this, there remains the assumption, or presumption, that some level of government has the primary—if not the sole—responsibility for supervising those offenders duly convicted in the courts. Because corrections largely is viewed as a governmental function, a basic philosophical question is often raised about the propriety of having private enterprise providing correctional services. In this regard, Logan (1987:35) notes that "The most principled objection to the propriety of commercial prisons is the claim that imprisonment is an inherently and exclusively governmental function and therefore should not be performed by the private sector at all, even under contract to the government."

To state the question most simply: should "free enterprise" be given the responsibility of running prisons? If so, to what extent should private services be utilized? Is there an ethical limit on correctional privatization? At the extreme, could the state contract with a private service provider to perform executions?

At one end of the spectrum, the free enterprise advocates believe that government should turn over to the private sector any and all services that could be provided at a better quality, less expensively, or even at the same cost. By contrast, critics like Robbins (1988) view corrections as an inherently governmental function, therefore it cannot be delegated. For Logan (1987:36) the central argument is that "Since all legitimate powers of government are originally, and continuously, delegated to it by citizens, those same citizens if they wish can specify that certain powers be further delegated by the state, in turn, to private agencies" (see also Mahoney, 1988). Additionally, Feeley (1991:2) believes that the central issue is not one of efficiency or effectiveness but *To what extent does privatization expand and transform the state's capacity to punish?* [Italics in original.]

If the decade of the 1980s provides any guidance, the issue will not be whether we will have privatization, but to what extent and under what circumstances privatization will be utilized. Privatization seems to be a fact of life in modern American corrections; and, while some may continue to struggle with the propriety of private prisons, the private sector seems to be committed to the long haul.

MOTIVATION ISSUES

To simply say that we have, or may have, correctional privatization is insufficient. Private or largely private entities already provide a wide range of correctional services. For example, many of the juvenile diversion programs developed in the wake of the Juvenile Justice and Delinquency Prevention Act of 1974 are private or quasi-private (Feeley, 1991; Schwartz, 1989). There also have been secure detention facilities as well (Mullen, 1984). Some of these programs are operated on a for-profit basis, but a large number of them are non-profit.

Therefore, we must recognize that there can be both for-profit and non-profit motivations behind correctional programs. While in all likelihood private, non-profit groups are going to be found in diversion programs or the "second system" (Rogers & Mays, 1987: 441–442), it is possible (although not as likely) that prisons—particularly at low security levels—could be operated on a not-for-profit basis as well. Realistically, however, the operation of secure prisons is sufficiently distasteful that only a fairly strong profit motive would lure many firms into the corrections arena.

ECONOMIC ISSUES

If we assume a profit motive for most private correctional operations, the essential question must be; what does the private sector bring to the table? The two obvious appeals are (a) a higher quality of service, and (2) a lower cost (Borna, 1986; Feeley, 1991). In the best case scenario, the private sector could offer both (Hutto, 1988). However, given the choice, state policymakers (and particularly legislators) generally will opt for lower costs and satisfactory quality. In most instances this may mean that what the private sector provides is no worse than what the public sector currently offers. In many cases, the private sector's main selling point is the ability to reduce the state's costs per inmate/day (see e.g., Sellers, 1989). The problem in this area is that a great deal of debate centers around how cost estimates are prepared, and what the state's current costs actually are.

SCOPE OF SERVICES ISSUES

Economic issues must be framed in the context of the scope of services desired by the governmental entity. Private providers advertise a broad range of services including financing, construction, partial service delivery (e.g., food service, health care, or education), prison industries, and total institutional operation (Feeley, 1991; Mahoney, 1988; Sexton, Farrow & Auerbach, 1985; Turner, 1988).

Private financing becomes desirable when a prison bond referendum seems difficult to sell to the public, or after such a referendum has been rejected (Borna, 1986). In such cases, the issue raised seems to be whether the will of the public has been subverted or circumvented by the public sector turning to a private financial consultant or bonding firm (see Borna, 1986; Mahoney, 1988; Mullen, 1984).

Construction has been an area where private corrections firms seem to have been particularly successful. The private sector promises, and typically delivers, faster and less expensive construction than the state can provide (Mullen, 1984). This is generally possible for two reasons. First, the private contractor can move more quickly to acquire a suitable site than can the state. States often are bound by statutory or other legal requirements to solicit offers of property and to hold public hearings concerning the potential locations of new prisons. When some communities counter with the NIMBY (not in my backyard) response, the land acquisition process can become politicized and protracted. The private sector, by contrast, simply finds the most suitable (i.e., affordable and least controversial) piece of property and purchases it.

Second, the state is often bound by cumbersome procurement codes in purchasing construction materials as well. Because all materials may have to go out for bid, the materials acquisition process may be prolonged and all bids may have to be granted to the lowest bidders meeting the minimum specifications.

What may take the state two to five years to complete—from design to final construction—a private contractor may be able to complete in 12 to 18 months. This difference is significant, since in the world of construction, time is money. Nevertheless, as Durham (1991:34) warns "whether the private or public sector is assigned the job of running American prisons, nobody at either the state or Federal level expects current building plans to handle the anticipated influx of new inmates."

There is probably no place where the private sector has had a greater impact on corrections than in the provision of specific institutional services. Three of the most common areas for partial privatization include food services, health care, and education. There are a variety of contractors in the food services area, and some of these companies supply food services to colleges, schools, and other public organizations.

The health care industry truly is big business in the United States, and some of the major service providers operate hospitals, clinics, and health maintenance organizations (HMOs) for the free world population. When a state seeks someone to provide health care to prison inmates, these companies are experienced and staffed to deliver such services. Prison health care services may include dental, mental health (counseling and substance abuse), and routine medical care. Specialized medical care such as OB/GYN services for female inmates and long-term care for inmates with AIDS may also be required (Hammett & Moini, 1990).

Education is another service that seems to lend itself to privatization. Educational services may include adult basic education (ABE), high school/GED courses, vocational education, and even college-level courses. While there are some private, for-profit service providers in this area, educational privatization most likely will come from local colleges, universities, and school districts and frequently will be delivered on a not-for-profit basis.

PERSONNEL ISSUES

There are a variety of concerns relating to private correctional personnel and typical questions concern: who are they? where will they come from? how much will they be paid? and will they have any type of job security? These are but a few of the questions that need to be answered in any move toward the private delivery of correctional services.

It is important to recognize that some private correctional facilities will be constructed to replace public ones, or a private contractor may be engaged to take over an already existing public facility. In both of these instances, the basic issue involves what will become of current public sector correctional employees. Because this is such a thorny problem, groups like the American Correctional Association have urged caution in reliance upon private sector corrections (Levinson, 1988). Many governmental employees' unions also see privatizing as substantially undermining the job security of their members (Mullen, 1984); thus, they routinely lobby against the movement to privatize. To alleviate such fears, many private contractors specify (or the state stipulates in the contract) that current employees will be retained under the new contract, to the maximum extent possible.

Therefore, we need to return to the question: who are these employees or, stated another way, what will their qualifications be? Given the national recruiting base from which many private correctional firms operate, there seems to be a fairly strong commitment to selecting the best qualified employees possible. Ironically, many private corrections workers are former state or federal employees, particularly those hired for supervisory or management positions. Private sector agencies use as a selling point to prospective employees not only a broader recruiting base, but a promotion potential not available in many states.

Although construction costs often capture the most public attention, over the life cycle of a prison as much as 90 percent of the total expenditures will be devoted to operations, and the bulk of these costs will be associated with personnel. Therefore, how can the private sector save money? There are two possible answers. First, the private sector could simply pay employees less. However, if private companies are committed to hiring quality personnel, and if they are committed or obligated to hiring current governmental employees, this may not be feasible or desirable (Henderson, 1988). Second, the private sector can pay the prevailing wage rate for its staff, but simply use fewer of them. Such a solution at first sounds contradictory to the goal of providing better, or at least comparable, service. However, one way to accomplish a personnel reduction is through the design or redesign of correctional facilities. If a private contractor can eliminate one post—a position that must be staffed continuously—great cost-savings can be realized, since it takes a personnel allocation of nearly five people to staff a post 24 hours per day and to allow for days off, holidays, sick leave, and the like. At a conservative figure of $30,000 per person (salary plus all fringe benefits), elimination of one post saves $150,000 per year.

Finally, there are two or three ways to approach the job security issue. In the most basic sense, some in the private sector would argue that competent job performance is the ultimate form of job security (Henderson, 1988). This may not be assurance enough for some employees, and in some instances employees may request employment contracts of specified lengths, with termination or buy-out procedures clearly specified. If all else fails, private employees can form or join labor unions, as many of their public sector counterparts have. In the end, public and private sector corrections personnel can take comfort in knowing that their job is not sought by a great many people, and while they can be replaced, the hiring of trained, dedicated employees is not a simple task. Therefore, it is highly unlikely that corrections managers, public or private, will act hastily or arbitrarily terminate most staff members.

LEGAL ISSUES

The legal issues surrounding the private provision of correctional services can be collapsed into two categories: litigation/liability and contract monitoring/performance. When it comes to dealing with legal problems, it is difficult to say which of these categories is most important. In all likelihood, given the potential legal problems posed by each, both are equally significant.

The litigation/liability category represents the legal challenges brought by prison inmates. As can be seen from the literature (see, e.g., Fairchild, 1984; Finn, 1984; Hanson, 1987; Mays & Olszta, 1989; Thomas, 1988), prison inmate litigation is extensive. In fact, federal and state prison and jail inmates file lawsuits relative to crowded living conditions, food quality, access to the courts, treatment programs, disciplinary procedures, and myriad other concerns. Inmate litigation has been one of the fastest growing segments of court dockets, especially for the federal district courts.

The essential question, then, must be: can states eliminate, or at least minimize, their legal liability for the way prisons and jails are operated and prisoners are treated? The answer in a word is "no." Because the state negotiates the contract and pays the per diem rate for inmates, the state is ultimately legally liable (Borna, 1986; Sullivan, 1989). Will a contract with a private firm in any way reduce liability? The answer here is "perhaps." If the contract is well-written and the contractor strictly adheres to the various stipulations (e.g., obtaining American Correctional Association accreditation for the facility), the sources of litigation should be reduced (Sellers, 1989:253). Can inmates continue to sue? Of course they can! Can they win? Probably not as often.

All of this is dependent, however, on the level of performance expected and the state's mechanism for monitoring the contract (Collins, 1987:32–33). It must be said initially that the state cannot, must not, allow the contract/contractor to go unmonitored (Sellers, 1989). No matter how professional, ethical, and conscientious contractors are, the state cannot take their word that they are doing the right thing in the right way. To have an unmonitored contract would be a complete abrogation of state responsibility to protect inmates and to act in the public interest.

Most states have developed one of two monitoring models. One way to monitor contract performance—what some might call quality control—is to establish a state oversight organization. This organization could be part of, and report to, the state legislature, but in most instances the contract monitoring entity will be part of the corrections department. Such an agency would conduct periodic site visits and inspections and would perform annual or semi-annual performance audits.

The second monitoring model utilizes state employees assigned full time to the privately operated facility. This arrangement provides on-site and continuous (but probably not as in-depth or rigorous) evaluation. Having state employees on the "inside" should insure routine contract compliance and help clarify those non-routine issues that arise periodically and unexpectedly.

CONCLUSION

To privatize or not to privatize, is *not* the question. It seems an inevitable fact of modern American corrections that there will be some degree of privatization. There is no doubt that private corrections holds out some hope for the problems currently plaguing prisons in this country and around the world. There is also no doubt that there are attendant problems with privatized correctional services. Henderson (1988:102) who speaks relatively favorably about the private provision of correctional services is quick to add that "Many people make outrageous claims for privatization. Privatization will not work in every system or with every kind of inmate. In terms of pure confinement, private corrections cannot necessarily do the job any better than government."

In all likelihood, we are entering what might be called the "public-private partnership" era (Cox & Osterhoff, 1991; see also Hutto, 1988; Turner, 1988). Some states will turn over some complete jails and prisons to private contractors, and many states will pursue privatization of some correctional services such as education, health care, and food services.

What will be the outcome of increasing privatization? Will the inmates fare better? Will the taxpayers benefit? Will anyone notice the difference? These and other questions guide the readings that follow. In large measure, the contributors to this volume have sought to do two things: (1) raise the important questions concerning privatization, and (2) where possible, provide definitive answers.

The book is divided into two major sections. The first section will address some of the global issues that provide the "context" of privatization. The second section deals with specific examples of privatization efforts, the consequences of privatization. When it comes to the thorny issue of privatization, this book seeks to shed a little light where there is already a lot of heat in the policy debate over the private provision of correctional services.

Point

Chain Gangs Are Right for Florida

by Sen. Charlie Crist

The official nickname of Florida is "The Sunshine State." The state has the environment of paradise. With gorgeous waters, sandy beaches and the cultural splendor of its major cities, Florida has a lot to offer both citizens and tourists alike.

But for the past few years, a more appropriate nickname for Florida would be "The Crime State." Criminals have murdered, raped, robbed and maimed innocent citizens. The statistics reveal a grim reality. In December 1994, the Federal Bureau of Investigation rated Florida number one in violent crime. In May 1995, the FBI reported that the three most violent cities in the nation were Florida's—Ft. Lauderdale, Tampa and Miami. And in November of 1995, the FBI released new and equally disturbing statistics which showed that Florida has three of the top five most violent cities in the nation—Miami, Gainesville and Tallahassee. According to the Florida Department of Law Enforcement, every three minutes and 39 seconds another violent crime is committed in Florida.

Sen. Charlie Crist (R) was elected to the Florida Senate in 1992. He sponsored an amendment to bring chain gangs back to Florida in May 1995. In December 1995, Florida became the third state in the United States to reinstitute chain gangs.

Perhaps most important in the long run, chain gangs serve as a deterrent.

As a state senator, it didn't take this kind of flood of frightening statistics for me to realize there was a problem. Constituents told me. They watch the news, as I do, and see the statistics played out over and over again. They tell me they are afraid to leave their homes at night.

In late 1994, when I was appointed chairman of the Ways and Means Subcommittee on Criminal Justice, which funds criminal justice programs in Florida, I decided to tour some prisons to see how money is spent on criminal justice. What I found was appalling.

Florida's prisons have basketball courts, sand volleyball pits, racquetball courts and baseball diamonds. Inmates enjoy weightlifting, arts and crafts, and amenities such as boccie balls for Italian-style bowling. The Florida Department of Corrections informed me that less than half of all inmates work, and many work for only about four hours a day. It was abundantly clear to me that inmates had too much freedom in prison.

Correctional officers told me that these amenities were necessary to keep inmates busy, so as to minimize the security risk that is caused by idle time. Yet, they also confessed to me that they would rather see inmates work.

It occurred to me, after touring a number of prison facilities, that Florida was sending the wrong message to criminals. In effect, we were telling criminals that if they commit a crime, they go to a place not unlike summer camp.

After seeing prisons and talking with state correctional officers and other officers who were interested in a better system of criminal justice, the answer seemed obvious: We needed to replace play with work.

Certainly inmates can work within the confines of the prison, and I believe they should. The prison system I envision is self-sustaining, where inmates grow their own food, do their own carpentry and plumbing, and handle the upkeep of the prison.

But I believe that convicted criminals should also work on our highways and byways, in visible places where would-be criminals can see the price of committing crime. Presently, nonviolent criminals do engage in this kind of work, but for obvious safety reasons, violent criminals cannot. That's inequitable. Chains provide additional security that, along with armed guards, keep our citizens and tourists safe while giving criminals the opportunity to work.

Chain gangs offer a number of benefits, particularly when they replace the kind of broken system we had in Florida. First, work on the chain gang is an appropriate punishment. It puts criminals to work. It gives them the opportunity to give back to the society they have taken from. Chain gangs and hard work ensure that prison is not pleasant, which is what society wants and criminals need.

Additionally, chain gangs are a useful prison management tool. Inmates work all day, so they are tired at the end of the day. This eliminates the need for recreation as a management tool during the day. I also support providing education to inmates at night.

Perhaps most important in the long run, chain gangs serve as a deterrent. They are a visible form of punishment that sends the message that if you commit a crime, you will be punished, and it will not be pleasant.

All this adds up to justice. Ultimately, it all adds up to freedom for law-abiding citizens. It means that we can get back the Florida where our children can play without fear, where our senior citizens can take evening strolls, where all of us can enjoy the environment, the beaches and the cultural splendor that make Florida the paradise that "The Sunshine State" should be.

Counterpoint

Chain Gangs Are Cruel and Unusual Punishment

by Rhonda Brownstein

Last year, with much fanfare, Alabama brought a sad and cruel part of American history back from the past—inmate chain gangs. More than 700 Alabama medium custody inmates now labor 10 hours a day busting rocks and picking up litter on the highways. The inmates, who receive no visitation during their entire six-month sentence, are handcuffed—arms above them—to a hitching post for the entire day if they "refuse to work" or disrupt others while working. The governor and prison commissioner claim that the chain gangs will deter crime and negative inmate behavior. They also claim that the program will save the state

Rhonda Brownstein is senior staff attorney at the Southern Poverty Law Center in Montgomery, Ala.

The reinstatement of chain gangs in Alabama was a shrewd political move, designed to appease the public's demand that the government get tough on crime.

money. Actually, the reinstatement of chain gangs in Alabama was a shrewd political move, designed to appease the public's demand that the government get tough on crime.

Will chain gangs work to deter crime? We may never know the answer to that question. But recent statistics and studies point to the fact that longer and harsher prison sentences will do nothing to curb crime. According to the Uniform Crime Reports and National Crime Survey, the prison and jail population in the United States doubled from 1985 to 1995 due to the move toward mandatory and longer sentences, more people being sent to prison instead of being placed on probation, and more restrictive parole and other release policies. Yet, during this same period, the overall rate of serious crime remained stable. In Florida, the incarceration rate in 1980 was 183 per 100,000. By 1989, the rate had increased to 311 people incarcerated per 100,000. Yet, during this same period, the per capita reported crime remained the same. And, despite the fact that the United States has the highest incarceration rate in the world, it also has one of the highest rates of violent crime. Incarcerating more inmates and lengthening prison stays has not served to deter crime.

On the other hand, recent studies suggest that education and jobs have some positive influence on both prison behavior and recidivism. A recent study by Anne Piehl, an assistant professor at Harvard, found that male inmates in the Wisconsin prison system who were enrolled in high school classes were 10 percent less likely to be rearrested four years after their release than those who did not participate in the program. Obviously, a 10 percent reduction in inmates nationwide would save a significant amount of tax dollars. Another study, by the Federal Bureau of Prisons, found that inmates enrolled in industrial work programs were less likely to commit disciplinary violations while in prison and were substantially less likely to be rearrested than other inmates.

Alabama's prison commissioner, however, believes that the "so-called rehabilitation programs" have created a "life of luxury" for inmates. Commissioner Jones' stated goal is to "break [those] suckers," Morris Thigpen, who formerly held Jones' position and now directs the National Institute of Corrections, disagrees. Speaking about the current movement toward making prison as harsh as possible, Thigpen states that "when you take men and women and take away all incentives and they've lost all hope, then you're creating a rather dangerous situation."

With 95 percent of all inmates in the United States returning to the streets at some point, we should be focusing on ways to deter future criminal activity. We must provide a wide array of community-based sanctions and rehabilitation programs, such as in- and outpatient drug treatment, education, training, supervised probation, community service and home confinement.

Chain gangs make a great photo opportunity for vote-conscious politicians. However, those who support them tend to overlook two points. First, for many, chain gangs are a painful reminder of the injustices of the post-bellum South. Although Alabama touts its chain gangs as modern and integrated, many cannot forget that, historically, chain gangs were developed as punishment for ex-slaves and their descendants who committed crimes. In the early 1900s, twice as many blacks than whites were on chain gangs. And today in Alabama prisons, where chain gangs are operated only in the disciplinary segregation unit, it is not unusual for the chain gang to be 90 percent African American.

Second, and just as important, intentionally degrading and humiliating inmates not only makes for bad corrections policy, it violates the Eighth Amendment to the Constitution. After all, as the U.S. Supreme Court has recognized; "The basic concept underlying the Eighth Amendment is nothing less than the dignity of man" (*Trop v. Dulles,* 356 U.S. 86, 100 [1958]).

Restorative Justice: The Concept

Movement Sweeping Criminal Justice Field Focuses on Harm and Responsibility

By Howard Zehr

"A revolution is occurring in criminal justice. A quiet, grassroots, seemingly unobtrusive, but truly revolutionary movement is changing the nature, the very fabric of our work."

These are the opening words in a recent publication of the National Institute of Corrections (NIC) characterizing the combined community and restorative justice movements. Author Eduardo Barajas Jr., a program specialist for NIC, goes on to observe that the changes extend beyond most reforms in the history of criminal justice: "What is occurring now is more than innovative, it is truly inventive... a 'paradigm shift.'"

The restorative justice movement has come a long way since probation officer Mark Yantzi and co-worker Dave Worth first pushed two shaking offenders toward their victims' homes in Elmira, Ontario, in 1974. Who could have imagined, when we began our version of victim/offender mediation—the Victim Offender Reconciliation Program, or VORP—in Elkhart, Ind., several years later that we were at the vanguard of a movement with the potential to revolutionize justice?

Crime as Harm

As Barajas' observation above implies, restorative justice is not a matter of adding some new programs or tinkering with old ones. Instead, it involves a reorientation of how we think about crime and justice. At a recent consultation of restorative justice and rehabilitation specialists sponsored by the NIC Academy, participants agreed that two ideas were fundamental: restorative justice is harm-focused, and it promotes the engagement of an enlarged set of stakeholders. Most of restorative justice can be seen as following from these two concepts.

Restorative justice views crime, first of all, as harm done to people and communities. Our legal system, with its focus on rules and laws, often loses sight of this reality; consequently, it makes victims, at best, a secondary concern of justice. A harm focus, however, implies a central concern for victims' needs and roles. Restorative justice begins with a concern for victims and how to meet their needs, for repairing the harm as much as possible, both concretely and symbolically.

A focus on harm also implies an emphasis on offender accountability and responsibility—in concrete, not abstract, terms. Too often we have thought of accountability as punishment—pain administered to offenders for the pain they have caused. Unfortunately, this often is irrelevant or even counterproductive to real accountability. Little in the justice process encourages offenders to understand the consequences of their actions or to empathize with victims. On the contrary, the adversarial game requires offenders to look out for themselves. Offenders are discouraged from acknowledging their responsibility and are given little opportunity to act on this responsibility in concrete ways. The "neutralizing strategies"—the stereotypes and rationalizations that offenders use to distance themselves from the people they hurt—are never challenged. So the sense of alienation from society experienced by many offenders, the feeling that they

RESTORATIVE JUSTICE SIGNPOSTS

We are working toward restorative justice when we...

I. Focus on the harms of wrongdoing more than the rules that have been broken;

II. Show equal concern and commitment to victims and offenders, involving both in the process of justice;

III. Work toward the restoration of victims, empowering them and responding to their needs as they see them;

IV. Support offenders while encouraging them to understand, accept and carry out their obligations;

V. Recognize that while obligations may be difficult for offenders, they should not be intended as harms and they must be achievable;

VI. Provide opportunities for dialogue, direct or indirect, between victims and offenders as appropriate;

VII. Involve and empower the affected community through the justice process, and increase its capacity to recognize and respond to community bases of crime;

VIII. Encourage collaboration and reintegration, rather than coercion and isolation;

IX. Give attention to the unintended consequences of our actions and programs; and

X. Show respect to all parties, including victims, offenders and justice colleagues.

—Harry Mika and Howard Zehr

---

themselves are victims, is only heightened by the legal process and the prison experience.

If crime is essentially about harm, accountability means being encouraged to understand that harm, to begin to comprehend the consequences of one's behavior. Moreover, it means taking responsibility to make things right insofar as possible, both concretely and symbolically. As our foreparents knew well, wrong creates obligations; taking responsibility for those obligations is the beginning of genuine accountability.

The principle of engagement suggests that the primary parties affected by crime—victims, offenders, members of the community—are given significant roles in the justice process. Indeed, they need to be given information about each other and to be involved in deciding what justice requires in this situation. In some cases, this may mean actual dialogue between these parties, as happens in victim/offender mediation or family group conferences, to come to a consensus about what should be done. In others, it may involve indirect exchange or the use of surrogates. In any eventuality, the principle of engagement implies involvement of an enlarged circle of parties as compared to the traditional justice process.

At the risk of oversimplifying, the restorative justice and the traditional justice approach—retributive justice—might be summarized as follows:

Retributive Justice
Crime
is a violation of the law, and the state is the victim.
The aim of justice
is to establish blame (guilt) and administer pain (punishment).
The process of justice
is a conflict between adversaries in which the offender is pitted against state rules, intentions outweigh outcomes and one side wins while the other loses.

Restorative Justice
Crime
is a violation or harm to people and relationships.

The aim of justice
is to identify obligations, to meet needs and to promote healing.

The process of justice
involves victims, offenders and the community in an effort to identify obligations and solutions, maximizing the exchange of information (dialogue, mutual agreement) between them.

To put restorative justice in its simplest form: crime violates people and violations create obligations. Justice should involve victims, offenders and community members in a search to identify needs and obligations, so as to promote healing among the parties involved.

Widespread Interest

Today's interest in restorative justice at the national level follows several decades of innovation and experimentation at the community and state levels. Victim/offender mediation programs have sprang up in at least 300 U.S. and Canadian communities. The Minnesota Department of Corrections has on staff a restorative justice planner who is working innovatively to help communities in that state develop new restorative approaches. Vermont has rethought the concept of probation, designing a "reparative probation" system for nonviolent offenders. Native American and Canadian communities are finding ways to put into operation some of their traditional approaches and values; these approaches also are being seen as part of a restorative justice framework. In academic and consulting fields, too, numerous restorative justice institutes and programs are emerging.

This interest in restorative justice is not limited to North America. Hundreds of victim/offender mediation programs have developed in European countries; Germany, Finland and England, for example, have many such programs. South Africa is writing a new juvenile justice code incorporating restorative principles. In New Zealand, restorative justice has served to guide and help shape the family group conference approach which is now the basis of that country's entire juvenile justice system.

Deciphering Terms

"Restorative justice" is a term which quickly connects for many people and therein lies both its strength and its weakness. Many professionals, as well as lay people, are frustrated with justice as it is commonly practiced and are immediately attracted to the idea of restoration. Restorative justice intuitively suggests a reparative, person-centered, common-sense approach. For many of us, it reflects values with which we were raised. As a result, the term has been widely embraced and used in many contexts.

But what do we mean by "restorative justice"? Will the term be used simply as a new way to name and justify the same old programs and goals? Many programs can be compatible with restorative justice if they are reshaped to fully account for restorative principles. If they are not reshaped as part of a larger restorative "lens," however, at best they will be more of the same. At worst, they may become new ways to control and punish.

Retributive vs. Restorative Justice

Retributive Justice	Restorative Justice
Problem	
defined narrowly, abstractly, a legal infraction	defined relationally, as a violation of people
only legal variables relevant	overall context relevant
state as victim	people as victims
Actors	
state (active) and offender (passive)	victim and offender primary, along with community and state
Process	
adversarial, authoritarian, technical, impersonal	participatory, maximizing information, dialogue and mutual agreement
focus = guilt/blame	focus = needs and obligations
"neutralizing strategies" encouraged	empathy and responsibility encouraged
Outcome	
pain, suffering	making things right by identifying needs and obligations; healing; problem-solving
harm by offender balanced by harm to offender	harm by offender balanced by making right
oriented to past	oriented to future

All this is not to say that there is such a thing as "pure" restorative or retributive justice. Rather, justice should be seen as a continuum between two ideal types. On the one end is our Western legal system. Its strengths—such as the encouragement of human rights—are substantial. Yet it has important weaknesses. Criminal justice tends to be punitive, conflictual, impersonal and state-centered. It encourages the denial of responsibility and empathy on the part of offenders. It leaves victims out, ignoring their needs. Instead of discouraging wrongdoing, it often encourages it. It exacerbates rather than heals wounds.

At the other end is the restorative alternative. Victims' needs and rights are central, not peripheral. Offenders are encouraged to understand the harm they have caused and to take responsibility for it. Dialogue—direct or indirect—is encouraged and communities play important roles. Restorative justice assumes that justice can and should promote healing, both individual and societal.

Criminal justice usually is not purely retributive. On the other hand, we rarely will achieve justice that is fully restorative. A realistic goal is to move as far as we can toward a process that puts victims, offenders and members of the affected community—and their respective needs and roles—at the center of our search for a justice that heals.

REFERENCE

National Institute of Corrections. 1996. *Community Justice: Striving for Safe, Secure and Just Communities.* LIS Inc. (March).

Howard Zehr is professor of sociology and restorative justice at Eastern Mennonite University and director of the Mennonite Central Committee, U.S. Office on Crime and Justice. Copies of the "restorative justice signposts" bookmark (and a list of other criminal justice resources) are available without charge from Literature Resources, Mennonite Central Committee, 21 S. 12th, Akron, PA 17501; (717) 859-1151; e-mail: see@mcc.org.

Rough justice in the youth courts

Labour's pledge to get tough on persistent young offenders could fall prey to a turf war between the Home Secretary and the Lord Chancellor

KIRSTY MILNE

Reeboks, a black leather jacket and an expression that says "I'm not here" are the uniform for teenagers at the youth court in Kingston upon Thames. A succession of boys, mostly 16 year olds who look a lot younger, slope before the magistrates to face charges of fare-dodging, theft, robbery and drink-driving.

Kingston, a pleasant riverside town in Surrey, has an alluring shopping centre, and shoplifting is a local speciality. Over the past couple of years magistrates have noticed an increase in mugging and threatening behaviour. At the railway station, a stop on the way to Chessington Zoo, groups of teenagers have taken to surrounding other children and demanding money (known as "taxing"). Sometimes gangs will get on trains at night and intimidate adults.

Proceedings in the youth court are brisk and business-like. But listening to the court clerk read out the charges, it is obvious that several of these youngsters were arrested as long ago as September. Only a few are sentenced on the spot. The three youth magistrates—who include a retired schoolteacher and a self-employed businessman—fine the fare-dodgers and a boy caught carrying cannabis in the town centre. Two cases have to be adjourned for pre-sentence reports from the local authority's youth justice team. Another is stalled while a defence lawyer tries to get crucial evidence from the police, and a fourth has run into problems with legal aid.

None of this would come as a surprise to the Home Secretary. Youth crime has been Jack Straw's crusade since he took on the home affairs brief from Tony Blair in 1994. In opposition he visited youth courts and police stations; he wrote policy papers; he faced outrage from penal reformers who felt he was demonising children and exploiting public fears.

The practical result was that Straw arrived at the Home Office having done his research and fought his political battles—on children's curfews, for example. The ground had been tilled in advance.

Perhaps this explains why Labour's pledge on youth crime—"fast-track punishment for persistent young offenders, by halving the time from arrest to sentencing"—is, of the five, the one in which No 10 has most confidence.

The pledge was chosen to symbolise reform of a system which, in Straw's view, was failing the public. It also had to offer voters a measurable change. Persistent offenders—the three per cent who commit a quarter of youth crime—wait an average of 142 days from the time they are arrested until the time they are sentenced. Fulfilling the pledge would mean getting that down to 87 days.

The interesting thing is that it does not lie in Straw's power to deliver the pledge. Ultimately it lies in the power of the Lord Chancellor, Lord Irvine of Lairg, whose department runs the courts system. The conjunction could not be more awkward, politically and personally. The Home Office and the Lord Chancellor's Department are a government turf war waiting to happen, while conflicts between Straw and Derry Irvine have already caused Whitehall comment. Irvine, Blair's mentor, is a self-important Cambridge-educated QC; Straw, who was also briefly a barrister, went to Leeds. With his Roundhead mentality, Straw is said to be one of the few ministers prepared to stand up to the Cavalier Lord Chancellor. If the two men cannot work together, it could torpedo the pledge.

It was Irvine who started the ball rolling, writing to magistrates within weeks of polling day to ask for their help in speeding up juvenile justice. He warned of an "adjournment culture", in which no one "expects that cases will be disposed of, or even progress, at the initial hearing". A 1996 Audit Commission report found that a young person appears in court four times during the average case; only 17 per cent are sentenced the first time.

No figures are yet available to show whether the Lord Chancellor's letter is having any effect. In Kingston, magistrates are already encouraged to ask why cases cannot be settled there and then, and to resist needless requests for adjournment from defence lawyers or the Crown Prosecution Service (CPS). "Benches have not always been as strong as they should be in challenging the professionals' pace," says Andrew Vickers, the justices' clerk.

But courts are not being left to their own devices. The wide-ranging Crime and Disorder Bill, which started its parliamentary passage in the Lords, gives Straw powers to set statutory time limits for dealing with young offenders. For persistent offenders, targets will be tougher. A Youth Justice Board, accountable to the Home Secretary, will monitor whether they are being met. Court budgets are already partly related to how many cases are heard, and how quickly, so the government is looking at performance indicators specifically tied to youth justice.

Statutory time limits will be piloted from autumn 1999. But some areas have already begun experimenting with "fast-tracking" for persistent young offenders. It can be done. Straw told the Commons before Christmas that in north Hampshire the average time between charge and sentence had dropped from 133 to 89 days over the previous year.

In Leeds, where a fast-tracking scheme long pre-dates the Labour government, the number of "persistent offenders" known to the youth court has plummeted from 30 to five. Some will be in custody. But the local magistrates' chairman, Raymond Curry, reckons "fast-tracking" helps others to keep out of trouble. It reduces the danger of "spree offending" while youngsters are out on bail. It also means probation or social services can move swiftly to get the culprit onto an appropriate scheme, such as the car repair programmes that have worked well with joyriders.

Half the delay in the system occurs before a court hearing is even scheduled, with the police and the CPS. In Kingston police are experimenting with a system of "short bail" for repeat offenders. They have a list of 16 previously cautioned-teenagers. If one of these is caught nicking CDs in Woolworth's, the arresting officer can get a prosecution started at immediately, cutting out much paperwork. Under an agreement with the court, a youngster picked up on Saturday will go before the bench on Tuesday.

"I don't want to put kids into the courts system who shouldn't be there," stresses Inspector Phil Harris. "Most youngsters who are cautioned—seven out of ten—never come to police notice again."

For others, he is hoping to set a "restorative justice" scheme, where shoplifters will be brought face to face with retailers. The fast-trackers would be the ones for whom court seems the only option.

Defining a "persistent" offender has been a source of friction between the Home Office and the LCD. Straw's white paper on youth crime (called, characteristically, *No More Excuses*) says it should cover ten to 17 year olds arrested after three previous offences—as well as "spree offenders" who accumulate a very long charge sheet in a very short time.

By contrast, the Leeds scheme only applies to youngsters who are facing multiple charges, have previous convictions and have committed offences on bail. Using the government's less stringent definition would expand the Leeds list from five to between 30 and 50.

Nor do individuals fall neatly into the category. There are two "persistents" before the juvenile justices in Kingston. One is a 16-year-old shoplifter with a thick file, addicted to heroin since the age of ten. Stealing to feed his habit, he is refusing treatment and seems unlikely to become, in the words of the magistrates' chairman, "a nice young gentleman". The other is one of a gang involved in a robbery, where logic demands that they be dealt with as a group.

After a morning in the youth court, it is clear that fulfilling the pledge depends on co-operation from a network of professionals or "agencies". It also depends on distinguishing between avoidable and unavoidable delays.

For instance, one case has to be adjourned because defence lawyers cannot get hold of a police video. Vital evidence, but available only from the arresting officer—who was out on the street.

Then there are cases which the magistrates must adjourn for background presentence reports from the youth justice team. These are required where the young person could be sentenced to custody or community service. In Kingston social services aim to write the report—outlining the child's background—within three weeks. The government is encouraging courts to use existing reports for persistent offenders, with verbal updates.

When it comes to legal aid two government aims collide: speeding up justice and holding down public spending. In order to rein in the legal aid budget, the LCD insists on elaborate evidence—benefit books, rent books, council tax bills, water rates—to prove entitlement. If one piece of paper is missing, the claim cannot be processed and the case cannot go ahead. Ministers are looking at postponing a means test until the case has started.

Other proposals are more controversial. The LCD is fighting a rearguard action against clause 40 of the Crime and Disorder Bill, which would let clerks take some decisions alone, without magistrates. For instance, in certain situations they could remand defendants in custody, a prospect that brought the Lord Chief Justice to his feet during the second reading. "Such a rule would erode the fundamental distinction between the justices and the justices' legal adviser," said Lord Bingham, "and in the longer term signal the demise of the lay magistracy, which would be an irreparable loss."

The government hopes it can create a virtuous circle, in which fast-tracking some cases promotes efficiency across the board. But the opposite could be true. It is easy to get agencies to give priority to a limited number of cases, says Curry. "But not everyone accepts that it's a good idea for all defendants to be dealt with quickly. Especially defence solicitors, who often seem to want to drag things out."

The government is thinking of fining lawyers who fail to meet court deadlines.

Alan Beith, the Liberal Democrats' home affairs spokesman, warns of the danger that fast-tracking "will simply create delays elsewhere in the system". He points out that other measures in the bill will create more work for courts. As well as introducing a whole new range of sentences—the child curfew, "parenting" and "reparation" orders—it transforms the existing formal caution into a "final warning", which would trigger work by local Youth Offending Teams. A final warning can only be given once: more trouble will pitch the offender into court.

What if courts cannot keep up with Straw's impatience? Magistrates are volunteers, after all. Kingston had to double the number of youth court sittings a year ago. The white paper makes it clear that Straw wants to press ahead with reform, sending first-timers before a "youth panel", rather than a court.

A decorous warning came this week from Anne Fuller, chairman of the Magistrates' Association. At a Nacro conference she observed that the government "wants everyone to be totally committed" to improving the system. This would mean extra work for magistrates. It seemed "counterproductive" to be heralding yet more radical changes within a couple of years.

An over-zealous Straw could find lay justices, who embody Blair's ideal of civic culture, looking to Irvine for protection against a persistent Home Secretary.

HIV/AIDS education and prevention programs for adults in prisons and jails and juveniles in confinement facilities—United States, 1994.

By the end of 1994, at least 4588 adult inmates of U.S. prisons and jails had died as a result of acquired immunodeficiency syndrome (AIDS), and during 1994, at least 5279 adult inmates with AIDS were incarcerated in prisons and jails.[1] Periodically conducted national surveys instituted in 1985[2] and sponsored by the U.S. Department of Justice's National Institute of Justice (NIJ) and CDC [Centers for Disease Control and Prevention] have documented the prevalence of human immunodeficiency virus (HIV)/AIDS and the incidence of sexually transmitted diseases (STDs) among adult inmates and confined juveniles.[*] In addition, these surveys have enabled an assessment of HIV/AIDS education and prevention programs in prisons and jails for adults and confinement facilities for juveniles. This report presents findings from the eighth survey, conducted in 1994, which indicate the need to increase HIV/AIDS education and prevention services among adult inmates and confined juveniles.

In the 1994 NIJ/CDC survey, questionnaires were sent to and responses received from the Federal Bureau of Prisons, all 50 state prison systems for adults, city/county jail systems with adult inmate populations among the largest in the country (29 [81%] of 36),[**] state systems for juveniles (41 [82%] of 50), and city/county systems with the largest populations of confined juveniles (32 [64% of 50).[***] Most questionnaires were completed by health services staff, but some portions were completed by other administrators. Although most systems for adults and juveniles include a number of individual facilities, systems were asked to provide single answers covering all of their facilities. However, for some questions, systems were asked to report the number of their facilities providing certain types of programs. Rates of AIDS and gonorrhea among the U.S. population were based on data reported by state health departments to CDC.

Prisons and Jails for Adults

Prison and jail systems for adults participating in the 1994 survey reported 5279 cases of AIDS among current inmates, representing 5.2 AIDS cases per 1000 adult inmates—a rate almost six times that of the total U.S. adult (aged ≥ 18 years) population (0.9 cases per 1000 population) (CDC, unpublished data, 1995). Based on mandatory testing of all incoming inmates or blinded studies, reported HIV seroprevalence rates of inmates ranged from <1% to 22%; 12 state systems reported rates >2%.[1]

HIV/AIDS education included interactive programs (e.g., peer-led programs and instructor-led sessions such as lectures, discussions, or question-and-answer periods) and passive programs (e.g., use of videotapes, other audio-visual materials, or written materials). Based on reports from all 51 state and federal systems, the percentage of systems providing instructor-led HIV/AIDS education in at least one of their facilities decreased from 96% in 1990 to 75% in 1994[1]. In 1994, of the 1207 state and federal facilities, 582 (48%) were providing instructor-led HIV/AIDS education programs, 90 (7%) were operating peer-led programs, 865 (72%) were using audio-visual materials, and 1068 (88%) were using written materials. Of the 80 federal, state, and city/county adult systems participating in the 1994 survey, 30 (59%) responded to a specific question that they would like to receive public health department assistance with their HIV/AIDS education programs.

Two state prison systems (Vermont and Mississippi) and four city/county jail systems (New York City; Philadelphia; San Francisco; and Washington, DC) reported making condoms available to inmates in their facilities. Of the 80 prison and jail systems participating in the 1994 survey, one city/county jail system reported making bleach available to inmates.[1]

Confinement Facilities for Juveniles

As of December 1994, the 41 state and city/county systems for juveniles participating in the 1994 survey reported a cumulative total of 60 cases of AIDS and four cases of AIDS among currently confined juveniles. The HIV seroprevalence among confined juveniles in six state systems and one county system was <1 %.[3] However, compared with the total U.S. population of equivalent age, the incidence rates for gonorrhea, a marker of high-risk sexual activity associated with HIV transmission, were 152 times and 42 times higher among confined juvenile females and males, respectively.[4] Twenty-six state systems reported a mean of 137 gonorrhea cases[****] per 1000 confined females during the 12 months preceding completion of the 1994 survey, compared with 0.9 cases per 1000 total U.S. females aged 15–19 years during 1994. Twenty-one state systems reported a mean of 25 gonorrhea cases per 1000 confined males during the 12 months preceding completion of the 1994 survey, compared with 0.6 cases per 1000 total U.S. males aged 15–19 years during 1994.[3,4]

Of 456 confinement facilities in the 40 state systems responding to the question, 31 (7%) were operating peer-led HIV/ AIDS education, 258 (57%) were providing instructor-led education, 246 (54%) were using audio-visual materials, and 270 (59%) were using written materials. Of the 73 state and city/ county systems for juveniles participating in the survey, 40 (55%) responded to the question that they would like to receive public health department assistance with their HIV/ AIDS education programs. One county system (Alameda County, California) reported making condoms available to juveniles confined in its facilities.[3]

Reported by: TM Hammett, Phd, R Widom, Abt Associates Inc, Cambridge, Massachusetts. National Institute of Justice, Office of Justice Programs, US Dept of Justice. Behavioral Intervention Research Br Div of HIV/AIDS Prevention, National Center for HIV, STD, and TB Prevention (proposed), CDC.

CDC Editorial Note: The findings in this report underscore the need to take advantage of important missed opportunities to provide HIV/AIDS prevention programs in prisons and jails for adults and in confinement facilities for juveniles.[5] These facilities are important settings for HIV/AIDS education and prevention efforts because of (1) high prevalences in their populations of HIV-infected persons and persons with risk factors for HIV infection[6]; (2) demonstrated occurrence of and continuing high potential for HIV transmission in these facilities through sexual activity and sharing of drug-injection equipment[7,8]; (3) eventual release of almost all adult inmates and confined juveniles to the community; (4) high rates of re-incarceration and re-confinement[9]; and (5) feasibility of providing HIV/AIDS education and prevention programs in these facilities.

Despite the established HIV/AIDS epidemic among adult inmates and high STD rates among confined juveniles, many facilities have not provided interactive HIV/AIDS education programs. In facilities for juveniles HIV/AIDS education often is presented as a curriculum unit of the school program, which many juveniles may not receive because of their short lengths of stay. Peer-led programs are provided in even fewer facilities for adults and juveniles, although such programs may be more credible and effective than those provided by educators affiliated with the correctional system for adults or the system for juveniles.[1]

Findings from the NIJ/CDC surveys presented in this report are subject to at least one limitation. Because the surveys did not include all city/county jail systems and because of possible underreporting by participating systems, the numbers of cumulative AIDS deaths and AIDS cases among current adult inmates reported in the survey probably were underestimated.

To assist in reducing the transmission of HIV in the United States, comprehensive and credible programs of interactive education, counseling, testing, partner notification, and practical risk-reduction techniques (e.g., safer sex and safer drug injection) should be implemented for adult inmates in prisons and jails and for juveniles in confinement facilities. In addition, because many adult inmates and confined juveniles have established patterns of high-risk behavior for HIV/AIDS, ongoing programs of support and counseling are needed to assist them in initiating and sustaining positive behavior change.

Although counseling, testing, and partner-notification programs have been implemented in some correctional facilities for adults,[10] few systems for adults or juveniles make available the means to practice risk reduction (e.g., condoms or bleach). Interviews with correctional administrators indicate that condom and bleach distribution have been rejected because such policies are believed to condone and encourage behavior prohibited to inmates. Public health agencies at all levels should collaborate with correctional systems for adults, justice systems for juveniles, and community-based organizations to strengthen HIV/AIDS education and prevention programs in facilities for adults and juveniles. Collaborative efforts could be used to formulate strategies for HIV/AIDS prevention and to implement comprehensive HIV/AIDS education and prevention programs. Finally, the needs of adult inmates and confined juveniles should be included in the community HIV/AIDS prevention planning process.

References

1. Hammett TM, Widom R, Epstein J, Gross M, Sifre S, Enos T. 1994 Update: HIV/AIDS and STDs in correctional facilities. Washington, DC: US Department of Justice, Office of Justice Programs, National Institute of Justice/US Department of Health and Human Services, Public Health Service, CDC, December 1995.
2. CDC. Acquired immunodeficiency syndrome in correctional facilities: a report of the National Institute of Justice and the American Correctional Association. MMWR 1986;35:195–9.
3. Widom R, Hammett TM. Research in brief: HIV/AIDS and STDs in juvenile facilities. Washington, DC: US Department of Justice, Office of Justice Programs, National Institute of Justice, April 1996.
4. CDC. Sexually transmitted disease surveillance, 1994. Atlanta, Georgia: US Department of Health and Human Services, Public Health Service, CDC, September 1995.
5. laser JB, Greifinger RB. Correctional health care: a public health opportunity. Ann Intern Med 1993;118:139–45.
6. Bureau of Justice Statistics. Correctional populations in the United States, 1991. Washington, DC: US Department of Justice, Office of Justice Programs, Bureau of Justice Statistics, 1993; publication no. NCJ-142729.
7. Mutter RC, Grimes RM, Labarthe D. Evidence of intraprison spread of HIV infection. Arch Intern Med 1994;154:793–5.
8. Mahon N. High risk behavior for HIV transmission in New York state prisons and city jails. Am J Public Health 1996 (in press).
9. Bureau of Justice Statistics. Correctional populations in the United States, 1993. Washington, DC: US Department of Justice, Office of Justice Programs, Bureau of Justice Statistics, 1995; publication no. NCJ-156241.
10. CDC. Notification of syringe-sharing and sex partners of HIV-infected persons—Pennsylvania, 1993–1994. MMWR 1995;44:202–4.

*In most states, offenders aged 18 years are handled by the juvenile justice system and confined in juvenile facilities; those aged >18 years are prosecuted in adult courts and incarcerated in prisons and jails. However, the cutoff age varies by state and even within some states on a case-by-case basis.

**The sample of 36 city/county jail systems for adults was selected to represent systems with large inmate populations and to provide geographic diversity. All 36 systems were among the 50 largest in the United States in inmate population in 1994. The Washington, D.C., system was considered a city/county system.

***The 50 city/county systems for juveniles selected for the survey included the largest confined populations in 1994 based on information provided by the Office of Juvenile Justice and Delinquency Prevention, Office of Justice Programs, U.S. Department of Justice.

****The NIJ/CDC questionnaire sought numbers of gonorrhea cases presumptively diagnosed and numbers of cases confirmed by laboratory findings during the preceding 12 months. Incidence rates for the 26 state juvenile systems providing the requested data were calculated based on the total of these two categories of cases. The reported means represent a simple average of the incidence rates in these 26 systems.

It's Time to Open the Doors of Our Prisons

Freeing first-time offenders is the compassionate answer. It also makes good economic sense.

By RUFUS KING

AMERICANS, ONCE SO KIND-HEARTED, have become lusty punishers. Since President Nixon's "war" on crime, the public has become increasingly intolerant of wrongdoers, a group with no lobbyists or spin doctors to look out for them. In the late 1960s, America, like most of the rest of the world, forsook capital punishment. Since reviving it almost a decade later, we have executed more than 500 people. Now governors brag about the number of death warrants they sign.

The U.S. prison population, 1.2 million not counting short-term jail inmates, is the largest in the Western world. A number of states are spending more on prisons than on schools, and along with the federal government are turning some of their prisoners over to private custody—so that skimping on accommodations directly boosts stockholders' dividends. Lawmakers trample one another to pose as tough crimefighters, and mandatory minimums force judges to hand out long sentences, sometimes life, automatically upon conviction. Parole programs have atrophied.

The situation is aggravated by America's hysteria over drugs. Self-administered opiates (heroin and morphine) and cocaine together cause fewer than 8,500 deaths per year—compared with tobacco, 430,000, and alcohol, 100,000 dead, plus millions drunk in the gutter or otherwise incapacitated. I don't think marijuana has ever killed anyone. Yet the White House campaign to be "drug free" not only costs billions, but concentrates on prohibition and punishment at the expense of notably cheaper and more effective treatment. The elaborate U.S. campaign to compel drug-crop growers abroad to give up their livelihoods is one of the most fatuous national efforts ever undertaken. Imagine Turks and Andeans trying to keep Yankee farmers from growing their truly deadly tobacco!

Nearly all the nation's prison systems are overcrowded, many critically. In state and federal prisons, more than half of all inmates are serving their time for nonviolent offenses. Some 30 percent are first offenders. African-Americans are a grossly disproportionate 49 percent. Drug-law convictions account for almost one fourth, and nearly one third of these are for simple possession. Genuine hardship cases abound, with stunning sentences for minor wrongs, the separation of parents and young children and a wide disproportion among convictions for identical offenses.

After working for many years in the development of criminal law, I've become increasingly concerned about our clogged prison system. My proposal to relieve the problem is simple: systematic use of pardon and commutation powers to clear out worthy first-offense long-termers to make room for serious felons. It should stir compassion and appeal to common sense. But there is another consideration that Americans may understand even better: costs. At an estimated $20,000 per year to hold each prisoner, we are spending more than $25 billion annually for simple, nonproductive warehousing of convicted offenders.

Altogether, our annual layout for corrections is more than $35 billion, curving steadily upward even as crime rates drop. We are developing a powerful "prison-industrial complex," a national growth industry exploiting today's hostility toward wrongdoers. There is scant evidence that long prison terms alone are causing the drop. Most observers credit other factors such as progress in reducing poverty, the improved economy, tighter gun laws and the increasing average age of the population. Criminologists agree that about-to-be lawbreakers don't look up penalties in the law books; they plan, if at all, on how to avoid being caught.

Every system for administering justice has, since ancient times, included some provision for tempering punishment, usually a power to pardon and commute sentences, vested in the executive. Royal pardons were well known to most of our European forebears. American presidents draw the power directly from the Constitution, and every state governor enjoys some such prerogative. Historically, the power has been freely, often liberally used, sometimes to grant amnesty to entire classes of offenders.

So I urge an immediate review of all sentences now being served in order to identify nonviolent first offenders held for disproportionately long terms, to release those who have paid their debts to society and are good risks, and to make room for menacing recidivists and other serious offenders.

'I'm urging an immediate review of all sentences to release those people who have paid their debt'

There would inevitably be a few Willie Hortons, but the process might be designed to include further screening in each case. Release should be strictly conditioned on good behavior and other factors where appropriate.

The president could initiate such a program simply by directive, or Congress could set up a new authority for it. And any governor or state legislature could give it a try. I only need to convince enough economy-minded people that some of the nation's prison-budget billions could be better spent elsewhere. Perhaps I've convinced you.

King is a Washington lawyer with a lifelong interest in criminal justice.

Index

A

Abramson, Marc, 171
abuse: associated with violent crime, 29; inmates and, prior to adulthood, 27–30; of women, in prison, 67–69
acquired immunodeficiency syndrome (AIDS), 206–207
activities, for elderly offenders, in prison, 91–92
Adalist-Estrin, Ann, 44, 45
ADAM drug-testing program, 34
Administrative Maximum Facility (ADX), 55
Alabama, chain gangs in, 197–198
Alabama Federal Intervention Syndrome, 82
Alcatraz, 55
alcohol, 32; and drug use among inmates, by mental health status, 106
Alexandria Adult Detention Center (AADC), 170, 172, 173
American Correctional Association (ACA), 76, 77
Amity Rightum, 52–53
Amnesty International, 68, 69
amphetamines. *See* prescription medications
Andrews, D. A., 142
anti-criminal modeling and reinforcement, 141
anti-criminal program components, 142
anti-psychotic drugs, 170
arrest data, 63
Asylums (Goffman), 171
Austin, James, 182
authority, 141
Aztecs, 75

B

Barajas, Eduardo, Jr., 199
barbiturates. *See* prescription medications
Barry, Ellen, 68–69
Bassoff, Evelyn, 86–87
Beck, Allen J., 89, 156
Bedlam. *See* mental institutions
Bell, James, 112–113
Between Prison and Probation: Intermediate Punishments in a Rational Sentencing System (Morris & Tonry), 149
Bloodsworth, Kirk, 127–128
Bonfire of the Vanities, The (Wolfe), 146
boot camps, 152, 159, 166
"brake fluid," 97
Brendtro, Larry, 112
"bride well," 10
Buentello, Sammy, 74, 75
Bureau of Justice Statistics (BJS), 23, 27–30, 38, 89, 100–110, 156
Bureau of Prisons (BOP), 111, 112, 114

C

Cabana, Donald, 136, 137
CAGE diagnostic instrument, 107
California, three strikes law in, 177–180
capital punishment, 135; in Illinois, 129–134; taxpayers pay for, 124
"carrot and stick" approach, 35
Cason v. Seckinger, 67
Center of Employment Opportunities (CEO) in New York City, 158, 159–160; cost of, 160; effectiveness of, 162–163
Centers for Disease Control and Prevention (CDC), 206, 207

chain gangs, 39, 40; in Alabama, 197–198; in Florida, 196–198
Chaser, interview with, 96–99
Chesney-Lind, Meda, 86
children, of offenders, 44–45
Children, Young Persons and Their Families Act of 1989, 115–116, 117
Chiles, Lawton, 182
chlorpromazine tranquilizers. *See* prescription medications
chronic offender, 91
clinical depressions, incarcerated Americans and, 46
Clinton, Bill, 153
cocaine, 31, 32, 51
Coder v. Lalor, 65
"coerced abstinence," 152; programs of, 35
community confinement and control (CCC), 152
community corrections strategies, 8
community resources, 141
community-based treatment, 52
community-oriented policing, 8, 9, 11, 150
complaints, by women inmates, 63
correctional goals, 10
correctional higher education, 186, 187–188
correctional officers, 45; life of, 56–61; responsible for abuse of women inmates, 67
correctional treatment: effective intervention of, 140–145; programs, 140
Corrections Clearinghouse (CCH) in Washington, 158; effectiveness of, 160
Corrections Mental Health Department, 31
cost failure, of prisons, 182–183
cost, of drug and alcohol-involved inmates, 53–54
Craig, Todd, 112
Crime and Disorder Bill, 204
Crime and Punishment in America (Currie), 46
crime, prevention of, due to education of prisoners, 184–189
crime victims' "bill of rights," 93
criminal justice, 199–202; American, 8–12; treatment programs, 34–35
Crossroads Community Correctional Center, 158, 159
"crowding crisis," 192
Crown Prosecution Service (CPS), 204
Cunningham, James, 113
Currie, Elliot, 46

D

Dakota Horizons, 112
David Wade Correctional Center (DWCC), Clinical Treatment Unit. *See* Forcht-Wade
day reporting and intensive supervision, 166
De Jong, Barbara, 45
Death at Midnight: The Confession of an Executioner (Cabana), 136
death penalty, 122–123; cost of, 124; flaws of, in Illinois, 129–134; reinstated, in New York, 135–137
death row: in Illinois, 129–134; race and, 123; wrongful sentence to, 125–128
Deeb, Muneer, 127

Department of Correctional Services (DOCS), 63, 64–65, 66
design capacity, 17
deterrence, 140
diazopene tranquilizers. *See* prescription medications
Differential Association Theory, 141
differential treatment, 143
disciplinary problems, among mentally ill inmates, 108
District of Columbia, prisons in, statistics of, 14, 15, 18, 23
diversion programs, 35, 36
Dix, Dorothea, 171
Drug Enforcement Administration, 51
Drug Treatment Alternative-to-Prison (DTAP) program, 35, 36
drugs, 34–36; criminal behavior and, among incarcerated men, 31–33; highest incarceration rate due to, 50–54
DSM-III-R, 31, 32
due process clause, 81–82
Duran Consent Decree, 76–77

E

Edgar, Jim, 182
education, as crime prevention, 184–189
effective intervention, of correctional treatment, 140–145
effective programs, for correctional treatment, 141
Eighth Amendment, 67, 81, 149
elderly offenders: care of, in Louisiana State Penitentiary, 93–95; needs of, 90–92
electric chair, 126
electronic monitoring equipment, 150, 165, 166
Epidemiological Catchment Area program, 101

F

families: at-risk, 44; family group conferences and, 117
Family and Corrections Network (FCN), 44
family group conference, 115–116
"fast-tracking," 204, 205
Federal Bureau of Investigation (FBI), 9, 51, 196
Federal Bureau of Prisons, 23, 35, 52, 68, 74, 185, 198
federal prison(s), 50; statistics of, 13–26
felony probationers, 151
female prisoners, 15, 19; characteristics of, 39–40
first-time offenders, 91, 208
flaws, in justice system, 125–128
Florida, chain gangs in, 196–198
Forcht, Martin L., Jr., 94
Forcht-Wade, 94
Forever Free, 53
Fourteenth Amendment, 81
"frank pledges," 9

G

gangs, in prisons, 74–75
Garber, Gertie, 190
GED programs, 184
general deterrence, 177, 178
Georgia, mandatory sentencing in, 176
Giuliani, Rudolph, 147
Godwin, Cory, 74, 75
Goffman, Erving, 171
Golden, Andrew, 125–126

209

Gooey, Kevin M., 30
Green, Mark, 62

H
habilitation, 146–147
Haney, Craig, 60
Hart, Peter D., 136
Hassine, Victor, interview with Chaser, as medication addict, 96–99
heroin, 31, 51
Higher Education Act, 185
high-risk probationers, 151, 152, 153
HIV/AIDS education and prevention programs, in correctional facilities, 206–207
Hobbes, Thomas, 135
Holbrook, Rick, 91
home detention, 165, 167
Home Detention Unit, 165, 166
Home Secretary vs. Lord Chancellor, 203–205
homelessness, among mentally ill inmates, 104
Horn, Martin, 155–156
"houses of corrections," 9
housing, for elderly offenders, 91
human rights groups, 67–69
Huskey, Bobbie, 92

I
illegal drugs and alcohol, associated with abused inmates, 29
inadequate education, among juvenile offenders, 184
incarcerated relatives, 29
incarceration, 10, 11, 44–45
index offenses, 178
indigents, 171
inmates, consequences of, for prison crime, 65
institutional drug treatment programs, 35
"intensive surveillance" programs, 149
interim emergency order, 80
"intermediate punishments," 149
intermediate sanctions, experimenting with, 148–154
intermediate sanctions programs (ISP), 148; participants, 151; program redesign, 152
intermediate targets, 144
Irwin, John, 182

J
Jacobs, Sonia "Sunny," 126–127
James v. Wallace, 80–81
job placement, for offenders, 157–164
justice-as-fairness, 140, 143
Juvenile Court Act, of Illinois, 178
Juvenile Justice and Delinquency Prevention Act of 1974, 193
juveniles, in federal prisons, 111–114

K
Key, Robert E. Lee, Jr., 126
Kleiman, Mark, 35, 152
Kozinski, Alex, 122

L
Lapp, Katie, 156
Latin Kings, 74
law enforcement approach, 9
Lawes, Lewis, 136
Leckey, Kevin, 113–114
legal issues, of correctional services, 195
Leslie, Donald R., 30
Levering, Richard, 59–60

Lichtenstein, Andrew, 46–49
"lifeguards," 163
Little, Tracy, 151–152
local jails, 15, 19, 50
Louisiana, and high incarceration rates, 14–15
Louisiana State Penitentiary (LSP), 93
Lucas vs. White, 68

M
Mahoney, Michael, 111
mandatory sentencing, 175–176
"mandatory-minimum laws," 175, 176
manic-depression, incarcerated Americans and, 46
manic-depressive disorder, 170
Man's Judgment of Death (Lawes), 136
marijuana. *See* drugs
Martinson, R., 140
Maryland Correctional Institution for Women (MCI-W), 70–73
Massachusetts Correctional Institution in Concord (MCI-Concord), 31, 32
McLaurine, William D., Jr., 91
McMillian, Walter, 126
medical care, for elderly offenders, 90–92
mental health, of inmates, 100–110; status of, 102
mental institutions, 170–174
mentally ill: incarcerated, in prison, 100–110; incarceration of, at Bedlam, 170–174; in prison, for violent crimes, 103
Mexican Mafia, 75
Michigan: mandatory sentencing in, 176; volunteer probation officers in, 190–191
military corrections statistics, 23–24
military jurisdiction, prisoners under, 15
Morris, Norval, 149
Moss, Andie, 68
motivation issues, of correctional services, 193
Mustin, Jim, 44
Myth of Mental Illness, The (Szasz), 171

N
National Center on Addiction and Substance Abuse (CASA), 34, 36, 50–54
National Corrections Reporting Program (NCRP), 24
National Council on Crime & Delinquency (NCCD), 182
National Institute of Corrections (NIC), 199
National Institute of Justice (NIJ), 149, 150, 206
National Institute of Justice Drug Use Forecasting System, 31
National Prisoner Statistics (NPS), 23, 24, 25–26
neighborhood probation, 152–153
"net repairing," 151
Neta, 75
"neutralizing strategies," 199–200
New Black Panthers, 75
New Mexico Department of Corrections, 76–77
New York State: mandatory sentencing in, 176; prison crime in, 62–66
New Zealand Experiment, for reforming juvenile justice, 115–119
Newman v. Alabama, 79
non-parental care, 28–29

non-violent crimes, 32
"nothing works" proclamation, 140

O
offender community service program, 191
Office of Juvenile Justice and Delinquency Prevention Comprehensive Strategy for Youth, 152
Olivarez, Jana, 190
open communication "friendship" models, 142
"Operation Night Light," 153
operational capacity, 17

P
PACE (Program Activities for Correctional Education) Institute, 158, 159
Palmer, Ted, 140
parental drinking, 29
Parole and Probation's Correctional Options Program, in Maryland, 166
parole boards, possible elimination of, 155–156
Partial Justice: Women, Prisons and Social Control (Rafter), 38
Partlow State School and Hospital, 80
Pataki, George R., 147, 155
"peace and service" orientation, 9
Penal Law, 65
People v. Vasquez, 65
personnel issues, of correctional personnel, 194–195
Peters, Howard, 182
Petersilia, Joan, 155
physical abuse, higher rates of, among mentally ill inmates, 105, 106
Piehl, Anne, 198
polarization, of sentencing, 149–150
police: historical review of, 8–9; juvenile offenders and, 115–116
Powell, Colin, 51
"practical life," 93
prescription medications, in prisons, 96–99
"preventive patrol," 9
Prison Fellowship Ministries, 44, 45
prison recidivists, 91
prisoners: in 1998, 13–26; and prior abuse as children, 27–30
prison-based education, recidivism rates lowered due to, 185
prison-based treatment, 52
"prison-industrial complex," 208
prisons, 181–183; capacity of, 15, 17, 21; crime in, 62–66; crowding of, in southern United States, 148–149; freeing first-time offenders, 208; riot in, at the New Mexico State Penitentiary, 76
privatization, of correctional service, 192–195
proactive corrections, 11
proactive policing, 11
proactive prison management, 90–92
probationers, and mental illness, 100–110; young adult, 165–167
problem-solving, 141
process and content of intervention, 144
Project READ, 184
Project RIO (Reintegration of Offenders), in Texas, 158, 160–161; effectiveness of, 161; cost of, 161–162
prosecution, of prison crime, 64
prosecutor misconduct, in Illinois, 131–132

psychological screening, 113
psychotropic medication, 97, 98
"public-private partnership" era, 195

Q

quality of interpersonal relationship, 141

R

radical nonintervention, 140
Rafter, Nicole, 38
rated capacity, 17
recidivism: and cost-benefit, 144; reduction of, and correctional costs, 157–164
reconviction, family group conferences and, 118
redistributive justice vs. restorative justice, 200–201
reform, of death penalty, 133–134
regimented offender treatment center (ROTC), 166
rehabilitation, 9, 11; for delinquent youths, 113
reinstating death penalty, in New York, 135–137
"rent-a-judge," 192
residential treatment programs, 52
restorative justice paradigm, 11, 199
riots, 63
Rives, Richard T., 82
Roberts, Burton, 146, 147
Roules, William, 56

S

Safer Foundation, in Chicago, 158–159; effectiveness of, 158–159; cost of, 159
Safir, Howard, 62
schizophrenia, 170; incarcerated Americans and, 46
scope of services, issues of correctional services, 193–194
"second chances," for juvenile offenders, 178
sentry men. See police
setting factors, 144
severe depression, 170
sexual crimes, 31–32
sexual molestation, of inmates, 67
sexually transmitted disease (STDs), 206, 207
"650 Lifer Law," 176
Smith, Brenda, 67
solitary confinement, 55
special medical programs, for LSP, 95

special needs facilities, for elderly offenders, 94–95
specific deterrence, 177, 178
spouses, of offenders, 44
Stanford Prison Experiment, 60
Starr Commonwealth Schools, for rehabilitating delinquent youths, 113
state prisons, 50; inmates of, identified as mentally ill, 101; inmates of violent and drug offenses, 20–21; parole violators in, 22; statistics of, 13–26
State Use Industries (SUI), prison industries program, 71
stories, of men and women, wrongfully sentenced to death row, 125–128
Straw, Jack, 203
street gangs, 74
student intern program, 190–191
substance abuse. See drugs
substance-abuse related crime, running in the family, 53
"supermax" concept, 55, 182
Supervision Management and Recidivist Tracking (SMART) Partnership, 154
Survey of Adults on Probation in 1995, 100, 109
Survey of Inmates in Local Jails in 1996, 100, 109
Survey of Inmates in State or Federal Correctional Facilities in 1997, 100, 109
system variables, 143
Szasz, Thomas, 171

T

Tenth Amendment, 78, 82
Texas prisons, crime in, 65
therapeutic integrity, 143
Thornburg, Dick, 150
three-strikes law, 44, 46, 175, 177–180
Tonn, Ron, 158
Tonry, Michael, 149
tough-on-crime platforms, 155
transition-to-trades initiatives, tailored to women inmates, 162
Traynor, Terry, 113
Tribune investigation, on capital punishment, in Illinois, 129–134
truth-in-sentencing laws, 93
Turner, Susan, 151

U

United States: largest prisons built in, 46–49; statistics of prisoners in, 13–26

U.S. Constitution, 78–83
U.S. Department of Justice (DOJ), 68, 150; report on women on probation, 89
U.S. felony probation, study of, 149
U.S. Supreme Court, 122, 125, 137
Utah, mandatory sentencing in, 176

V

Vesey, Bonita M., 171, 172
victimization surveys, 63
victim/offender mediation programs, 201
victims, family group conferences and, 117–118
violent crime, 31–32; death penalty, least effective way, of reducing, 136–137
Violent Crime Control and Law Enforcement Act of 1994, 35, 93
violent recidivists, mentally ill inmates as, 103
Vocational Opportunity Training and Education (VOTE), 162
voluntary treatment programs, 35
volunteer probation officer program, 190–191
Volunteers in Corrections (VIC), 191

W

Weeks, David, 65
"well-known law," of delinquency programs research, 141
white inmates, and mental illness, 102
White, Rachelle, 165–167
Wilson, Pete, 175
Wickersham Commission, 9
Wolfe, Tom, 146
women inmates: abuse of, 67–69; daughters of, following life of crime, 86–88; equality for, 37–41; life stories of, 70–73; on probation, 89
Women Prisoners vs. District of Columbia Department of Corrections, 67
"workhouses," 9
Wyatt v. Stickney, 79–80

Y

Youth Aid Section, 116, 118
Youth Court, 116, 203–205

Z

Zimbardo, Philip, 60

AE Article Review Form

We encourage you to photocopy and use this page as a tool to assess how the articles in **Annual Editions** expand on the information in your textbook. By reflecting on the articles you will gain enhanced text information. You can also access this useful form on a product's book support Web site at **http://www.dushkin.com/online/**.

NAME: DATE:

TITLE AND NUMBER OF ARTICLE:

BRIEFLY STATE THE MAIN IDEA OF THIS ARTICLE:

LIST THREE IMPORTANT FACTS THAT THE AUTHOR USES TO SUPPORT THE MAIN IDEA:

WHAT INFORMATION OR IDEAS DISCUSSED IN THIS ARTICLE ARE ALSO DISCUSSED IN YOUR TEXTBOOK OR OTHER READINGS THAT YOU HAVE DONE? LIST THE TEXTBOOK CHAPTERS AND PAGE NUMBERS:

LIST ANY EXAMPLES OF BIAS OR FAULTY REASONING THAT YOU FOUND IN THE ARTICLE:

LIST ANY NEW TERMS/CONCEPTS THAT WERE DISCUSSED IN THE ARTICLE, AND WRITE A SHORT DEFINITION: